Natural Protest

Crane and Egan have signposted the long path of environmental activism in American history, from the early Republic to the day before yesterday. Everyone interested in environmentalism in the U.S. will want to know these stories, and grasp the larger picture that Crane and Egan present.

—**J. R. McNeill,** author of *Something New Under the Sun: An Environmental History of the 20th-Century World*

Natural Protest brings together contributions that expand our understanding of the multiple currents within environmentalism, both past and present, and provide a fresh lens in looking at some of the critical battles and efforts to expand the discourse that have made environmentalism such a complex, exciting, and continually evolving social movement.

—**Robert Gottlieb,** author of *Reinventing Los Angeles: Nature and Community in the Global City*

The essays in *Natural Protest* push readers to think harder about the rich history of American environmental activism. Because the authors mostly are up-and-coming scholars, this collection also gives a first taste of wonderful work to come.

—**Adam Rome,** author of *The Bulldozer in the Countryside: Suburban Sprawl and the Rise of American Environmentalism*

From Jamestown to 9/11, concerns about the landscape, husbanding of natural resources, and the health of our environment have been important to the American way of life. *Natural Protest* is the first collection of original essays to offer a complete social and political examination of environmental awareness, activism, and justice in contemporary America. Editors Jeff Crane and Michael Egan have selected the finest new scholarship in the field, establishing this complex and fascinating subject firmly in the forefront of American historical study.

Focused and thought-provoking, *Natural Protest* presents a cutting-edge perspective on American environmentalism and environmental history, providing an invaluable resource for anyone concerned about the ecological fate of the world around us.

Contributors: Kevin C. Armitage, Elizabeth D. Blum, Jeff Crane, Michael Egan, Philip Garone, John Hausdoerffer, Kevin R. Marsh, Will McArthur, Robert W. Righter, Sarah L. Thomas, Adam Tompkins, Frank Uekoetter, Sylvia Hood Washington.

Michael Egan is Assistant Professor in the Department of History and the director of the Sustainable Future History Project at McMaster University. He is the author of *Barry Commoner and the Science of Survival: The Remaking of American Environmentalism.*

Jeff Crane is Assistant Professor in the Department of History at Sam Houston State University.

Natural Protest
Essays on the History of American Environmentalism

EDITED BY

MICHAEL EGAN AND

JEFF CRANE

 Routledge
Taylor & Francis Group

NEW YORK AND LONDON

First published 2009
by Routledge
270 Madison Avenue
New York, NY 10016

Simultaneously published in the UK
by Routledge
2 Park Square, Milton Park, Abingdon, Oxon
OX14 4RN

Routledge is an imprint of the Taylor & Francis Group, an informa business

Typeset in Minion by Prepress Projects Ltd, Perth, UK

Printed and bound in the United States of America on acid-free paper by Edwards Brothers, Inc.

Library of Congress Cataloging in Publication Data
Natural protest : essays on the history of American environmentalism / editors, Jeff Crane and Michael Egan ; contributors, Kevin Armitage ... [et al.].
      p. cm.
Includes index. 1. Environmentalism—United States—History. I. Crane, Jeff. II. Egan, Michael, 1974–
GE197.N38 2008
333.720973—dc22

                       2008020822

ISBN 10: 0–415–96268–4 (hbk)
ISBN 10: 0–415–96269–2 (pbk)

ISBN 13: 978–0–415–96268–1 (hbk)
ISBN 13: 978–0–415–96269–8 (pbk)

For Janice and Jennine

Contents

Figures

Contributors

Kevin C. Armitage is a visiting assistant professor in the Department of History at Miami University in Ohio. A graduate of the University of Kansas, he has published numerous essays and is the author of *Knowing Nature: Nature Study and American Life, 1873–1923*, forthcoming from the University Press of Kansas.

Elizabeth D. Blum is an associate professor in the Department of History at Troy University. She is a leading scholar in African American environmental history, having published articles and chapters in a number of sources. Her book, *Love Canal Revisited: Race, Class, and Gender in Environmental Activism* (University Press of Kansas, 2008), explores the connections in activism between several groups at the famous crisis. She is currently working on a historical examination of the environmental messages delivered to children through pop culture.

Jeff Crane is an assistant professor in the Department of History at Sam Houston State University. His scholarship has focused on nineteenth- and twentieth-century protests against dams on the Kennebec, Elwha, and other rivers, the efforts to restore rivers and their fisheries through dam removal, and the origins of conservation in Missouri in the 1930s. His manuscript *Finding the River: The Environmental History of the Elwha River* is currently under review. He has published articles on the topic of dams and dam removal in *Columbia* and *Oregon Historical Quarterly*.

Michael Egan is an assistant professor in the Department of History at McMaster University and director of the Sustainable Future History Project. He is the author of *Barry Commoner and the Science of Survival: The Remaking of American Environmentalism* (MIT Press, 2007) and a number of articles on the history of environmentalism in journals including *Environment and History, Organization & Environment, New York History,* and *Natur und Kultur.*

Philip Garone is an assistant professor in the Department of History at California State University, Stanislaus. He received his PhD, as well as an MS in ecology, from the University of California at Davis. His research focuses on the intersection of environmental history and ecology, particularly in relation to wetland history and conservation. He has published on California water issues revolving around the 1980s ecological disaster at Kesterson National Wildlife Refuge. He is currently completing a manuscript for the University of California Press on the environmental history of the wetlands of California's Great Central Valley.

John Hausdoerffer is Director of Environmental Studies and assistant professor of Environmental Studies and Philosophy at Western State College. His research interests focus on the intersection of environmental ethics, social justice, and popular culture, particularly in nineteenth-century America. He is also the author of a forthcoming book with the University Press of Kansas on George Catlin, native justice, and the ethics of nature.

Kevin R. Marsh is an associate professor in the Department of History at Idaho State University. He is the author of *Drawing Lines in the Forest: Creating Wilderness Areas in the Pacific Northwest,* published by the University of Washington Press. He has also published articles on environmental history in *Western Historical Quarterly* and *Oregon Historical Quarterly.*

Will McArthur teaches history at Arizona State University-Polytechnic, where he has been recognized as Honors Disciplinary Faculty. His research concentrates on the intersections of race, social justice, suburban life, and environmentalism. He is currently completing his dissertation, "'It Seems Like We Should be on the Same Side': The Sierra Club, Social Justice, and Environmentalism, 1945–75." Recognized as a distinguished teacher, he also writes and lectures on a variety of pedagogical subjects.

Robert W. Righter is a research professor at Southern Methodist University. His work focuses on environmental history and the history of the American West. He has written or edited six books, including *Wind Energy in America: A History* (University of Oklahoma Press, 1996) and, most recently, *The Battle over Hetch Hetchy: America's Most Controversial Dam and the Birth of Modern Environmentalism* (Oxford University Press,

2005), winner of the Hal K. Rothman Book Prize for the best book in western environmental history. He is presently working on a new book entitled *Windfall: Harvesting Electricity from the Wind,* to be published by the University of Oklahoma Press.

Sarah L. Thomas is a PhD candidate at the University of California at Berkeley. Her research focuses on the impact of postwar land development on rural communities and on the evolution of local and state land use policies.

Adam Tompkins received his MA in history from Pennsylvania State University and is currently a PhD candidate in the Department of History at Arizona State University. His dissertation uses regional case studies to investigate farmworkers' campaigns for pesticide reform from the 1960s until the present. His research interests include historical issues relating to environmental justice, social justice, and environmental activism.

Frank Uekoetter is Dilthey Fellow at the Research Institute of the Deutsches Museum in Munich, Germany. He is the author of numerous articles in English and German on environmental history, agricultural history and the history of science and technology, and the history of social movements. His books include *The Green and the Brown: A History of Conservation in Nazi Germany* (Cambridge University Press, 2006). His book *The Age of Smoke: Environmental Policy in Germany and the United States, 1880–1970* is forthcoming with the University of Pittsburgh Press.

Sylvia Hood Washington is a research associate professor at the University of Illinois School of Public Health's Environmental & Occupational Health Sciences Division and an affiliate of the University's Institute for Environmental Science and Policy. She is the past national project director of the EJ/Environmental Health Project for African American Catholics that was jointly sponsored by the U.S. Conference of Catholic Bishops' Environmental Justice Office and Knights of Peter Claver/Ladies Auxiliary; and executive producer of the project's film *Struggles for Environmental Justice and Health in Chicago: African American and Catholic Perspectives.* Dr. Washington is member of the Aldo Leopold Foundation Board, a charter member of the University of Illinois-Chicago's Environmental Justice Board, and a member of the Illinois EPA Environmental Justice Advisory Board. She is editor-in-chief of the *Environmental Justice* journal published by Mary Ann Liebert Publishers. She teaches interdisciplinary courses in environmental history/ethics/environmental health and environmental justice courses at DePaul University and the University of Illinois School of Public Health. Washington is the author of *Packing Them In: An Archaeology of Environmental Racism in Chicago, 1865–1954* (Lexington Books, 2005) and co-editor of *Echoes from the Poisoned Well: Global Memories of Environmental Injustice* (Lexington Books, 2006). She has received a NSF professional development grant, "Engineering, Infrastructures and Environmental Justice," to complete her third book, *The Color of Trees: African American Struggles for Sustainable Communities, 1915–1975.*

Acknowledgments

This book's genesis was in 2002 at the American Society for Environmental History's annual meeting in Denver. We had organized a session titled "Roundtable on Environmentalism Unbound: Dimensions of the Environmental Movement," which included a number of junior and senior scholars working on different aspects of the history of environmentalism. The very large room was filled to capacity and we both came away from that session thinking that there was a growing interest in how we might historicize American environmentalism. This volume is an extension of the conversation we began then. We are very grateful to the audience at that session for their engaging questions and to our fellow panel participants, Linda Lear, Vera Norwood, Frank Uekoetter, Maril Hazlett, Robert Gottlieb, and Samuel P. Hays, who provided an inspiring commentary to the proceedings.

At Routledge, Kim Guinta was enthusiastic about our original plans at our first meeting and provided good encouragement and advice; she has been instrumental in shepherding this book through the publishing process. She and Matthew Kopel also exhibited inhuman patience with a couple of novice book editors. Our friend and mentor, Paul Hirt, provided valuable insight on editing a volume of essays and working with contributors. And we should thank the authors in this volume for their hard work, attention to detail, and willingness to collaborate. An Arts Research Board grant at McMaster University helped defer the cost of images throughout the book.

One of the great pleasures of working on this project has been the opportunity—indeed, the excuse—to stay in regular contact with each other when work has taken us some 1,500 miles apart. Our families are our anchors and source of motivation, especially our wives, to whom this book is dedicated.

Michael Egan & Jeff Crane
April 2008

Introduction

MICHAEL EGAN & JEFF CRANE

In the aftermath of the first Earth Day (22 April 1970), when more than 20 million people took to the streets in the largest demonstration in American history, the biologist and environmental leader Barry Commoner wrote *The Closing Circle*, a treatise on the nature and severity of the post-World War II environmental crisis. Commoner's book offered an accessible and compelling evaluation of the crisis brought on by new and polluting technologies and provided a template to help the public understand how natural and industrial systems interacted. Commoner's "Four Laws of Ecology" warned Americans that their actions and technologies needed to adhere to certain basic ecological rules. Among Commoner's laws of ecology was the assertion that "everything is connected to everything else." This truism suggested that destruction or exploitation of the physical environment could result in a series of unanticipated ripples throughout the ecosystem, but it also tied Commoner's environmental activism to a deep and longstanding tradition. Indeed, a century earlier, while tramping through the Sierras, John Muir had observed "when we try to pick out anything by itself, we find it hitched to everything else in the Universe."[1] Both evoked an appreciation for nature upon which human welfare depended, but they are also suggestive of different generations of American ecological awakening. Commoner and Muir came from very different worlds and brought starkly different priorities to their environmental concerns. And yet Commoner was retreading and reconfiguring paths that had been similarly retrodden and reconfigured by Muir many years before. Both recognized an interconnection, not, perhaps, with specific earlier actions or points of concern, but with the larger idea that if everything

1

is hitched to everything else in the universe, then our societies, politics, and economies needed to be much more cognizant of the environment.

This book investigates a variety of sites and sources of American environmental protest, bringing together fresh scholarship from a number of historians interested in the history of American environmentalism. Individually and collectively, the essays stress the importance of acquiring a deeper and more nuanced reading of environmental activism throughout American history. This exercise is designed to challenge the traditional narrative associated with American environmentalism. This is an important discussion insofar as it helps to enrich our reading of the past. In addition to these scholarly merits, this history also possesses political relevance in helping contemporary environmentalists to situate their interests and concerns within a larger historical context. History is a key determinant in the politics of identity; people, places, and ideas are invested in having a history, because that narrative shapes public perceptions of their place in contemporary politics. As a result of contributing to the history of American environmentalism, this volume is also engaging in a more pressing discussion of environmental activists' place in the larger discourse of current political debate. So much of contemporary politics of identity are caught up in historical interpretations of people, places, and ideas that the careful study of history makes an important contribution that stretches well beyond the academy.

Natural Protest seeks to make two major contributions to the existing discourse on the history of American environmental activism, one of complication and one of integration. First, it aims to identify directions in which historians might complicate the history of American environmentalism. The intention of this collection is not to explode or critically deconstruct the traditional narrative of American environmental protest. Rather, this collection continues the efforts to complicate and show the complexity of the forms of protest, conflict, and opposition that have marked American history. Furthermore, this collection emphasizes and demonstrates that environmental protest is long-lived and, in fact, as American as apple pie, baseball, and environmental destruction. Second, this collection will help to move beyond the simplistic portrayals of protest that have predominated in American society. The reality of protest is much more interesting and further scholarship should help promote useful analysis or discussion of social action toward the environment.

Natural Protest explores sites of environmental protest in order to show that the roots of American environmental activism and ecological thinking run much deeper and across a wider swath of American history than is typically perceived. Contemporary environmentalism is an amalgam of various social and ecological interests, which makes definition—contemporary and historical—both awkward and misleading. This is further evidenced by the selection of essays in this anthology, which investigate varied perspectives from the intellectual foundation for environmental activism to action on the ground. Traditional dichotomies between naturalists and humanists, or distinguishing land use alternatives—conservationism, utilitarianism, and preservationism—and anthropocentric and biocentric worldviews breed exclusivity and forms of classification that are historically unwarranted. It is sufficient to note that some of the most interesting work within the field in recent years focuses on previously unrecognized ecological protests and on communities that are typically relegated to the margins of this discussion. This volume puts traditional and marginal narratives in conversation with each other and draws connections between them while also coming to terms with the incommensurability of many of their tenets.

Indeed, in attempting to identify the character of American environmentalism through its history, we have reached the conclusion that no singular "movement" really exists, and, more to the point, it is unclear whether ecological protest really had a clear and singular point of origin. Environmental interests are not exclusively the domain of intellectuals and an urban elite. Instead, quite frequently, environmental protest is taken up by people who would not call themselves environmentalists at all and would not associate their activities with any kind of movement. Put another way: to concentrate on a collective, institutional history of environmental organizations is to necessarily overlook the lifeblood of American ecological activism, which is the product of a more organic social function. This is the double entendre of our title—natural protest—and it also serves as our thesis, which weaves together the following essays. To talk of a "movement" marginalizes important features of environmental protest. Similarly, to talk of a "mainstream" environmentalism misses the point, too, and creates an awkward relationship between artificial centers and peripheries of environmental action. Historicizing a mainstream environmental movement leaves no room for the more recent internal criticisms of environmental justice, for example, whose roots and perspectives are no less motivated by "environmental" concerns. Similarly, a mainstream movement has some difficulty in reconciling consistency and continuity between land use and public health reform as foundational planks. From our twenty-first-century vantage point we can see that the landscape of American environmentalism is, somewhat paradoxically, defined by its diversities: diversity of personnel, diversity of philosophies, diversity of resources, diversity of priorities, diversity of spaces, diversity of strategies and tactics.

By this, though, we do not mean to claim that the history of American ecological protest has been a disorganized, incoherent mess. It has, at times, comprised a cacophony of voices and interests, but historians and environmentalists ought to embrace this complexity, especially since a better understanding of this past can only lead to a more promising future. Instead, methods of working toward a more sustainable future have varied across time and place. The enduring consistency—and the focal point for the studies that follow—is the history of human relationship with nature, which is the centerpiece of environmental history. Often and aptly, histories of environmentalism straddle environmental history and social history; *Natural Protest* does this too, but stresses the connection to the environment as its anchor. Stated generally, the project of environmental history is to illuminate the important role that the physical environment plays in human history and culture. This collection, however, aims to do something more specific: namely, to demonstrate the variety and profusion of America's efforts to improve the ecology of our lives and their work through action and protest. Through various case studies the essays in this volume adhere to the notion that environment profoundly shapes the human life process; ecology molds life and ecological issues inhere in all human activity.

From Jamestown to 9/11, landscape, natural resources, and environmental health have been central to the American ethos, psyche, and condition. How the American public has responded to changes in the physical environment is an important bellwether of larger trends and changes in American culture. Economies and livelihoods remain deeply connected to the environment, as do patterns of recreation and community identity. Health is also dependent on a healthy environment. Combined, these interests constitute the foundation of American politics and popular culture. The environment is historically important; consequently, how Americans have fought to use and protect the environment is an important feature of American history. The essays in this collection draw connections and build bridges between environmental history and American history writ large. And this practice strikes at the core of the volume's second contribution, which seeks to implant the history of American environmentalism more earnestly into mainstream American history and historiography. This is, fundamentally, an American history. Through various case studies, the essays in this volume contend that ecology is life and that ecology resides at the center of all human activity. Moreover, in their social and cultural contexts, *Natural Protest* glimpses Americans acting throughout their history upon their most basic democratic rights. No single volume could hope to be totally comprehensive, but the essays that follow offer a thumbnail sketch of this vital history to suggest its relevance and complexity and to point toward avenues of further inquiry for students and scholars alike.

For example, although Muir's and Commoner's iterations on the interconnectivity of ecosystems and their component parts suggests elements of intellectual consistency across the twentieth century, these two luminaries came from and lived in vastly different worlds and their interests in promoting broader social awareness about ecological systems stemmed from divergent priorities. Muir worried about the wholesale devastation of American natural beauty by industrial powers that threatened the aesthetic and spiritual virtue of place and soul; Commoner witnessed the introduction of new hazards from the petrochemical industry that put human health firmly within the purview of ecological concern. Muir's rhetoric was profoundly religious; Commoner's distinctly secular. But these trends reflected basic changes not just in the American environmental consciousness, but also in American history.

The essays in this volume suggest similar relationships between George Catlin, Liberty Hyde Bailey, and Rachel Carson and point to concomitant connections between places, ranging from the central California wetlands to urban centers to the construction of dams in Maine. Their interests and sites of protest vary and sometimes conflict—as do the players involved—but the reader is urged to look for connections between the essays and across the sections. *Natural Protest* is divided into five sections, suggestive—roughly— of chronological and thematic features that help to organize our reading of American environmental activism.

Thanks to critical work by Theodore Steinberg, Richard W. Judd, and others, we now have a clear understanding of how far environmental protest extends back in American history. For example, in *Nature Incorporated: Industrialization and the Waters of New England* Steinberg shows that there were vociferous conflicts over the future of resource use in the very beginning of the industrial revolution in late eighteenth-century America.[2] In the New England region, a tradition of common use of resources had persisted through the colonial era and into the early republic. Brian Donahue's *Great Meadow: Farmers and the Land in Colonial Concord* demonstrates a pattern of land use and exchange, a use of the commons, predating industrial capitalism, that was both sustainable and productive.[3] But as rivers were dammed and factories built, the commons system fell apart. Dams not only flooded upstream meadows, destroying pasturage, they also blocked river transport and stopped the passage and spawning of anadromous fish, which were a critical part of the subsistence and trade of this region and era. With the rise of industrial capitalism and the corresponding need for hydromechanical power, necessitating the damming of rivers and controlling the flow of water on those rivers for foundries, sawmills, and textile mills, the traditional users of these rivers and the ecosystems along the rivers found their way of life threatened. The opposition to a dam on the Kennebec River of Maine in 1835, as described by Jeff Crane, clarifies and extends the historiography of opposition to dams in early American history. The dam on the Kennebec

River in Augusta, Maine, was constructed in order to provide hydromechanical power for the creation of a textile mill economy. The vision of the town boosters was to create an industrial mill town on the scale of Lowell, Massachusetts, and damming the river was a critical step in industrial production as it had been everywhere in the Northeast before this point. The very meaning and uses of these rivers and their resources lay in the balance and those Americans opposing dams or demanding fish passageways realized that their way of life was endangered by these dams and, of course, by the industrial revolution.

Another feature of the industrial revolution consisted of the transformation of the urban landscape. Rapid population growth put intense strains on urban infrastructures while new manufacturing practices—emphasizing the use of fossil fuels to power production—posed new health hazards. In "Organizing Environmental Protest," Michael Egan challenges the traditional reading of urban environmental concerns arising late in the nineteenth century. His account of public agitation against the distribution of "swill milk" brings together urban and public health historiographies in his hunt for the ancestors of environmental activism and continues a discussion initiated by Robert Gottlieb in his seminal book, *Forcing the Spring: The Transformation of the American Environmental Movement*.[4] Gottlieb traced connections between 1960s environmentalism and various forms of social activism that preceded it to demonstrate that American environmentalism is a richer and more fundamental feature of the American landscape than had previously been assumed. Another central tenet of his book was the key assertion that race, class, and gender were instrumental in the construction of this social activism, challenging the notion that environmental issues have traditionally been the purview of white and middle-class males. Sylvia Hood Washington points to similar issues in her more recent book, *Packing Them In: An Archaeology of Environmental Racism in Chicago, 1865–1954*.[5]

Building on these notions and continuing the link between race and the environment, another way of looking at the peoples and environments of the nineteenth century is to examine Indian removal as indicative of the cultural and political contexts of the era, but also as an expression of ecological power relations. Building on important debates in cultural environmental history, John Hausdoerffer explores the intellectual origins of Euro-American environmental impulses. The artist George Catlin is one of the forerunners of American environmental activism, having famously proposed the creation of a national park as a place to admire wild nature. But, as Hausdoerffer points out, Catlin's portraits were also a manifestation of manufacturing a popular consent regarding Indian policy and the opening of new landscapes. Catlin was unquestionably a defender of American Indians, but his lament for the imminent passing of a people contributed in complicated ways to the politics of his era.[6] In *Rivers of Empire: Water, Aridity, and the Growth of the American West*, Donald Worster employed Karl Wittfogel's theory of a hydraulic society to show that the control of nature ensured the control of people.[7] Hausdoerffer suggests that in a popular culture setting the control of ideas leads to the control of nature.

One of the critical stages in the development of American environmentalism is the rise of conservationism and the conservation movement at the beginning of the twentieth century. As is true of much of what this collection examines, the term *movement* is misleading because of the variety and disparity of concerns and actions, not to mention the profusion of groups with different backgrounds, philosophies, and agendas. Therefore it may be more productive to speak of a conservation era while acknowledging and exploring the complications of this time. Samuel P. Hays really began this conversation with *Conservation and the Gospel of Efficiency*.[8] In this study, he focused on the conservationists as part of the Progressive era. Simply put, conservationists were managers, public officials, fisheries experts, forestry scientists, and such, concerned with the rational and scientific management of natural resources for sustainable present and future use. In this sense, they were supporters of rational and efficient capitalism *and* responsible stewards of the land. Although conservationists often wielded political power, their attitudes and actions in many cases represented a form of protest. Protest against wasteful economic and environmental practices, protest against laissez-faire capitalism, and protest against individualism and greed run wild. That protest was limited in its tacit acceptance of capitalist land and resource use and exploitation as the best use for the environment but this was a realistic position in the political economy of the time.

Further complicating our understanding of this era, Kevin C. Armitage provides an innovative and compelling interpretation of the conservationists through his study of Liberty Hyde Bailey. Arguing that the traditional histories of the Progressive era conservationists have focused too much on the embrace of science and bureaucracy, and that there has been too much reliance on the traditional division between the scientific conservationists seeking to manage nature efficiently and the preservationists who sought to set aside nature for other reasons, such as spiritual and aesthetic benefits, Armitage uses Bailey, a forgotten conservationist, as a model of complexity of thought that has been forgotten or ignored. Bailey believed that nature had to be used and interacted with in multiple ways in order for a democratic society to flourish or exist. Furthermore, this approach would help nature flourish. Healthy nature and democracy, according to Bailey and Armitage, were irrevocably intertwined. Arguing against simple technocracy and pure science for science's sake, he insisted that true nature study and use fueled and strengthened democracy. Because of this, Bailey argued for an education system that emphasized the study of science through the study of nature.

This argument for complicating our view both of conservationism and human relations with nature intersects with another important piece of conservationist scholarship. Nancy Langston's *Forest Dreams, Forest Nightmares: The Paradox of Old Growth in the Inland West* effectively critiques the confidence in science displayed by forestry management in the Blue Mountains of the Pacific Northwest during the Progressive era.[9] It has been argued that not only was the use of science critical to the conservationists in their efforts to sustainably manage natural resources, it was also believed that science could be employed to make nature much more productive, to improve on nature. This line of thought was found in fisheries management efforts, in reclamation, and of course, as Langston argues, in the management programs of forestry experts in the early twentieth century. In fact, however, they too often got the science wrong. This misunderstanding of the forest ecology of the Blue Mountains led to grievous mistakes in forest management policy, doing great damage to the environment of this region. Furthermore, Langston's description of the foresters as alienated from and even frightened of this landscape reinforces Bailey's concerns over establishing healthy and intelligent relationships between humans and nature. According to Armitage, Bailey believed that normative relationships with the land and resources created confusion about nature and human society. Frightened foresters would not have surprised Bailey at all.

Robert Righter's essay on the legendary Hetch Hetchy fight blurs the categories of conservation and preservation, concentrating on the strong preservationist ethos and activism of the early twentieth century. Preservationism in this era is best understood through John Muir, who helped create the Sierra Club, helped create Yosemite National Park, and led the failed efforts to block a dam on the Tuolumne River in Yosemite. Muir, a deeply spiritual man who saw evidence of God's handiwork and beauty throughout nature, felt that sacred places were refuges deserving the highest level of protection. The relationship between humans, nature, and spirituality is another significant avenue of inquiry that warrants attention. Whereas many of the earlier essays stress economic interests as a motivation for environmental protection, much preservationist rhetoric is imbued with a more moral line of persuasion. This is present in Roderick Frazier Nash's classic work, *Wilderness and the American Mind*, but more recent work, such as Thomas R. Dunlap's *Faith in Nature: Environmentalism as Religious Quest* and Mark Stoll's *Protestantism, Capitalism, and Nature in America*, also investigate the role of nature in spiritual awareness.[10]

Regardless of the spiritual value of nature in general and the Hetch Hetchy Valley specifically, the leaders of San Francisco sought more water for their growing city and they decided damming the Tuolumne River was the answer. According to Righter, the Hetch Hetchy fight pitted preservationists against utilitarians and also created rifts in the Sierra Club as members of that group fought about the best uses of nature. In fact, like Armitage, Righter complicates the dichotomy of utilitarians against preservationists seemingly embodied in the Hetch Hetchy fight. Many of the key actors in this drama were torn, trying to balance between the values of preserving important natural places and the need to provide resources for human society; many of the tensions of environmentalism in the twentieth century are seen in this fight. As Righter points out, this was an unusual fight to have so early in American history when so much of American society's momentum was behind unquestioned growth and development.

Other unusual fights over the environment occurred in the 1920s and 1930s. The environmentalism of the interwar years is an interesting and complex phenomenon that has been examined by several historians. Most consistent with Philip Garone's contribution to this collection, Paul Sutter argues in *Driven Wild: How the Fight against Automobiles Launched the Modern Wilderness Movement* that the increasing popularity of the car and recreational travel was central to the expanding wilderness movement.[11] Showing that the use of nature, through tourist travel by car, created a love of nature while also threatening its health through road building, Sutter makes the case that use, rather than the preservationist impulse alone, played a critical role in the creation of wilderness areas. Similarly, Garone demonstrates how in the interwar years, in California's Central Valley, use and recreation were pivotal in private and public efforts to protect crucial wetlands habitat for migratory waterfowl.

Although the environmental struggles in the first half of the twentieth century are often cast in terms of federal and state governments imposing environmental measures on landowners and resource users, in some cases, activists and private landowners found that government programs and bureaucracy violated their own efforts to protect the land. Garone explores this very issue in his chapter examining the fight by duck hunters and cattle ranchers to protect vital waterfowl habitat in the Central Valley of California from Bureau of Reclamation irrigation projects in the 1930s and on. Garone shows the dramatic decline of critical wetlands, with approximately 90 percent of wetlands in the Central Valley disappearing to development, agriculture, and irrigation prior to 1930. As this valley was an important flyway for migratory waterfowl, local duck hunting clubs and cattle ranchers created a cooperative program allowing both to use the land while protecting critical wetland habitat—an area close to 100,000 acres. The Bureau of Reclamation's massive 1930s irrigation program for this valley, the Central Valley Project, threatened to take away the necessary water rights, thereby leading to the destruction of this last remaining piece of important wetlands habitat.

This threat led to the organization of "an unlikely coalition of duck hunters and cattle ranchers," which fought to save the Grasslands, creating a campaign that grabbed national attention, protected the wetlands, and also compelled the Central Valley Project to consider and mitigate its impacts on fish and wildlife for the first time. Whereas this effort proved important in promoting the importance of wetlands, thereby eventually halting the loss of wetlands in California and leading to international recognition of the Grasslands wetlands' significance for migratory waterfowl and biodiversity, the cooperative effort of businessmen and hunters to force a powerful federal agency dedicated to development to seriously address environmental issues is yet another environmental story that defies the parameters of the traditional environmental history narrative and demonstrates the very complexity of American environmental protest.

World War II constituted something of a technological revolution in the United States. Between 1939 and 1945 government funding of scientific research and development grew exponentially. The motivation was to harness the ingenuity of American science and technology for the war effort, but after the war's conclusion the government grip on research and development increased even further, creating what President Dwight Eisenhower called a "military–industrial complex." Government control of science drastically altered the shape and direction of American natural protest. New landscapes, not least the human body, came under threat from new, human-made pollutants. Nuclear fallout, synthetic chemicals, and other hazards proliferated. Like Egan, Frank Uekoetter shows that health as an environmental issue preceded this technological turn. Nevertheless, his concentration on air pollution after World War II and the growing concern over air pollution certainly suggest a marked change in priorities, which serves as a key catalyst in Adam Rome's *The Bulldozer in the Countryside: Suburban Sprawl and the Rise of American Environmentalism*.[12] The rise of an environmental health science that could both measure and monitor air quality is part of a larger social and medical movement that identified a relationship between health and ambient environments.[13] Whereas expert knowledge was used during the Progressive era to manage lands and resources, new kinds of scientific expertise after World War II specified how Americans might manage healthy living and working environments.

Citizen participation in determining what constituted a healthy environment contributed to this significant shift in natural protest. In "A Call to

Action," Sarah L. Thomas notes the new role of science and technology as well as the new role of scientists. Two key themes are central to her chapter: a newfound discussion of risk as it pertains to environmental health, and activist scientists' role in communicating that risk to an increasingly concerned public. Like Egan's interpretation of the crusading journalist Frank Leslie, Thomas's reading of *Silent Spring* in its historical context is one in which an informed public, armed with the necessary scientific information, is galvanized into action. Thomas's essay contributes to a growing body of scholarship that engages with scientists and their public role as it pertains to the environment. Rachel Carson was one of a number of public scientists who sought to develop and disseminate accessible scientific information to a public anxious to learn about the hazards around them. This larger scientists' movement was the cornerstone of Donald Fleming's classic essay, "Roots of the New Conservation Movement," in which he introduced the idea of the "politico-scientist."[14] Carson, Commoner, Paul Ehrlich, René Dubos, Margaret Mead, and others not only reframed the nature of environmental protest by providing technical information to grassroots organizations throughout the United States, but they also reframed the polity of science by forcing expertise outside the academy.

Another characteristic of natural protest after World War II involves the proliferation of voices and participants, which expanded even further the discussion of priorities raised in the previous section. As Gottlieb noted, race, class, and gender were present in environmental activism long before World War II, but their presence in environmental politics certainly became more prominently felt during the 1960s and 1970s. Invoking the Temptations' "Ball of Confusion," Sylvia Hood Washington surveys the widespread and diverse responses to Earth Day within African American communities and among African American leaders. To suggest a single, monolithic African American response to Earth Day and to the environmental movement, she argues, is problematic and historians should recognize that natural protest occurs within historical contexts that necessarily transcend singular and local issues.

Even with the growing emphasis of science and the more direct influence of race, class, and gender, elements of the old conservationist and preservationist impulses continue to shape and drive many natural protests. The wilderness movement, which played a role in the fight for Hetch Hetchy, evolved and expanded throughout the twentieth century, and the preservationist ethos that so influenced John Muir became a rather prominent feature of the overall framework of American environmentalism after World War II. Perhaps the preservationist drive was best articulated in the fight to protect Echo Park in the late 1940s and 1950s. This environmental conflict, described by Mark W. T. Harvey in *A Symbol of Wilderness: Echo Park and the American Conservation Movement*, demonstrates the effectiveness of environmental efforts as well as the importance of fighting to preserve significant and beautiful natural places. Like the earlier Hetch Hetchy fight, this became a national campaign. Unlike the Hetch Hetchy fight, the Echo Park activists defeated the Bureau of Reclamation and protected the threatened site. The defense mounted by the Sierra Club and Wilderness Society against the U.S. Bureau of Reclamation propelled them and vocal leaders such as David Brower and Howard Zahniser into national prominence. Wallace Stegner's *This is Dinosaur: Echo Park Country and its Magic Rivers,* a collection of essays about and images of Echo Park, the canyon where the Yampa and Green Rivers meet, mobilized sentiment in favor of preservation of this beautiful and important site and as Harvey argues, success in this effort generated momentum for greater achievements of environmental protest such as the passage of the Wilderness Act several years later.[15]

The preservationist impulse is critical to Kevin Marsh's essay, in which he examines the fight to preserve wilderness areas in Oregon from the postwar era through the 1970s. Like Harvey, he shows that this protest arises in opposition to the excesses of a federal agency, in this case the United States Forest Service (USFS). Noting that wilderness preservation had been part of the Forest Service's mandate in the pre-World War II years, Marsh demonstrates that the aggressive cutting of forests in the postwar years, with little effort to preserve habitat, ran up against a growing groundswell in support of wilderness preservation. He argues that this fight to preserve wilderness from a logging-obsessed USFS in the postwar years was at least as important as Echo Park in gaining support for the creation and passage of the Wilderness Act.

The focus of Marsh's chapter is the effort to protect the French Pete wilderness and show that as the counterculture gained strength and joined the wilderness fight, it not only reinforced the French Pete wilderness advocates, thereby strengthening that effort, but also brought a new set of goals and philosophies into the movement and American environmentalism overall. Therefore, according to Marsh, the effort to save French Pete is significant not only for the preservation of wilderness and other environmental victories but also because American environmentalism grew more complex, with a broader range of goals and strategies. This creates a more comprehensive and sophisticated environmental movement but also, like so many of the protest movements of this era, introduced divisive elements that would break down the cohesiveness of American environmentalism in the 1980s.

In a similar vein to Marsh's examination of the French Pete wilderness fight, Elizabeth D. Blum finds a strong correlation between the protest movements and counterculture of the 1960s and 1970s and the ecumenical response to the environmental crisis of Love Canal. She demonstrates that the leadership of the Ecumenical Task Force to Address the Love Canal Disaster (ETF) came from backgrounds of activism or protest on a variety of issues including opposition to the Viet Nam War, civil rights efforts, other environmental crises, nuclear disarmament, and gay rights. In contradiction to the efforts led by Lois Gibbs, the ETF created a theological response to the crisis that sought to not only deal with the immediate problem presented by leaking chemical pollutants but also question and challenge the dominant ideas of American capitalism and the uses of the environment that led to this crisis in the first place. Their philosophical approach changed over time as the leadership shifted from the emergency response they began with to articulating an argument for Christian stewardship and ecofeminism that would help reestablish a healthier relationship with nature than the one that had developed—one that could lead to a disaster like Love Canal. Furthermore, while they embraced a scientific, technical response to industrial pollution, it was a response informed by a desire to force businesses to be moral and responsible in their actions. If industrialists could not create a technological solution to the dangerous pollutants and waste they created, then it was immoral to create that waste in the first place. This chapter helps us to understand the response to Love Canal in a broader sense and see the effort to reevaluate human relations with nature.

Adam Tompkins's essay follows neatly from Blum's, but on the other side of the country, in the same Central Valley in which Garone's bird hunters had sought to protect wetlands some decades earlier. In providing an account of concerns over exposure to pesticides, Tompkins also echoes themes of risk and the polity of science from Thomas's chapter on Rachel Carson. It is interesting, however, to observe the evolution of science in public environmental politics over the intervening period. Tompkins's local victims are marginalized—yes—but there also appears to be a growing use of science, scientists, and scientific findings by all parties in his case study, indicating a shift in the use of science and medical professionals. This phenomenon and the complexities inherent therein expand upon Sylvia Noble Tesh's *Uncertain Hazards: Environmental Activists and Scientific Proof*, which shows how the interaction between experts and the public and the use of science is frequently muddied by the urgency with which activists and legislators are required to act.[16]

Also starting from the margins, Will McArthur asks the question that is fundamentally at the center of this book: "What or who is an environmentalist?" McArthur traces the history of a struggle over the Grand Canyon in the early 1980s, and pits local and national branches of the Sierra Club against each other and against Havasupai. His essay brings the volume back to addressing ideas about ecology and Indians some 150 years after Catlin, but also to revisit land use issues. On the one hand, McArthur's piece provides an interesting perspective on environmental justice insofar as he explores who has access to nature and natural resources in a manner not dissimilar to Laura Pulido's *Environmentalism and Economic Justice: Two Chicano Struggles in the Southwest*, whereas on the other he chronicles some of the deep-seated divisions within national environmental organizations, identified in Mark Dowie's *Losing Ground: American Environmentalism at the Close of the Twentieth Century*.[17]

Where we are now, with oil at well over $100 a barrel, global climate change threatening weather patterns and biodiversity, the discovery of myriad chemicals contributing to previously unanticipated health hazards, and ongoing reticence among many key players entrenched within the Beltway and industry, is a confusing and problematic time and place. On a more local level, many communities face more immediate and pressing concerns than these larger global phenomena. The accounts that relate successful cases of ecological activism might inspire hope and persistence; the more declensionist narratives might identify the intractability of environmental concerns and serve as cautionary tales or as lessons that stress how seriously we must take the protection of our environment. Each essay also highlights the varieties of peoples and natural protests that make up American history. And, collectively, these essays might remind students, scholars, and Americans alike that these current problems have antecedents in the past that warrant our attention and that the origins of the environmental crisis we are currently facing can and should be hitched to a context that is a part of the American historical universe. It is also worth remembering, as these essays remind us, that environmental protest of all forms, springing from different classes, regions, ethnicities, races, and eras, has always been a central part of American society. Just as nature has made America wealthy and powerful, protest has always marked American's responses to natural degradation, pollution, and land and resource use. In a time of increasing environmental peril it is helpful to understand that environmental protest has long been and remains a pivotal part of the American political landscape.

Notes

1   John Muir, *My First Summer in the Sierra* (1911, San Francisco: Sierra Club Books, 1988), 110.
2   Theodore Steinberg, *Nature Incorporated: Industrialization and the Waters of New England* (Cambridge: Cambridge University Press, 2003). See also Richard W.

Judd, *Common Lands, Common People: The Origins of Conservation in Northern New England* (Cambridge, MA: Harvard University Press, 2000).

3   Brian Donahue, *The Great Meadow: Farmers and the Land in Colonial Concord* (New Haven, CT: Yale University Press, 2004).

4   Robert Gottlieb, *Forcing the Spring: The Transformation of the American Environmental Movement* (Washington, DC: Island Press, 1993).

5   Sylvia Hood Washington, *Packing Them In: An Archaeology of Environmental Racism in Chicago, 1865–1954* (Lanham, MD: Lexington Books, 2005).

6   For ecology and Indians, see Shepard Krech III, *The Ecological Indian: Myth and History* (New York: W. W. Norton & Co., 2000); and Mark David Spence, *Dispossessing the Wilderness: Indian Removal and the Making of the National Parks* (New York: Oxford University Press, 2000).

7   Donald Worster, *Rivers of Empire: Water, Aridity, and the Growth of the American West* (New York: Oxford University Press, 1985).

8   Samuel P. Hays, *Conservation and The Gospel of Efficiency* (Cambridge, MA: Harvard University Press, 1959).

9   Nancy Langston, *Forest Dreams, Forest Nightmares: The Paradox of Old Growth in the Inland West* (Seattle: University of Washington Press, 1996).

10 Roderick Frazier Nash, *Wilderness and the American Mind* (New Haven, CT: Yale University Press, 1967); Thomas R. Dunlap, *Faith in Nature: Environmentalism as Religious Quest* (Seattle: University of Washington Press, 2004); and Mark Stoll, *Protestantism, Capitalism, and Nature in America* (Albuquerque: University of New Mexico Press, 1997). On wilderness, see also Michael Lewis (ed.), *American Wilderness: A New History* (New York: Oxford University Press, 2007).

11 Paul S. Sutter, *Driven Wild: How the Fight against Automobiles Launched the Modern Wilderness Movement* (Seattle: University of Washington Press, 2004).

12 Adam Rome, *The Bulldozer in the Countryside: Suburban Sprawl and the Rise of American Environmentalism* (New York: Cambridge University Press, 2001).

13 Christopher C. Sellers, *Hazards of the Job: From Industrial Disease to Environmental Health Science* (Chapel Hill: University of North Carolina Press, 1999). See also Gregg Mitman, *Breathing Space: How Allergies Shape Our Lives and Landscapes* (New Haven, CT: Yale University Press, 2007).

14 Donald Fleming, "Roots of the New Conservation Movement," *Perspectives in American History* 6 (1972), 7–91. See also Frederick Buell, *From Apocalypse to Way of Life: Environmental Crisis in the American Century* (New York: Routledge, 2003); Michael Egan, *Barry Commoner and the Science of Survival: The Remaking of American Environmentalism* (Cambridge, MA: MIT Press, 2007); Linda J. Lear, *Rachel Carson: Witness for Nature* (New York: Henry Holt, 1997); and Donald Worster, *Nature's Economy: A History of Ecological Ideas* 2nd edition (New York: Cambridge University Press, 1994).

15 Mark W. T. Harvey, *A Symbol of Wilderness: Echo Park and the American Conservation Movement* (Seattle: University of Washington Press, 2000); and Wallace Stegner, *This is Dinosaur: Echo Park Country and its Magic Rivers* (New York:

Alfred A. Knopf, 1955). See also Harvey, *Wilderness Forever: Howard Zahniser and the Path to the Wilderness Act* (Seattle: University of Washington Press, 2007).

16 Sylvia Noble Tesh, *Uncertain Hazards: Environmental Activists and Scientific Proof* (Ithaca, NY: Cornell University Press, 2001). See also Linda Nash, *Inescapable Ecologies: A History of Environment, Disease, and Knowledge* (Berkeley: University of California Press, 2007).

17 Laura Pulido, *Environmentalism and Economic Justice: Two Chicano Struggles in the Southwest* (Tucson: University of Arizona Press, 1996); and Mark Dowie, *Losing Ground: American Environmentalism at the Close of the Twentieth Century* (Cambridge, MA: MIT Press, 1995).

CHAPTER 1

"Fancy Foreshadowed a Magnificent Destiny"

The Market Revolution and the Kennebec River Dam Fight

JEFF CRANE

The Kennebec River of Maine is well known in some circles for its central and highly publicized role in the efforts of environmentalists to remove dams in order to restore rivers and fisheries. In 1999, by order of the Federal Energy Regulatory Commission (FERC) the Edwards Dam in Augusta was removed to restore threatened anadromous fish such as short-nosed sturgeon, American shad, Atlantic salmon, striped bass, herring, and other species. It was the first major dam in the nation to be removed by a FERC order for environmental reasons and the positive benefits of the dam removal, the immediate and dramatic improvement of the river ecosystem and numerous fish species, have energized environmental groups to take on other dams in watersheds in Maine and across the nation. A general and widespread river restoration movement has emerged as a vibrant new direction in American environmental activism. The current efforts to restore the river and its fisheries reflect dramatic changes in the way Americans think about nature and also frames the back-end of a debate over river use that started in the Kennebec River Valley in the 1830s.

Looking back over the contours of American history we are often misled by the general assertions of progress argued in textbooks, syntheses, and the broad descriptions of eras in American history. The mid-nineteenth century was central to the expansion of the American economic system and the cornerstone to America's future economic prosperity. Therefore it is easy to view that era as one in which Americans equally and enthusiastically supported economic development and likewise shared in its benefits; neither assumption is accurate. In the case of the Kennebec Dam, significant protest arose along the Kennebec River in opposition to the dam. This protest is primarily articulated through petitions to the Maine state legislature opposing approval of the charter to build the dam. These petitions are remarkable documents, generally well written, passionate, and comprehensive in revealing the variety of reasons for opposing the dam. Furthermore, the petitions reveal splits in communities over the building of the dam. Many towns had pro-dam and anti-dam petitions but they were all consistent in citing economic factors, either positive or negative, for their support for or opposition to the proposed dam.

The incorporation of the Kennebec Dam Company in 1834 provided an impetus for dissent against intensive economic development, the transformation of the landscape, and the shrinking of "the commons," referring to a pattern of land use in which residents shared access to rivers and fisheries, pasturage, and forest resources, among other things. This pattern had remained largely intact in the Northeast until the Market Revolution. Brian Donahue argues in *The Great Meadow: Farmers and the Land in Colonial Concord* that in some communities such as Concord, Massachusetts, a sustainable economic system that worked within the limits of the environment had been created. This system collapsed in the face of industrialization and the destruction of the sustainable pattern of land use, cooperation, and exchange.[1]

Whereas economic interests drove motivations both for and against the dam, objections were also at least partially fueled by a strong concern for the river ecology. The subsistence and economic activities of many Kennebec Valley residents were deeply dependent on a healthy river ecosystem and their opposition to the proposed dam demonstrated an understanding of the ecological damage the dam would create with a corresponding impact on their own way of life. They protested the production of energy at this site because it would threaten their own economic well-being by damaging fisheries and blocking transportation on the river. The fight over a river and its uses was in fact a fight over the nature of the future economy and the role of individual Americans in that economy.

The traditional organization of environmentalism into a primarily late nineteenth- and twentieth-century movement divided in the early stages between conservationists, preservationists, and activists focused on urban sanitation has made it hard to categorize opposition of the sort seen on the Kennebec River in the early nineteenth century. In fact, they fought economic development that would damage the river environment and the fisheries and hurt many residents of the valley economically. As Laura Pulido argues in *Environmentalism and Economic Justice: Two Chicano Struggles in the Southwest,* much of what constitutes environmentalism is an effort to protect one's community and environment from capitalist development and corresponding deterioration. If there is a link between natural protest and capitalist development, the opposition to the Kennebec Dam in 1834 constitutes a site at which we might need to reconsider the traditional organization of the history of American environmentalism.[2]

The course of American history is framed around a number of key events familiar to most Americans such as the Revolution and the Civil War. The lesser-known intervening period referred to as the Market Revolution is as important to American society and history as any of the wars perceived as pivotal to the American experience. The Market Revolution refers to the period from roughly 1820 to 1850 and took place primarily in the Northeast; it was characterized by the dramatic growth of transportation infrastructure such as improved roads, canals, steamboats, and railroads, and a concomitant and unprecedented economic expansion. Moreover, this marked the edge of an expanding capitalist system that was sweeping the world. American communities worked hard to find their niche in this burgeoning economy. Businessmen and laborers alike had to become nimble, flexible, and aware of and responsive to change as the world was transformed around them. Furthermore, they were compelled to understand not only how they could benefit from these changes but also the threats presented to their interests and lifestyles.[3]

Although the Market Revolution provided more jobs, created great wealth, and laid the industrial foundation of America's emerging modern capitalist economy, this all came at great environmental cost. Nature, wealth accrued over centuries in the form of trees and fertile soil and healthy fisheries, for example, as William Cronon argues in *Nature's Metropolis,* subsidized this convulsive economic growth. The harvest of forests, breaking of ground for farms, and damming of rivers for foundries, textile mills, and saw mills all destroyed the natural environment. The destruction of grasslands and forest habitat led to a corresponding decline in many animal and bird species. The devastation of river ecosystems from log drives, dam construction, overharvesting of fish, and erosion created precipitous drops in fish populations by the 1850s in the Northeast. The catalog of environmental devastation is a long and daunting one. The wealth of nature, as Donald Worster called it, drove this process of growth and nature suffered dramatically as a result.[4]

If it were a simple formula of wealth versus degraded nature, understanding this era might be more difficult. But the conversion of nature to capital and the creation of industrial capitalism served other deep-seated American needs. Charles Sellers provides a powerful explanation of the forces driving changes during this period and in this region, arguing that the lack of an aristocracy and post-feudal institutions, such as those found in Europe, created a great deal of freedom for American entrepreneurs and drove the pursuit of wealth because the rich would become America's aristocracy.[5] An ideology promoting the pursuit of wealth was essential to the emerging market. Max Weber's work in *The Protestant Ethic and the Spirit of Capitalism* (1930) showed that production and the wealth bestowed upon successful laborers in a market economy provided a way to demonstrate one's piety. Drawing on Weber's analysis, Sellers explains the role of Calvinism in the emerging economy of the market revolution:

> While revitalizing traditional piety against market corrosion, Calvinism also became the spiritual medium of capitalist transformation by sanctifying worldly work as religious duty and wealth as fruit of grace . . . As God seemed kindlier, the environment more manageable, and their fate more dependent on their own abilities, they could no longer see themselves as sinners helplessly dependent on the arbitrary salvation of an all-powerful God.[6]

While religious beliefs and personal philosophy enabled and encouraged the expansion of the capitalist economy into the hinterlands, other structural changes were necessary as well. Several factors were integral to the expansion of the market economy. The expansion and improvement of transportation networks through roads, canals, and railroads facilitated the flow of commodities, capital, and credit thereby expanding the reach of the market. The expansion and extension of credit through the creation of a national bank as well as state and local banks was fundamental to the growth of the market because providing centralized credit allowed for dynamic and explosive business growth. Another important factor in the marketplace was the increase in government power, particularly through the creation of eminent domain and Supreme Court decisions favoring the expansion of a commercial, industrial economy over the preservation of traditional economic uses of land, water, and other resources.

Roads, railroads, and canals extended the market further into a countryside that until the arrival of a new turnpike or canal had been primarily a mixed economy of subsistence agriculture, hunting and fishing, barter, and limited wage work. Easier shipping of goods and correspondingly lower shipping rates made it possible for farmers to engage more actively with the marketplace and offer their goods for cash sale. These farmers, devoting more of their agricultural production to the market rather than to subsistence, also began replacing home production of needed goods with the purchase of necessary items from the manufacturing centers of the Northeast, thereby providing more capital for the expansion of the market. And although private capitalists had invested in canals and roads, it was only with the chartering of turnpikes and the state support of canals and roads that the transportation revolution, so intrinsic to broadening and opening markets, expanded south, west, and north from the port cities of the Northeast.[7]

As the Market Revolution expanded from its base in the northern Atlantic states and capitalists cast their eyes to the margins of Anglo-American society in pursuit of riches, the Kennebec River in Augusta became a central tool in the process of transforming the surrounding landscape, industrializing the Augusta economy, and converting nature's capital to cash. Interest in dam construction in Augusta clearly began in 1818 when Ephraim Ballard Jr., the son of Martha Ballard, the famous midwife of Hallowell and Augusta, surveyed the site at Cushnoc and boldly asserted that he would be able to build a dam for $25,000. The river's topography gave him reason for confidence. The dam would sit at the very head of the tidal zone, and by covering the dangerous rapids at Cushnoc it would extend river navigation a much greater distance, conceivably all the way to Waterville, fifteen miles upstream.

This desire to create and improve transportation routes and use rivers for hydromechanical power reflected the powerful, transforming impulses of the Market Revolution and those people participating in and guiding the process. Ballard's idea drew little interest at that time but surfaced again with an article published in the Augusta paper, the *Kennebec Journal*, in 1825. The proponent of the idea in 1825, Luther Severance, was a man clearly tuned in to the zeitgeist of that era. Born in Montague, Massachusetts, a mill town in that state's western Pioneer Valley, he could clearly see the value of water power to industry and commerce. Having worked as a political newspaper writer in Philadelphia and Washington, D.C., he would have understood and been influenced by the forces of the Market Revolution. In the January 15, 1825, issue of the *Kennebec Journal*, Severance elucidated the benefits of a national transportation system: "Every thing which tends to connect the commercial interests, and increase the mutual dependence of one state on another, and to connect all with the capital, must tend to strengthen the ties which unite the states in one political community."[8] He was calling not only for greater economic growth but also for a stronger sense of nationalism, created by expanding markets. When he proposed the dam in Augusta, Severance extolled the benefits in the language of all boosters eyeing the landscape and imagining the numerous ways in which natural resources could be converted to capital:

> This state affords numerous facilities for machinery moved by water power. Many streams run into our river, some of which are used already, principally for sawing timber . . . but we would invite public attention to the project of making a dam across the Kennebec river, at the small island a few hundred yards above the bridge, in this town . . . inexhaustible quarries of excellent stone exist on both sides of the river . . . steam boat navigation . . . may be afforded to Waterville . . . a dam once made here, there would be ample water power to move more machinery, perhaps, than is at present in operation in all the New England states.[9]

Responding to the expressed interest in a dam, the U.S. Army Corps of Engineers surveyed the river. Although nothing came immediately of this effort, support gradually coalesced for the dam. The Kennebec Dam Company was organized as a corporation and applied for a charter from the Maine State Legislature to build a dam in 1834.[10]

This was not the first dam to be built in the Northeast and where dams had been built before, there was frequently opposition. Protests against dams emerged early in American history largely as a result of conflict between competing economic interests and the tension between a market-oriented, industrial-driven economy versus traditional subsistence activities and pre-industrial capitalist practices. In "Dams, Fish, and Farmers: Defense of Public Rights in Eighteenth Century Rhode Island,"[11] Gary Kulik illustrates the conflict between traditional users of the river and fish and those seeking to build dams for power generation. Increasing dam size is an important development in this historical period, for as the author points out, as long as dams were used for small-scale grain mills they were perceived as an extension of the agricultural economy and therefore not considered a threat to the existing economic order. Furthermore, they demonstrated greater flexibility in allowing fish passageways to be built in order to sustain anadromous fisheries and occasionally closed operations during spawning runs.[12] In fact, these early dam builders were subject to laws favoring subsistence gatherers of fish and the maintenance of anadromous fish runs.[13]

The right to the river and its fish was codified in colonial law as well and continued into the early part of the Market Revolution. The law so favored the traditional uses of the river that disgruntled fishermen and farmers had the right to remove dams prior to a determination by a court as to their legitimacy if they threatened fish runs. Although colonial law supported the continued use of rivers for numerous subsistence activities it also codified the right of mills to build dams to generate mechanical power and cause some upstream flooding, requiring only that they provide suitable fish passageways, a reasonable requirement. As long as mills served as an integral part of the local economy and were generally small in scale, conflict was rare and subdued. The production of blast furnaces and cotton mills, with their larger scale and greater need for power, led to emerging conflicts over dam construction. One key moment was the fight over the Furnace Unity dam in 1748 on the Blackstone River in Rhode Island. Complaining that the dam blocked the passage of fish, upstream residents convinced the local justice of the peace to order that the dam open for fish passage. According to Kulik:

> The two owners, referring to the plaintiffs as "certain malicious persons," petitioned the General Assembly in October 1748 to void the court's directive. The owners claimed that salt-water fish were not hindered, that breaking the dam would not promote the passage of fish, and moreover, would spoil a "useful grist mill now standing in such dam." The owners, however, made no claim for the local utility of the furnace. Their petition was signed by thirty-seven freemen. Even if some of them were furnace workers, it is apparent that local opinion was divided. The General Assembly agreed with the furnace owners and their supporters, its reasoning unknown, and preserved the dam.[14]

Farmers and commercial fishermen opposed this dam and others like it, the energy behind these protests arising from an increasing distrust of "corrupt and arbitrary power." Additionally, their discomfort with the shifting economic system is evident in their efforts to block dams and require the builders to build fish passageways. According to Kulik, "it was no accident that conflict over fish and conflict over empire overlapped in time and elicited similar fears—the fear of arbitrary power and corrupting influence, and the fear that rapacious private interests might overwhelm a fragile, and traditionally defined, public good."[15] Although farmers dependent upon fish for extra subsistence continued their opposition to dams, the shift to an expanding market economy and increasing industrialization doomed their efforts.[16]

Conflict over dams arose in other locations throughout New England as well. In the first half of the nineteenth century farmers upstream of the Bilerica Dam on the Concord River in eastern Massachusetts used the courts to protest the building of the dam and later efforts to raise the height of the dam to create an even larger upstream reservoir. Important hay-producing meadows were flooded, which resulted in a variety of other environmental impacts including softening of the soil—making it harder to harvest—and a conversion of beneficial feed plants to riparian vegetation less palatable to cattle. Their protests, except for temporary victories, failed to block the expansion of the dam as the courts favored industrial development in that time period.[17]

Opposition to the building of the Kennebec Dam clarifies the nature of the debate over the expansion of the economy and corresponding changes to the environment in the early part of the Market Revolution. As Theodore Steinberg writes in *Nature Incorporated: Industrialization and the Waters of New England*:

> Not only the conflict over the workplace, over wages and hours, but the struggle to control and dominate nature is central to industrialization. The face-to-face relations of power in the factory should be supplemented with a broader vision of conflict going on outside the factory walls. That struggle, at least in part, is over who will control the natural world and to what ends. Industrial capitalism is as much a battle over nature as it is over work, as likely to result in strife involving water or land as wages or hours.[18]

The Kennebec River, then, became the rope in yet another tug-of-war over the nature of capitalism in this region. The central conflict in the fight over the future of the river and its fisheries was one over the meaning of the river itself. Would it remain an ecosystem of multiple uses, a common available to all for small-scale economic activity and subsistence as well as providing a waterway for transportation of people and goods? Or, conversely, would the Kennebec be harnessed for hydromechanical production, providing power for the expanding industrial revolution and, in the process, changing the meaning of the river to power source and little more? Damming the river would necessarily cut the Kennebec Valley residents off from their traditional river uses while further compelling them to join a wage-labor economy that many were leery of and some strongly opposed.[19]

Petitions lodged against the dam evinced a clear understanding of how it would harm the abundant, ecologically healthy, and economically important fisheries of the Kennebec River. Plentiful runs of Atlantic salmon, shad, and alewives, among others, would be prevented from reaching upriver spawning grounds, thereby wiping out an important subsistence base and economic resource for inland farmers and laborers. A petition submitted by citizens of Georgetown in 1834 explained the fisheries' importance to people living along the river.

> Construction of the dam would injure Georgetown, which has less fertile soil for agriculture and which is dependent on two primary other activities—mills & fishing. The dam would make passage of logs difficult and

therefore more expensive and drive Georgetown mills out of business . . . the destruction of fishing privileges would be infinitely more disastrous in its consequences—a large number of our citizens derive their only subsistence from salmon, shad, alewive [sic] and cod fishery.[20]

The petition proceeded to illuminate the importance of fishways (passage-ways for spawning fish to cross the dams) to healthy fish runs and the eco-nomic importance of the Kennebec River to Maine's economy. The language employed is strongly economic in tone, displaying a clear understanding of the impacts the dam would have on fisheries and those economically depen-dent on the fish. The petition also argued for preserving traditional economic practices, such as logging and fishing, in the face of dominance or dislocation by the emerging industrial economy.

> The preservation of the salmon, shad, and alewives in the Kenebec [sic] . . . depends entirely on the free passage afforded them up and down the river. The salmon and shad fishery are a source of considerable profit . . . and create much capital in the state. Many men are employed in tak-ing and curing the fish . . . the alewives are important as a considerable article of trade, as bait for fishermen and as the means of alluring the cod fish to our shores. The cod fishery is perhaps as important as all the above taken together and this fishery depends entirely on the preserva-tion of shad & alewives. On these several fisheries many of our citizens are entirely dependent for the means of livelihood.[21]

Opponents of the dam clearly understood that the river was the basis for a complex and wide-ranging economy and damming the river would not only change the meaning of the river and destroy its fisheries, it would also undermine jobs throughout the region, further affecting the health of ocean fisheries dependent on the life produced by a free-flowing river. Interestingly, opponents understood and explained the long and complex ecological chain reaching from the Kennebec River and its tributary streams into the Atlan-tic and the economically and environmentally important cod fishery. This was a nuanced and sophisticated defense of the river and an older economic model, indeed.

The argument against the dam on the basis of damage to existing econo-mies is most clearly spelled out in the petition against the dam prepared by some residents of Greenfield in 1834, after other citizens of the town had presented a petition to the legislature supporting the dam. The opposing pe-tition specifically explored how the dam would hurt the river transportation economy, with the authors explaining their argument in depth and provid-ing tremendous detail to support their points. A good example of this is the explanation of the impact of the proposed dam on logs being transported downstream:

> Logs in rafts are frequently run from Ticonic bay, and still more frequently from the dead water in Sidney to Hallowell, Gardiner and places below. Under the improved navigation this must cease to be the case, because they cannot be so run over the dam; logs destined for these places must then in future be run singly & caught in tide waters, this we apprehend would subject owners of this species of lumber to a considerable expense.
>
> Ship timber to the amount of from 2500 to 3000 tons is annually run down the river from Sebasticook River to Bath, it is usually run in rafts of about 100 tons, as the timber must be rafted at the dead waters in Winslow & then run to Bath. But the rafts must be inevitably be broken upon passing over the dam & great expense must be incurred in collecting and re-rafting it below; besides it will be subject to considerable loss by some portions being sunk; under the improved navigation we are constrained to say this business must be abandoned.[22]

The petition clarified the nature of the economic conflict taking place regarding the future use of the river. In fact, loggers and lumber companies in this era could never be confused with environmentalists. Heavy logging along the Kennebec River caused severe ecological damage including habitat loss, erosion, and a great deal of damage done to river bottoms by the log drives mentioned above. This had a deleterious impact on the river ecosystems, devastating fish populations. The Edwards Dam would not only interfere with the loggers' economic practices, it would also add to the environmental damage done to the river and, therefore, to the fisheries. These dam opponents were fighting not to preserve the ecology of the Kennebec River for its own sake but rather for the Kennebec River as a tool for timber transport, one of the many uses of the river before the building of the dam. Not only did this petition explain the environmental and economic impacts of the dam but it also argued that the spring freshets would tear out the dam, a prediction which quickly proved prescient.

Arguments about damaging economic change were reinforced by the use of examples of historical precedent to illustrate the inevitable destruction to the Kennebec River's fisheries that would result from the damming of the river in Augusta. For example, opponents of the dam in Woolwich sent a petition to the Maine Legislature explicating the impact of dams on fisheries by citing the destruction of other rivers' fisheries by dams in Maine.

Where streams of any magnitude have been obstructed by dams it has ever destroyed the fish ascending the streams. When the waters of the Androscoggin were obstructed by dams, it proved the destruction of a vast quantity of salmon which till then, had annually ascended that stream; and should the Kennebec be obstructed by a dam, from shore to shore, we believe the various tribes of fish . . . would be cut at a stroke.[23]

The citizens of Woolwich demonstrated their clear understanding that dams had destroyed fisheries in the past and the same fate was inevitable for Kennebec River fish. Such environmental destruction would threaten their very livelihoods. Yet another petition elucidated the damage a dam would render:

That the preservation of this species of fishery has been considered by our ancestors, as well as ourselves to have an important bearing in the community, not only because it contributes so largely in feeding a vast population, and by causing considerable money to circulate in the country, but that these river fish attract the fish in the sea to approach our shores, and thereby provide employment for all those engaged in the cod & mackerel industries. But as time passes on we find by sad experience that the river fish, if not others, are rapidly diminishing year by year from some cause or other, and the time must soon arrive . . . when the fish will be utterly exterminated.[24]

The petition from Greenfield also mentioned the impact on salmon, warning of the dam's potentially devastating impact on the salmon fishery, arguing that an important economic resource of "$3000 to 5000" would be lost. The opponents to the dam penning this petition also pointed out that the salmon "afford to a class of people at one season a cheap living, and are a source of considerable profit to a portion of our citizens. But this business must vanish and give way to the 'march of improvement.' "[25] The last lament against progress or "improvement" reveals the petitioners' concern with the damage that economic development would do to their traditional economic activities. Accordingly, the dam opponents argued for the preservation of more traditional economic uses of the river as well as subsistence, in short, a preservation of the commons. Furthermore, they also provided a limited critique of industrial development, with the rhetoric of the Greenfield petition foreshadowing the later conservation movement with its argument for the preservation of fish for their economic benefits.

Regardless of current debates, petitions against the dam in the 1830s laid out in precise detail what the consequences, environmental and economic, would be. This ecological and economic protest was one of complexity, revealing a concrete understanding of what the "march of progress" would do to the river and their own economic and subsistence practices. These opponents tried to stop the transformation of the Kennebec River from a commons and river that could be used in multiple ways by different people from different economic classes—from the farmer supplementing his diet with salmon to the logging industry trying to move lumber downstream—to merely an industrial river serving the interests of local men of wealth,[26] transforming Augusta into yet another textile mill town. "Thus, we believe, the industry, enterprise, and business of the whole Kennebec County will be brought into bondage for all coming time, and most injuriously affected by this project to 'make Augusta the greatest manufacturing town in New England.'"[27] This point was reiterated in the Georgetown petition, which stated:

> Your remonstrants cannot believe that from the great interest your honorable bodies have always manifested for the preservation of their fisheries, as well as the great injury that will be inflicted upon them, that your honorable bodies will not authorize an obstruction, which directly tends to impoverish one part of the community for the possible benefit of another.[28]

Those dependent on shad, salmon, and alewives for subsistence and commercial sale recognized the threat proposed by the dam in Augusta. Their petitions did not so much question progress as they beseeched the state to intercede on their behalf to protect their own economic interests and subsistence needs. This conflict was not between economic systems—subsistence farmers vs. capitalists—but, rather, a fight over how nature could be best employed, and by whom, for economic gain. In short, what kind of capitalist economy, and benefiting whom, would emerge during the Market Revolution? Furthermore, this was a conflict over control of the commons: the Kennebec River and its fisheries resource. Indeed, it has been widely noted that many settlers in New England and Maine sought to balance subsistence activities with economic participation in the expanding market and yet opponents found themselves in the minority. This model allowed them to maintain their freedom from wage labor while trying to pursue the yeoman ideal but also striving to advance themselves economically and improve their quality of life through the purchase of manufactured goods. For this strategy to work they had to maintain access to common resources such as lumber, fish, and game species. Richard Judd, for example, demonstrates that these farmers understood this and passed a number of laws and sent in numerous petitions in their efforts to maintain access to and preservation of "the commons."[29] The alternative strategy favored by capitalists was one of intensive development and extraction of resources. Private logging companies sought to clear land completely and mill owners needed to control the river in order to provide power for the conversion of logs to lumber and to convert cotton into textiles. This intensive development necessitated exclusive control of the commons and brought dam proponents and opponents face to face in a conflict over the best way to use the river. Furthermore, the extension of this capitalist model of economic development necessitated a larger wage-earning labor force and closing the commons would help create that work force, much like the earlier enclosure movement in Great Britain. The supporters of intensive private development won control of the Kennebec River in Augusta, and the dam assured that many of those trying to pursue a mixed economic lifestyle would be compelled to provide wage labor in the expanding market economy.

A minority of Maine representatives and senators gave voice to those opposing the dam as the charter underwent votes in both houses. Opposing senators forced debate for two days, expressing concern over the potential impact on fisheries, navigation problems, and possible downstream flooding caused by the dam, reiterating the concerns elucidated in the opposition petitions. At the end of the second day the charter passed by a vote of fifteen to seven.

> In the House the bill excited a lengthy and spirited debate. Mr. Chadwick of Gardiner was strenuous in opposition, manifesting a great regard for the interests of the citizens of Augusta and a desire to protect them against "a power" he perceived in the bill "which the kings of England were not allowed to exercise."[30]

Others joined in his protest but the charter easily passed the house of representatives by a vote of 126 to 27. The interests of economic development and the dominant attitudes favoring growth and industrialization rendered the dam inevitable for a growing and ambitious Augusta. Completed in 1838, the dam immediately devastated the river fisheries. Repeated washouts of the dam by spring freshets triggered persistent calls to block the rebuilding of the dam and continuing demands for the construction of fish passageways.[31]

Although local business leaders and manufacturers envisioned the prosperous future that the dam would usher in, they had no intention of picking up axes and shovels and laying their hands to the task of building a large dam. Local labor was unequal to the task, necessitating a large migration of workers, in this case French Canadians and Irish, into Augusta to provide the muscle power to complete the project. Author Nathaniel Hawthorne observed on a visit in 1837 that the Irish lived in horrible conditions, in "squatters colonies of sod huts and shacks." Many of the French Canadians came south to earn money by working on the dam and returned to Canada with their earnings. Others stayed on and settled in the Kennebec Valley.[32]

In his 1870 history of Augusta, James W. North described the bustle of activity in the Augusta area in the 1830s, noting that the increased importance of regional banks and larger amounts of currency in the local economy stimulated business growth:

> Augusta was in a thriving condition. Real estate had risen "within six months from fifty to one hundred per cent," and it was expected to rise much more upon the completion of the Kennebec dam, "the stockholders in which were most ready to buy at increasing prices."[33]

The author proceeded to describe a frenzy of speculation and sales in "wild lands, timber lots, water power . . . corner lots, granite quarries, buildings and stocks." Local boosters were optimistically anticipating the benefits that would accrue to them from the dam's construction. An article in a March 1835 issue of the *Kennebec Journal* predicted the future eminence of Augusta:

> We take great pleasure saying that we are now well assured that men of capital have taken a great part of the stock in the dam at this place . . . Practical and scientific men who have examined the river, unite in opinion that the dam will create a water power superior to that at Lowell, besides having the advantage of schooner navigation—the raw materials of all manufacturers can be shipped here directly from the ocean, or brought down the river in boats. Lumber can be sawed without limit, and put directly into vessels without being put into the water, such a water power, in the centre of a fertile and populous country, and with such advantages of navigation, must be of immense value. And then as to the lumber; many believe there is as much pine timber on the waters of the Kennebec as there is on the Penobscot. At any rate, the amount is very great, and must employ a vast number of saws for ages to come.[34]

This exaggerated prose of natural abundance and the potential preeminence of the writer's own town is typical booster rhetoric; it was often undermined by later harsh realities. Speculation increased as a result of the intended Kennebec dam, as investors saw their town industrializing and becoming a possible center for the expansion of the market with the concomitant profits for those prescient enough to sink their money into land and resources in the anticipation of growth. Augusta boomed as a result. Local investors looked to the model of the Lowell mills for what might happen in their own community as a consequence of developing local water power. According to North,

"The successful operation at Lowell, a few years previous, was continually suggestive of large profits. A greater power than that at Lowell was to be created, and fancy foreshadowed a magnificent destiny awaiting Augusta in the future."[35]

As the market extended its reach into interior Maine local residents prepared themselves for the prosperity and wealth they were sure would follow. But the interest in the possible profits that could be conferred by construction of a dam in Augusta was not limited to citizens of Maine. Boston investors also sank their money into the proposed project. This investment by Boston capitalists typified a pattern of the Market Revolution in which the capital of eastern seaboard trading ports was invested in the hinterlands of the expanding market.[36]

All of this investment and speculation created a frenzy of creative destruction of nature and construction of the dam, mills, and homes. Nathaniel Hawthorne, visiting a friend and investor in the dam, described dam construction in 1837:

> Beyond the road rolls the Kennebec, here two or three hundred yards wide. Putting my head out of the window, I can see it flowing steadily along the straightaway between wooded banks; but arriving nearly opposite the house . . . the current is further interrupted by the works of the mill-dam, which is perhaps half finished, yet still in so rude a state that it looks as much like the ruins of a dam destroyed by the spring freshets as like the foundations of a dam yet to be. Irishmen and Canadians toil at work on it, and the echoes of their hammering and of the voices come across the river and up to this window.[37]

Hawthorne then described the flow of the river and the logs drifting downstream on its current, explaining, too, the use of the river as a transportation route for already milled boards. He provided a vivid portrait of the dam under construction:

> Chaises and wagons occasionally go over the road, the riders all giving a passing glance at the dam, or perhaps alighting to examine it more fully, and at last departing with ominous shakes of the head as to the result of the enterprise. My position is so far retired from the river and mill-dam, that, though the latter is really rather a scene, yet a sort of quiet seems to be diffused over the whole. Two or three times a day this quiet is broken by the sudden thunder from a quarry, where the workmen are blasting rocks; and a peal of thunder sounds strangely in such a green, sunny and quiet landscape.[38]

The dam construction site became the center of the commerce in town as the productive capacity of the completed dam would symbolize, to many residents of Augusta and the region, the emergence of the town as an industrial power. Although hopes ran high for the profits the dam would generate, destructive weather introduced other realities into the dreams of the residents of Augusta and investors in the dam and mills. A severe storm struck the region in January 1839. Strong winds from the south brought heavy rain to wash away the snow. The water was four feet deep in downtown Hallowell (a few miles downstream of Augusta) and the wind damaged buildings and chimneys. While the dam withstood the rising river the pressure of the backed-up water washed away part of the bank wall on the west side of the dam. The following May heavy rains led to a breaching of the already damaged dam and washed away the recently completed mills. Private homes were swept away by the swollen river as it washed away shorelines.[39] The failure of the dam and the destruction of the mills struck a depressing blow to the Augusta business elite, who saw the dam and the industry it would engender as the centerpiece of the developing Augusta economy. Locals moved quickly to bring the river back under useful control. Responding to pressure from the legislature, which had voted to rescind the company's charter if they could not convincingly prove that they would have the dam rebuilt within two years, the repairs of the dam were completed in 1841 and industry quickly followed. Although the dam would be breached numerous times by spring floods, it would continue to serve an important economic function in Augusta. In 1842 a saw-mill was constructed on the east side of the river and a machine shop was also built. A cotton factory and mills were built in 1845 and 1846. Although Augusta, Maine, never became another Lowell, Massachusetts, as dam advocates had hoped and projected, the power provided by the dam supported a growing industrial economy.[40]

In addition to growing industrial production, by the mid-nineteenth century the Kennebec River and the Augusta–Lewiston region occupied a central place in the Maine logging economy. Typically, the operations along the Kennebec River were larger than operations on other Maine rivers. One particularly large firm owned approximately 400,000 acres of land along the Kennebec River and during the Civil War was producing around 24 million board-feet of lumber a year from those lands. With a complement of 228 oxen, 125 horses, and 860 humans, this was clearly a large-scale logging company that benefited from development along the river. Whereas this supports the logic of development and market expansion, it also confirms the fear of small landowners and businessmen that their practices would be eclipsed and subsumed by large-scale production, whether by textile mills or logging operations.[41]

The impact of the dam on the Kennebec River's fish was immediate and abrupt. The fish were no longer able to pass upstream to their spawning grounds, thus beginning a period of fisheries collapse on the Kennebec River. For the very short term the barrier created an excellent fishing hole, stopping fish in their upstream migration and causing them to mill about below the dam in confusion. According to North,

> Salmon, which had a free passage to ascend the river during the two seasons the dam was open, were taken in great numbers after it was closed, in 1841. One night in June of that year, one hundred and fifty were taken at Augusta of an average weight of seventeen pounds each.[42]

The fish runs declined quickly afterwards as the few runs returning from pre-dam days dwindled to nothing and a below-dam fishery emerged that was a shadow of the river's former prodigious production. When the dam was breached again by a flood in 1870, some called for the creation of functional fish passageways to restore the river's once great fish runs. North recounted the conflict in a diatribe against the fish passageways, reflecting the dominant political economy that had emerged during the Market Revolution and the naturally conservative attitude of pro-business historians but also the complete rejection of any sense of natural resource stewardship:

> When the proprietors were ready to move they requested the assistance of the city to relieve them from the burden and damage of a fishway which the law required to be made, and which competent authority was urging them to build. The law relating to fishways was doubtless passed by the legislature without knowledge of its operation upon enterprises of the magnitude contemplated at Augusta. Here is a dam nineteen feet high above tide water, on a large river, subject to sudden and great rises, upon which a large manufacturing capital is to be invested by the most wealthy and experienced manufacturers in the country. This, if successfully carried out, will be of incalculable value to the valley of the Kennebec and the whole state, and while encouraged by wise and fostering laws, should such enterprises be subject to other laws creating serious obstacles to their execution? Can it be doubted that the permanent interest of the States is to foster manufactures rather than the inferior fisheries? One gives constant and profitable employment to industry almost unlimited to extent, and in its operation stimulates every other branch of business; the other is in its operation a short period of the year, and does not so directly promote any other interest. If it should be said that each may be fostered without injuring the other, it should recollected that capitalists

will not be persuaded that it can be done, and will shun our State if, in exhibiting its unrivaled water powers, it should show the irritating and burdensome incumbrances [sic] of fishways inseparably connected with them.[43]

Besides rejecting any commitment to resource conservation this reflected the bias toward industrial production over fish as an economic resource and emphasized the use of the river as a source of industrial power exclusively over the preservation of fisheries or as a commons for many uses. Moreover, it reflects the dominance of the political economy that so many dam opponents had feared. Accordingly, the fish passageways were not built until much later and were never successful. The river would remain an industrial tool and continue its ecological decline over the next century until the dam was removed in 1999.

The petitions, representing the opposition to the dam, provided a complex, detailed, and highly prescient critique of the impacts the dam would have on the river's fisheries and the access of Kennebec Valley residents to the commons of the river, primarily fish for subsistence and sale. Moreover, the opponents of the Kennebec dam also understood that this was a conflict between competing capitalist economic systems—a traditional pattern of capitalism based on a mix of subsistence, trade and barter, and sale, which included a commons accessible to all, versus the industrial capitalism of the Market Revolution, which would cut off access to the commons and displace many of the lower class from their traditional economic practices into wage-labor jobs. The petition from Woolwich stated the conflict well:

After taking in to view the advantages for men of capital & rich corporations to invest their funds—the immense water power in every section of the state but partially employed—that the great mass of our frontier population are of the lower class in point of wealth and derive a valuable part of their support from the fisheries . . . and in fact a grant to the petitioners [the Kennebec Dam Company], the *many* would be injured whilst the *few* might be benefited: your remonstrances believe that your Hon. Body will not countenance an enterprise so injurious to a large section of the state.[44]

Although the opponents understood the impacts the dam would have, they chose to hope against hope or failed to see that the tide had turned decisively behind development over preservation of the commons.

Understanding the historical debate over this dam, even acknowledging that a debate over dams existed in 1834, is of great historical value. The debate over the Kennebec dam provides critical insight into the history of incommensurable differences when it comes to natural resources and thereby suggests a lens through which we might consider natural protests in the "prehistory" of American environmentalism. Moreover, it is of historical import to comprehend how accurate many of the opponents' predictions were. This does not imply that those inclined to protect the environment are necessarily or uniformly right in their impulses, but it does point to the historical and political significance of public participation and its role in environmental decision-making.

But there is a further point that is worth elaboration. Specifically, opponents of the dam, and one would have to assume the dam's proponents as well, clearly understood the ecological damage that would ensue from blocking the river. Regarded as Luddites opposed to progress at the time and over the course of history, they, in fact, provided an important critique and dissent. This is important not only in regards to the debate taking place in the 1830s but also because of current environmental debates and discourse. Too often, the opponents of environmental reform in the current era refer to the relevant era (in this case the Market Revolution in the Northeast) as a time of innocence, rendering the environmental and social costs of widescale and intensive development as unanticipated mistakes rather than a cold-blooded calculus of ecological and social tradeoffs for capitalist development and greater wealth. Anyone engaged in environmental activism has heard the refrain of "we didn't know what we were doing then but now it would be too expensive and difficult to fix the problem." If we gain a clear, historical understanding of these early processes and the clear-eyed understanding of the ecological and social costs of development, does that necessarily change the tenor of discourse in the current period? Is there a way to negotiate environmental reform today that includes historical thinking and, in fact, points out that opponents of development were often correct in their gloom-and-doom predictions? Furthermore, in late-stage capitalism, with an increasing focus on ecological restoration, can and should the ecological intelligence of early development opponents be employed rhetorically to push the momentum for restoration projects such as dam removal?

The end of the river's upstream shad, alewife, and salmon fisheries seemed a small sacrifice to those erecting mills, harvesting and processing logs, and building an industrial economy in the heart of the Kennebec River Valley. While the local industrial economy benefited from the construction and consequent rebuilding of the dam, the river began a long process of decline that entailed the devastation of numerous fish species as well as the overall river ecosystem. By the middle of the twentieth century the Kennebec River would more closely resemble an industrial sewer, filled with human effluent, industrial pollutants, and increasingly devoid of life. This was the final, long-term cost, one not figured into the cost of doing business but predicted long before, when many residents of the Kennebec River Valley opposed the Kennebec Dam.

Notes

1 Brian Donahue, *The Great Meadow: Farmers and the Land in Colonial Concord* (New Haven, CT: Yale University Press, 2004).

2 Laura Pulido, *Environmentalism and Economic Justice: Two Chicano Struggles in the Southwest* (Tucson: University of Arizona Press, 1996).

3 Donald Meinig, *The Shaping of America: A Geographical Perspective on 500 Years of History*, vol. 1, *Atlantic America, 1492-1800* (New Haven, CT: Yale University Press, 1988), 312.

4 William Cronon, *Nature's Metropolis: Chicago and the Great West* (New York: W. W. Norton & Company, 1992); Donald Worster, *The Wealth of Nature: Environmental History and the Ecological Imagination* (Oxford: Oxford University Press, 1994).

5 Charles Sellers, *The Market Revolution: Jacksonian America, 1815–1846* (New York: Oxford University Press, 1991), 21.

6 Sellers, *The Market Revolution*, 30.

7 Ibid., 44.

8 Luther Severance, *Kennebec Journal*, 15 January 1825.

9 Ibid., 30 July 1825.

10 Edward Seabury Coffin, "The Untold Story of the Great Kennebec Dam at Augusta" (Augusta, unpublished, 1991), 1, 2.

11 Gary Kulik, "Dams, Fish, and Farmers: Defense of Public Rights in Eighteenth Century Rhode Island," in Steven Hahn and Jonathan Prude (eds.), *The Countryside in the Age of Capitalist Transformation: Essays in the Social History of Rural America* (Chapel Hill: University of North Carolina Press, 1985).

12 Kulik, "Dams, Fish, and Farmers," 33–35.

13 Ibid., 28.

14 Ibid., 34–35.

15 Ibid., 36.

16 Ibid., 43–46.

17 Brian Donahue, "Dammed at Both Ends and Cursed in the Middle: The 'Flowage' of the Concord River Meadows, 1798–1862," in Char Miller and Hal Rothman (eds.), *Out of the Woods: Essays in Environmental Essays* (Pittsburgh: University of Pittsburgh Press, 1997).

18 Theodore Steinberg, *Nature Incorporated: Industrialization and the Waters of New England* (New York: Cambridge University Press, 1991), 15–16.

19 Petitions flooded in from surrounding communities supporting or opposing the proposed dam. Roughly one-third opposed the dam. The petitions are stored at the Maine State Archives (MSA) in Augusta, Maine.

20 Georgetown petition against Kennebec Dam, 1834, MSA.

21 Ibid.

22 Ibid.

23 Woolwich petition against Kennebec Dam, 1834, MSA.

24 Philipsburg petition against Kennebec Dam, 1834, MSA.

25 Greenfield petition against Kennebec Dam, 1834, MSA.

26 As Alan Taylor points out in *Liberty Men and Great Proprietors: The Revolutionary Settlement on the Maine Frontier, 1760–1820* (Chapel Hill: University of North Carolina Press, 1990), the five officers of the Kennebec Dam Company were elite members of the community who had accrued a great deal of their wealth from rents collected from tenant farmers in the previous generation.

27 Greenfield petition against Kennebec Dam, 1834, MSA.

28 Georgetown petition against Kennebec Dam, 1834, MSA.

29 Richard W. W. Judd, *Common Lands, Common People: The Origins of Conservation in Northern New England* (Cambridge, MA: Harvard University Press, 2000).

30 James W. North, *The History of Augusta: From the Earliest Settlement to the Present Time* (Augusta, ME: Clapp and North, 1870), 571–72.

31 Ibid.

32 Ibid.; Coffin, "The Untold Story," 4–6.

33 North, *History of Augusta*, 569.

34 *Kennebec Journal*, 18 March 1835.

35 North, *History of Augusta*, 569.

36 Ibid., 574.

37 Nathaniel Hawthorne, *The American Notebooks* (Columbus: Ohio State University Press, 1972), 34–35.

38 Ibid., 35.

39 North, *History of Augusta*, 598, 599.

40 Ibid., 608–10.

41 David C. Smith, *A History of Lumbering in Maine 1861–1960* (Orono: University of Maine Press, 1972), 43.

42 North, *History of Augusta*, 610–11.

43 Ibid., 790–91.

44 Woolwich petition against Kennebec Dam, 1834, MSA.

CHAPTER 2

Organizing Environmental Protest

Swill Milk and Social Activism in Nineteenth-Century
New York City[1]

MICHAEL EGAN

This essay is a fraud. It offers an account of efforts to end the distribution of swill milk in New York City in the decades prior to the Civil War. Swill milk was milk drawn from cows living in cramped urban dairy barns and fed the cheap (and nutritiously dubious) slop from neighboring distillery factories. Urban dairy workers milked these diseased and dying cows, and sold their milk to the urban poor at discount prices. The essay is a fraud, because it trades on the anachronistic notion that the urban reformers who pushed for quality control and public health were early environmentalists. They certainly would never have called themselves environmentalists; environmentalists and environmentalism are products of a more recent time. Nor would these urban health reformers have considered that their protests contained elements of ecological thought; the German Darwinist Ernst Haeckl coined the term *oecology* only in 1866 to refer to the interaction of species within a specific region. Nevertheless, in hindsight, we can identify various practices and trends that we now associate with environmentalism in these early urban reform movements, and as such, they warrant our attention if we are to understand the origins and dynamics of American environmental protest. Just as social and environmental advocates today challenge industry on issues of environmental risk and risk to human health, nineteenth-century opponents of swill milk engaged in methods of organization and practices consistent with twentieth-century environmentalists and—also similarly—sought integration into the political debate to achieve control of polluting or hazardous or unsavory industrial practices.

More importantly, however, nineteenth-century reformers shared intrinsic interests with modern environmentalists and this, too, deserves our attention, if only because it enriches our reading of the history of environmentalism. In contemporary urban spaces, a variety of planning and health issues have been cast as environmental problems. Sewage treatment, waste disposal, the use and reuse of space, and the planning of green areas have all attracted input—and sometimes ire—from environmental groups. The problem, however, is that this urban activism has frequently been regarded as a post-World War II phenomenon, spurred by suburbanization, urban blight, and economic downturns that left many cities in decay. This essay means to stress the truism that even before a language of natural protest united activists under an environmental umbrella, efforts to protect health and establish sustainable communities were a predominant feature of the American urban landscape. And in so doing, this essay suggests that as historians we might sensibly listen for echoes through the past as a means of identifying potential relationships that might enrich our reading of the past. To do so permits us to draw better lines over and across time that help us to appreciate complexities inherent in historical study.

Too often histories dismiss the origins of American natural protest by waving deftly at a conservation movement that grew out of the Romantic naturalism of the early nineteenth century. Pastoral love of nature typically interpreted industrial urban centers with their smokestacks, railroads, noise, and cramped living as the apotheosis of the evils it condemned. As a result, there was no room for specific action to address urban problems within the traditional lament for nature. Casting so narrow a net fails to appreciate the social dimensions of American environmentalism and restricts the possible parameters of its history, which in turn marginalizes the potential of the movement. Indeed, this limited definition dismisses from the spectrum of the environmental movement themes such as public health, environmental justice, and urban reform, many of which preceded the conservation movement, which enjoyed its entry into the mainstream during the Progressive era. Such a dismissal has serious contemporary political implications. As Marcy Darnovsky notes, "excluding urban reformers from the history of environmentalism can seem to imply that those who take up similar issues today are latecomers to, or even worse, interlopers in, environmental politics."[2] Rather, this essay seeks to identify roots of American environmentalism in histories of public health and social activism.

Social activism arises in response to the discovery of an objective problem.[3] In the instance of the development of swill milk dairies, its origins were innocent enough. As New York's population grew after 1830, the amount of enclosed pasturage available for cows shrank noticeably. The establishment of dairy stables in urban enclosures was common and often a necessity without the means of refrigeration and rapid transportation. Many rural dairies were not equipped with the economic or technological means to supply milk to larger, distant urban populations. As a result, large dairy herds were kept on New York's West Side near 16th Street; both dairying and butchering took place in the city.[4]

Facilities for healthy dairy production were available, but all too often the power of the market economy prevailed and dairymen opted for less expensive alternatives. It was cheaper to crowd the cows into cramped, filthy quarters, with little light or ventilation; the stalls were very rarely cleaned as sanitation cost money. In a further effort to reduce costs and maximize profits, city stable owners discovered that after a period of enforced semi-starvation, cows could be persuaded to eat distillery slop. A marriage of convenience was arranged between brewers and dairymen, who located their dairies next to distillery manufactories and fed the cows the waste from the distilleries' fermentation process; this boiling hot swill was channeled straight into the stable troughs. Dairymen had a constant and ready food source for their cattle and distillers were turning a profit on their waste.[5] Without sewers, the disposal of waste in antebellum New York City was an expensive and time-consuming process; that cows would consume the distillery waste was a significant solution for distillery owners.[6] Although swill had a relatively high nutritional value, it required supplementation with hay and grain to provide a healthy diet for the cows, which were already living in deplorably unhygienic conditions. Although they had reduced costs by taking on distillery waste, most dairy owners showed little inclination to raise their overheads in order to supply their livestock with a more wholesome diet. As a result, the milk from cows fed on alcoholic dregs smelled strongly of beer and displayed a tendency to coagulate into a hard lump.[7] Not surprisingly, diseases were also commonplace in these urban stables, because of the close quarters, the cows' lack of access to proper ventilation, and their limited diet. Nevertheless, dairymen continued to milk their diseased herds and sold the milk daily to consumers. The diseased milk was a pale blue color, so the dairymen adulterated it with magnesia, chalk, and plaster of paris to give it a rich, creamy texture and appearance.[8] Cows rarely survived for more than a year in these conditions, being milked until they died—the last milking being performed "posthumously"—and their meat then being sold to butchers who then distributed the diseased meat to more consumers (Figure 2.1). By 1835 there were an estimated 18,000 cows in New York and Brooklyn being fed distillery slop and by the 1850s, more than two-thirds of New York City's milk came from distillery herds.[9]

Public criticism of this practice emerged during the 1820s and 1830s, but neither the city nor the state felt compelled to restrict the growing swill milk industry. Their reluctance was based on a series of related factors. First, most of the wealthy city-dwellers, who might have presented a stringent challenge to the legislators' political hegemony, were in the process of insulating themselves from the urban poor. As New York grew, members of the upper class started a migration from decidedly urban areas, surrendering those neighborhoods to immigrants and the city's poor. Furthermore, the wealthy were predominantly unaffected by and therefore uninterested in the debate as they could afford good, rural milk from farms in Westchester, Queens, and Connecticut.[10] For the urban poor, however, there was no alternative to the swill milk.

A second factor explaining lawmakers' reluctance to control the production and distribution of swill milk was based on the premise that governmental regulations impinged upon the freedom of the market economy.[11] Moreover, by the 1830s, New York's integration into the world market made it impossible—logistically and ideologically—for the city government to maintain its

Figure 2.1 A cow too weak to stand is strung up to be milked in a swill milk dairy stable. *Frank Leslie's Illustrated Newspaper*, 15 May 1858, 374.

control over economic regulation. The city's exceptional population growth in the following decades—New York's population quadrupled between 1830 and 1860—forcibly changed the context of city politics and urban living. The swill milk controversy emerged and was fought during a period in which civic politics was experiencing growing pains while trying to reinvent itself. Out of the eighteenth-century system that bred stiff controls came a new industrial system of machine politics pitting special interests against reformers. Furthermore, by the mid-1830s the locus of political power shifted away from the central City Hall and established itself within the political interests of the city's separate wards. The conflict over swill milk was prolonged, then, by the efficiency with which the swill milk distributors immersed themselves into this new and still-developing system. Many of the swill milk stable owners were in fact respected members of the community, further entrenching official reluctance to act against them.[12] The opponents of the sale of unhealthy milk were far less effective in learning the new ropes.[13]

Benevolent societies were the first to come to the defense of the powerless urban poor. A substantial increase in humanitarian reform sentiment spread across the United States—and, indeed, the western world—in the century after 1750. By the 1830s, the second Great Awakening galvanized a resurgence in humanitarian activity.[14] That a growing humanitarianism should develop simultaneously with an increase in industrialism was hardly coincidental. However, reformers' motivations were not simply a genuine desire to help the marginalized. Rather, benevolent societies invariably functioned to advance their own interests.[15] With an increase in industrialization and its subsequent urbanization, significant populations of oppressed workers and destitute immigrants were crowded into filthy, unventilated tenements. Their living conditions and opportunities for work—never mind their prospects of upward mobility—were meager at best. Many critics of nineteenth-century humanitarianism and benevolent societies saw benevolent societies' actions toward the poor as an effort to maintain a social hegemony that would discourage the growing hordes of immigrants and downtrodden citizens from resisting oppression. By helping just enough to appease those who could not help themselves, the humanitarians were also protecting their own desirable lifestyle.[16]

More often than not humanitarianism in the early nineteenth century was infused with religious piety and therefore lacked the secular pragmatism that might have contributed to solving social crises. This was certainly the case with early resistance to swill milk by such benevolent societies as the New York Temperance Society (NYTS) and the Association for Improving the Condition of the Poor. For example, in February 1838 the New York Female Reform Society—composed of evangelical women from the elite classes—proposed distributing charity to those living in destitution that they deemed virtuous and receptive to religious doctrine. Most of the poor, they concluded, were not deserving of charity, as they were either intemperate or (worse) Catholic or both.[17] Moreover, whatever help was provided by benevolent societies was predominantly spiritual rather than political; such activity was not designed to manufacture legislative change. Help was offered piecemeal with strings attached, but benevolent societies were generally unwilling to embark on significant social change for the poor and oppressed.

Some were, however, more deliberate in their efforts to help New York's growing poor masses. The first concerted attack against swill milk came from Robert M. Hartley, the corresponding secretary for the NYTS since 1833. In his investigation of distilleries Hartley discovered that they sold slop to dairymen. Having initially fought for temperance, he accidentally fell into the milk question and, in 1842, published *An Essay on Milk*, a comprehensive history and treatise on the social significance of milk as a nutritional substance. In the essay, Hartley turned his attention to the immoral practices of the urban milk trade and condemned the sale of swill milk. He characterized the typical stall as holding 2,000 cows in the winter, while noting the unhealthy conditions in which the cows were kept.

In raising an alarm against swill milk, Hartley sought to kill two birds with one stone. Ever the temperance advocate, Hartley alerted his readers to the connection between urban dairies and distilleries and noted that many distilleries were in financial straits. "In order that the expenses may not exceed the profits, the slop must be turned to good account; hence a milk dairy . . . [is an] indispensable adjunct to every distillery."[18] Hoping to break the entire ring, Hartley proposed "let the customers withdraw their patronage, and the business of these milkmen will be broken up, and a check given to the business of distillation."[19] If the distilleries could be closed, then the dairy owners would be forced to look elsewhere for food for their cows, hopefully improving the condition of the dairies. In concluding, Hartley insisted that "we see no relief, but in the entire prevalence of temperance principles."[20]

After chastising the swill milk traders, Hartley did offer some solutions. He noted that supply of wholesome milk from the country did not meet the city's demand and appealed to country dairymen to better organize their resources in order to profit from increased sales in New York City. Hartley addressed the persistent question of distance from New York and insufficient means with which to transport and refrigerate the milk by pointing to the extension of the railway that already crossed the Hudson River to Orange, Sullivan, and Rockland Counties. He also noted the imminent construction of the New York and Albany railroad, which would connect the city with the counties of Westchester, Putnam, and Dutchess, as well as adjoining portions of Connecticut.[21] Indeed, the combination of train and canal made possible the delivery of milk to New York from Goshen—seventy miles away—in five or six hours.

Hartley emphasized that the purchase of swill milk was unnatural, but this lacked pragmatic value for the poor who were left with no choice. He could not escape the fact that swill milk was still produced less expensively than country milk. At the time Hartley was writing, the sale of pure country milk could no longer be a profitable endeavor at less than 6¢ a quart, while adulterated swill milk could be sold at profit for 3¢ a quart.[22] Nevertheless, he seemed oblivious to the widespread nature of poverty in New York. The reform-minded editor of the *Tribune*, Horace Greeley, estimated that in 1845 at least two-thirds of New Yorkers subsisted on no more than $1 per week per person. "On this pittance, and very much less in many thousands of instances, three hundred thousand persons within sight of Trinity steeple must pay City rents and City prices." Estimates also suggested that between 50,000 and 75,000 New Yorkers were forced to resort to charity. Furthermore, during the 1840s the economy froze with the weather during the winter months as the canals were closed and ocean commerce was reduced.[23] The difference between 3¢ and 6¢ was likely more significant than Hartley realized.

Hartley's campaign rang of divine righteousness and his attack on two insalubrious industries pointed to the woes of nineteenth-century industrialism and urbanization, but much of his efforts fell on deaf ears, mainly because the political actors to whom he appealed were strong supporters of the swill milk trade. After the publication of Hartley's book, resolutions were presented to the city's Board of Aldermen, calling for a special committee to investigate the swill milk question, but the Board took no action on these recommendations and did not appoint a committee.[24] This inactivity was due in no small measure to Hartley's strong demands. After claiming that swill milk was responsible for the city's high infant mortality, he insisted that trade between distilleries and dairies be terminated.[25] His request fell on deaf ears in large part because he offered no acceptable alternative to supplying the city's destitute with more wholesome milk that was comparably priced. Proposing that rural dairies should form associations so that country milk could be available for all of New York's inhabitants, he grossly misjudged the amount of milk required and the manner in which it might be transported to the city before it soured or went bad. Furthermore, Hartley did not recognize the complexity of the milk industry and the fact that many of the rural dairies—who produced wholesome milk—also had interests in the distillery stables. In 1858, the *Daily Tribune* noted that several rural dairies rotated their cows between urban and rural stables. Milk was produced and sold less expensively in this manner and a distinct division between pure and swill milk was almost impossible.[26] Caught in his righteous humanitarianism, Hartley also failed to appreciate the relative expense of country milk even when it was incorporated into combines. Although the Orange County Milk Association was distributing 7,000 quarts a day to the city, there was no corresponding decline in the sale of swill milk.[27]

Hartley's other failing was his inability to escape his evangelical background. Throughout his career, Hartley saw a distinct relationship between poverty and depravity and he deplored both; poverty was caused not by the economic failures of recent years—over which his class had presided—but by moral deficiencies in the poor themselves. He excused the epidemics that regularly afflicted the city as God's retribution for sin. Among the victims of the 1832 cholera outbreak, for example, more than 40 percent of the dead had been Irish Catholic. Hartley, like many others of his class, failed to make the connection with the fact that Irish immigrants were also among the most numerous inhabitants of the city's squalid tenements.[28]

John H. Griscom's career in public health mirrors but also represents a foil for Hartley's.[29] Hartley's contemporary, Griscom was a Quaker who in 1842 was appointed City Inspector and conducted a thorough study of city health and concluded that the city's unsanitary conditions represented a distinct social problem that needed to be addressed. Whereas his predecessor's annual review had very briefly listed a series of health-related statistics for the year, Griscom labored over the city's mortality statistics and provided fifty-five pages of commentary. His central argument was that preventive action should be the focal point of public health. Griscom was particularly concerned about the city's crowded, unventilated housing and its general filth. His model for preventive action called for the regulation of the construction of housing and for a comprehensive drainage and sewage system to alleviate the buildup of toxic substances.[30] Griscom also proposed replacing politically appointed health wardens with a team of impartial medical experts.

Not surprisingly, his recommendation of controls and checks and balances on both the market and the government did not sit well with pro-market economy authorities, who categorically dismissed Griscom's survey. No doubt the Board of Aldermen who convened to consider Griscom's recommendations were particularly unwilling to eliminate more than thirty political appointments—a form of machine politics patronage to favorites—in order to fill them with independent medical personnel.[31] Furthermore, Griscom was not re-appointed as City Inspector. With the help of city reformers, however, Griscom published his study in 1845 under the title *The Sanitary Conditions of the Laboring Class of New York*.[32] In demonstrating the unnatural quality of city life, Griscom also lauded the healthy—natural—life of the country. In so doing, he compared the life and physique of the "savage" with that of the wan and slight New Yorker. In nature, the "savage" was living in a more healthful environment. In promoting the healthy lifestyle in the country, Griscom anticipated the "rigorous life" mantra of the early twentieth-century Progressive era.[33]

Griscom's study is significant, because he broke from conventional wisdom by refusing to blame the poor for the unsanitary living spaces in which they were confined. Like members of the modern environmental justice movement, he perceived deep-seated connections between social and environmental problems; "for Griscom, dirt was a symptom of poverty, not its cause."[34] Indeed, in light of the cholera outbreak in 1849 and the Astor riot the same year a degree of radicalism was entering New York; excusing the plight of the poor or the sick as simply the result of their own immorality only fueled the fires. Within this broad spectrum of social and public health problems, swill milk provided a plausible and focused platform upon which to base the efforts of social and environmental reform. Milk consumption took place in almost any home with children and swill milk's ubiquity contributed significantly to the city's growing health problems. But neither Griscom's nor Hartley's manuscript was published widely or made readily available for more than a select group of readers. Although Griscom and Hartley continued to participate in the movement and their early works were certainly catalysts for later improvements, the initial lack of reception to their ideas is attributable to their inability to organize a sustained and pragmatic attack on city legislators who remained reluctant to regulate markets. Their solutions, too, failed to resolve the myriad and inchoate difficulties involved in the distribution of city funds for large projects while they also antagonized the interests of the aldermen who voted on them.

The worsening of the swill milk situation, however, helped galvanize further support. In 1847, distemper or "cow fever" broke out in the swill stables near the South Ferry.[35] The disease spread rapidly through the crowded stables and was uniformly fatal, until it was discovered that cows could be inoculated by slitting their tails and inserting parts of a dead cow's lungs. The tail generally swelled and rotted off, but only 20 percent of the inoculated cows died.[36] Inoculated cows, cows suffering from distemper, and dead cows were all milked, however, and their milk continued to be distributed among the urban poor. Even at the height of the epidemic, the swill milk remained the only milk that many poor New Yorkers could afford. For 1843, before the epidemic hit the swill stables, the City Inspector of New York reported that children under five years of age represented 4,588 of the 13,281 deaths reported in the city. In 1856, 13,373 children under the age of five died, but the number of deaths of people over the age of five had hardly changed at all. Whereas in 1843 children under five had represented roughly one-third of all deaths, by 1856 they represented more than 60 percent of all deaths.[37]

Concerned about the widespread disease among cows and the increase in infant mortality, the New York Academy of Medicine set up a committee to investigate the swill milk stables in 1848. The committee found that conditions under which the cows were kept were atrocious and unacceptable. The larger stables kept 2,000 to 4,000 cows confined in unventilated stalls, which—combined with their inadequate diet of distillery slop—led to the easy transmission of disease throughout the entire herd. Running, ulcerated sores all over their bodies, missing teeth, sore feet, hair loss, and consumptive lungs were just some of the common ailments listed by the committee. After a chemical analysis of the milk, the committee found that the milk contained only one-half to one-third the amount of butter fat found in country milk and concluded that the distillery milk was very likely the cause of scrofula and cholera infantum, which had claimed so many of the city's young. On 1 March 1848, the committee's chair, Dr. Augustus Gardner, presented two resolutions to the Academy: that swill milk was "not only less nutritious than that of unconfined and well-fed animals, but is positively deleterious, especially to young children," and that city officials should take action against the swill milk dairymen "as in their wisdom they may think fit."[38] The Academy accepted Gardner's report, but the resolutions were tabled until further evidence could be obtained. The Gardner report was not published by the Academy until 1851, and even then its condemnation of swill milk was not spread publicly. Although Gardner and Griscom both persisted in their fight, they received little assistance from the powerful body of respected health authorities. Indeed, the Academy did not really act again upon the swill milk issue until it gained widespread publicity in the city's newspapers.

The swill milk campaign was one of the first journalism crusades in history. The "power of the press" highlighted the dangers of the swill milk trade and galvanized support for the movement against the practice among its readership. The *Daily Tribune* published a long article and editorial on 26 June 1847, attacking swill milk for containing "*positively* noxious properties." The article was anonymously written "by a scientific gentleman of the highest character," who pointed to swill milk as being responsible for the excessive infant mortality numbers in the city and concluded by chastising city officials for not acting. "What other city," the article asked, "would allow 100,000 quarts of impure, demonstrably diseased milk, to be distributed every week among its inhabitants?"[39]

Among the more vociferous (and successful) antagonists of the swill milk dairy industry was the journalist Frank Leslie. In May 1858, Leslie's weekly newspaper, *Frank Leslie's Illustrated Newspaper*, devoted extensive time and energy to researching and exposing the social and moral ills of the "nefarious and revolting trade."[40] Leslie's challenge to the industry was comprehensive as he increased public awareness, articulated the health risks associated with the swill milk, publicized the trade routes taken by the distributors, and attacked the political machine that looked the other way. "Shall these manufactories of hell-broths be permitted longer to exist among us?" he boldly queried.[41] Previous attempts to counter and arrest the abuses of the milk trade had been unsuccessful, but Leslie's attack—complete with vivid illustrations— demonstrated the power of pictorial journalism.[42] Compared with Hartley and Griscom, Leslie combined the distribution of information and advocacy with a more confrontational position that made it very difficult for authorities to dismiss or ignore him.

Leslie joined the ranks of public health officials and benevolent societies that opposed the distribution of diseased milk. His prose—often melodramatic and always full of panache—was designed to stimulate reaction from its readers, but it also rang of goodwill and concern for his fellow citizen:

> In presenting to our readers the sickening details connected with the distillery milk manufacture which prevails to an alarming extent in both New York and Brooklyn, we are animated solely by a desire to benefit our fellow-citizens, to expose the shameless frauds which are every day perpetrated under the eyes and with the full cognizance of the public authorities, and to break up a system which, by the wholesale distribution of liquid poison, is decimating our population, bringing death into a thousand homes, and demoralizing the general health of the city. . . . Ours has been no pleasing task! we should not have selected it for pastime or amusement! we would rather have shunned it as we would avoid a place infected by the plague; but a sense of public duty and the powerful lever of faithful and accurate illustrations taken on these leper spots . . . prompted us to pursue our present course, and the hope of ameliorating a great evil has encouraged us to persevere.[43]

But his participation in the attack of the swill milk industry does not exactly qualify as being wholly altruistic, as the popularity of his exposé effectively saved his business. In 1857, Leslie claimed to have 90,000 subscriptions, but he was embroiled in a fierce battle with the newly established *Harper's Weekly*. By the end of 1858, Leslie boasted a subscription total of 140,000 with special issues selling considerably more copies. This rise in subscriptions was likely directly attributable to Leslie's investigation of the swill milk controversy; during his exposé Leslie reduced and eventually eliminated his gossip columns in favor of presenting news and editorials. While he still competed with *Harper's* for the illustrated newspaper market, Leslie established his newspaper as a first-rate publication of investigative journalism.[44]

Nevertheless, Leslie's exposé was powerful and it attacked not just the men directly involved in the production and distribution of swill milk; after his initial flurry of articles exposing the trade, Leslie struck at the political machine that condoned it. By 1858, some sixteen years after Hartley published his essay on the history of milk and fourteen years since Griscom had derided the sanitary conditions of the city, civic authorities still had not imposed any restrictions on the sale of swill milk. The resistance to reform remained intractable, owing largely to the dairy owners' political sway. Leslie noted that the high profits realized from swill milk production had made the dealers a potent lobby against reforms. In 1856, for example, the Brooklyn Common Council passed a law requiring ample room for dairy cows, but within a couple of months the Council buckled under the pressure of the swill milk dealers and passed an amendment exempting urban swill milk distilleries. By 1858, one anonymous, prominent official told Leslie it was unlikely that the authorities would take action: "They dare not do it! *Don't you know that every one of those cows has a vote?*"[45]

Leslie's coverage of the diseased milk trade did, however, provoke a series of formal inquiries, the first by a committee of city officials altogether too friendly with the swill milk dealers to provide a balanced report. Indeed, the *Daily Tribune* mocked the investigation as an example of political corruption.

> After giving the swill-milk venders ample time to brush up and 'make it all right' for the official visit, Alderman [Michael] Tuomey yesterday led his Committee up to Johnson's distillery, looked about a little, found all in tolerably good condition, took a drink at the corner groggery, got a few samples of milk from cows, and rode back to City Hall.[46]

Tuomey issued reassuring reports, but Leslie challenged his credibility and his connections to the industry. His attacks against the committee members were particularly ruthless. Leslie called Tuomey "a barefaced, shameless rascal" and was even more disparaging of Tuomey's second, Alderman E. Harrison Reed, who "in all that constitutes the scurrilous blackguard and mouthy poltroon is Tuomey's superior."[47] He further escalated his mockery of the committee's work and findings by printing a now-famous cartoon of three aldermen whitewashing a stump-tailed cow (Figure 2.2).[48] After the whitewashing cartoon, Leslie was indicted for criminal libel, but after a hearing marred by violence the action was dismissed by the grand jury. It was blatantly obvious that, as incriminating as Leslie's cartoon had been, it was not libelous.

Responding to growing tensions, the Board of Health decided to appoint a new committee to conduct a more thorough study. Two reports resulted from

Figure 2.2 Three New York City aldermen charged with investigating the swill milk industry shown "whitewashing" a diseased, stump-tailed cow and her owner. *Frank Leslie's Illustrated Newspaper*, 17 July 1858, 110.

this second study. The majority report, signed by Tuomey and Reed, found the stables and the conditions of the cows to be adequate, but recommended that the stables receive better ventilation. Critics of the report—who then submitted the minority report—complained that the investigation sought to protect the dairymen and that the committee spent most of its time putting Leslie's charges on trial.[49] Charles H. Haswell submitted the minority report that presented a stark criticism of all facets of the swill milk industry. Witnesses had admitted that diseased cows were regularly milked and that urine was occasionally—through accident or negligence—added to the milk.[50] Haswell listed four objections to the swill dairies: crowded stalls, widespread disease, unsanitary milking process, and the slaughter of diseased cows for meat. On 14 July 1858, the Council discussed the majority and minority reports and opted in favor of the corrupt majority report. No concessions were made to appease the angry committee members; even a resolution requiring that distillery dairies post signs on their carts that read "Swill-fed Milk" was rejected.[51]

With no resolution in sight, Leslie dedicated himself to persevering in his crusade. Accompanying his vivid illustrations were extensive lists of the

Figure 2.3 False advertising of swill milk with a "country wagon" pulled up to a distillery yard. *Frank Leslie's Illustrated Newspaper*, 8 May 1858, 368.

routes taken by the distillery milk carts, the numbers of the houses to which they delivered, the locations of the depots that advertised their milk as "country pure," the names of the owners of the cows, and the false inscriptions on the carts that carried the swill milk around the city (Figure 2.3). Leslie did achieve some success as some milk distributors started to buy country milk and he was quick to publish these small victories along with his weekly stories. Mitchell and Blain, from Fulton Market, wrote Leslie to "thank you for your exposure of the Swill Milk trade. We have changed our milkman, and now use none but the best Country Milk."[52]

Given the impotence or unwillingness of city officials to act, Leslie likely saw his crusade as an attempt not just to raise public awareness, but also to arouse public action. Like the later muckrakers of the Progressive era and, later, the scientists who participated in environmental protest after World War II, he understood that informing the public could lead to meaningful reform. In 1848, the inhabitants of a small town near Elberfeld, Germany, burned a swill milk distillery to the ground and drove out the owners, after officials had not acted. By drawing on this example early in his exposé, it is possible that Leslie was hoping to incite a similar reaction in New York if reforms were not enacted.[53] What Leslie did not know or neglected to mention was that the events in Elberfeld were part of a greater uprising associated with the Revolution of 1848. Leslie also left out the fact that the Prussian state eventually crushed such civil disobedience. Nevertheless, Leslie promoted his exposé as the catalyst for social change and stoked the fires of public activism. "During the past week," he wrote the week after he first broke the story, "it has been the subject of serious and animated discussion in almost every house. . . . Each one asked himself, 'How could I be so supine as to sit quiet and never make an effort to cleanse this foul nest for humanity's sake, if not from personal motives?'"[54] Again, in attempting to stir public activism, Leslie wrote, "every man who rests in the vain and selfish security that he is 'safe' is a traitor to the cause, and gives comfort and help to the general enemy."[55]

Besides challenging the moral goodness of men involved in the urban dairy trade as well as those who did not act against it, Leslie also attacked the swill milk distributors' gender identity. Gail Bederman notes that the popular conception of "manliness" in the mid-nineteenth century was associated with a man's strength of character and a duty to protect and guide those weaker than himself, namely his family or his employees.[56] By referring to the New York and Brooklyn milkmen as scoundrels and modern Herods, Leslie was implying that their immorality made them less than manly.[57] And he went even further, referring to swill milk dairy owners and distributors as "'milkmaids,' with large beards and excessive dirt."[58] In so doing, Leslie openly provoked gender stereotypes that hearkened back to pre-industrial Europe, where milking was seen as women's work. Leslie continued referring

Figure 2.4 "Attack of the milkmaids." Frank Leslie's artist is accosted in Skillman Street, Brooklyn, between two swill milk stables. Note the artist's noble stance in contrast with the slovenly mob. *Frank Leslie's Illustrated Newspaper*, 15 May 1858, 384.

to "milkmaids" in subsequent issues of his paper, even illustrating an "attack of the 'milkmaids'" on one of his artists (Figure 2.4).[59] The image clearly showed an upright, strong, and noble artist defiantly preparing to meet a dirty and raucous horde of "milkmaids." In persisting with attacks on the swill milk distributors' gender, Leslie sought to further demonstrate gender differences that would antagonize his adversaries.

In contrast to the immoral, effeminate "dairymaid," Leslie was recognized as a masculine savior for his moral crusade. In appreciation of his efforts, Leslie was presented with a gold watch and chain, the inscription reading "in behalf of the mothers and children of New-York, as a grateful testimonial of his Manly and Fearless Exposure of the Swill Milk Traffic."[60] Leslie even promoted himself as more masculine during the controversy after a meeting in which Alderman Reed suggested that only dignity prevented him from doing Leslie bodily harm. In response, Leslie submitted that—in spite of his great patience—he was glad not to have been "within hearing of that cowardly and wretched maligner," or else "[that] hawk's bill which ornaments [Reed's] Aldermanic face would certainly have been rubbed, thumb-and-fingerwise, to a very 'fine point' indeed."[61] Even as Leslie presented the members of the swill milk trade and their political allies as effeminate and less than men, he sought to exemplify and articulate an aggressive masculinity of morality whose central goal was the defense of the home against corrupt polluters of milk and bodies.

Conscious that increased numbers would maintain the momentum of the actions he had begun, Leslie also worked to persuade the strong temperance movement to join his crusade. Attacking both the distilleries and the swill milk at the same time, Leslie pointed up the irrevocable relationship between the two:

> Wherever large masses of people congregate, thus creating a great demand for milk, *a distillery springs up at once*, and while this *furnishes fiery alcohol which makes fathers and husbands drunkards, loafers, and, perhaps, murderers*, the filthy cow stables, which hang around it like bloated parasites, dispense *the poison that deals death to the mothers and children*.[62]

In broadening the scope of the protest, Leslie was attracting more people to the movement. If the plight of urban women and children was not enough to attract middle- and upper-class women to the movement, perhaps relating the environmental problems with swill milk to their own benevolent issues such as temperance and family problems associated with alcohol would. Furthermore, Leslie was demonstrating how swill milk had an impact on men as well as women and children. By expanding the issue to one of public health in general, Leslie found a broader base, though ultimately insufficiently so. Where Hartley's prosaic attempts to galvanize public sentiment into action had failed, Leslie's persistence and sensationalism was highly effective. The illustrations no doubt brought to life the conditions in the swill stables, but his message was also heard by far more people. Leslie also managed a sustained attack that appeared serially in his newspaper, whereas Hartley's book was not followed by further writings that reached a wide audience.

Timing, however, may ultimately have been the critical factor. By the late 1850s railroad expansion was making the transportation of country milk to the city an ever-increasing possibility. The supply of milk continued to grow and milk associations began forming, dropping the overall cost of wholesome milk. The feasibility of bringing country milk to the city spurred a different legislative body into action against the distillery milk traders. In 1861, Otsego County Senator Francis M. Rotch proposed a bill to stop the sale of swill milk in New York City. Inspired perhaps by some of Hartley's suggestions regarding the potential economic growth of rural dairies almost twenty years earlier, Rotch might have seen an economic opportunity for his rural constituents if the swill milk trade were abolished. As the travel time between New York City and outlying counties got continually and dramatically shorter, a cost-effective alternative to swill milk presented itself. The senate passed the bill, but the assembly rejected it. The following year, however, the law was enacted and it represented the first Milk Law to be passed in New York State. The law made the sale of "any impure, adulterated, or unwholesome milk" a misdemeanor and punishable by a fine of fifty dollars or a jail sentence in default of the fine. The law further outlawed the feeding of cows on food that would produce unwholesome milk—an attack on distillery slop—and imposed stricter laws of stable conditions.[63] That the law was passed at the state rather than the municipal level suggests that the distillery and urban dairy owners still held considerable sway in city politics.

Although this legislation represented a monumental victory in the fight against swill milk, distributors quickly found loopholes, namely in the law's vagueness regarding what constituted "adulterated" or "unwholesome" milk under the statute. An amendment in 1864 specifically defined "the addition of water or any substance other than a sufficient quantity of ice to preserve the whole milk while in transportation" to be an adulteration.[64] Given that the swill milk required adulteration to even look like milk, the amendment legally put an end to the production of swill milk in Manhattan. But in Brooklyn the swill milk trade was still protected by the local amendment passed in 1856 protecting swill milk businesses within the city limits. As late as the turn of the century, swill milk was still produced and sold in Brooklyn. The

Department of Health, formed in 1866, entered the fray in 1873, banning—
and making specific reference to—swill milk as part of the sanitary code.[65]
As the swill dairies decreased in number and were pushed further from the
city, their owners found it increasingly difficult to manage both production
and distribution, while lower prices for milk from the countryside hurt them
through competition. The division of labor ultimately ruined the political
power of the swill milk trade; as the milk industry grew, the interests of milk
producers were often in conflict with those of the distributors and what had
once been a formidable political lobby was in shambles.

But was this really a significant environmental victory? The protest against
bad milk was ultimately successful, but it took almost twenty years for public health advocates to realize the changes they sought. The growth of the
activism and the amount of pressure it could exert on the political machine
depended largely on its support base, which grew slowly and ineffectively,
allowing its opposition to build a powerful political lobby. Opponents to
the swill milk trade enjoyed a relative victory, but it was not entirely due to
their own efforts. That it took more than twenty years after the initial, concerted alarm over swill milk to realize any kind of control over the industry
is testament to the disorganized nature of the early protest against it and the
lack of interest in this issue on the part of the community leaders. Leslie's
efforts must be recognized as the most effective public condemnation of the
distillery milk trade, because his exposé directly and aggressively attacked
the political machine in a manner that administrators could not ignore. Leslie also struck a chord with a wider audience and galvanized action from a
broader support base than did efforts from smaller groups. But the protest
was ultimately hampered by not effectively outlining a distinct problem or
organizing in a manner that would exact change. Swill milk was accepted as
the problem, but activists could not agree amongst themselves whether it was
the production or the distribution that should be challenged. Furthermore,
reformers disagreed on whether the feeding of distillery slops to the cows,
the stable conditions, the unethical business practices of the dairymen, or the
lack of municipal licensing within the milk industry presented itself as the
central target for civil objection. In spite of these internal conflicts, however,
the lobby was likely never sufficiently strong to represent any legitimate challenge to the status quo.

That such demands were not realized quickly—indeed as late as 1904 only
six American cities used dairy inspectors—speaks more to difficulties in
organizing a politically potent protest than it does to a lack of social and environmental concern.[66] Whereas the heated battle over swill milk dissipated
after state legislation was passed in the 1860s, the 1906 Food and Drug Act
represented a more official closure of sorts, with more stringent, enforceable,

and enforced laws against the production and distribution of contaminated or dangerous food products. It finally took a dramatic expansion of state and federal regulatory powers at the beginning of the twentieth century to bring meaningful reform to the problem of contaminated and adulterated foods.

As a rule, environmental protest must move from the public sphere into the political arena in order to exact change that might solve or mitigate the existing environmental problem.[67] To receive political attention the public organization must be sufficiently broad and vocal enough that legislators feel pressure to act. Central to any success, then, is the process of organizing responses to perceived environmental problems. Intrinsic to organizing responses is galvanizing the public into action through impressing upon them the potential hazards. In New York City's battle over swill milk, the organizational process that resulted in a growing and concerted attack on the distributors of swill milk and their political allies slowly found ways to engage the public while pushing for political action. In different capacities, Hartley, Griscom, and Leslie sought to inform the public about the nature of the hazards inherent in the distribution and consumption of swill milk. Among the three, Leslie's newspaper provided him with the widest audience. And when Leslie insisted that the sale of adulterated milk be outlawed, he also advocated creating clear standards: "Milkmen should be licensed, and the license should be granted only upon positive evidence of a dairy of grass or hay fed cows."[68] This argument might have galvanized a concerned public and readership, but it also focused on legislators who could act. Nevertheless, although the initial movement to ban swill milk was premised on a strong social and moral ethic, it lacked a focused foundation upon which it could build the bigger structure of an effective political movement. Moreover, New Yorkers with political sway were hard to engage; they had access to fresh country milk because they could afford it.

These factors are useful to keep in mind, because they are present in more recent environmental struggles. In many instances, the dissemination of information is a form of political activism. And the problem of arousing the urban elite is also a common problem in twentieth-century American environmentalism. Those with means are able to protect themselves from environmental harm; bottled water, organic fruits and vegetables, and healthier communities are contemporary expressions of this.[69] And this is an intriguing and problematic feature of the larger American environmental consciousness: there is little collective or altruistic spirit in much natural protest. Since World War II, the major environmental victories—halting aboveground nuclear weapons testing, removing lead from gasoline, and the bans on some heavy metals and synthetic pesticides—have been those that affected all Americans. Nuclear fallout, for example, was not discriminatory along race or class lines in where it fell; it threatened everyone. The same is true of the release of lead into the air. American environmentalists have been less successful when addressing health and environmental problems that are more local in their nature, because it becomes harder to gain support from people who are not affected by the harm.

Notes

1 A version of this essay was published as "Organizing Protest in the Changing City: Swill Milk and Social Activism in New York City, 1842–64," *New York History* 86 (Summer 2005), 205–25. I am grateful to the New York State Historical Association for their permission to reprint this essay here.

2 Marcy Darnovsky, "Stories Less Told: Histories of US Environmentalism," *Socialist Review* 22(4) (1992), 11–54. Quotation is from p. 28. Modern environmentalism certainly owes much to figures such as Henry David Thoreau, George Perkins Marsh, Gifford Pinchot, and Theodore Roosevelt. From their conservationist principles came a parks system, forest silviculture and management, and the championing of serene nature as a place for reflection and spiritual renewal. Such systems, management tools, and expanded notions of human ethics have been critical in shaping a "green" agenda, but critics note that they are inherited from a predominantly white and male ancestry. Indeed, conservation and wilderness preservation have played a significant role in the growth of the environmental movement and their interests are notably central to the agendas of the "Group of Ten," the nation's ten largest environmental organizations. Given the cultural and ethnic breadth in contemporary American demographics and the ubiquity of environmental problems, historical perceptions of a strictly conservationist agenda require revision. This singular root of modern environmentalism, I submit, is as historically problematic as Frederick Jackson Turner's frontier thesis; both are awkwardly ethnocentric and suffer from a positionality that makes the incorporation of non-white and non-middle-class concerns exceedingly difficult.

3 Focusing on environmental lobbies and their organization over time constitutes an important avenue for historical study. Frank Uekoetter proposes that analyzing the process of the organizing of responses to environmental problems represents an intriguing new direction for environmental histories. By locating social perceptions of divergences between objective natural conditions and certain political, economic, or cultural norms and values, an organizational approach, he argues, offers the historian an opportunity to gauge the degree to which societies are able to recognize, control, and regulate their environmental impact. This organizational approach, therefore, allows historians to contribute to contemporary environmental discussions in a more relevant manner. Frank Uekoetter, "Confronting the Pitfalls of Current Environmental History: An Argument for an Organisational Approach," *Environment and History* 4 (1998), 31–52.

4   John Duffy, *A History of Public Health in New York City, 1625–1866* (New York: Russell Sage Foundation, 1968), 427–39.

5   Interestingly, this kind of practice serves as a precursor for modern ideas surrounding industrial ecology, in which industries consume each other's waste, thereby reducing the amount that requires disposal. Modern industrial ecology is currently regarded as a paradigm for more sustainable industrial practices. For a brief introduction to modern industrial ecology, see David Salvesen, "Making Industrial Parks Sustainable," *Urban Land* (February 1996), 29–32.

6   During the first half of the nineteenth century, the institutional limitations of New York's political system hindered the ability to legislate for the construction of the infrastructure that was necessary to realize an adequate sewage system. For a history of the construction of New York sewers, see Joanne Abel Goldman, *Building New York's Sewers: Developing Mechanisms of Urban Management* (West Lafayette, IN: Purdue University Press, 1997). For the history of the development of antebellum New York politics, see Amy Bridges, *A City in the Republic: Antebellum New York and the Origins of Machine Politics* (Cambridge: Cambridge University Press, 1984).

7   Norman Shaftel, "A History of the Purification of Milk in New York, or, 'How Now, Brown Cow,'" in Judith Walzer Leavitt and Ronald L. Numbers (eds.), *Sickness and Health in America: Readings in the History of Medicine and Public Health* (Madison: University of Wisconsin, 1978), 277.

8   The adulteration or watering down of milk had previously been a serious issue of contention, especially since the water used was invariably contaminated. Physicians continued to fight against the adulteration of milk, but this issue was largely secondary to the protesters of swill milk.

9   Duffy, *A History of Public Health*, 427–39; Shaftel, "A History of the Purification of Milk in New York," 277. For the "posthumous" milking of cows, see Shaftel, "A History of the Purification of Milk in New York," 278. For summaries of the origins of the "swill milk" controversy, see also Edwin G. Burrows and Mike Wallace, *Gotham: A History of New York City to 1898* (Oxford: Oxford University Press, 1999), 788; Budd Leslie Gambee Jr., *Frank Leslie and his Illustrated Newspaper, 1855–1860* (Ann Arbor: University of Michigan Department of Library Science, 1964), 69–72; Frank Luther Mott, *A History of American Magazines, 1850–1865* (Cambridge, MA: Harvard University Press, 1938), 456–58; Kenneth T. Jackson (ed.), *The Encyclopedia of New York City* (New Haven, CT: Yale University Press, 1995), 308–9.

10   The wealthier classes did eventually get behind the movement to ban the distribution of swill milk, but generally on the premise that the odor of the distillery stables permeated through the city. For them, it seems that their motivations were spurred less by the social crisis of unhealthy milk, and more by their interest in preserving their comfortable mode of living. By mid-century, the wealthier classes were also in the midst of a migration uptown, away from the swill milk battleground.

11   For a description of the market economy in antebellum America, see Charles
     Sellers, *The Market Revolution: Jacksonian America, 1815–1846* (Oxford: Oxford
     University Press, 1991).

12   In Brooklyn, for example, Samuel Bouton was a dairyman and also served as
     alderman from the Seventh Ward in 1836, 1837, 1842, and 1843. Jacob Judd,
     "Brooklyn's Health and Sanitation, 1834–55," *Journal of Long Island History* 7(1)
     (1967), 40–52.

13   For a variety of perspectives on political change and the emergence of the indus-
     trial metropolis during the middle of the nineteenth century, see Bridges, *A City
     in the Republic*; Goldman, *Building New York's Sewers*; Edward K. Spann, *The New
     Metropolis: New York City, 1840–1857* (New York: Columbia University Press,
     1981); Sam Bass Warner Jr., *The Urban Wilderness: A History of the American City*
     (Berkeley: University of California Press, 1995); Sean Wilentz, *Chants Democratic:
     New York City and the Rise of the American Working Class, 1788–1850* (Oxford:
     Oxford University Press, 1984); Stuart M. Blumin, *The Emergence of the Middle
     Class: Social Experience in the American City, 1760–1900* (Cambridge: Cambridge
     University Press, 1989); and Carroll Smith Rosenberg, *Religion and the Rise of the
     American City: The New York City Mission Movement, 1812–1870* (Ithaca, NY:
     Cornell University Press, 1971).

14   See, as introduction, Sellers, *The Market Revolution*, 202–36.

15   Thomas L. Haskell, "Capitalism and the Origins of the Humanitarian Sensibil-
     ity, Part 1," *American Historical Review* 90(2) (1985), 339–61. See also Haskell,
     "Capitalism and the Origins of the Humanitarian Sensibility, Part 2," *American
     Historical Review* 90(3) (1985), 547–66; and Paul Boyer, *Urban Masses and Moral
     Order in America, 1820–1920* (Cambridge, MA: Harvard University Press, 1978).

16   Haskell, "Capitalism and the Origins of the Humanitarian Sensibility, Part 1."

17   Burrows and Wallace, *Gotham*, 620.

18   Robert M. Hartley, *An Historical, Scientific and Practical Essay on Milk as an Arti-
     cle of Human Sustenance* (New York: Jonathan Leavitt, 1842), 112.

19   Ibid., 113.

20   Ibid., 348.

21   Ibid., 335.

22   Ibid., 326–27. Hartley conceded that 6¢ a quart was the bare minimum price for
     country milk being delivered and that prices were generally higher.

23   *Daily Tribune*, 9 July 1845. Cited in Spann, *The New Metropolis*, 71–72. Spann
     notes that by the 1860s, railroad construction and more manufacturing signifi-
     cantly improved the winter economy.

24   Duffy, *A History of Public Health*, 428–29.

25   Hartley, *An Essay on Milk*.

26   *Daily Tribune*, 28 May 1858, 5.

27   Shaftel, " A History of the Purification of Milk in New York," 278–79.

28   Burrows and Wallace, *Gotham*, 785. In *The Cholera Years*, Charles E. Rosenberg
     traces the evolution of American thinking about disease during the mid-

nineteenth century. Concentrating on New York's numerous cholera epidemics during the period, Rosenberg notes that "cholera in 1866 was a social problem; in 1832, it had still been, to many Americans, a primarily moral dilemma." Charles E. Rosenberg, *The Cholera Years: The United States in 1832, 1849, and 1866* (1962; Chicago: University of Chicago Press, 1987), 228.

29 For a comparison of Hartley and Griscom, see Charles E. Rosenberg and Carroll Smith-Rosenberg, "Pietism and the Origins of the American Public Health Movement: A Note on John H. Griscom and Robert M. Hartley," in Leavitt and Numbers (eds.), *Sickness and Health in America*, 345–58.

30 Such demands mirror the demands made by postwar suburban groups.

31 Duffy, *A History of Public Health*, 302–7.

32 John H. Griscom, *The Sanitary Conditions of the Laboring Class of New York* (New York: Harper & Brothers, 1845). Martin V. Melosi notes the influence of the English sanitarian Edwin Chadwick on Griscom and the title of his work. Chadwick had, in 1842, published his *Report on the Sanitary Condition of the Labouring Population of Great Britain* and corresponded with Griscom during the 1840s. Martin V. Melosi, *The Sanitary City: Urban Infrastructure in America from Colonial Times to the Present* (Baltimore: Johns Hopkins University Press, 2000), 43–72. For more on Chadwick and the European influence on American notions of public health, see Christopher Hamlin, *Public Health and Social Justice in the Age of Chadwick: Britain, 1800–1854* (Cambridge: Cambridge University Press, 1998).

33 For a study of masculinity during the Progressive era, see Gail Bederman, *Manliness and Civilization: A Cultural History of Gender and Race in the United States, 1880–1917* (Chicago: University of Chicago Press, 1995).

34 Burrows and Wallace, *Gotham*, 785.

35 S. Rotton Percy, "Report of the Committee on City Milk," *Transactions of the New York Academy of Medicine*, 2 March 1859, 97–149. Reference to "cow fever" is on pp. 104–6.

36 Ibid., 104–6. Percy posited that the inoculation was "a needless piece of folly," and that there was no evidence that the fever was contagious.

37 *Frank Leslie's Illustrated Newspaper*, 8 May 1858, 359.

38 Augustus K. Gardner, "Report of a Committee Appointed by the Academy of Medicine, upon the Comparative Value of Milk Formed from the Slop of Distilleries and Other Food," *Transactions of the New York Academy of Medicine*, 1 March 1848, 31–49. Quotations are from p. 49.

39 *Daily Tribune*, 26 June 1847, 2. John Duffy suggests that the author of this article was very likely Dr. Augustus Gardner, who wrote extensively on the topic of swill milk as chair of the New York Academy of Medicine. Duffy, *A History of Public Health*, 429.

40 *Leslie's*, 15 May 1858, 369.

41 *Leslie's*, 22 May 1858, 385.

42 Gambee, *Frank Leslie and His Illustrated Newspaper*. Gambee notes that issues in early 1858 had very few pictures, likely because Leslie's illustrators were busy researching and drawing for the swill milk exposé.

43 *Leslie's*, 8 May 1858, 353.

44 Gambee, *Frank Leslie and his Illustrated Newspaper*, 68–72.

45 *Leslie's*, 15 May 1858, 379.

46 *Daily Tribune*, 28 May 1858, 4.

47 *Leslie's*, 10 July 1858, 90; 24 July 1858, 120.

48 *Leslie's*, 17 July 1858, 110. Reed, one of the whitewashers, was defeated for alderman that fall.

49 C. H. Haswell, *Reminiscences of an Octogenarian of the City of New York, 1816–1860* (New York: Harper & Brothers, 1896), 511–12.

50 *Majority and Minority Reports of the Select Committee Appointed to Investigate the Character and Conditions of the Sources from which Cows' Milk is Derived* (New York: Charles W. Baker, 1858), 24–28.

51 Duffy, *A History of Public Health*, 433–34.

52 *Leslie's*, 15 May 1858, 384.

53 *Leslie's*, 8 May 1858, 353, 359.

54 *Leslie's*, 15 May 1858, 378.

55 *Leslie's*, 22 May 1858, 385.

56 Bederman, *Manliness and Civilization*, 11–12. The gender mixing in which Leslie engaged was a time-tested rhetorical strategy that dated back to the ancient Greeks. For a discussion of masculinity and Athenian politics, see John J. Winkler, "Laying Down the Law: The Oversight of Men's Sexual Behavior in Classical Athens," in David M. Halperin, John J. Winkler, and Froma I. Zeitlin (eds.), *Before Sexuality: The Construction of Erotic Experience in the Ancient Greek World* (Princeton, NJ: Princeton University Press, 1990), 171–209.

57 The reference to modern Herods comes from *Leslie's*, 8 May 1858, 359.

58 *Leslie's*, 8 May 1858, 353. There is a considerable amount of scholarship on the interpretation of gender in the dairy industry. In most western countries, women lost their predominant role in the dairying industry as production became centralized and mechanized. Interestingly, the introduction of machines shifted the balance of power in the industry from women to men. For the masculinization of the machine, see Carolyn Merchant, *The Death of Nature: Women, Ecology, and the Scientific Revolution* (San Francisco: Harper & Row, 1980). For a good introduction to the literature on dairy history, see Lena Sommestad, "Gendering Work, Interpreting Gender: The Masculinization of Dairy Work in Sweden, 1850–1950," *History Workshop Journal* 37 (Spring 1994), 57–75. For American examples, see also Joan Jensen, *Loosening the Bonds: Mid-Atlantic Farm Women, 1750–1850* (New Haven, CT: Yale University Press, 1986); Jensen, "Butter Making and Economic Development in Mid-Atlantic America from 1750–1850," *Signs* 13 (Summer 1988), 813–29; Deborah Valenze, "The Art of Women and the Business of Men: Women's Work and the Dairy Industry c. 1740–1840," *Past and Present*

130 (February 1991), 142–69; and Sally McMurry, "Women's Work in Agriculture: Divergent Trends in England and America, 1800–1930," *Comparative Studies in Society and History* 34(2) (1992), 248–70.

59 *Leslie's*, 15 May 1858, 384. The accompanying story and further references to "milkmaids" are in *Leslie's*, 15 May 1858, 380–81.

60 *Leslie's*, 19 February 1859, 186.

61 *Leslie's*, 24 July 1858, 120.

62 *Leslie's*, 22 May 1858, 385.

63 *New York State Laws*, 85th session, chapter 467, 23 April 1862, 866–67.

64 *New York State Laws*, 87th session, chapter 544, 2 May 1864, 1195–96.

65 *New York Department of Health Sanitary Code*, 2 June 1873.

66 William T. Howard, *Public Health Administration and the Natural History of Diseases in Baltimore, Maryland, 1797–1920* (Washington, DC: 1924), 120–21.

67 For a discussion of environmental concerns and the power of the political machine, see Samuel P. Hays, *Conservation and the Gospel of Efficiency: The Progressive Conservation Movement, 1890–1920* (Cambridge, MA: Harvard University Press, 1959). For an example of more recent environmental politics, see Hays (with Barbara D. Hays), *Beauty, Health, and Permanence: Environmental Politics in the United States, 1955–1985* (Cambridge: Cambridge University Press, 1987).

68 *Leslie's*, 15 May 1858, 379.

69 Andrew Szasz, *Shopping Our Way to Safety: How We Changed from Protecting the Environment to Protecting Ourselves* (Minneapolis: University of Minnesota Press, 2007).

CHAPTER 3

"That Shocking Calamity"

Revisiting George Catlin's Environmental Politics[1]

JOHN HAUSDOERFFER

Introduction: A Tale of Two Portraits

In October of 1832, the American artist and essayist George Catlin (1796–1872) took a brief hiatus from his six-year journey to the distant headwaters of the Missouri River. Having dedicated his career to recording and advocating for Indian cultures and environments, Catlin returned to St. Louis to paint Black Hawk, the recently defeated Sauk leader of the Black Hawk War and prisoner in Jefferson Barracks. Catlin painted several individual portraits of Black Hawk and his compatriots, but two portraits of note emerge—one that he promoted with pride and a still relatively unknown one that he did not promote. Each represents a different side of George Catlin's complicated relationship with Native American struggles.

The first is Catlin's "Black Hawk, Prominent Sauk Chief," among Catlin's most famous Indian portraits (Figure 3.1). Catlin knew this painting would reach a broad audience. He also knew, given the popular mystique surrounding the Black Hawk War, that this portrait would bring fame and legitimacy to his declaration that "nothing short of the loss of my life, shall prevent me from visiting [Indian] country, and of becoming their historian."[2] He featured the painting in his classic 1841 memoir of his western journey, *Letters and Notes on the Manners, Customs, and Conditions of North American Indians*, and

Figure 3.1 George Catlin, "Black Hawk, Prominent Sauk Chief" (1832). Catlin's celebrated portrait of Black Hawk is typical of the nineteenth-century lament for the noble savage. Smithsonian American Art Museum.

highlighted the painting in his public galleries, lectures, and performances across the United States and Europe throughout the 1830s and 1840s. He emphasized the portrait in extensive advertising for his shows, recognizing the surge in recognition it would bring to his artwork. His father Putnam, to whom George Catlin often reported the success of his artwork and galleries, said in a family letter, "[George] mourns the dreadful destiny of the Indian tribes . . . but unquestionably that shocking calamity will greatly increase the value of his expertise & works."[3] Indeed, Catlin mourned sincerely and painted earnestly to preserve and celebrate the memory of a displaced people. He also understood the social and financial capital that emerged from representing those "destined to fall"—an increasingly rare commodity, as defeated tribes quickly became public curiosities. Since that time, stretching its popularity into the twenty-first century, the Black Hawk painting has continued to draw audiences to Smithsonian displays of Catlin's work.

The other portrait from that day is much more obscure, hard to find both in Catlin's publications at the time as well as in public treatments of Catlin's work since. "Black Hawk and Five Other Saukie Prisoners" never made it into

Letters and Notes and was not emphasized in Catlin's lectures. It has not been commemorated (in his time or ours) as an example of Catlin's commitment to free his audiences "as far as possible from the deadly prejudices which [Americans have] carried . . . against this most unfortunate and most abused part of the race of his fellow man."[4] This painting is quite different from more conventional Catlin portraits. Rather than depicting Black Hawk in a digni-fied pose, dressed in traditional garb, and distinguished in the "noble savage" mode, this second portrait features Black Hawk and his warriors in chains—a near-documentary representation of their prison conditions (Figure 3.2).

Catlin's second Black Hawk portrait is markedly different and presents a different kind of Indian politics. He set out to paint American Indians as noble icons of vanishing cultures, but as he sketched the conquered Black Hawk and his men in their cell, Neopope, one of Black Hawk's countrymen, pleaded for Catlin to include their shackles in each portrait. As Benjamin Drake narrated in his 1838 account of the event, Black Hawk's ally Neopope "seized the ball and chain that were fastened to his leg, and raising them on high, exclaimed with a look of scorn, 'make me so and show me to the Great Father.'" In demanding his shackles be included in the portraits, Neopope asked Catlin to show the world that their fight for their lands continued.

Figure 3.2 George Catlin, "Black Hawk and Five Other Saukie Prisoners" (1861/1869), oil on card mounted on paperboard. Paul Mellon Collection. Image courtesy of the Board of Trustees, National Gallery of Art, Washington. Catlin's lesser-known second portrait of Black Hawk, painted at the behest of Neopope, Black Hawk's countryman, who insisted that the Sauk chief be painted in his chains.

He asked Catlin to portray them as neither brutal nor noble savages, but as displaced yet dynamic dissidents of an unjust system. He asked Catlin, famous for public laments for the plight of Indians, to move beyond white lament and to use his art to support their protest. "Refusing to paint him as he wished," despite the fact that Neopope "kept varying his countenances with grimaces, to prevent [Catlin] from catching a likeness," Catlin chose instead to portray each subject "as though free and at repose." Only decades later, in the 1860s, did Catlin grant Neopope's wishes; only much later, long after Black Hawk was dead and the Saukie destroyed did Catlin paint the warriors in their chains in a painting that was first shown in Europe in 1870.[5] Perhaps Catlin did not want to humiliate Black Hawk and his people by showing them so confined. Perhaps Catlin hoped he could subvert President Andrew Jackson's and the mainstream papers' descriptions of Black Hawk as savage and undeserving of sovereignty, by portraying the Sauk leader as a caring, proud, and thoughtful person. Nevertheless, Catlin's "refusal" in the 1830s to publicly portray a chained Black Hawk reflects an ironic and inadvertent alignment with the very political powers that framed Black Hawk as savage and deserving of violent removal—it contributes to assumptions that Black Hawk's social contributions lie in a memorialized past.

It may seem odd to those familiar with Catlin to suggest any alignment between Catlin and the political forces driving Indian removal. After all, in addition to Catlin's efforts to dispel Indian stereotypes and to preserve their traditions through his art, Catlin was also the first to promote a national park as an alternative to extractive uses of western environments that economically necessitated and culturally justified the displacement of Indian cultures. He famously declared:

> what a beautiful and thrilling specimen for America to preserve and hold up to the view of her refined citizens and the world, in future ages! A *nation's Park*, containing man and beast, in all the wild and freshness of all their nature's beauty![6]

Of this park he said, "I would ask no other monument to my memory, nor any other enrolment of my name among the famous dead, than the reputation of having been the founder of such an institution."[7] Catlin offers historians the rare example of an environmental thinker who predated Rachel Carson and Aldo Leopold by over a century. More importantly, Catlin offers an example of an early environmental thinker who understood the cultural and human consequences of environmental damage. When Catlin lamented Indian "extermination," he simultaneously criticized slaughtered buffalo and devastated prairie, revealing a sophisticated grasp of the intersection of cultural health and environmental diversity.

Catlin challenged the prevailing mood of his times as powerfully as did his innovative national park idea when he chose to paint Black Hawk with dignity, in the midst of a society that caricatured the Sauk leader as savage. At the same time, however, Catlin's decision to promote the painting of Black Hawk (and thus Black Hawk's movement) as a noble savage of the past, rather than the painting that features Black Hawk as an active agent of resistance, raises critical questions concerning the tradition of protest that Catlin established in promoting the preservation of Indian cultures and environments. It raises questions about the fine line between recording a memorial of a people and supporting a movement for Native American land and life. To what extent did Catlin advance the preservation of complex Indian relations with and rights to native environments? To what extent did Catlin's efforts inherently accept the injustice of cultural displacement and environmental exploitation in pursuit of an inadvertently imperial form of preservation—the preservation of icons of nature at the cost of sustaining viable cultural relations with nature? To what extent did Catlin inadvertently silence and appropriate the voice of Black Hawk to promote his own, although humanitarian and preservationist in essence, vision for the continent? These questions ultimately raise the enduring question: "Who speaks for nature?"

This essay seeks to negotiate these questions concerning Catlin's environmental politics through revisiting the larger context of his environmental ideologies, including but also looking beyond his celebrated call for a "nation's Park." In revisiting the ideologies underlying Catlin's literary and artistic work, this essay argues that as much can be learned about Catlin's environmental politics in places like Black Hawk's cell as in the open "natural" spaces of his imagined park. This reading neither lauds Catlin as a preservationist nor condemns him as an imperialist, but interrogates him as a pioneering, highly well-intentioned, yet quite problematic "green capitalist." That is, Catlin set out to establish a new ethical course for an emerging entrepreneurial society, attempting to blaze a path to success and notoriety through preserving and generating appreciation for an abstracted "Nature." However, his ethical entrepreneurship disengaged audiences from considering active Indian protests against the exploitation of their lands. Even Catlin's park preserved a *concept* of vanishing "Nature" that fueled the very environmental practices he protested. With Catlin, natural protest transforms, ironically and unintentionally, into cultural consent. I explain this in four sections: the environmentally destructive ideologies of Catlin's times; Catlin's expressed ethical goals and environmental commitments; the way in which Catlin's ethical goals consent to those problematic ideologies; and the larger implications of Catlin's environmental ideologies for the history of environmental protest.[8]

Jacksonian America

George Catlin confronted a subtle blend of oppressive forces interwoven into the daily fabric of American life. The Jacksonian era that Catlin criticized—the period between the 1828 election of Andrew Jackson and the beginning of the antebellum period in 1848—relied on sophisticated ideologies that perpetuated inequalities.

On one hand, it was an "Age of Democracy," with non-property-owning Anglo-American males earning the right to vote, and with economic opportunities arising for all classes of Anglo-Americans. But this unprecedented age of expanding political and economic opportunity for Anglo-American men emerged during a bleak time for Indians, blacks, workers, women, and the environment. Cultural and environmental injustices collectively served as prerequisites for Anglo-American opportunity.

For example, the opportunity to settle the West and the economic promises of timber, cotton, wheat, cattle, and minerals required the availability of Indian homelands. American leaders of the day believed that a society with surging immigrant and urban populations could not maintain the promises of democratic opportunity for whites without "empty" land to settle or "unlocked" raw materials to transform into wealth. This ideology fueled Andrew Jackson's controversial 1830 Indian Removal Act, resulting in the removal of cultures from their homelands—from the Seminole of Florida to Black Hawk's Sauk of Illinois; Jackson's and his constituents' belief in Anglo-democratic opportunity resulted in the removal of 70,000 members of native peoples in the 1830s. Most infamously, this decade of mass removal led to the "Trail of Tears," during which 4,000 Cherokee died on the forced journey from Georgia to Oklahoma.[9]

With Indians removed, their cultural and environmental practices were replaced with the exhaustive, early capitalist extraction of raw materials fueling a global market revolution. Slave labor intensified as a central tool for extracting raw materials rapidly and cheaply in these "new" western lands. In these territories, slavery expanded with such intensity that in many sections of Georgia, Louisiana, and Texas slaves constituted well over 50 percent of the population. Ironically enough, as the historian Quintard Taylor points out, displaced Indians such as the Cherokee and Creek mimicked these intensive agricultural practices with their own slaves in Indian Territory. As with Jackson's justification of Indian Removal, slavery was described as a "positive good." The paternal plantation owner was defined as protecting "inferior" beings from the confusing poverty of cities or the uncivilized darkness of Africa. As John Calhoun said in 1850, "We see [slavery] now in its true light, and regard it as the most safe and stable basis of free institutions in the world."[10]

In addition to "available" land and resources, and in addition to the economic utility of a dehumanized labor force, new methods of transporting and producing materials provided the basis for the new wealth and opportunity of this "democratic" age. Canals, steamboats, and railroads opened the once-distant timber, wheat, minerals, and cotton of the continent's interior to urban centers and ports such as New York and Charleston as if they were next door. Places once the distant homes of native cultures and ecosystems could now be transmuted fluidly, without limitations imposed by human or natural geography. From eastern cities, the places of the West could be defined as commodities, as simplified economic parts of whole, complex cultural and ecological systems. These economic parts could be transported with ease to the emerging factories of the Northeast. The factories, powered by dammed rivers and overworked laborers, functioned in tandem with the "free" labor of Southern slavery and the "free" resources of previous Indian lands to generate an economic explosion for American cities.[11]

A new middle class developed rapidly, as merchants, factory managers, financiers, and lawyers were in high demand to maintain this growing market economy. Again, development and opportunity rested on the shoulders of domination, as the factories that enabled these opportunities particularly exploited young, disempowered, lower-class female workers who could not marry into the emerging middle class. Just as with Indian removal and slavery, the very limitations of rights and opportunities for women *supported* the levels of production necessary for white males to pursue the socio-economic liberties promised by this "democratic" age.[12]

The collective human tragedies of Indian removal, slavery, factory exploitation, and patriarchy produced tremendous wealth and opportunity for the culturally privileged, but also resulted in dramatic environmental devastation. During a single person's lifetime in this period, the passenger pigeon went extinct on account of habitat loss, the buffalo dwindled in numbers from approximately 30 million in 1830 to a few thousand in the 1880s (with 5 million slaughtered in just three years), and forests the size of Europe were mowed down in North America. Throughout Catlin's prime (1830s and 1840s) the economic and political prosperity of male Anglo-Americans rested upon what the contemporary eco-feminist scholars Greta Gaard and Lori Gruen call (with reference to interlinking injustices in our own era) "the mutually reinforcing oppression of humans and the natural world." These were not separate, coincidental, human and environmental tragedies. They "mutually reinforced" one another, both materially and ideologically. Materially, "free" land and labor from Indians, blacks, working-class immigrants, and women collectively enabled the feverish pace at which environments were depleted, as the capital stored by nature over millennia was rapidly depleted to subsidize dramatic economic growth. Ideologically, the view that "naturally" inferior blacks, "naturally" savage Indians, and "naturally" nurturing women were all better off under paternal white males allowed for these material injustices to be named something other than unjust. The practices that critics of the time called injustice, domination, and oppression were rhetorically reconfigured into "natural" pursuits of democracy, freedom, and opportunity.[13]

George Catlin and the Art of Protest

Thus, as a citizen who questioned the exploitation of Indian lands and cultures, Catlin faced a complex and interconnected system of oppression. To effectively identify, question, and protest the driving source of environmental problems in this age, George Catlin needed to also challenge injustices of race, class, and gender as well as long-rooted and long-unexamined philosophies that rhetorically justified such injustices as destined liberties. Indeed, there have been few figures in the history of environmental protest who understood the need to delink mutually reinforcing forms of oppression, particularly in the nineteenth century, but Catlin embodied a rare case of an individual who tried. Catlin conscientiously challenged the practices of his age in five ways: he subverted negative Indian stereotypes; he redefined the value of western landscapes; he criticized the consumptive practices and general apathy of the American populace; he asked for changes in government frontier policy; and he sought to ethically detach his own endeavors in the West from exploitive institutions of expansion.

First, Catlin challenged negative stereotypes. As he said in *Letters and Notes*, "the Indian's misfortune has consisted chiefly in our ignorance of their true native character and disposition . . . inducing us to look upon them in no other light than that of a hostile foe." Later in the same essay he asserted that Americans have "too often recorded them but a dark and unintelligible mass of cruelty and barbarity." Jackson's expansionist policies relied heavily on dominant assumptions that Indians were "savages." The clearest example of Jackson's simultaneous justification of savage stereotypes and environmental displacement came in his Second Annual Message in 1830, six months after signing the Indian Removal Act: "what good man would prefer a country covered with forests and ranged by a few thousand savages to our extensive Republic, studded with cities, towns, and prosperous farms . . . and filled with the blessings of liberty, civilization, and religion?" Catlin, through the basic but vital act of painting humanizing portraits of demonized societies, protested the very logic of Jackson's removal claims and military policies.[14]

Catlin's western portraits also challenged the prevailing ideology that the spaces of the West were "savage forests" awaiting "the blessings . . . of civilization." His paintings showed the pre-"settled" West as open yet complete as an Indian homeland. Unlike nineteenth-century painters such as John Gast and Frances Palmer, Catlin in his paintings (e.g. Figure 3.3) did not show incomplete or empty landscapes, awaiting the arrival of miners, loggers, farmers, wagons, trains, steamboats, and cities.[15] In showing these spaces as complete, Catlin challenged the combined ideology that the spaces were untamed wilderness and that the people inhabiting those "forests" were in turn savage, requiring removal to allow for settled lands and thus civilized people.

Beyond contradicting the imagery of Indians and nature that enabled displacement policies, Catlin protested the daily practices of his readers and audiences. "Reader! . . . The buffaloes (the quadrupeds from whose backs your beautiful robes were taken, and whose myriads were once spread over the whole country, from the Rocky Mountains to the Atlantic Ocean) have recently fled before the appalling appearance of civilized man." Directly linking his audience's consumer choices to the extinction of a species offered a direct, activist approach to preservation.[16]

Furthermore, Catlin questioned the structural policies of fur trade companies and the government. He extended the critique of his audience to a criticism of how fur companies traded alcohol for hides with impoverished, desperate Indian societies plagued with disease, alcoholism, and few economic alternatives. "Oh insatiable man, is thy avarice such! Wouldst thou tear the skin from the back of the last animal of this noble race, *and rob thy fellow-man of his meat, and for it give him poison!*" Going even further than linking fur trade to native alcoholism, he demanded policy change within

Figure 3.3 George Catlin, "River Bluffs, 1320 Miles above St. Louis" (1832). Smithsonian American Art Museum. Gift of Mrs. Joseph Harrison Jr., Washington, DC.

the government, particularly towards those tribes that had yet to confront frontier conditions of greed, poverty, alcohol, guns, and buffalo slaughter. He stated:

> Our government should raise her strong arm to save the remainder of them from the pestilence which is rapidly advancing upon them. We have gotten from them territory enough, and the country which they now inhabit is most of it too barren of timber for the use of civilized man; it affords, however, the means and luxuries of savage life, and it is to be hoped that our government will not acquiesce in the continued willful destruction of these happy people.

Thus, he not only challenged dehumanizing stereotypes and consumer behaviors, but called for direct political intervention to preserve cultural health and natural resources of American Indians.[17]

Finally, Catlin hoped present a model that would allow them to avoid culpability for Indian "extermination."

> The humble biographer or historian, who goes amongst them from a different motive, *may* come out of their country with his hands and conscious clean, and himself an anomaly, a white man dealing with Indians, and meting out justice to them; which I hope it may be my good province to do with my pen and my brush . . . having done them no harm.

Catlin sought to withhold consent from systems of removal, to do "no harm." "If in my zeal to render a service and benefit to the Indian, I should have fallen short of it, I will, at least, be acquitted of having done him an injury." Catlin hoped that if he could not fulfill his intentions ("I have flown to their rescue") he could at least provide a model for his society on how to thrive on American industrial wealth and fame without participating in the injustices that underlie that very prosperity.[18]

The Environmental Ethics of Cultural Vanishing

Catlin's five challenges to society found continuity in his grand vision for a "*nation's Park*." Catlin envisioned his national park during his 1832 expedition, while overlooking the Yellowstone River. He vividly described this place, while sitting in "the very heart or nucleus of buffalo country," and supplemented this description with his artwork—paintings of an Indian hunting in winter, of wolves attacking a buffalo, and of a buffalo bull in his wallow. Catlin quickly moved from artistic and ethnographic recording to social and environmental protest when he reported that buffalo deaths came from a combination of "desperate" Sioux and the "indefatigable men" of America, from white fur traders to white consumers—including his readers. He pointed out that Americans are "always calling for every robe that can be stripped from these animals' backs" resulting in a "wild and shorn country."[19]

Catlin began to imagine alternatives to the destruction of the bison. He suggested that if Americans really needed robes, they should invest "in machines for the manufacture of *woolen robes*, of equal and superior value and beauty; there by encouraging the growers of wool, and the industrious manufacturer, rather than [consuming] . . . the last of the animals producing [buffalo robes]."[20] Catlin cried out against the destruction of "this animal in all its pride and glory," and connected buffalo with "the peace and happiness (if not the actual existence) of the tribes of Indians who are joint tenants with them, in the occupancy of these vast and idle plains." This is the context in which he imagined his famed "nation's Park," expanding from Mexico to Canada in "almost one entire plain of grass."[21]

Catlin's park represented his call for a new vision of the West in the mind's eye of the American public. While sitting in "the shade of a plum tree," in the "grass on a favorite bluff," Catlin imagined that he was suddenly transported above the earth.

> I was lifted up upon an imaginary pair of wings, which easily raised and held me floating in the open air, from whence I could behold beneath me the Pacific and the Atlantic Oceans—the great cities of the East, and the mighty rivers.

In this reverie, he imagined that "the world turned gently around." He saw the whole, rotating earth from a fresh perspective, not caught up in the desperation of the Sioux or the greed of fur companies. He claimed a moment of transcendent clarity. As he looked down from space at foreign parts of the round earth, he expressed nostalgia for "the vast and vivid green, that is spread like a carpet over the Western wilds." He realized that the vast green home of the buffalo is unique only to this relatively small place in the world, to his imagined park. This uniqueness saddened him. Focusing his gaze back on the western plains, he pictured buffalo being slaughtered and Indian cultures vanishing along with the buffalo, along with the species on which the Plains Indian economy and worldview relied.[22]

He rose above the geographic and the ideological fray in this reverie.

> It may be that *power* is *right*, and voracity a *virtue*; and that these people, and these noble animals, are *righteously* doomed to an issue that *will* not be averted. It can be easily proved—we have a civilized science that can

easily do it, or anything else that may be required to cover the iniquities of civilized man in catering for his unholy appetites.

Catlin expressed frustration that the iniquities of cultural removal and environmental devastation were deemed civil, and institutionalized into daily life to the point that no one challenged them.[23]

From the point of view of his culture's mainstream ideologies it would have been wrongheaded to question a scientifically predicted vanishing, but in this rare, brief moment Catlin questioned "unholy appetites" and the "proofs" that legitimized them. He continued, with sad sarcasm:

> We have a mode of reasoning (I forget what it is called) by which all this can be proved; and even more. The *word* and the *system* are entirely of *civilized* origin: and latitude is admirably given to them in proportion to the increase of the civilized wants.

Catlin understood that the ideologies of his time ("the *word*") functioned to justify and maintain an economy that required cultural and environmental exploitation ("the *system*"). So when he says that "*power* is *right*," he says it ironically, showing that his society with all of its civilized science and prosperity was really at its base a "might makes right" society, in which reason was twisted to explain away the "iniquities" of "power."[24]

Alas, Catlin's reverie ended. He returned to earth both geographically and ideologically. He imagined a radical critique of the political economy of America at the time, saw its hypocrisy, and then retreated. He retreated, because deep down, deeper than his concern about the loss of these lifeways, he believed they were "destined" to vanish. As he says in the introductory section of the same book, "civilization [is] destined, not only to veil, but to obliterate the grace and beauty of nature." Like his withdrawal of support for the visual protest in Black Hawk's cell, here Catlin stopped imagining after briefly wondering if some new system could provide for buffalo health, "whose numbers would increase and supply [Indians] with food for ages and centuries to come."

> But such is not to be the case—the buffalo's doom is sealed, and with their extinction must assuredly sink into real despair and starvation, the inhabitants of these vast plains, which afford for the Indians, no other possible means of subsistence; and they must at last fall a prey to wolves and buzzards, who will have no other bones to pick.

Although revealing an early understanding that societies rely on intricate connections within ecological systems, Catlin returned to tacitly accepting his period's root ideology—like it or not (and he certainly did not), it is carved into the plan of nature that these Plains systems (both human and nonhuman) will vanish. He found himself left with ethnography rather than protest as the closest thing to an ethical enterprise in this context of "extinction." As with his ideas for woolen robe manufacture and for a national park, Catlin looked for solutions through a new kind of capitalist consumption. He did not promote the dynamic persistence of autonomous Indian lifeways, but aimed to inspire a more ethical consumer-based capitalism—a proto-green consumerism.[25]

In fact, in arguing for his park, he claimed that without a park to draw spectators, the plains were "useless to cultivating man." He desired the expansion and perpetuation of the American economy, and he sincerely wanted Indian peoples to benefit from it. In fact, Catlin wanted them to benefit through continuing their practices inside his park for spectators and through conversion to western economies and beliefs outside his park.

> If [Americans] would introduce the ploughshare and their prayers amongst these people, who are so far separated from the taints and contaminating views of the frontier, they would soon . . . be able to solve to the world the perplexing enigma, by presenting a nation of savages, civilized and Christianized (and consequently *saved*) in the heart of the American wilderness.

Perhaps this could have led to a market for woolen robes, perhaps to a massive park, but at least in the worst case scenario Catlin could excuse himself as one who set out "from a different motive," while serving an "innocent" market in art and science. Furthermore, he could at least console himself because he had proposed a solution to Indian and environmental destruction.[26]

No matter what, from Catlin's perspective, he would have preserved a record of images, a "production of a literal and graphic delineation of the living manners, customs, and character of an interesting race of people, who are rapidly passing away from the earth—lending a hand to a dying nation." Despite the possibilities of what might have been preserved beyond just his canvas if everyone had drifted into and inhabited his literary dream of a new Plains, Catlin regressed to ideologies of vanishing and artistic preservation of a soon-to-be-vanished "Nature."[27]

The very ideologies of vanishing that justified Jackson's view of removal as the remaining ethical choice for Indians thus tempered the thrust of Catlin's goals of natural protest. Although in his reverie he made connections between the wealth of buffalo-based ecosystems and the health of Indian economic and social systems, and although he in turn connected social injustices with environmental devastation, his acceptance and participation in ideologies of vanishing (throughout this text and his larger career) contradicted the active future of actual environments and cultures.

One final example from *Letters and Notes* epitomizes the tremendous extent to which Catlin's sincere ethical intentions were undermined by his own collusion in the ideology of cultures and environments destined to vanish. In 1832, just as he began to venture beyond Ft. Leavenworth, Catlin shot a buffalo while on a now infamous buffalo hunt with two fellow frontiersmen. The buffalo did not die immediately, but stared at Catlin as it struggled to live. Catlin, instead of finishing it off immediately, "drew from my pocket my sketch-book, laid my gun across my lap, and commenced taking his likeness. He stood stiffened up, and swelling with awful vengeance, which was sublime for a picture." Continuing this process "I rode around him and sketched him in numerous attitudes, sometimes he would lie down, and then I would sketch him; then throw my cap at him, and rousing him on his legs, rally a new expression, and sketch him again." Finally, he finished drawing this "buffalo bull, whom I then shot in the head and finished."[28]

In the same work in which Catlin criticized the evils of the buffalo trade, his desire to "preserve" the buffalo merged with his acceptance of its vanishing from its original context. He sought to preserve scientific knowledge of all parts of the buffalo before it vanished, so he felt compelled to study it even as it suffered and he participated in its eradication. His art and his violence are intimately connected in this scene. Yet it was not violence to Catlin, because he valued the act as the pursuit of knowledge of "Nature" rather than an act of aimless slaughter (it turns out that the buffalo was too old to have meat appetizing enough to eat). His goal to preserve "Nature" before it vanished triumphed over the life of an animal, in spite of the individual animal's pain, and in spite of Catlin's personal depletion of a threatened population. Preserved "Nature" justified actions not condoned elsewhere in the text. Catlin's unexamined ideologies, shared with the very perpetrators of injustice that Catlin so adamantly criticized, contradicted his earnest and visionary natural protest. Effective protest in an age of mutually reinforcing ideologies and modes of domination required a level of cultural critique far beyond Catlin's combination of concern, lament, and action for peoples and places. The level of protest found in his rhetoric and literary vision proves limited when contradicted by actions such as slaughtering a buffalo or refusing to promote his painting of dissident Sauks in chains. Moreover, even within his rhetoric and vision, effective environmental protest would have required him to reject—one of the most often told yet least well understood features of his epoch—the vanishing of peoples, places, and things. Such a rejection, in turn, would have led to different actions. That is, without his belief in inevitable vanishing, his decision to kill the buffalo and to sanitize the state of political prisoners would have lost their justification as altruistic acts of recording the final remnants of a lost cause for the sake of posterity.[29]

Catlin and the History of Environmental Politics

In October 1872, George Catlin died at the age of 76, forty years after visualizing "*a nation's Park*" from a solitary vantage point overlooking the Yellowstone River. Coincidentally, he died in the same year that President Ulysses S. Grant dedicated 1,600 square miles of Wyoming Territory as Yellowstone National Park. The official statute read that the park would be "set apart as a public park of pleasuring ground for the benefit and enjoyment of the people." This sounds not unlike Catlin's 1832 declaration that the park would be "for America to preserve and hold up to the view of her refined citizens and the world, in future ages!"[30]

Catlin's park symbolizes the unsettling questions that he posed about the buffalo trade, negative stereotypes of Indians, and the subsequent extermination of Indian societies. In this way, Catlin's vision for a park marks him as a pioneer of social and environmental protest in the American West, a pioneer who attempted to expand views and uses of the West beyond industrial extraction.

Perhaps more importantly, the historical Yellowstone Park also epitomized the ideology that contradicted Catlin's expressed ethical intentions. Yellowstone exemplified Catlin's hope for a gentler form of capitalist expansion in a post-Indian world. In turn, Yellowstone embodied the way in which Catlin abstracted and extracted this post-vanished-Indian "Nature" from environmental and cultural relations in order to preserve and sell palatable icons of that "Nature."

Just as Catlin's call for a park should be celebrated for its innovation, of course, Yellowstone should be seen as a significant development in the history of preservation. Proponents argued that it was "a great breathing space for the national lungs." The statute establishing the park suggested that the industrial extraction of "timber [and] mineral deposits" from the park would be prohibited. Thus the statute nationally recognized and protected the intrinsic value of certain environments, framed by scenic "monumental" landscapes, in the face of intense exploitation of the continent. But even Yellowstone was not free from being valued as a commodity that could be used to make a profit.[31]

Yellowstone emerged in the midst of a new tourist economy that eventually brought millions per year to the West, to momentarily escape urban anxiety and enjoy some semblance of the fabled yet disappearing frontier experience. Railroads, a rising economic force in America, recognized the potential profits from offering these western experiences. In fact, Yellowstone was originally promoted by the powerful railroads of late nineteenth-century America. Jay Cooke's Northern Pacific Railroad lobbied Congress and heavily advertised the park throughout the 1870s. In similar instances, the Northern Pacific promoted Rainier National Park in 1897; the Great Northern pushed for Glacier National Park in 1899; the Union Pacific advocated for the Grand Canyon while the Southern and Central Pacific Railroads supported Yosemite. These railroad companies, also the driving force behind opening the prairies and forests of the West to aggressive timber harvesting, cattle ranching, wheat farming, mining, and cotton planting (and, central to my earlier argument, a critical factor in the demise of the buffalo), pushed for parks that would not allow the extraction of raw materials. The central asset of these regions, equally profitable (from the railroad's point of view) as meat, hides, wheat, and ore, was what Yellowstone's statute called "natural curiosities, or wonders . . . in their natural condition." Even the Hayden Survey's scientific letter to Congress on behalf of Yellowstone argued for the preservation of a place where people could see "freaks and phenomena of Nature" along with "wonderful natural curiosities." Nash concludes that "Yellowstone's initial advocates were not concerned with wilderness; they acted to prevent acquisition and exploitation of geysers, hot springs, waterfalls, and similar curiosities."[32]

The construction of a "natural" landscape of curiosities and freaks, prepared for the public's viewing pleasure, distracted the public from the complex, 10,000-year history of the area's environment and culture. Defending a nationalist natural space during a time of manifest destiny, proponents argued that Yellowstone offered Americans a heritage rooted in the beauty of God's work. Contrasted with Europe's claim to an ancient connection to place, based on ruins of cities, cathedrals, and castles, America could connect to an exceptional and ancient past through "Nature" on their newly adopted continent.[33]

The belief in a "Nature" outside environmental and cultural relationships ignored the fact that God or "Nature" alone did not carve Yellowstone. Indians had used, changed, and shaped much of the environment found by American tourists in 1872. Shoshone, Crow, and Blackfoot Indians had "immeasurably" altered the ecosystem of the region over a *longue durée*. Over these millennia, Indian hunting practices forced megafauna to extinction, while broadcast burnings of forests and prairies regenerated nutrients requisite for diverse vegetation and, in turn, grazing for diverse species of animals. Slowly, tribes molded the land to their needs and the "natural" landscape that emerged was one that served Indians' needs well but signified wilderness to Americans.

Just as in Catlin's art, preservation meant decontextualizing individuals and landscapes; preservation of Yellowstone meant ignoring and obfuscating the history that helped shape the "natural" flora and fauna of this place.[34]

The outcome of the plan to incorporate Indian cultures in Yellowstone also changed in consequence of this view of an essential "Nature" separated from cultural history and context. Since policy makers assumed that Indian cultures had no role in ecological history, these tribes were deemed incapable of meeting a criterion of ownership rigidly defined through the private use of property and the taming of "wilderness." On account also of a fear that a native presence would scare off tourists, Yellowstone Park Superintendent Philetus Norris and railroad interests erased this environmental and cultural reality from their promotions of the park. Norris told tourists that Indians historically avoided the Yellowstone region owing to a primitive fear of spirits haunting the geysers. In fact, Indians cooked food in those geysers, but such information did not fit a construction of cultureless nature that could guarantee pleasure, renewed vitality, and self-discovery for the white American consumer. The Shoshone, Sheepeater, and Bannock tribes of Yellowstone had been physically removed to Idaho in the 1870s. The park *conceptually* removed them for another century. This removal represents a culmination of the ideology of vanishing that Catlin's culture offered to him, and that ultimately derailed his ethical intentions. Given the five interconnected ways (discussed earlier) that Catlin earnestly sought to challenge his society— fighting stereotypes, criticizing consumer behavior, envisioning better policy, imagining preserved cultures and environments, and seeking personal immunity from participating in displacement—the ideological contradictions of Catlin's work and of Yellowstone's founding provide a strong testament to the power of these historical ideologies of vanishing people and cultureless "Nature." These entrenched, unexamined ideologies provide evidence of how hard it was for anyone, even a George Catlin, to defy such ideologies in hopes of enacting effective environmental protest.

With Yellowstone, not only was this packaged "Nature" separate from geography, it also shrouded environmental and cultural realities. In the context of the era's new market economy, this separation unintentionally yet conveniently distracted mass audiences from ethical quandaries involved in producing and consuming the influx of commodities. The most viable connection between George Catlin and Yellowstone National Park exists in the fact that both erased environmental and cultural relations to produce a "Nature" for mass consumption. Just as Catlin's work was driven by his belief in future vanishing, so Yellowstone National Park's promoters benefited from erasing Indians from the past landscape of the park—rendering it "Nature." Just as Catlin felt that he had found a way to prosper from explosive, capitalist systems of expansion without being complicit in its unjust byproducts, so Yellowstone National Park was constructed as a profitable alternative to exploitative, extractive uses of the West.

Catlin and the founding of Yellowstone thus represent early examples of "green capitalism." Each perpetuates a deep belief in the profit motive and in economic growth as forces for generating ethical benefits from an economic system that had devastated lands and peoples. In both cases, however, Catlin and the early founders of Yellowstone National Park participated (probably inadvertently) in ideologies of vanishing that led to further removal of peoples from their lands and to an idea of preservation based on a post-Indian, post-vanished "Nature."

Conclusion: The Trouble with "Nature"

This "Nature" is a fantasy. Catlin had two moments in 1832 in which he saw an opening to reject assumptions of vanishing and thus to protest the dangerous mirage of cultureless "Nature." One opportunity came when he looked down upon the earth in a state of reverie, wondering for the briefest of moments if there was any way to think of a future for buffalo lands and autonomous native cultures. The other was looking across a prison cell at Black Hawk and his people, wondering if he should paint them in their chains.

The Black Hawk War, after all, began as an Indian protest against the very realities Catlin lamented. In Black Hawk's cell, however, Catlin's reaction to such a protest shows the grand and ethically dangerous canyon that stretches between lament and protest. Two short years after Jackson signed the Indian Removal Act into law in 1830, Black Hawk led Sauk and Fox Indians back into their traditional territory in present-day Illinois. White settlers strongly resisted this move, and Black Hawk's action sparked latent fears in local white settlers, resulting in the short war. The Black Hawk War ended brutally, with Sauk men, children, and women slaughtered by Illinois militia, U.S. Army, and Sioux warriors as they fled across the Mississippi. One hundred and fifty of Black Hawk's 1,000 people died in this fight.[35]

Andrew Jackson tried to co-opt this tale of conflict for himself. Jackson, struggling in the North to gain support for his removal policy, used the Black Hawk War as a vindication for Indian removal in the midst of an election year. He preyed on dormant Northeastern fears of what happens when Indians neither assimilate *nor* remove *nor* vanish—they revert to savage behavior, as exemplified in Illinois. Jackson imprisoned Black Hawk and other Sauk leaders in St. Louis. Far from solitary confinement, this imprisonment became a popular media spectacle, and Jackson devised it in order to show why his Removal Act was necessary and inevitable.[36]

In 1832, Black Hawk and his co-leaders sat in Jefferson Barracks in St. Louis as public curiosities, receiving visitors such as Washington Irving and George Catlin. As discussed earlier, Catlin did not recognize the Sauk request that they be publicly depicted as trapped in jail and shackled in chains. The painting that does show them in chains was not published in his main work and is rarely included in discussions of Catlin today. To distribute the more accurate painting would have contradicted Catlin's central assumption that Black Hawk and the Sauk were bound to vanish. Such an accurate rendering of the imprisonment would convey Black Hawk, the Sauk, and Native Americans as active and influential contributors to the American dialogue on how best to expand its republic, rather than as memorialized icons of "nature's beauty" abstracted to compassionately make room for "ploughshares" and "prayers." Furthermore, it would have fundamentally undermined the ideology of vanishing Indians, providing a dissenting voice to the dominant ideology of expansion and removal.

The image Catlin chose to publish ironically decontextualized Black Hawk from his continuing struggle—it inadvertently initiated his vanishing. In Catlin's painting, not only did Black Hawk's chains vanish, but so do any reminders of the barbarity of the policy of removal and of Black Hawk's legal, spiritual, and deeply historical claims to his native environments. But from Catlin's combined view as an artist and as a believer in the inevitable vanishing of Indians, paintings and shows were the only hope, the best methods to preserve the essential, visual "Nature" that these vanishing peoples and environments embodied.

If we look to Catlin as an early preservationist, we must honestly look to him as one who defined preservation specifically through this lens of vanishing. His "preservation" was not a fight for sustaining economic and ecological relations. His was an iconography of nature, not a politics of nature. However, he saw this iconography as an ethics of nature. He saw it as a way to prosper in a capitalist society without promoting extractive and corrupting injustices, all the while endorsing appreciation of beauty, lamenting dying peoples, and preserving icons of extinguished cultures, including even a park that would demonstrate past reality in a select group of exhibited peoples.[37]

In Black Hawk's cell, Catlin was presented with the opportunity to anticipate a more modern ethic for social and environmental justice, in the same way that the bluff above the Yellowstone River allowed him to fashion an early conservationist perspective on national parks that has since swept the globe. That is, Black Hawk's cell offered Catlin a clear choice to demand that displaced peoples no longer suffer from exploitive environmental practices, and reciprocally to declare that America care for environments in order to enable the autonomy of suffering cultures. Out of ethical intentions rooted in unexamined ideologies, he chose instead to preserve a "Nature" constructed out of a lamented yet accepted vanishing.

Catlin's story teaches humbling lessons about how complicated environmental protest was and can be, about how hard it was and is to identify and take on the underlying, "mutually reinforcing" ideologies that drive and justify environmental injustices. Of course, Catlin operated within context and cultural blind spots as much as we do today. So how do we, with both our own ethical intentions and our own unexamined ideologies, avoid such contradictions? In the twenty-first century, as we look to a climate crisis in which over a billion poor are predicted to lose the life-giving waters of vanishing Himalayan glaciers by 2035, as we witness the Inuit sue the United States in protesting a new kind of Indian removal resulting from melting ice, Black Hawk's cell symbolizes a missed but still available environmental opportunity to engage with the protests of the disempowered. It calls upon us to involve the displaced as active participants in sustainable solutions, rather than accepting their vanishing as the inevitable consequence of a "natural" cycle. In fact, if we hope to promote a livable planet for global cultures, Black Hawk's cell must inspire us to imagine an environmental ethics without "Nature."[38]

Notes

1 This article borrows from my manuscript *Catlin's Lament: Indians, Manifest Destiny, and the Ethics of Nature*, a book-length study currently under contract with University Press of Kansas and scheduled for publication in 2009. I would like to give special thanks to Michael Egan, Jeff Crane, Joan Burbick, Paul Hirt, T. V. Reed, Noel Sturgeon, LeRoy Ashby, Tony Zaragoza, Bill Niemi, Dave Plante, Kalyani Fernando, Nancy Jackson, George Miles, Tom Lynch, Tyson Hausdoerffer, and Karen Hausdoerffer for their support and thoughtful comments on this project.

2 George Catlin, *Letters and Notes on the Manners, Customs, and Conditions of North American Indians*, vol. 1 (New York: Dover Publications, 1973), 2.

3 Putnam Catlin, *The Letters of George Catlin and His Family: A Chronicle of the American West*, ed. Majorie Roehm Catlin (Berkeley: University of California Press, 1966), 127.

4 Catlin, *Letters and Notes*, vol. 1, 7.

5 Rosemarie Bank, "Staging the 'Native': Making History in American Theater Culture, 1828–38," *Theater Journal* 45(4) (1993), 476; Benjamin Drake, *Life and Adventures of Black Hawk, with Sketches of Keokuk, the Sac and Fox Indians, and the Black Hawk War* (Cincinnati: George Conclin Press, 1846), 202–3. See also Joan Elliot Price, "Robert Sully's Nineteenth-Century Paintings of Sauk and Winnebago Indians," *Wisconsin Academy Review* 45(1) (Winter 1998–99), 22–23.

6 Catlin, *Letters and Notes*, vol. 1, 261–62.

7 George Catlin, *Notes of Eight Years' Travels and Residence in Europe*, vol. 1 (New York: Burgess, Stringer, & Co., 1848), 62. This moment has inspired many environmental historians to locate Catlin at the origins of American environmentalism, at the genesis of natural protest. Catlin's writings have been anthologized in such readers as Jeanne Nienaber Clarke and Hanna J. Courtner (eds.), *The State and Nature: Voices Heard, Voices Unheard in America's Environmental Dialogue* (Upper Saddle River, NJ: Prentice-Hall, 2002), 31–36; Roderick Frazier Nash, *American Environmentalism: Readings in Conservation History*, 3rd ed. (New York: McGraw-Hill, 1990), 31–35; Robert Finch and John Elder (eds.), *Norton Anthology of American Nature Writing* (New York: W. W. Norton, 2002), 129–39. Historians since the early 1970s have celebrated and questioned the role of his park in the history of environmental protest. See Roderick Frazier Nash, *Wilderness and the American Mind* (New Haven, CT: Yale University Press, 1967), 100; Roderick Frazier Nash, "The American Invention of National Parks," *American Quarterly* 22(3) (Autumn 1970): 726–35; John Opie, *Nature's Nation: An Environmental History of the United States* (New York: Harcourt Brace College Publishers, 1998), 370–71; Benjamin Kline, *First along the River: A Brief History of the US Environmental Movement* (San Francisco: Acada Books, 2000), 35; David Mazel, "George Catlin, the Death of Wilderness, and the Birth of the National Subject," in Michael Branch, Rochelle Johnson, Daniel Patterson, and Scott Slovic (eds.), *Reading the Earth: New Directions in the Study of Literature and Environment* (Moscow: University of Idaho Press, 1998), 130; Ronald Weber, "'I Would Ask No Other Monument to My Memory': George Catlin and a Nation's Park," *Journal of the West* 38(1) (1999), 19; Jeffrey Meyers, *Converging Stories: Race, Ecology, and Environmental Justice in American Literature* (Athens: University of Georgia Press, 2005), 67. Nash recognizes Catlin as the first to consider the National Park idea. Opie and Kline each feature Catlin's park as a turning point in American conservation, with Kline resurrecting Nash's view that Catlin's "arguments for preserving wilderness in the United States initiated the idea for national parks and, in particular, the creation of Yellowstone National Park." Conversely, other scholars have questioned the environmental contribution of Catlin's imagined park. Mazel's article critiques the park as "decidedly problematic, for the notion of rendering an entire people into a living tableau is clearly the product of an *imperialist* sensibility, while the idea of deploying such a 'specimen' to an admiring world just as clearly suggests a nationalist sensibility." Weber seconds Mazel's concern: "Surely Plains Indians would have recoiled from the indignity of this manner of maintaining their way of life." Finally, Jeffrey Meyers, in his 2005 book *Converging Stories*, questions the political implications of Catlin's park: "Catlin's emphasis is on how such a park would reflect on the 'refined citizens' of the United States, rather than on American Indians themselves." This essay seeks to negotiate these contrasting historical claims regarding Catlin's environmental ambitions.

8 "Ideology" is a concept central to this article. For a basic definition, see Carla Freccero, *Popular Culture: An Introduction* (New York: NYU Press, 1999), 158;

Philip Deloria, *Indians in Unexpected Places* (Lawrence: University Press of Kansas, 2004), 9. "Ideology" refers to the unexamined assumptions that provide the foundation for cultural belief systems and socio-economic practices. Freccero, a cultural theorist, defines ideology as "the way a society explains itself to itself; a certain way of presenting the world that passes itself off as the truth of the world, that seems so self-evident that we take it as the truth." Ideology, then, is *not a conscious justification* of particular social practices like slavery or environmental devastation. Ideology is *the tacit base of assumptions* regarding what is natural about society that enables a society to accept its own practices, institutions, and beliefs as just—such as the view of Catlin's time that the plantation owner can best care for the "naturally inferior" black slave or that nonhuman living systems instrumentally serve human social systems as merely a store of commodities. As Deloria, a historian, states, "ideologies, in other words, are not, in fact, true, but, as things that structure real belief and action in a real world, they might as well be."

9   For a succinct discussion of the transformation of the West into a commodity mindset, see Theodore Steinberg, *Down to Earth: Nature's Role in America's History* (New York: Oxford University Press, 2002), 55–70. For a more in-depth discussion, see William Cronon, *Nature's Metropolis: Chicago and the Great West* (New York: W. W. Norton, 1991), Part II. For discussions of the Trail of Tears and other consequences of Jackson's Indian Removal Act, see Sean Wilentz, *The Rise of American Democracy: Democracy Ascendant 1815–1840* (New York: W. W. Norton, 2007), 205; John Ehle, *Trail of Tears: The Rise and Fall of the Cherokee Nation* (New York: Anchor Books, 1989); David S. Heidler and Jeanne T. Heidler, *Indian Removal* (New York: W. W. Norton, 2007), 41, 175, 221.

10   Quintard Taylor, *In Search of the Racial Frontier: African Americans in the American West, 1528–1990* (New York: W. W. Norton, 1998) 62; James M. McPherson, *Ordeal by Fire*, vol. 1, *The Coming of War* (New York: McGraw-Hill, 1993), 32, 50.

11   William Cronon, *Nature's Metropolis: Chicago and the Great West* (New York: W. W. Norton, 1991), 33, 70; Charles Sellers, *The Market Revolution: Jacksonian America, 1815–1846* (New York: Oxford University Press, 1991), 41–44; Ted Steinberg, *Down to Earth: Nature's Role in American History* (New York: Oxford University Press, 2002), 70.

12   Jan Lewis, "The Republican Wife: Virtue and Seduction in the Early Republic," *William and Mary Quarterly* 44(1) (1987), 699–703; Sellers, *Market Revolution*, 242, 405–7.

13   John Steele Gordon, "The American Environment: The Big Picture is More Heartening than All the Little Ones," *American Heritage* (October 1993), 37; Kline, *First Along the River*, 26; Greta Gaard and Lori Gruen, "Ecofeminism: Toward Global Justice and Planetary Health," in Andrew Light and Holmes Rolston III (eds.), *Environmental Ethics* (Malden, MA: Blackwell Publishing, 2003), 277.

14   Catlin, vol. 1, 8–9; Andrew Jackson, "Second Annual Message, December 6, 1830" in Jeanne Nienaber Clarke & Hanna J. Courtner (eds.), *The State and Nature:*

Voices Heard, Voices Unheard in America's Environmental Dialogue (Upper Saddle River, NJ: Prentice-Hall, 2002), 28.

15 For an example of one of Catlin's paintings that shows a pre-Anglo, pre-industrial landscape as complete rather than vacant, see Figure 3.3.

16 Catlin, *Letters and Notes*, vol. 1, 261.

17 Ibid., 260–61.

18 Ibid., 225, 255, 16.

19 Ibid., 249.

20 Ibid., 263.

21 Ibid., 261.

22 Ibid., 258–59. For discussions of buffalo-based ecosystems and Native American economies, see Shepherd Krech, *The Ecological Indian: Myth and History* (New York: W. W. Norton, 1999), 123–50; Winona LaDuke, *All Our Relations: Native Struggles for Land and Life* (Cambridge, MA: South End Press, 1999), 139–62; Richard Manning, *Grassland: The History, Biology, Politics, and Promise of the American Prairie* (New York: Penguin Books, 1995).

23 Catlin, *Letters and Notes*, vol. 1, 260.

24 Ibid.

25 Ibid., 2, 262–63.

26 Ibid., 261, 184.

27 Ibid., 3.

28 Ibid., 26.

29 Ibid., 260.

30 Roderick Nash, *Wilderness and the American Mind* (New Haven, CT: Yale University Press, 1967), 108.

31 Ibid., 114. For a detailed discussions of "monumentalism," as opposed to "environmentalism," as an early attraction to National Parks, see Alfred Runte, *National Parks: The American Experience* (Lincoln: University of Nebraska Press, 1997), 29–33.

32 Nash, *Wilderness*, 108, 113, 108. See also John Opie, *Nature's Nation: An Environmental History of the United States* (New York: Harcourt Brace College Publishers, 1998), 398.

33 Runte, *National Parks*, 38.

34 Alston Chase, *Playing God in Yellowstone: The Destruction of America's First National Park* (Boston: Atlantic Monthly Press, 1986), 105.; Krech, *The Ecological Indian*, 23.

35 Anthony Wallace, *The Long Bitter Trail: Andrew Jackson and the Indians* (New York: Hill & Wang, 1993), 108.

36 Bank, "Staging the Native," 475. See also Robert J. Moore, *Native Americans: A Portrait: The Art and Travels of Charles Bird King, George Catlin, and Karl Bodmer* (New York: Stewart, Tabori, and Chang, 1997), 28.

37 Catlin understood the economic benefits that emerged from portraying infamous Indian figures. See Paul Reddin, *Wild West Shows* (Chicago: University of Illinois

Press, 1999), 12: When Osceola, a Seminole prisoner of U.S. wars, died after Catlin had painted a portrait of him, Catlin immediately "paid one printer $83.25 in a six-week period for 5,100 'advertisements,' 350 circulars, 1,000 handbills, 200 prospectuses for his prints of the Seminole leader Osceola, and 2,000 copies of his catalog. This totaled 8,650 items, or about 206 pieces of printed materials per day."

38 *United Nations Environment Program*, "The Environment in the News," www.unep. org/cpi/briefs/2007May10.doc; Richard Black, *Inuit Sue over US Climate Policy*, http://news.bbc.co.uk/1/hi/sci/tech/4511556.stm.

CHAPTER 4

"The Science-Spirit in a Democracy"

Liberty Hyde Bailey, Nature Study, and the Democratic Impulse of Progressive Conservation

KEVIN C. ARMITAGE

Some persons have supposed that the "contentment" of the nature-lover implies unvexed indifference to the human affairs of the time, and therefore it makes for a kind of serene and weak utopianism; but to my mind, the outlook to nature makes for just the reverse of all this. If nature is the norm, then the necessity for challenging and amending the abuses that accompany civilization becomes baldly apparent by very contrast. The repose of the nature-lover and the assiduous exertion of the man of affairs are complementary, not antithetical, states of mind.[1]

—Liberty Hyde Bailey, *The Outlook to Nature*, 1905

Writing against the "stress and fury" of World War I, the horticulturalist, educator, and conservationist Liberty Hyde Bailey (1858–1954) contemplated the relationship between the conservation of natural resources and peaceful, democratic life. Bailey reasoned that because material wealth ultimately derived from the natural world, a just and democratic society must ensure the fruitfulness of nature. "The lesson of the growing abounding earth is of liberality for all, and never exploitation or very exclusive opportunities for the few," argued Bailey. "More iniquity follows the improper and greedy division of the resources and privileges of the earth than any other form of sinfulness."[2] Bailey thus linked conservation to democratic liberty. For participatory government to thrive, the entire public needed to share and conserve the flourishing, abounding earth.

Yet for Bailey democracy entailed much more than the sustainable and equitable distribution of resources. Crucially, a humane society must enable "the expression of individualism, but for the public good." Indeed, Bailey argued that individual flourishing was necessary for social well-being. Given the interrelationship between individual character and democratic fulfillment, Americans must "avoid the mechanistic standardization of society," because "Democracy cannot be maintained on the mental habits of quantity-production."[3] Because individualism and democracy supported each other, the standardized "mental habits" of rationalized industrial processes posed grave threats to democracy: "Much of our public organization for efficiency is essentially monarchic in its tendency," claimed Bailey. "It is likely to eliminate the most precious resource in human society, which is the freedom of expression of the competent individual."[4] If democracy is the best way to harmonize individual and social development, society must guard against the cultural effects of industrial production that standardized individual identity.

Given the antidemocratic nature of the "processes of standardization" which were "justified in . . . manufacturing results rather than in . . . human results," it followed that scientific research should be used to connect people to the natural world rather than to help institute industrial monotony.[5] Yet many people experienced science as "dry . . . what we teach as science drives many people from nature."[6] If science education devolved into rote memorization and repetition, it depersonalized the relationship between the student and the object of scientific investigation—nature. Science, however, was not inherently alienating. Scientific inquiry brought Bailey closer to the natural world because it did not "imply any loss of mysticism or of exaltation: quite the contrary. Science but increases the mystery of the unknown and enlarges the boundaries of the spiritual vision."[7] Bailey gained this satisfaction because for him science fostered humane values as well as technical expertise. In his view, society should not only cultivate the instrumental ends of the professional researcher, but also many other kinds of interactions with the natural world: "Sometimes it seems as if scientists think that they have all the right of way in the subjects which they espouse; but there is more than one way of interpreting nature."[8] For Bailey, conservation, which fostered both awe and knowledge, was essential to the material wealth and mental well-being of democratic society.

Bailey's concerns for democracy, personhood, and the manner in which the public related to science and nature sharply contrasts with the way most historians have understood progressive conservation. Environmental historians have considered progressive conservation not as an expression of democracy, but rather as a utilitarian, bureaucratizing force that centralized power in the hands of experts. Most historians work within Samuel Hays's rich analytical frame, which viewed conservation as "above all . . . a scientific movement" whose essence was "rational planning" and "efficient development."[9] According to this view, the progressive conservation movement was an acute departure from the individualism and romantic nature love of nineteenth-century figures such as Emerson, Thoreau, Whitman, and Melville, in favor of scientific management and its corollary interests in technology and efficiency. Even those historians who have defended the democratic nature of conservation by linking social equity to the efficiency derived from applied science delineate a tradition that, with the exception of John Muir, largely turned its back on its nineteenth-century forebears.[10] The interpretation of conservation as bureaucratic and celebrating efficiency above all suggests that the typical conservationist was a scientist who yoked individual expertise to federal power, giving conservation the utilitarian and dispassionate caste of objective, quantifiable science. More recent, revisionist accounts of progressive conservation also accept that conservation was primarily an exercise in expertise and state power—even as they question whether its use of the state was benign.[11]

Furthermore, historians have conflated science with utilitarianism, and thus created a circular rationale for the utilitarian interpretation of conservation: conservationists were utilitarian because they embraced science, and vice versa. Using Bailey and the nature study movement he championed, I propose another view: that conservation can best be understood as a debate over the social use of science and expertise in a democracy.[12] Rather than uncritically embracing a vague notion of "science," progressive conservationists such as Bailey fought to support modern science and rational inquiry as well as to maintain a plethora of individual, spiritual, and aesthetic relationships with nature—relationships often dismissed by Bailey's contemporary critics and modern historians alike as mere "sentimentalism." Rather than flights of fancy, conservationists sought multiple kinds of relationships with nature to bridge the antimodern and modernizing tendencies within the conservation movement. Nature study conservationists such as Bailey encouraged romantic nature love to preserve individualism against the depersonalizing drill of industrial civilization while also supporting an approach to modern science that was civically engaged and attuned to the richness of democratic experience. Rather than narrowly functional, Bailey's approach to conservation is best understood as pragmatic, for as we shall see, Bailey and John Dewey shared deep commitments to public education, to using science to promote democracy and the public good, and to preserving unique, individual relationships with the natural world. Eschewing narrow-minded technocracy, conservationists like Bailey drew upon their roots in nineteenth-century romanticism as they tried to reconcile individualism, science, and modern bureaucracy. Consequently, like many other conservationists, Bailey spent a great deal of energy theorizing the appropriate relationship between humans and nature. Analyzing Bailey's wealth of written material and actions as a conservationist reveals a picture of the conservationist as a moralist, not a technocrat, as a committed democrat deeply concerned with the relationship between civic life and modern science, rather than a bureaucrat suspicious of the decision-making capabilities of everyday people.

Though a prominent intellectual widely known and read during his lifetime, Liberty Hyde Bailey is now a largely overlooked figure in the history of progressive conservation.[13] Dubbed by one historian the "philosopher of country life," Bailey was a remarkable figure, perspicacious, wide-ranging in his academic interests and achievements, a passionate philosopher not just of country life, but of conservation and nature study.[14] His abiding interests in conservation, rural life, and education were forged through his childhood experiences on the family farm in South Haven, Michigan, located about one mile inland from Lake Michigan. Named "Liberty" like his father to express the strong anti-slavery views of his family, Bailey grew up on a working farm, one well known for its apple orchards and innovative horticultural techniques. Despite the death of his mother when he was five, Bailey led a happy childhood absorbed in observing local flora and fauna as he explored nearby streams and woodlands. A signal part of his childhood occurred as he witnessed the rapid disappearance of passenger pigeons.[15] As with many Progressive era conservationists, the extermination of passenger pigeons— once easily the most numerous birds on the North American continent— transformed him into a conservationist who defended nature for both utilitarian and aesthetic reasons. At age fifteen, he read an essay on birds to the State Pomological Society at South Haven that asked farmers what "is more useful [than birds] in destroying the myriads of insects which infest our vegetation?" He noted that thousands of "noxious insects . . . are destroyed by these harmless songsters, yet the selfish man dooms them to destruction." Furthermore, he emphasized that birds "have powers of music unequaled by works of art," qualities that "lend life and vivacity to the dullest place."[16]

Bailey continued stumping for aesthetic and practical conservation in his rural Michigan community. He was influenced in his outreach to rural people by the farmer's cooperatives known as the Grange, and he used this model to broach aesthetic and conservation issues to the rural populace. Delivering a paper before the Michigan State Horticultural Society in 1885 that advocated the preservation of natural stream banks and other wild places, Bailey called upon farmers to preserve native trees and to adapt wild shrubs and flowers to the farm and garden landscape. All of these measures would help farm efficiency as well as give a facelift to the surrounding countryside. Moreover, Bailey advocated planting trees and shrubs to provide a border for wetlands and to beautify untillable areas such as roadsides.[17]

Bailey's activism and academic interests led him to invite Professor William James Beal of the Michigan Agricultural College to lecture in South Haven in 1882. Beal and Bailey impressed each other, and Bailey enrolled at Michigan Agricultural College the following year. Beal, a follower of Louis Agassiz, instructed Bailey in scientific methodology and botany by using live plants rather than preserved specimens. Upon graduation Bailey apprenticed with the nation's leading botanist, Harvard's Asa Gray.

A mere year later in 1884, Bailey received an offer to become a professor of horticulture at Michigan Agricultural College. Gray advised his student against taking the position, arguing that botany was science whereas horticulture was mere gardening. Bailey, however, already chafed at such hierarchies of knowledge and at distinctions between pure and applied science. This was a view that Bailey maintained throughout his life. He asserted that there was "as much culture in the study of beet roots as in the study of Greek roots." According to Bailey, the split between theory and practice divided disciplines that should be allied. He bemoaned what he perceived as the needless prejudice embodied by Gray that separated the botanist from the

Figure 4.1 Liberty Hyde Bailey speaks to a group of extension students in what he considered the best classroom with the best equipment: the outdoors.

horticulturist. Bailey accepted the position. Four years later, when Cornell University offered Bailey a professorship, he accepted it on condition that he could develop horticulture as he saw fit. Beginning at Cornell in 1888, Bailey tried to unify theory and practice through his research in horticulture and in the education of children through his support of the nature study movement.

Bailey devoted much of his professional career to promoting nature study as a means to connect people with the natural environment. He became nature study's chief theoretician. A leading part of the "new education," nature study used instruction in basic natural history such as plant identification, animal life histories and school gardens to promote the skills needed to succeed in industrial life while at the same time cultivating the spiritual growth that nature study advocates felt modern life occluded.[18] The pedagogy rejected the rote memorization, repetition, and recitation of the traditional school. The critique extended to modern science. The empirical, formal, and disciplinary spirit of scientific investigation too easily lent itself to the traditional pedagogy of catechism and memorization that so repelled reformers committed to new and innovative methods of instruction. As the writer Edward H. Eppens observed in the *Critic*, scientific precision could turn "what was once a free, unfettered delight to all who could love a flower," into "stumbling over its italicized Latin name." A solely professional and bureaucratic interest in the outdoors was a means to "bridle" nature appreciation and "break" it "into a business."[19] Bailey concurred: "All youths love nature" he wrote, "none of them, primarily, loves science. . . . A rigidly graded and systematic body of facts kills nature-study; examinations bury it."[20] In this manner nature study proponents critiqued both the limits of scientific knowledge and traditional pedagogy. In their place they advised immersing young students in the broader aims of nature study.

Though nature study was not meant to be instruction in science, its advocates hoped to stimulate a fascination with living things and a love of inquiry that might, in the mature individual, flower into scientific investigation. Thus Bailey declared that nature study was "a revolt from the teaching of mere science" because rather than formal experimentation it endeavored to help "every person . . . live a richer life." Nature study pedagogy insisted that direct contact with nature would impart to children the beginnings of a scientific mindset and simultaneously enhance their spiritual development. The proponents of nature study argued they could foster the child's healthy maturation if the child developed "sympathy" with nature. Sympathy was a key term in the nature study lexicon. "If one is to be happy, he must be in sympathy with common things," wrote Bailey. "He must live in harmony with his environment."[21] By "sympathy" nature study advocates meant not only a deep-seated affinity, but also a harmony that affected both humans and nature. They defined sympathy in the same way as the philosopher William James: an "expansive embracing tendency."[22] Nature study advocates believed that this expansive, embracing tendency prompted a future interest in science. "Knowledge begins in wonder," maintained Bailey. As the individual matures, systematic investigation can shape the sense of wonder and eventually become scientific. By fostering wonder, "nature-study prepares the child to receive the science-teaching."[23]

Nature study advocates theorized their pedagogy's contribution to conservation by introducing ethical sentiment to guide individual action and the scientific endeavor. If moral concern guided individuals' actions toward nature, they would become conservationists as a matter of simple principle. Lamenting the stunning devastation of the natural order, Bailey averred that "we find ourselves in the epoch of destructiveness, which is born of lack of sympathy and responsibility and is therefore a kind of enmity."[24] To combat this enmity, nature study offered a spiritual and practical education that emphasized conservation, the "child's true relation to his environment."[25] Charles B. Scott's widely read *Nature Study and the Child* explained that nature study fostered conservation because it emphasized that the child

> owes something to the world about him. He protects what he once destroyed. He takes care of the flowers which before he trod upon. The birds are his friends. He is learning to love them. . . . He is adapting himself to his physical environment; not merely appropriating, but giving in return.

The key to adapting rather than merely appropriating was the development of sympathy. "Without sympathy" argued Scott, "nature study may be . . . disastrous in its effects on the child's environment." The disaster occurs because ethics do not inform and constrain the investigations of science. Without ethical sentiment to guide scientific inquiry, "Our wild-flowers will be pulled up, our birds destroyed, our shade-trees mutilated ('sacrificed to the cause of science')." Such science students become not conservationists but "cold blooded anatomists and collectors." Instead, if teachers develop sentiment as well as science, students will "care for or work for nature."[26]

Like Bailey, his contemporary John Dewey (1859–1952) also viewed education as a means of individual and social development, and also reacted to "the horrors" of World War I by thinking deeply about the relationship between education, science, the natural world, and democracy.[27] The similarities in thought between Dewey—America's greatest philosopher of democracy—and Bailey are striking. Dewey championed a broad conception of science.

For Dewey, science was not a rarefied process accessible only to intellectuals, but rather a "purification and intensification" of ordinary methods of thought. Scientific judgment is simply the refinement of everyday cognitive virtues, and "the native and unspoiled attitude of childhood, marked by ardent curiosity, fertile imagination, and love of experimental inquiry, [that] is near, very near, to the attitude of the scientific mind."[28] In short, science was commonplace "experience becoming rational." Because science was rooted in the everyday knowledge, it was not "remote, aloof, concerned with the sublime" but rather "found indigenous in experience." At the same time, because science was attached to everyday thinking, if it was taught in a manner that ignored this grounding "it remains a body of inert information." Should teachers highlight facts divorced from scientific methods of investigation, science teaching would fail because "there is no magic attached to material stated in technically correct scientific form."[29] Though not motivated by facts alone, ordinary people could thrive by applying scientific methodology to everyday problems. If the processes of scientific thought are demystified, they could be used for solving the problems faced by individuals, communities, and nations. For Dewey, learning to think scientifically was an essential resource for modern democratic societies.

Bailey also viewed scientific methodology as a boon to democratic self-governance, and like Dewey he championed a broad conception of scientific inquiry rooted in public interest and participation. "What is the purpose and what [is] the value of our widespread teaching of science," queried Bailey, "if not that the mental attitude is to be applied in all the horizons of life?" The "great gains" from science were found not in technology or even in the advance of knowledge, but in the "mental postures" of everyday people.[30] For Dewey, resistance to the use of science derived from an "aristocratic" heritage that undervalued "applied knowledge" while exalting "pure knowledge" because historically "slaves and serfs" performed "useful" labor as opposed to the "pure theorizing" of the leisured.[31] Though Bailey did not historicize resistance to science in such a manner, he very much defended the wide use and democratic viability of the scientific method. Because science was a species of truth, one that was open and straightforward, Bailey asked if it was "not time to introduce into politics the attitude of the open mind . . . [and] to approach public questions in something of the spirit with which we approach the problems of science?" In this manner science could revolutionize politics and revitalize democratic decision-making. "Science is free to all men so far as they are able to understand. It is no discriminator of persons. . . . It shuts no doors, but it opens many."[32]

Both of these thinkers also recognized the potential destructiveness that science, unmoored from moral foundations and combined with industrial might, could wreak upon nature and society. Bailey understood that society could apply "our vastly attained power to new machineries of destruction, new oppressions of power, even until war itself becomes a vast chemism and mechanism." Americans were using the knowledge gained from the scientific endeavor not for "great mental stimulation" but for "accumulation that comes of new ruinations and completer tyrannies." This destructiveness was not inherent to scientific methodology, however, but occurred because "not yet have we threaded our science into the fabric of democratic society." Should such a democratic quilt come into being, society could guide science and keep its energies working toward human ends. "If we apply our science constructively here [to rural life]" wrote Bailey, "as it must necessarily be applied in the main, we shall have a vast foundational element to hold us in check."[33] Bailey held that the ties to the land typifying rural life would ground the use of science in ways that benefited the body politic, a topic to which we shall return.

Like Bailey, Dewey held a broad conception of science that was not narrowly material, but instead accounted for a wide range of human experience.[34] Indeed, Dewey harshly criticized positivist science. Dewey postulated science as a method of investigation shaped by the values of a community of inquiry and tested against pragmatic standards. Thus for Dewey, science was "wholly a moral matter, an affair of honesty." The methods and results of science could not be divorced from the society that produced them. An ideology of "pure science" is nothing more than the "rationalization of an escape . . . a shirking of responsibility."[35] Dewey's conception of the scientific endeavor, then, was intended to allow myriad kinds of experience to flourish: "If the proper object of science is a mathematico-mechanical world (as the achievements of science have proved to be the case), then how can the objects of love, appreciation—whether sensory or ideal—and devotion be included within true reality?" It is worth emphasizing that Dewey insisted upon the basic reality of aesthetic and moral traits; Dewey described them as "found, experienced, and not to be shoved out of being by some trick of logic."[36] Given the reality of these many traits, Dewey argued for the reconciliation of aesthetic appreciation with scientific practice. Without such an appreciation he feared that "mankind might be become a race of economic monsters, restlessly driving hard bargains with nature and with one another, bored with leisure or capable of putting it to use only in ostentatious display and extravagant dissipation."[37]

Given his wide-ranging goals of deriving aesthetic pleasure and inciting critical inquiry from contact with nature, it is not surprising that Dewey joined with Bailey in supporting the nature study movement. Dewey's interest in nature study was longstanding. In 1897 he gave an address to the parents and teachers of his Laboratory School (often referred to as the "Dewey School") at the University of Chicago, presenting a detailed account of how the school's practices related to his theoretical principles.[38] In it he described nature study this way:

> Both nature study (that is the study through observations of obvious natural phenomena) and experimental work are introduced from the beginning. . . . The earth is, perhaps, the focus for the science study as practically all of the work relates to it sooner or later, and in one way or another.[39]

Dewey wished to blend into the school a holistic and integrated curriculum that reflected his romantic understanding of the integrated character of knowledge itself.

A holistic view of nature also helped spur sympathy for nonhuman life. "When nature is treated as a whole," argued Dewey, "its phenomena fall into their natural relations of sympathy and association with human life." Although nature study was used to "instill the elements of science," its chief goal was to cultivate "a sympathetic understanding of the place of plants and animals in life and to develop emotional and aesthetic interest."[40] The tending of classroom animals is important because it "teach[es] humaneness to animals and a general sympathy for animal life."[41] Meanwhile, nature study advocates adopted Deweyan language to describe their pedagogy. "The nature-study method," wrote the widely read nature study advocate Maurice A. Bigelow, "consists largely in *learning by doing*."[42]

Dewey maintained his belief in the efficacy of nature study long after he left the Laboratory School. Moreover, his philosophical work continued to insist upon the active role of nature in human life. In his landmark 1916 text *Democracy and Education*, Dewey theorized nature as an active historical agent. "This setting of nature," wrote Dewey, "does not bear to social activities the relation that the scenery of a theatrical performance bears to a dramatic representation; it enters into the very make-up of the social happenings that form history." Dewey's philosophical and pedagogic goal of replacing Cartesian dualisms with holistic thinking led him to advocate a method for studying the past that combined narrative and natural history. It remains a good example of progressive educators searching for romantic pedagogy that integrated rather than categorized human knowledge. Dewey argued that if history failed to consider its basis in the natural environment it lost its vitality as a discipline. "When this interdependence of the study of history, representing the human emphasis, with the study of geography, representing the natural, is ignored," wrote Dewey "history sinks to a listing of dates with an appended inventory of events." Dewey ridiculed the teaching of history that overlooked the influence of nature as a "literary fantasy." Indeed, history that ignored the agency of nature became a literary fantasy because "in purely literary history the natural environment *is* but stage scenery."[43]

Though both Dewey and Bailey displayed the inordinate faith in education typical of progressive reformers, they also understood that education in and of itself would not guarantee democracy. It must impart democratic values. Dewey and Bailey each warned of the threat posed by oligarchy—what Dewey defined as the "attempt to monopolize the benefits of intelligence"—to democratic education.[44] For Dewey, schools needed to inculcate democratic practice by becoming a community of democratic inquiry. Bailey also worried that education could be perverted to oligarchic ends. "The fundamental concept in a democracy is that government and other forms of public action are expressions that inhere in the people themselves," wrote Bailey. Therefore education must work for "personal and social" ends rather than "to safeguard and support a super-imposed State."[45] For these thinkers, public education was an expression of democracy that simultaneously safeguarded against its enemies.

This deep intertwining of the "new education" with conservation highlights another problem with historians' understanding of conservation. Though historians universally acknowledge that conservation shared many values with progressivism—most prominently the aforementioned science, technology, and efficiency—rarely have historians taken note of the organizational intersections between conservation and other progressive institutions. But as nature study demonstrates, conservation was deeply embedded in progressivism not only in the realm of ideology but also through the democratic reform of social institutions. This is particularly important in the case of education, for it shows the commitment to humanitarian values and practices that existed alongside conservationist faith in science and efficiency. Such belief in education demonstrates conservationist commitment to democratic means of social development.

A second institutional overlap between progressive reform and conservation occurred in the form of the country life movement. During the first two decades of the twentieth century, an increasingly urban America granted tremendous cultural significance to farmers and rural life. Indeed, urbanites, newly anxious with concern about the state of farmland America, devoted unprecedented attention to rural affairs and rural people. This concern was often economic, as the farm economy remained vital to overall commercial health. Yet the concern was also social and cultural, for many Americans worried that the nation was becoming unmoored from the vital qualities of rural life that, mixed with moral individualism, created the best components of the American character.

Such anxieties were expressed by a bevy of progressive professionals—educators, religious leaders, businessmen, politicians, and social scientists—who believed that the promise of urban cultural opportunity was drawing the people of best character to the city. ("The social fascination of the town" surmised Bailey, "will always be greater than that of the open country."[46]) A blighted countryside would harm the economy and deplete the natural conditions that fostered the moral development of the American people. Even confirmed urbanites such as Frederic C. Howe, author of *The City: The Hope of Democracy*, warned in 1906 of the debilitating effects of a civilization deprived of contact with the green world. "Human life seems to require a ground wire to the sod, a connection with Mother Earth to maintain its virility," argued Howe.[47] Other reformers worried that the depopulated countryside would no longer provide the "fresh blood" that would "repair the physical, mental and moral waste" of the city.[48] For many of these reformers contact with nature was a primary means of moral training and thus urban life by definition veered away from virtuous action. "Trees everywhere exert a moral influence," declared California Superintendent of Public Instruction Ira G. Hoitt in 1888, "that fact we know and feel in our every day's experience."[49]

The rural reform movement was steeped in similar Jeffersonian rhetoric. Country life mythologies contended that people close to the soil supported democratic, honorable, and stable social orders. Trees, in other words, exerted a moral influence. Though the values championed tended to replicate the concerns of middle-class Anglo-Saxons—thrift, hard work, stability—they were promoted for the cause of democratic flourishing. Nor was Bailey a stranger to such sentiments. "The farmer is the fundamental fact in democracy," argued Bailey, "not merely because he produces supplies, but because to him is delegated the keepership of the earth."[50] Bailey viewed this "keepership"—he termed the farmer a "trustee"—as an intensely moral endeavor. The farmer is responsible for ensuring the fertility of the land so that its "productiveness . . . must increase from generation to generation. He must handle all his materials, remembering man and remembering God. A man cannot be a good farmer unless he is a religious man."[51] The keepership worked both ways. By handling God's materials, the farmer was imbued with moral clarity; by providing the moral bedrock of society, the farmer was the indispensable foundation of democratic society.

A belief in the need to reform rural institutions brought the disparate concerns of country life advocates together. The reforms they posed were neither utilitarian nor romantic in nature, but a mix of hardheaded economic and institutional reform with attempts to nurture the culture and personhood of rural people. Given these typically disparate concerns, the progressive reformers of the country life movement focused on education, for it addressed both the moral and sociological quandaries that drove country life reform efforts. Education could enhance rural culture and thus help rural life maintain its role as wellspring of the American conscience. Moreover, rural children could learn the fundamentals of modern science and its application to the problems of agriculture. No part of the school curriculum promised to address the disparate concerns of country life activists more than nature study. Nature study at once promised the contact with the soil that assured proper moral development while also nurturing the curious and analytic habits of the scientific worldview that fostered agricultural efficiency.

The country life movement thus hoped to alter rural life so that it would produce good citizens, men and women of character who would temper degenerate (most often urban) social habits and transform antiquated agricultural practices. At the center of the country life movement, then, was an essential contradiction: country lifers wished to modernize the countryside while at the same time revitalizing many established aspects of its culture. Deeply concerned with tradition while also committed to the progressive improvement of social institutions, country life reformers attempted to control social change by tempering it with moral regeneration. For country life reformers, scientific agriculture must harmonize with moral belief. Put another way, country life reformers felt that the modernization of rural life needed to occur without the ostensibly corrupting influences of modern culture. Behind the country life movement, then, was an intellectual suspicion of modern culture yoked to the zest for progressive social transformation and embrace of science and technology that ensured modern culture would thrive.

For Bailey, the tensions and contradictions within country life ideology were not constraining but an opportunity to implement many reforms. "It is a public duty . . . to train the farmer [so] that he shall appreciate his guardianship," asserted Bailey. This duty focused the entire society's attention upon the farmer, and thus opened avenues for civically mature and responsible democratic change. "The farmer cannot keep the earth for us without an enlightened and very active support from every other person," wrote Bailey. That support included "safeguards from exploitation and from unessential commercial pressure." Key to social health was land ownership. Persons who work the land "should have the privilege of owning it." The trend in tenant occupancy was dangerous "because the practice in tenancy does not recognize the public interest in fertility . . . [it] is largely an arrangement for skinning the land."[52] Beyond ecological considerations, "the aristocracy of land is a very dangerous power in human affairs. It is all the more dangerous when associated with aristocracy of birth and of factitious social position."

Again the situation of the farmer spoke to the health of the entire democracy, because if "rigid aristocracy in land connects itself with the close control of politics, the subjugation becomes final and complete."[53] Bailey insisted that great aggregations of wealth corrupted democracy. Genuine self-government relied upon the democratic social control of natural wealth and beauty.

Tenancy and other questions regarding ownership and distribution of resources were bound up with the larger problem of individuality and independent judgment in the citizenry. Bailey argued that as society became more bureaucratized, or in Alan Trachtenberg's brilliantly telling phrase, "incorporated," it became "more difficult . . . for the person to find himself."[54] The remedy came from "contact with the earth" because interaction with nature tended "to make one original or at least detached in one's judgments and independent of group control." Independent judgment formed the basis of democratic decision-making: "We can never successfully substitute bookkeeping for men and women. We are more in need of personality than of administrative regularity." In short, "we must protect the person from being submerged in the system."[55] Contact with nature reinvigorated the bureaucratically stamped individual because nature, almost by definition, is unique, thus allowing authentic experience to thrive. Of the many kinds of interactions with nature sought by the nature study movement, they all held in common the essential trait of individuals developing personal skills and sympathies. Hence the long tradition of using contact with the natural world to live, as Thoreau stated, "deliberately." Unlike society, natural environments did not make social claims upon people, and thus interactions with nature helped produce distinctive and sovereign individuals. In this manner, farmers produced the cultural as well as the material building blocks of democracy. But this process worked only if the farmer remained independent. "When the farmer is a free land-owner and is not a peasant," noted Bailey, "he resists the standardizing process."[56]

Bailey's philosophy of nature study assumed that it could help modernize the countryside and stabilize the rural economy, as well as alleviate the alienation that comes from the narrow instrumentalism inherent in the market mentality. The farmer who sees in his crops "only clods and weeds, and corn," wrote Bailey, leads an "empty and a barren life." Conversely, the "knowledge of soil and atmosphere, of plant and animal life that makes [the farmer] an intelligent producer, puts him in sympathetic touch with these activities of nature." For nature study advocates, sympathy created happiness. Thus Bailey asserted that nature study must begin with "an interest in the things with which the farmer lives and has to do, for a man is happy only when he is in sympathy with his environment."[57]

For Bailey, the renewal of country life must therefore begin with a spiritual rather than economic revitalization. Much extension work in agriculture missed this point. "The burden of the new agricultural teaching has been largely the augmentation of material wealth," wrote Bailey. "Hand in hand with this new teaching, however, should go an awakening in the less tangible but equally powerful things of the spirit." In the last analysis, then, Bailey would "make farm life interesting before I made it profitable."[58] Bailey's close colleague at Cornell, the widely read nature study expert Anna Botsford Comstock, concurred with Bailey's position. "The ideal farmer is not the man who by hazard and chance succeeds," wrote Comstock.

> He is the man who loves his farm and all that surrounds it because he is awake to the beauty as well as the wonders which are there; he is the man who understands as far as may be the great forces of nature which are at work around him, and therefore he is able to make them work for him.[59]

Moreover, the spiritual relationship with nature would serve the utilitarian end of keeping children on the farm. Bailey and many other country life reformers proclaimed nature study as a means to enhance rural cultural vitality, for a "sympathetic knowledge of nature will in the end be more satisfying than much of the amusement that the town has to offer."[60] The fascinating world of natural history would give rural people the cultural and intellectual satisfaction assumed to exist only in highbrow, urban culture. With their cultural lives thus fulfilled, creative and intelligent people would choose to remain farmers. As the journalist Sidney Morse, writing in *Craftsman*, contended,

> the interrelation of scientific thought and intellectual culture with the physical contact of Nature robs the latter of its monotony and instills into it the supremest joy: all of these are lessons which the farmer's boy of our day and his children are to learn.[61]

Nature was not only a material object subject to efficient development, but also a means to enhance cultural vitality and intellectual acuity.

The nationwide concern for country life also elicited a federal response, one initiated, appropriately enough, with a speech given by Liberty Hyde Bailey. In 1907 the Michigan Agricultural College invited Bailey, one of its most prominent graduates, to deliver the keynote speech at its semicentennial celebration. Bailey seized the opportunity to expound upon the crisis in rural life and his proposed remedies. Among the audience at Bailey's speech was President Theodore Roosevelt. A year later Roosevelt asked Bailey to chair a presidential committee on country life, the Country Life Commission. In this manner the country life movement became intertwined with Roosevelt's conservation policies. Roosevelt later recalled,

> I doubt if I should have undertaken to appoint a commission if I had not been able to get Director Bailey for its head, and no man in our country did better work for the country than he did on that commission.[62]

Bailey headed the commission that featured a who's who of country life intellectuals, including the sociologist Kenyon Butterfield; the conservationist and head of the United States Forest Service Gifford Pinchot; the editor of *World's Work*, Walter Hines Page; and Henry Wallace of *Wallace's Farmer*. To gain knowledge about the country life crisis, the committee sent out questionnaires to roughly 550,000 country residents; over 115,000 responded. Butterfield conducted research into the country church, and Wallace inquired into farm labor tenancy. The commission also encouraged country people to hold meetings in which they examined rural problems and subsequently forwarded their ideas to the commission. Thousands of such meetings were held. Bailey in particular wished for rural people to lead the reforms of their lives and institutions. The commission made its final report to the President in January 1909. Roosevelt forwarded the report to Congress, but Congress, carping with the executive branch and aggrieved at not being consulted about the commission, refused to fund printing of the document and ordered the commission to desist its activities. Congressional hostility, along with a lack of interest in the commission by President William Howard Taft (who took office shortly after the report was completed), ended the work of the commission with the submission of its report.

Despite the lack of congressional response, the Country Life Commission prompted legislation that led to the U.S. Parcel Post System, federally funded rural electrification, and a nationwide extension service. The commission also focused a great deal of its efforts on the reform of education. One question from the commission's questionnaire, "Are the schools in your neighborhood training boys and girls satisfactorily for farm life?," elicited a resoundingly negative response from respondents across the nation. The commission noted that "there is demand that education have relations to living, that the schools should express the daily life, and that in rural districts they should educate by means of agriculture and country life subjects."[63] The education that the commission envisioned extended well beyond technical instruction in agriculture. "As a pure matter of education," wrote the commission, "the countryman must learn to love the country and to have an intellectual appreciation of it." The commission report, edited by Bailey, cited nature study, among other curricular possibilities, as a way to ensure that agriculture "color the work of rural public schools."[64] Progressive nature study met these demands because it imparted the latest methods of scientific agriculture while at the same time bestowing the moral foundation that country life reformers wished to impart.

Bestowing that moral foundation demanded wide-ranging relationships with the environment that repudiated the vision of nature as red in tooth and claw promoted by social Darwinists. Bailey, a fervent defender of evolution by natural selection, ridiculed the idea that physical power alone drove natural change, terming it "a false analogy and a false biology . . . a misconception of the teaching of evolution." Among the many problems with this formulation was that "man is a moral agent; animals and plants are not moral agents."[65] Nature simply did not conform to the image that social Darwinists imparted to it. For example, those who justified war by citing the struggle for existence were "confusing very unlike situations." A more thoughtful analysis discovers that the "military method of civilization finds no justification in the biological struggle for existence." The point was a crucial one because commitment to democracy meant repudiating false analogies about society and nature. "Democracies are not established on the nineteenth century dogma of the struggle for existence," explained Bailey. "The current construction of the struggle is to excuse selfishness."[66]

Rather than combat, warfare, or other forms of physical destruction, Bailey viewed adaptation as the central fact of the natural world. Accordingly, adaptation was nature's key lesson for human society. "If one looks for moral significance in the struggle for existence," argued Bailey, "one finds it in the fact that it is a process of adjustment rather than a contest in ambition." Indeed, "the final test of fitness in nature is adaptation, not power." The lesson for society is that "Adaptation and adjustment mean peace, not war." Rather than projecting a bloody struggle for existence onto nature, we should see that such a view makes a "mockery" of the natural world on "a June morning." For Bailey, the "fullness of every field and wood is in complete adjustment. The teeming multitudes of animal and plant have found a way to live together, and we look abroad on a vast harmony, verdurous, prolific, abounding." Without slipping into pure sentimentalism—Bailey recognized the "capture and carnage" in nature—he nevertheless repudiated those simplistic ideologies that used analogies to nature as a way to justify regressive social policy.

Adaptation entailed more than an accurate understanding of the natural world. For Bailey, human society must adapt to the realities of environments, and it was precisely the openness and flexibility of democratic societies that made democracy the best way for society to interact with nature. The responsiveness of democracy was important because it could match the variety of nature itself. The diversity of natural environments made necessary the many different responses humans must have to their surroundings. In place of the social and mental rigidities that so worried Bailey, farmers should cultivate a creative and ecological worldview. "A good part of agriculture is to learn how to adapt one's work to nature," noted Bailey; the successful farmer needed "to fit the crop scheme to the climate and to the soil and the facilities."[67] But creativity should be tempered by humility. Humans are part of the natural world, and thus should have a humble attitude toward creation. "Evolution is the point of view of otherism and altruism," wrote Bailey. Not all things exist "merely to please man." Recognizing this reality "is one of the first steps toward a real regard for the rights of others, and consequently toward elimination of selfishness."[68] By recognizing human embeddedness in nature we are best able to understand environmental limits and adapt our practices to them.

Bailey's evolutionary outlook prompted his theorization of the relationship between society and nature emphasizing the kinship existing between humans and the rest of nature. Like all of Bailey's thought, it mixed moral injunction, evolutionary naturalism, great regard for farmers, and commitment to democracy. In its dedication to a nature-centered, "biocentric" worldview—Bailey coined the term "biocentric"—Bailey's thought was more radically ecological than any of his peers save John Muir. Bailey is thus one of the most important precursors of contemporary environmental philosophy, but is rarely cited by either the popular essayists or academic philosophers of this vibrant intellectual community.

Bailey articulated his philosophy most fully in his 1915 text, *The Holy Earth*. Bailey worked from the injunction that "the earth is divine, because man did not make it. We are here, part in creation." Because humans are part in creation, "Nature cannot be antagonistic to man, seeing that man is a product of nature." Being part of creation also gives humankind rights: "We come out of the earth and we have a right to the use of the materials." If people kept in mind the divinity of creation, there would be "no danger of crass materialism." Bailey also emphasized in his writings about evolution that the earth does not exist solely for humans. "The living creation is not exclusively man-centered: it is biocentric," argued Bailey. By "biocentric" Bailey did not draw the same conclusions as modern-day deep ecologists, but simply that "the creation, and not man, is the norm." Recognizing this fact, "we lose our cosmic selfishness and we find our place in the plan of things." Despite the airy quality of this theorizing, Bailey, always the pragmatist, did not "mean all this, for our modern world, in any vague or abstract way."[69] Bailey's philosophy was grounded in and by the prosaic world of farmers and other everyday people.

Though we live in a biocentric world, we rarely recognize it as such. Bailey argued that the first and most important consequence that stems from this lack of recognition of our biocentric world is that "our dominion has been mostly destructive." People fail to "exercise the care and thrift of good housekeepers . . . this habit of destructiveness is uneconomical in the best sense, unsocial, unmoral." Biblical texts may have granted "dominion" to human beings, but people have "no commission to devastate." Because humans are unmoored from our obligations to the earth, "we have not yet learned how to withstand the prosperity and the privileges that we have gained by the discoveries of science." But in the era of conservation,

> Society now begins to demand a constructive process. With care and with regard for other men, we must produce the food and the other supplies in regularity and sufficiency; and we must clean up after our work, that the earth may not be depleted, scarred or repulsive.[70]

It was farmers, of course, who produced with regularity and sufficiency. Bailey's biocentric worldview placed special emphasis on the importance of rural people to society. The farmer is "the agent or the representative of society to guard and to subdue the surface of the earth; and he is the agent of the divinity that made it." This recognition did not absolve urbanites of responsibility, for the farmer needed "enlightened and very active support from every other person" in the society. Among the obligations that the larger society had to the farmer was "to provide liberally at public expense for the special education of the man on the land." Because of the farmer's "joyful" privilege of producing staple goods for society, this education must be "secular" and "technical." At the same time it must "introduce the element of moral obligation" that the farmer has to earth and to society, a result that "cannot be attained until the farmer and every one of us recognize the holiness of the earth." Nor can society afford to leave farmers out of the political conversation. Rather, society must "do everything it can to enable those in the backgrounds to maintain their standing and their pride and to partake in the making of political affairs."[71] Again, the philosophy of the holy earth demanded democratic participation by the "background" members of society.

Nor does the immersion into the biocentric worldview create selfishness. According to Bailey, selfishness was more likely to arise from "occupations that are some degrees removed from the earth." "The naturist," on the other hand, "desires to protect the plants and the animals and the situations for those less fortunate and for those who come after." This regard for the poor and the future were inescapable corollaries of the biocentric worldview. "The best kind of community interest attaches to the proper use and partitioning of the earth," argued Bailey. It is a "communism that is dissociated from propaganda and programs." Bailey railed against the "sinfulness" of "vast private estates" that "shut up expanses of the surface of the earth" from regular people. Despite this criticism of landed aristocracy, Bailey remained wary of government ownership of land, generally favoring mixed plots of public and private landholdings. Because "the ultimate good in the use of land is the development of people," all citizens should "have the right and the privilege to a personal use of some part of the earth."[72] Bailey argued repeatedly that because we are all subject to natural forces, nature herself was "one vast democracy." "Whatever may be our high fortune among our fellows," wrote Bailey, "we come back to the earth, to the earth that gave us birth."[73] Just as nature does not discriminate in how it affects people, society should eliminate arbitrary social barriers that restrict access to the earth's treasures.

Despite Bailey's reverence for farmers and his concern for soil fertility and similar issues, he refused to reduce his advocacy for rural people and conservation to purely utilitarian ends. "The proper caretaking of the earth lies not alone in maintaining its fertility or in safeguarding its products," declared Bailey. "The lines of beauty that appeal to the eye and the charm that satisfies the five senses are in our keeping." Indeed, "no one has a moral right to contribute unsightly factory premises or a forbidding commercial establishment to any community. The lines of utility and efficiency ought also to be the lines of beauty." It was for the working class that beauty must be made available: "it is due every worker to have a good landscape to look upon," argued Bailey. Nor did the veneration of beauty forestall use. Because people are part of nature, we should not fear modification of natural landscapes. "There is unfortunately a feeling abroad that any modification of a striking landscape is violation and despoliation."[74] For Bailey, this feeling arose from unexamined and untenable assumptions that set use and conservation, humans and nature, against each other.

Bailey did understand that the way to preserve some natural beauty was to keep it beyond human interference. He favored the preservation of the "supposed wasteplaces" of the earth: "I am glad to see these outlying places set aside as public reserves." Moreover, "some pieces and kinds of scenery are above all economic use and should be kept wholly in the natural state." For most lands, "the first responsibility of any society is to protect them, husband them, bring them into use, and at the same time teach the people what they mean."[75] Bailey recognized many ways that land might be used; these uses included various activities, not just agricultural production. "One may have land merely to live on," declared Bailey. "Another may have a wood to wander in. Another may have a shore, and another a retreat in the mountains." The many kinds of land provided many kinds of use—utilitarian, aesthetic and spiritual—for citizens across the country.

So too, must all people have access to the natural world. Though Bailey favored the creation of public reserves, he warned that society "must not so organize and tie up the far spaces as to prevent persons of little means from securing small parcels." Nor did Bailey believe that access alone determined democratic control of resources: they must be protected "from rapacious citizens who have small social conscience."[76] Because "the product" of democracy was "self-acting men and women," the independent citizenry must guard against public and private institutions that would curb access to the natural world.[77]

Self-actualization may not have been efficient, but it created the kinds of citizens that allowed democracy to thrive. Precisely because Bailey was typical among conservationists in his concern for beauty, democracy, and the enchantment of nature and society, his thought forces us to recognize a morally sophisticated and democratically centered conservation movement. Following Bailey's thought, then, leads to three general themes that all force reconsideration of progressive conservation and its relationship with modern environmentalism.

According to the interpretation of conservation as efficiency, the more radical preservationists (such as John Muir) opposed conservationists. The supposed split centered on the utilitarian and scientific conservationists who favored the wise use of nature versus the aesthetic and spiritual preservationists who argued for the permanent protection of sacred, spectacular lands. Scientific forestry competed against national parks. For ostensibly utilitarian conservationists, modern science abraded the legacies of Emerson and Thoreau, as they embraced scientific expertise, modern management, and industrial technology. These historical divisions, the story goes, are repeated in contemporary environmentalist debates. Reform-oriented, utilitarian environmentalists obsessed with how many parts per million of various pollutants are safe for the public consumption are opposed by radically biocentric deep ecologists who insist upon the moral and legal rights of nature itself—or, in Bailey's words, that the earth is holy.[78] Thus the history of twentieth-century environmentalist thought is boxed into a neat, well-wrapped package.

But as Bailey's ideas and actions demonstrate, that package is too small and too tightly bound to accommodate the complexities of conservationist ideology. Most importantly, the diversity of nature itself demanded many responses from human society—responses that don't fit into conservationists or preservationist molds. Bailey wished to preserve some places and develop others. He fought to increase both farm fertility and efficiency, and to make society think about the many types of relationships with nature that it wished to foster. Like most conservationists, Bailey understood that the human relationship with nature was many-sided and always changing, and not constrained by one single dominant kind of interaction. Progress could mean many different things—and pose profound dilemmas for those searching for relationships with the natural world that are viable for the long run. The farmer's complicated relationship with the soil typified the complex ways that conservationists sought to reform social interaction with nature.

Questions of conservation were also deeply mixed with debates about civic organization and democratic reform. Bailey was not aloof from the possibilities or the problems of modern science. Rather than blindly embracing science and technology as a utilitarian conservationist, he fought to foster science while simultaneously tempering it with moral deliberation and democratic purpose. Like John Dewey he argued that utilitarian, aesthetic, and spiritual interactions with nature all fulfilled deep needs intrinsic to the human animal. Conservationists criticized, indeed were repulsed by, the notion that narrow, bureaucratic expediency could function as a social philosophy. In other words, Bailey and Dewey were deeply concerned with the kind of ethical and democratic character that conservation and education could foster in the citizenry. They believed conservation should foster citizenship, not technocracy. If conservation helped enrich rural people economically and spiritually, it would simultaneously create the kinds of citizens upon which democracy depends. In voicing this concern they drew upon the democratic legacies of American romanticism.

Last, insofar as science dampened the diversity of human relationships with the natural world, society must temper it with the kind of populist individualism encouraged by nineteenth-century Romantic thought. Bailey did not turn his back on this tradition, but drew upon it to deepen his criticism of incorporation and his thinking about how contact with nature could revitalize Jeffersonian individualism. In this manner, preservation of nature was deeply bound with the struggle to maintain individualism and a coherent identity against the dislocations of industrial modernity. Conservationists thus approached different issues with different values, all dependent upon the particularities of the case at hand. There was no overriding conservationist or preservationist ideological commitment. In the end, conservationists such as Bailey believed that the best hope of mediating the relationship between humans and nature was education—and even education could at best give people tools of evaluation rather than overriding ideological maxims. It is this legacy, rather than untenable splits in ideology, that demonstrates the vitality of conservationist thought and its continuing relevance to the profound social and ecological issues of our own time.

Notes

1   Liberty Hyde Bailey, *The Outlook to Nature* (New York: Macmillan, 1911), 7.
2   Bailey, *The Holy Earth* (New York: New York College of Agriculture and Life Sciences 1980 [1915]), 13, 31.
3   Bailey, *What Is Democracy?* (Ithaca, NY: Comstock, 1918), 87.
4   Bailey, *The Holy Earth*, 89.
5   Bailey, *What Is Democracy?*, 64–65.
6   Liberty Hyde Bailey, *The Nature Study Idea* (New York: Doubleday, Page & Company, 1903), 87.
7   Bailey, *The Holy Earth*, 6.

8   Bailey, *The Nature Study Idea*, 94.

9   Samuel P. Hays, *Conservation and the Gospel of Efficiency: The Progressive Conservation Movement, 1890–1920* (Cambridge, MA: Harvard University Press, 1959), 2. Hays went so far as to argue that the moral crusade for conservation was a mere revulsion with materialism that inhibited the real business of conservation. "It was especially difficult," argues Hays "to approach resource development in a rational manner when one's major political support now came from groups who looked upon the problem in moral rather than economic terms." Hays, *Conservation and the Gospel of Efficiency*, 146. My perspective on Hays is similar to that of Charles T. Rubin. See Charles T. Rubin, "Preface," in Charles T. Rubin (ed.), *Conservation Reconsidered: Nature, Virtue and American Liberal Democracy* (New York: Rowman & Littlefield, 2000). For recent scholarship on conservation that follows Hays's angle of investigation, see the work of Benjamin Kline, who summarized progressive conservation as "the proper use of the nation's natural resources as determined by the scientific standards of the times and regulated by objective bureaucrats." Benjamin Kline, *First along the River: A Brief History of the U.S. Environmental Movement*, 3rd ed. (Lanham, MD: Rowman & Littlefield, 2007), 53.

10 The most prominent proponent of this line of argument is J. Leonard Bates, who concluded that conservation "was an effort to implement democracy for twentieth-century America, to stop the stealing and exploitation, to inspire high standards of government, to preserve the beauty of mountain and stream, to distribute more equitably the profits of this economy." Despite this brief concern with "beauty," Bates's account accepts the supposedly wholly utilitarian character of conservation. See J. Leonard Bates, "Fulfilling American Democracy: The Conservation Movement, 1907 to 1921," *Mississippi Valley Historical Review* 44(1) (June 1957), 57.

11 For studies that detail the local effects of conservation policy, see Karl Jacoby, *Crimes against Nature: Squatters, Poachers, Thieves and the Hidden History of American Conservation* (Berkeley: University of California Press, 2001); Mark David Spence, *Dispossessing the Wilderness: Indian Removal and the Making of the National Parks* (New York: Oxford University Press, 1999); and Louis Warren, *The Hunter's Game: Poachers and Conservationists in Twentieth-Century America* (New Haven: Yale University Press, 1997). For an argument that examines the rural origins of conservation, see Richard Judd, *Common Lands, Common People: The Origins of Conservation in Northern New England* (Cambridge, MA: Harvard University Press, 1997). For urban conservation see David Stradling, *Smokestacks and Progressives: Environmentalists, Engineers, and Air Quality in America, 1881–1951* (Baltimore: Johns Hopkins University Press, 1999). For the ambiguous legacy of conservation on the resources themselves, see Nancy Langston, *Forest Dreams, Forest Nightmares: The Paradox of Old Growth in the Inland West* (Seattle: University of Washington Press, 1995); and Joseph E. Taylor III, *Making Salmon: An Environmental History of the Northwest Fisheries Crisis* (Seattle: University of Washington Press, 1999). David Stradling has compiled a fine collection of

documents that express some of the complexity of Progressive era conservation. See David Stradling, *Conservation in the Progressive Era: Classic Texts* (Seattle: University of Washington Press, 2004).

12 Other scholars are reexamining the democratic and civic aspects of Progressive era conservation. See, in particular, Ben A. Minteer and Robert E. Manning (eds.), *Reconstructing Conservation: Finding Common Ground* (Washington, DC: Island Press, 2003); and Ben A. Minteer, *The Landscape of Reform: Civic Pragmatism and Environmental Thought in America* (Cambridge, MA: MIT Press, 2006). Minteer devotes a chapter to Bailey, correctly placing him in a tradition of civic pragmatism that extends to Lewis Mumford, Benton MacKaye, and Aldo Leopold. My essay incorporates, supports, and extends Minteer's important work.

13 Bailey is nearly absent from the historiography of progressive conservation. One of the important initial examinations of conservation during the environmental era, Donald Worster's *American Environmentalism: The Formative Period, 1860–1915*, included a section on Bailey. Yet few scholars followed Worster's lead. See Donald Worster, *American Environmentalism: The Formative Period, 1860–1915* (New York, NY: Wiley, 1973), 223–31.

14 William L. Bowers, *The Country Life Movement in America, 1900–1920* (Port Washington, NY: Kennikat Press, 1974), 45. For Bailey's biography, see Philip Dorf, *Liberty Hyde Bailey: An Informal Biography* (Ithaca, NY: Cornell University Press, 1956) and A. D. Rodgers, *Liberty Hyde Bailey: A Story of American Plant Sciences* (Princeton University Press, NJ: 1949).

15 For more on passenger pigeons, see Jennifer Price, *Flight Maps* (New York: Basic Books, 1999), 1–55.

16 Cited by Margaret Beattie Bogue, "Liberty Hyde Bailey, Jr. and the Bailey Family Farm," *Agricultural History* 63(1) (Winter 1989), 39.

17 Bogue, "Liberty Hyde Bailey, Jr. and the Bailey Family Farm," 46.

18 The literature on educational progressivism is vast. Interested readers should begin with Lawrence A. Cremin, *The Transformation of the School: Progressivism in American Education, 1876–1957* (New York: Vintage, 1964); Herbert Kliebard, *The Struggle for the American Curriculum, 1893–1958* (Boston: Routledge and Kegan Paul, 1986); William J. Reese, *Power and the Promise of School Reform: Grassroots Movements during the Progressive Era* (Boston: Routledge and Kegan Paul, 1986); and Diane Ravitch, *Left Back: A Century of Failed School Reforms* (New York: Simon & Schuster, 2000). Two important essays are Timothy L. Smith, "Progressivism in American Education, 1880–1900," *Harvard Educational Review* 31(2) (Spring 1961), 168–93; and William J. Reese, "The Origins of Progressive Education," *History of Education Quarterly* 41(1) (Spring 2001), 1–24.

19 Edward H. Eppens, "Nature-Study à la Mode—A Protest," *Critic* 45 (August 1904), 149.

20 Bailey, *The Nature Study Idea*, 41.

21 Ibid., 4, 31.

22 Quoted by Louis Menand, "William James and the Case of the Epileptic Patient," in Louis Menand, *American Studies* (New York: Farrar, Straus and Giroux, 2002), 21.

23 Bailey, *The Nature Study Idea*, 41.

24 Liberty Hyde Bailey, *Universal Service* (Ithaca, NY: Sturgis and Walton, 1919), 18.

25 Clayton F. Parker, "Are Children Naturally Naturalists?," *The Nature-Study Review* 4(1) (January 1908), 29.

26 Charles B. Scott, *Nature Study and the Child* (Boston: D. C Heath, 1902), 126–27.

27 The recent revival of interest in pragmatism has resulted in a number of excellent interpretations of Dewey. Highlights include Larry A. Hickman, *John Dewey's Pragmatic Technology* (Bloomington: Indiana University Press, 1990); Robert Westbrook, *John Dewey and American Democracy* (Ithaca, NY: Cornell University Press, 1991); Alan Ryan, *John Dewey and the High Tide of American Democracy* (New York: W. W. Norton, 1995); David Fott, *John Dewey: America's Philosopher of Democracy* (New York: Rowman & Littlefield, 1998); Jay Martin, *The Education of John Dewey* (New York: Columbia University Press, 2003.) Scholars are also reevaluating pragmatism for its potential contributions to environmental philosophy. See Andrew Light and Eric Katz (eds.), *Environmental Pragmatism* (New York: Routledge, 1996). Two essays that examine Dewey in particular are William Chaloupka, "John Dewey's Social Aesthetics as a Precedent for Environmental Thought," *Environmental Ethics* 9(3) (Fall 1987), 243–60; and Kevin C. Armitage, "The Continuity of Nature and Experience: John Dewey's Pragmatic Environmentalism," *Capitalism Nature Socialism* 14(3) (September, 2003) 49–72.

28 Standard references to John Dewey's work are to the critical edition, *The Collected Works of John Dewey*, edited by Jo Ann Boydston (Carbondale and Edwardsville: Southern Illinois University Press, 1969–91), and published as *The Early Works* (EW), *The Middle Works* (MW), and *The Later Works* (LW). Whenever possible I have cited the original source, followed by its reproduction in the critical edition. I followed these designations with volume and page number. Dewey, *How We Think* (1910), MW 6:179.

29 Dewey, *Democracy and Education* (1916), MW 9:233, 229.

30 Liberty Hyde Bailey, "The Science-Spirit in a Democracy," *Nature-Study Review* 12(1) (January 1916), 8.

31 Dewey, *Democracy and Education* (1916), MW 9:237.

32 Bailey, "The Science-Spirit in a Democracy," 5, 8.

33 Bailey, *Universal Service*, 22–23, 26.

34 Dewey is widely misunderstood on this point. For one clarification, see James T. Kloppenberg, "Democracy and Disenchantment: From Weber and Dewey to Habermas and Rorty," in James. T. Kloppenberg, *The Virtues of Liberalism* (New York: Oxford University Press, 1998), 82–99.

35 Dewey, *The Public and Its Problems* (1927), LW 2:344–45.

36 Dewey, *Experience and Nature* (1925), LW 1:110, 14.

37 Dewey, *Reconstruction in Philosophy* (1920), MW 12:152.

38   For a history of the Laboratory School, see Ida B. DePencier, *The History of the Laboratory Schools: The University of Chicago 1896–1965* (Chicago: Quadrangle, 1967); and Katherine Camp Mayhew and Anna Camp Edwards, *The Dewey School* (1936 New York: Atherton, 1965). See also Alan Ryan, "Deweyan Pragmatism and American Education," in Amélie Oksenberg Rorty (ed.), *Philosophers on Education: New Historical Perspectives* (New York: Routledge, 1998), 394–410; as well as Cremin, *The Transformation of the School*. On Dewey's Laboratory School pedagogy, see Herbert Kliebard, *The Struggle for the American Curriculum*. See also Laurel N. Tanner, *Dewey's Laboratory School: Lessons for Today* (New York: Teachers College Press , 1997).

39   John Dewey, "The University Elementary School, Studies and Methods," *University Record*, 21 May 1897.

40   Dewey, *Democracy and Education*, MW 9:221; *Schools of Tomorrow* (1915), MW 8:272.

41   Dewey, *Schools of Tomorrow* (1915), MW 8:271.

42   Maurice A. Bigelow, *Nature-Study Review* 2(3) (March 1906), 91. Emphasis in original.

43   Dewey, *Democracy and Education*, MW 9: 219.

44   Dewey, "Education from a Social Perspective" (1913), MW 7:115–16.

45   Bailey, *What Is Democracy?*, 41.

46   Bailey, *The Holy Earth*, 26.

47   Frederic C. Howe, *The City: The Hope of Democracy* (New York: Charles Scribner's Sons, 1906), 33.

48   Henry Wallace, "The Socialization of Farm Life," cited by William L. Bowers, *The Country Life Movement in America, 1900–1920* (Port Washington, NY: Kennikat Press, 1974), 36. Other writers claimed urban life enervated formerly healthy rural people. The urban resident must therefore sleep regularly, eat well, exercise, and get to nature as often as possible. See Ada Patterson, "Country Life in the City," *Pittsburgh Gazette Times*, 16 April 1911, 2.

49   Ira G. Hoitt, quoted in United States Commissioner of Education *Annual Report*, 1887/88, 159–60.

50   Bailey, *What Is Democracy?*, 96.

51   Bailey, *The Holy Earth*, 24.

52   Ibid., 26, 37, 36.

53   Ibid., 33. Bailey broadened the critique to include international relations as well. Peace would result only from just distribution of land and resources. "Neighborliness," wrote Bailey, "is international."

54   Bailey, *The Holy Earth*, 88. Alan Trachtenberg, *The Incorporation of America: Culture and Society in Gilded Age America* (New York: Hill & Wang, 1982).

55   Bailey, *The Holy Earth*, 89.

56   Bailey, *What Is Democracy?*, 99.

57   Bailey, *The Nature-Study Idea*, 82, 65.

58   Ibid., 80, 81.

59   Anna Botsford Comstock, *Handbook of Nature Study* (1911, Ithaca, NY: Comstock, 1986), 22.

60   Bailey, *The Outlook to Nature*, 53.

61   Sidney Morse, "The Boy on the Farm: And Life as He Sees It," *Craftsman* 16(2) (May 1909), 199. One thing that almost all reformers and almost all rural residents could agree upon was the desperate need to reform rural schools. The actual structures that housed rural schools were often not fit for farm animals, let alone learning. Children either froze near drafty windows or baked near a single potbellied stove. The slab seats induced blisters, as did the birch rods that teachers used to maintain discipline. Teachers were often poorly trained, and their classroom curricula were subject to the whims and biases of the communities they served. Primary school children were usually lumped into one large grade with older children who were given the task of instructing the younger ones. School attendance itself was often voluntary and occurred only when farms could spare the labor. Moreover, rural people tended to view formal education as impractical "book learning" that made little pragmatic difference to their lives. In rural communities education occurred as families, neighbors, and churches socialized children; schools needed to demonstrate practical results if they were to be accepted into this process. The travails of rural education were well enough known to inspire a play by M. R. Orne, *The Country School: An Entertainment in Two Scenes* (Boston: Walter H. Baker, 1890). See David B. Tyack, "The Tribe and the Common School: Community Control in Rural Education," *American Quarterly* 24(1) (March 1972), 3–19. The subject of rural schools and the life of rural children is generally understudied. Some primary sources that investigated the situation of rural schools include Ellwood P. Cubberley, *Rural Life and Education: A Study of the Rural-School Problem as a Phase of the Rural Life Problem* (Boston: Houghton Mifflin, 1914); Clifton Johnson, *The Country School in New England* (New York: D. Appleton, 1895); and Marion G. Kirkpatrick, *The Rural School from Within* (Philadelphia: J. B. Lippincott, 1917). One recent volume that has begun to redress this historiographic gap is Pamela Riney-Kehrberg, *Childhood on the Farm: Work, Play, and Coming of Age in the Midwest* (Lawrence: University Press of Kansas, 2005).

62   *The Cornell Countryman* 11 (December 1913), 88. Roosevelt's letter praising Bailey can be found online at: http://rmc.library.cornell.edu/bailey/commission/commission_8.html#.

63   Cited by Cremin, *The Transformation of the School*, 83.

64   *Report of the Commission on Country Life* (New York: Van Rees Press, 1911), 123.

65   Bailey, *The Holy Earth*, 57, 56. Defense of evolution was typical of nature study advocates. Despite their fervent belief in the moral power of contact with the natural world, I have found not a single nature study author who repudiated Darwinian evolution, and many who staunchly supported it.

66   Bailey, *What Is Democracy?*, 86.

67   Bailey, *The Holy Earth*, 53, 56, 60, 11.

68   Bailey, *The Outlook to Nature*, 175.

69   Bailey, *The Holy Earth*, 13, 11, 6, 23, 16.

70   Ibid., 14, 15, 16, 17.

71   Ibid., 17, 26, 30.

72   Ibid., 31, 32, 34.

73   Bailey, "The Science-Spirit in a Democracy," 10.

74   Bailey, *The Holy Earth*, 78.

75   Ibid., 35, 78, 39.

76   Ibid., 35, 39.

77   Bailey, *What Is Democracy?* 36.

78   For deep ecology, see Arne Naess, *Ecology, Community and Lifestyle: Outline of an Ecosophy*, trans. and ed. by David Rothenberg (Cambridge: Cambridge University Press, 1980); Bill Devall and George Sessions, *Deep Ecology—Living as if Nature Mattered* (Salt Lake City: Gibbs Smith, 1985); Sessions, *Deep Ecology for the Twenty-First Century* (Boston: Shambhala, 1995).

CHAPTER 5

The Hetch Hetchy Controversy

ROBERT W. RIGHTER

Just before midnight on Saturday 6 December 1913, the U.S. Senate finally voted on the Raker Act: forty-three yeas, twenty-five nays, and twenty-seven absentees. It was the culmination of a thirteen-year struggle by San Francisco to gain the right to dam a spectacular glacial river valley within Yosemite National Park. Michael O'Shaughnessy, the Chief Engineer of San Francisco, was jubilant. He and his San Francisco delegates had been listening intently to floor debate from the balcony for six days. Now victory was at hand. They gleefully returned to the Willard Hotel, intent on raising a few glasses of whiskey to their triumph. However, Sunday had arrived, and the bartender could sell no liquor. Still pleased, but unable to satisfy their expectations, they toasted their triumph with cold water—not so satisfying, but perhaps more symbolic.[1]

Within a few days O'Shaughnessy and the San Franciscans were riding the rails west in plenty of time for Christmas. The Chief Engineer thought of the holidays, but mainly of the great project that lay ahead. For the next twenty years the Hetch Hetchy water project, aimed at bringing a bountiful supply of water to San Francisco, would dominate O'Shaughnessy's life. The keystone to his efforts was the O'Shaughnessy Dam, which created the Hetch Hetchy reservoir. At the 1923 dedication O'Shaughnessy spoke against those who opposed construction of the dam, arguing that the dam and reservoir was the place "Where Beauty and Utility Wedded."[2]

Without a doubt the valley represented beauty, and the dam, utility. Whether it was a successful wedding is still in doubt. Although the Hetch Hetchy fight was the first national protest against destruction of a dramatic natural area, it is still an issue today, nearly 100 years after the passage of the Raker Act. There are many who still believe that it was a bogus marriage and should finally terminate in a divorce, represented by the tearing down of the great dam.[3] Although no one can say, it is very possible that people reading this account may see the Hetch Hetchy Valley restored within their lifetimes.

We may take up the story in 1903. In January of that year the Mayor of San Francisco, James Phelan, and his City Engineer, C. E. Grunsky, were feeling pleased because the Hetch Hetchy Valley would soon be city property. They had purchased much of the land and had filed the necessary water claims and paperwork. Concluding the deal hinged only on approval from Ethan Hitchcock, Secretary of the Interior, which seemed a sure thing. Both Phelan and Grunsky envisioned that soon sawyers would be cutting trees and bulldozers would be preparing the dam site.

But in a remarkable decision, Secretary Hitchcock denied the city's request.[4] He determined that his first obligation was to protect Yosemite National Park, of which the Hetch Hetchy Valley was an important part. San Francisco's Attorney, Franklin K. Lane, appealed in December 1903, but the secretary denied his appeal. Soon after, Hitchcock justified his action to President Theodore Roosevelt:

> If natural scenic attractions of the grade and character of Lake Eleanor and Hetch Hetchy Valley are not of the class which the law commands the Secretary to preserve and retain in their natural condition, it would seem difficult to find any in the Park that are unless it be the Yosemite Valley itself.[5]

The secretary's ruling would have been a perfect time for San Francisco to abandon its desire to dam the Hetch Hetchy Valley. There were other possibilities, at least three of which would provide the city a pure, abundant source of water while avoiding the invasion of a national park. If city leaders had taken up one of those alternatives they would have saved the city money, the national park would not have been violated, and the Tuolumne River would still flow through the valley. Instead, they persisted, for the city had purchased land and perfected water rights. San Francisco had made its choice, and to change directions would be difficult.

Had it not been for the San Francisco earthquake and fire of 18 April 1906, it is doubtful that San Francisco could have prevailed. On that April morning, at 5:12 a.m., the city shook. Buildings fell, power lines separated, gas lines broke, and of course, water mains ruptured. Many people never woke. Some of those who did perhaps wished they had not. With overturned kerosene lamps and broken gas mains, fire engulfed four square miles in the city center for four days. The earthquake was a natural disaster that few San Franciscans could blame on anyone, save those who viewed the event as God's wrath unleashed on a sinful, pleasure-loving city. However, the fire was another matter. As the flames spread across the city, firefighters and citizens called for water but found little. The violent shaking had broken many of the main lines, and the hydrants provided little more than a trickle. As citizens watched the flames leaping ever higher, they looked for answers. It was only natural to blame the Spring Valley Water Company, who owned the water mains, for the fiery tragedy. In truth, it mattered not a whit if the broken water mains were city-owned or private, yet some believed the destruction could have been avoided with Hetch Hetchy water.

The earthquake and fire became not only a holocaust but a catalyst, reigniting the Hetch Hetchy solution. Help came from Washington. On the floor of the United States Senate, Nevada Senator Key Pittman pronounced:

> I saw the hillside covered by homeless people. I saw such suffering as I never expect to see again, and I know that a lot of it was caused by reason of the inefficient system of water that was being supplied to the people of San Francisco. I know it was largely due to the greed of that water monopoly in its efforts to spend as little as possible to grasp just as much as possible, and I never want to see such a condition again exist in any city.[6]

Help also came from President Roosevelt's cabinet. Even before the earthquake, Gifford Pinchot, head of the United States Forest Service, had expressed sympathy for San Francisco's designs on Hetch Hetchy. After the quake he wrote to the City Engineer, Marsden Manson, that he hoped that the city could "make provision for a water supply from the Yosemite National Park, which will be equal to any in the world. I will stand ready to render any assistance which lies in my power."[7] More help from Washington emerged when Hancock resigned as Secretary of the Interior, to be replaced by James Garfield, who happened to be a good friend of Pinchot. Garfield had never agreed with Hitchcock's preservationist stance on Yosemite National Park, and soon would reverse that decision.

Perhaps at this point we should pause to examine just what this fight was all about. First, Hetch Hetchy, a U-shaped glacial valley, lay within Yosemite National Park. It featured waterfalls, dramatic granite cliffs, and an impressive meadow bisected by the smooth-flowing, gin-clear Tuolumne River. It was, by all accounts, identical in glacial origin with Yosemite Valley, although smaller and not quite as spectacular. Perhaps Josiah Whitney, the famed Harvard geologist, had it right when he pronounced that "if there were no Yosemite, the Hetch Hetchy would be fairly entitled to world-wide fame." Describing the 1,800-foot glacier-carved cliffs and the waterfalls with surprising passion, he noted that "were they anywhere else than in California, they would be considered . . . wonderfully grand."[8]

John Muir visited the valley in 1871 when it was largely untracked and unknown. Alone, he sauntered up and down, east and west, describing cliffs, waterfalls, and various wonders. He seemed to bond with the valley and his rhapsodic prose reflected his infatuation. "Imagine yourself in Hetch Hetchy," wrote Muir. "It is a bright day in June; the air is drowsy with flies; the pines sway dreamily, and you are sunk, shoulder-deep, in grasses and flowers."[9] He exulted in the vertical landscape, the high mountain meadow, the granite, the ancient oaks and pines, and the sparkling waterfalls. Yosemite Valley often claimed his attention and passion, but the Hetch Hetchy Valley, a geological replica, did not suffer Muir's neglect. The valley represented all that he loved, and it would never be far from his thoughts until his death in 1914.

Almost every environmental fight needs a leader who is passionate, eloquent, and committed for the long haul. Muir was. As he aged, however, he turned over much of the responsibility to young William Colby, the energetic secretary of the Sierra Club. Colby devised much of the political "in

Figure 5.1 Looking up Hetch Hetchy Valley from Surprise Point. Photo by Isaiah West Taber. Source: *Sierra Club Bulletin*, 6(4) (January 1908), 211. Photo courtesy of the Sierra Club.

the trenches" strategy that proved so effective in countering San Francisco's desires. Yet without Muir's eloquence there would have been no fight. His passion could not help but win admiration and support, nationwide. Who could not be moved by his fervor? "Dam Hetch Hetchy! As well dam for water-tanks the people's cathedrals and churches, for no holier temple has ever been consecrated by the heart of man."[10] In this impassioned plea, Muir, by a stunning theological comparison, conveyed on the valley not only his ardor but an ethical right to exist.

Contrasting Muir's philosophy with two of his antagonists tells us much about the issue. First let us consider Gifford Pinchot, America's first trained forester as well as President Theodore Roosevelt's close confidant. Pinchot firmly supported San Francisco's claims to the valley, following the Progressive dictum of the "greatest good for the greatest number for the longest time." Yet in 1890 Muir and Pinchot had been good friends, often hiking and camping together. In the Grand Canyon a trifling incident revealed their differing views toward nature. Pinchot recalled that when they "came across a tarantula he wouldn't let me kill it. He said it had as much right there as we did."[11] Muir defended the life of one of the most feared spiders known to man. Pinchot, reflecting his utilitarian approach towards nature, could see no reason why the tarantula should live, and was quite prepared to crush its life away: it had no real benefit to man that he could identify. Muir intervened because of his respect for all life, sentient or not. Every living being had its place in the broad scheme of things, and "lord man" should not needlessly intervene or attempt to divine what that purpose might be. Pinchot was inclined to exert his power through a well-placed boot stomp. Muir urged, indeed demanded, human restraint. If we can substitute a valley for the tarantula, we can understand what was at the heart of their disagreement over Hetch Hetchy.

Muir's other antagonist was the San Francisco Mayor, James Phelan. If one were to characterize the Hetch Hetchy fight through two personalities, Phelan and Muir would be reasonable choices. Phelan was rich, powerful, honest, cultured, committed, and imbued with a sense of noblesse oblige for his city. He realized that San Francisco was ideally located, except for water. Surrounded on three sides by salt water, we can imagine Phelan, with his penchant for poetry, looking out over the hills of his city and reflecting on Samuel Coleridge's "Rime of the Ancient Mariner":

Water, water every where,
And all the boards did shrink;
Water, water, every where
Nor any drop to drink.[12]

Phelan surveyed the city and dreamed of its commercial and cultural success. To realize that dream the city needed fresh water in large quantities. Looking to the Sierra Nevada mountains for a reliable, pure supply of water, he found the Hetch Hetchy Valley with the Tuolumne River flowing through it. It was a perfect reservoir site. The river, if dammed, would supply the city's water needs for at least 100 years. As an added bonus, the proposed dam would provide water storage for a significant hydroelectric plant. In 1900 Phelan made a commitment to bring Hetch Hetchy water to the city, and for the rest of his life (he died in 1930) he fought to fulfill that obligation. Phelan's friend, novelist Gertrude Atherton, remembered "he could talk the hind legs off a donkey, and when he applied himself to win a point he won it."[13] For Muir, Phelan would provide a worthy adversary.

Phelan's instincts were urban, and when he experienced the outdoors, as he often did at his manicured Montalvo estate, his idea of roughing it was to have a barbeque complete with chilled wine, linen, and uniformed servants.[14] In essence, Phelan's compass point in life was anthropocentric: he truly appreciated the creations of human beings. Nature, when present in his life, was a mere backdrop for music, poetry, sculpture, grand architecture, and art. The night before the San Francisco earthquake Phelan enjoyed the performance of Enrique Caruso as Don José in the opera *Carmen*.[15]

That same fateful night John Muir was in the Arizona desert examining deposits of petrified wood.[16] Unlike Phelan, he was never at home in the city. While Muir was comfortable in his well-tended orchards across the bay in Martinez, he was never more at ease than in the pinnacles of the High Sierras. Muir was more biocentric, consumed by geologic formations, and enchanted by flora, birds, trees, mountains, meadows, rushing water, and even petrified wood. California historian Kevin Starr summarized the two men: "For Phelan, California was the splash of baroque fountains in a sun-drenched plaza. For Muir and his fellow Sierra Club members, . . . California was a trek through the High Country."[17]

The two men looked on the Hetch Hetchy Valley through the prism of their beliefs, and what they saw was quite different. From their appositional points of view spring many of the arguments the two sides advanced. At issue was the meaning of progress and whether the United States had reached the point where it might wish to preserve landscapes of special beauty as an expression of American grandeur, even if that might inconvenience material needs. For Phelan that point had not been reached. For him, a great dam symbolized human determination and ingenuity, an edifice that would enhance nature and yet serve the human needs of his city. Muir did not believe that humans could enhance the magnificence of nature, at least not in a mountain sanctuary. In many ways, this debate was the opening salvo of a century's worth of conflict over "the highest and best use" of natural areas.

As previously noted, San Francisco lost the first round of this fight. However, the earthquake and fire ultimately, and somewhat ironically, worked to the city's advantage. In July 1907 the new Secretary of Interior James Garfield traveled to San Francisco to meet with recently elected Mayor Edward Taylor and other city leaders. Garfield encouraged the group to reapply for a permit for use of the Hetch Hetchy Valley as a city reservoir. In early May 1908, the City Engineer, Marsden Manson, formally asked that a permit be issued. Four days later Garfield approved the request. What became known as the "Garfield Grant" represented a significant victory for the city. It encompassed Phelan's efforts and ideas and harmonized with the Progressive social philosophy championed by Gifford Pinchot and President Theodore Roosevelt. With the Garfield Grant in place, bolstered by a socially acceptable philosophy, it seemed that the bulldozers would soon be preparing the valley for its fate.

But not so fast. The small but dedicated group of people constituting the Sierra Club was beginning to stir. Founded in 1892 by Muir and many educated San Francisco Bay Area friends as an outdoor recreation group, the club took a special interest in the California mountains. Leaders had counted on the Department of the Interior to protect the park and Hetch Hetchy from exploitation, but by the summer of 1907 they realized that their trust had been misplaced. With the messianic Muir in the lead, San Francisco's dam intentions suddenly faced determined opposition. Muir had already emerged as a brilliant defender of nature through his scientific publications on the glacial origins of the Yosemite region, but even more by his writing in respected magazines such as *Century*. No one in the nation could write with such passion and eloquence about his mountains, and no one was more committed. Ecological protest requires commitment and often sacrifice. Although close to seventy, Muir was prepared to make that sacrifice. The fact that the Hetch Hetchy Valley lay within the boundaries of Yosemite National Park made it particularly meaningful. Muir and his friend Robert Underwood Johnson, *Century* magazine editor, were largely responsible for creation of the park in 1890, and they were not about to see one of its features become a bathtub for San Francisco without a fight. Therefore, they would defend the sanctity of the new park and the valley.

Between 1907 and 1913 Muir, Johnson, J. Horace McFarland, the Sierra Club, the Appalachian Club, and various other organizations waged a furious fight, challenging the right of any organization, public or private, to infringe on the embryonic national park system. But organizing protest did not come easily. A considerable number of the club's members were San Franciscans. They were torn, many believing that a reliable water supply for their city superseded the sanctity of the national park. Such a person was Warren Olney, a founder of the club, an avid mountaineer, and a great admirer and friend of Muir. However, Olney had moved to the East Bay and now served as mayor of Oakland. From that perspective the line between public good and national park protection became blurred. He struggled. Reluctantly, he stepped across the line to the San Francisco side. In the years to follow he would argue consistently for San Francisco. But this was not without personal anguish, bordering on a Greek tragedy. Later his daughter revealed that after twenty years of pioneering service and close friendships his resignation from the club was a bitter pill. So bitter, she recalled, that "the Hetch Hetchy project was never afterward a permissible topic of conversation in our household."[18]

Olney's dilemma was not unique. Many within the club were ambivalent, so much so that as a political lobbying group the club was ineffective. The Sierra Club spent too much time and energy fighting within itself. Given the situation, in December 1909, Secretary William Colby called for a special Hetch Hetchy election. The result was that 589 members supported Muir and the Board of Directors, while only 161 opposed. The club melted away with resignations, but although smaller in number it was more committed in cause. It could now speak with one voice in its opposition to San Francisco's water development plan.

But the Sierra Club was largely a regional group confined to California. This fact was noted by Edmund Whitman, a Boston attorney dedicated to saving the valley. Whitman suggested that Hetch Hetchy needed a national voice. Muir concurred. By April of 1909 William Colby created, largely through his own initiative, the Society for the Preservation of National Parks. Muir served as president, but the Advisory Council revealed that Hetch Hetchy was going national. Members such as Allen Chamberlain of Boston, Asahel Curtis of Seattle, Harriet Monroe of Chicago, J. Horace McFarland of New York, John Noble of St. Louis, and C. H. Sholes of Portland gave an indication of the geographical diversity of the council. Contrary to some advisory councils, these members were all active. They gave of their time and talent, and on occasion their money.[19]

In contesting San Francisco's plans and the Garfield Grant, the Society for the Preservation of National Parks initiated a pamphlet campaign. The Society issued the first one, titled "Let Everyone Help to Save the Famous Hetch Hetchy Valley and Stop the Commercial Destruction Which Threatens Our National Parks," in November 1909.[20] It was widely distributed, particularly in the halls of Congress. It contained quotations from newspapers and magazines, photographs of the valley, and some of Muir's most powerful "sermons" stressing the folly of San Francisco's scheme. In the next three years the Society sponsored at least three more tracts, thousands of which were distributed throughout the nation. An isolated valley became better known.

In the meantime the Hetch Hetchy Valley issue had moved into the House Committee on the Public Lands, and shortly thereafter, the Senate Committee on the Public Lands. In both appearances the "nature lovers" came out well, and San Francisco emerged rather battered. In the Senate eloquent testimony came from Harriet Monroe, the Chicago poet and founder of *Poetry* magazine. She spoke of her camping visit to Hetch Hetchy, calling it a garden of paradise, unequaled elsewhere in America. The Bostonian Edmund Whitman had also spent time in the valley, but he particularly praised the magnificent twenty-mile Grand Canyon of the Tuolumne River. He envisioned building a scenic road so that others might enjoy the canyon, an idea that would horrify Sierra Club members today.

San Francisco's engineers and statisticians seemed quite ineffective when confronted with the eloquence of the nature lovers. It appeared that the engineers with their slide rules and cost–benefit analyses were being outmaneuvered by a bunch of seemingly useless visionaries. The hydrologists believed that such people who gazed at stars, reflected on running water, or described the effervescent world of a water ouzel could be easily swept aside by hard science and utilitarian thinkers. These defenders of Hetch Hetchy, like Henry Thoreau, eschewed the supposedly real world of business and making a living, preferring to spend their days in baffling ways. In the engineers' eyes these people were welcome to waste their time, but they should not be permitted to enter into a debate on or even comment on the practical water and power needs of cities and societies. Yet the congressmen were listening to such testimony, and it was evident that those who argued with emotion won the day. A reporter for the *San Francisco Call* wired home that Congress had turned to "a lot of talk about 'babbling brooks' and crystal pools." Nothing much could be done until "the New England nature lovers exhaust their vocabularies."[21]

The political world of Washington only turned worse for San Francisco's interests. In March 1909 William Howard Taft assumed the presidency of the United States. San Francisco's sympathetic triumvirate of Roosevelt, Pinchot, and Garfield was gone, replaced by Taft and his new Secretary of the Interior, Richard Ballinger. To make matters worse, in October 1909 President Taft requested that Muir guide him on a visit to Yosemite Valley. We can be assured the new president was briefed on the Hetch Hetchy situation. Taft was so charmed by Muir that he asked that the famed naturalist accompany Secretary Ballinger on a visit to the Hetch Hetchy Valley, then only accessible by a nine-mile trail.

We know little of what transpired on the Muir–Ballinger visit to Hetch Hetchy, but Muir was optimistic, writing to Colby that "all seems coming our way, and the silly thieves and robbers seem at the end of their scheme."[22] Muir's analysis proved correct, and by the end of February 1910, Secretary

Ballinger ordered San Francisco to "show cause" why the Hetch Hetchy Valley should not be deleted from the Garfield Grant. The city would have to provide conclusive proof that it needed the valley—not an easy task. For the valley defenders the Ballinger order was the high point and as the historian Holway Jones noted, "it appeared that the fight was won and that nothing . . . could stem the tide of victory."[23]

Once more the momentum had swung, this time to those who wished to protect the valley from San Francisco, reserving it for tourists and future generations. However, San Francisco confounded the valley defenders by deciding it could and would "show cause" why it must have the controversial valley. Instead of exploring other water alternatives, the city contracted with John Freeman to redesign the project and show that other alternative sources were simply not adequate. Freeman, headquartered in Providence, Rhode Island, was the top civil engineer in the country, commanding a $200 a day fee. To carry out Freeman's ambitious plans, San Francisco hired Michael O'Shaughnessy, a very able civil engineer who would become the builder of the Hetch Hetchy system. Freeman and his staff produced a massive 400-page study to show the photographic beauty of reservoirs, and also to demonstrate the folly of any alternative water source.[24] San Francisco distributed copies of this lavishly illustrated tome to every member of Congress.

Other reports were produced, and it became the Board of Army Engineers' job to make sense of them and then advise Secretary Ballinger. Everyone acknowledged that these professional engineers knew how to deal with questions of natural resources. They made decisions by the force of their calculations and their facts, which few could dispute. Even the valley defenders were willing to defer to their expertise. When the board finally recommended the Hetch Hetchy site, the nature lovers were disappointed, but they should not have been surprised. The board was not truly objective: it gave no weight to national park status, scenic value, and tourist use—the very issues on which the Sierra Club based its case. A body of engineers was ill-equipped to answer questions regarding the growing importance of the national parks and the direction of American culture regarding leisure time, outdoor recreation, and a need to escape the burgeoning cities.

Given the board's obsession with cost and water quantity, the result was no surprise. However, the final outcome was. On an unrelated issue, Forester Gifford Pinchot accused Secretary Richard Ballinger of corruption regarding the granting of coal leases in Alaska. The controversy received much publicity, and finally President Taft fired Pinchot in January 1910. Ballinger, under heavy pressure, resigned a year later. The new Secretary of the Interior, Walter Fisher, now inherited the whole Hetch Hetchy mess. Wrestling with the issue, he decided he did not have the legal authority to make a decision.

Fisher believed that his predecessor interior secretaries had overstepped their authority in the matter. Recourse for San Francisco, he argued, must come from the Congress of the United States. It was a strange decision, perhaps motivated by Fisher's ambivalence. Earlier, in 1907, Secretary William Garfield had sought out and received the United States Attorney General's opinion that he did have authority to grant San Francisco the valley. But legal interpretations can, and did, change with political administrations.

The last chapter in the long struggle took place in early 1913. Both the House and Senate staged lengthy debates. What was the nature of the new national park system? Should the lands designated by Congress as parks be given protection from invasion? Should public and private interests profit from the parks? A multitude of issues emerged but much of the congressional debates focused on farmers' water rights. The Modesto and Turlock irrigation districts had senior water rights on the Tuolumne River, and San Francisco reluctantly had to acknowledge those rights. Another issue complicating this debate was the growing fight between public and private power. Young Senator George Norris of Nebraska cared little about the water issue. He believed that the benefits of Hetch Hetchy flowed less from water and more from electricity.[25] Who would control this hydroelectricity? Would it be the City of San Francisco or the newly created private power company, Pacific Gas and Electric (PG&E)? Norris was convinced that Muir and the Sierra Club were mere pawns to the Pacific Gas and Electric Company. He, and a number of other legislators, felt that if Congress denied San Francisco the valley, private power would soon snatch it up. The environmentalists never could shake accusations that their efforts supported the power companies. It was a major reason why they lost.

The power controversy gives added meaning to the Hetch Hetchy fight, for it was the opening debate of the public-versus-private power conflicts that would dominate the world of electricity for half a century. For San Francisco, the provision in the Raker Act (Section 6) that prohibited the city from ever selling power to a private utility caused thirty years of controversy, culminating in Secretary of the Interior Harold Ickes taking the city all the way to the Supreme Court of the United States.[26] Ickes won, but still today PG&E serves the city and periodically the wrath of public power advocates rains down on city leaders.

With the passage of the Raker Act in December 1913, the alliance of environmental groups lost the fight. Perhaps more than anything it was a victory of perceived human needs over nature's rights. There were charges of elitism: that the valley defenders cared more for pristine nature and, indeed, would sacrifice the legitimate needs of the masses of humanity. Senator Marcus Smith rose on the Senate floor to declare that "we all love the sound of whispering winds amid the trees, but the wail of a hungry baby will make us forget it for the while. . . . You lovers of nature," he continued, "will do well to give less attention to nature's beauties and more sympathy to the wants of men. Love nature all you please, but do not forget its crowning glory—man."[27] But even without Senator Smith's eloquence, the fate of Hetch Hetchy Valley was sealed when President Woodrow Wilson appointed Franklin K. Lane as Secretary of the Interior. A past San Francisco Attorney General, Lane had long advocated San Francisco's desires. It was a serendipitous appointment, for Wilson cared little about public land issues or conservation concerns. Once in power, Lane used his office to see that the Raker Act passed, and when it reached the president's desk, Wilson signed it into law without hesitation.

From the perspective of approximately 100 years, it is quite remarkable that this fight occurred at all. For the first time in American history, two competing visions of nature clashed at Hetch Hetchy, as the valley became a symbol of aesthetic and spiritual values challenging immediate, material ones. Congress vigorously debated the matter. To many Americans these arguments over an obscure valley were baffling. During the debate, Senator James A. Reed of Missouri expressed incredulity that the Senate went "into profound debate [and] the country is thrown into a condition of hysteria" over a valley that no one had heard of, let alone visited. Furthermore, he wondered, how come "when we get as far east as New England the opposition has become a frenzy." Clearly Hetch Hetchy had become a lightning rod for conflicts between use and non-use, between development and scenic appreciation, and ultimately between practical needs and nature tourism. Should progress be measured solely by technological advance, often won at the expense of nature? For a small but growing number, the answer was no. To their minds, the ascendancy of technology and materialism symbolized American civilization gone wrong. It was time to listen to the earnest voices of "nature lovers" such as Muir, whose values perhaps reflected the future, rather than only to the hydraulic engineers with their charts and benefit projections.

Historians have often portrayed the Hetch Hetchy struggle as a fight between wilderness and development.[28] The nature lovers, however, did not ignore economic arguments. Nevertheless, although the valley was nine miles from the nearest wagon road, no one favored continued wilderness. In fact, Muir, the Sierra Club, members of the Adirondack Club, and many others advocated for a road that would open the valley to tourism. Once in the valley visitors would find hotels, cabins, restaurants, trails, and a whole infrastructure to support thousands of people.[29] Using the success of Switzerland as an example, Colby and Muir argued that in time the tourism worth of the Hetch Hetchy Valley would exceed the value of San Francisco's water and power. They pointed out that San Francisco's gain would be California's loss. These arguments, important as they were, could not save the valley from San Francisco's perceived immediate needs.

In arguing as they did, John Muir and the Sierra Club did not ignore San Francisco's water needs, but suggested, indeed insisted, that there were other Sierra Nevada sites outside of the national park that could serve the city equally well. Muir and the defenders' argument proved prophetic when, in the 1920s, the cities of Oakland, Berkeley, and Richmond developed their own water supply from the Mokelumne River (one of San Francisco's options) at much less cost, no environmental fight, and without the invasion of a national park.

Reflecting on the long Hetch Hetchy fight, its significance cannot be denied. It was the first time in the nation's history that Americans made a concerted effort to stop what the majority of people considered progress. Before it was done, the fight involved Presidents Theodore Roosevelt, William Howard Taft, and Woodrow Wilson, as well as five Secretaries of the Interior, two national foresters, and three San Francisco mayors. It was the seminal environmental fight, attracting the attention of the nation, becoming a model and a rallying cry for numerous battles over land use in the past century and continuing into this one.

The city emerged triumphant on the political front, but now it would have to take on the daunting task of building a dam and aqueduct system deep in the Sierra Nevada mountains. Construction would not be easy. First the city built a rough road into the valley. But to transport all the workers, materials, and equipment necessary to do the job, the city constructed and operated the sixty-seven-mile Hetch Hetchy Railway. In 1918 San Francisco began construction of the massive O'Shaughnessy Dam, completing the effort in 1923. By 1938 engineers had raised the dam to its present height, inundating the valley under many fathoms of water. The Hetch Hetchy system now provides San Francisco and thirty towns in the Bay Area with abundant, clean water.[30]

As we look back on the Hetch Hetchy fight, we must ask whether San Francisco should have fought for possession of the valley, and then made it the centerpiece of its complex water and power system. For many the answer was no. The constructed system was so immense that for fifty years it produced more water than the city and neighboring towns could consume. The tremendous cost of building a water system made it difficult for the city to establish a municipal power system. Although the Raker Act of 1913 clearly anticipated that San Francisco should have the benefit of public power, the city lacked the financial resources to purchase the Pacific Gas and Electric Company infrastructure. Today, as earlier mentioned, San Franciscans are served still by the PG&E. But beyond the expense, San Francisco politicians and engineers ignored viable alternatives to Hetch Hetchy. Three, possibly more, alternatives could have served that city's water requirements, sparing both expense and Yosemite National Park. The leaders of San Francisco stubbornly insisted on forging ahead with its overly ambitious plan.[31]

In regard to the national parks, the controversy left a significant legacy. Hetch Hetchy provided an example of what should not happen in a national park: scenic lands should not be sacrificed for a water and power supply. One way to assure there would be no repeat was the creation of an agency exclusively dedicated to administering and protecting the parks. The National Park Service Act of 1916 created that agency and its mission. In large measure the people involved with Hetch Hetchy were the same men and women who fashioned and fought for the creation of the National Park Service. The connection between the Hetch Hetchy fight and the establishment of the National Park Service is indisputable. Such leaders as Horace McFarland, Frederick Law Olmsted Jr., Stephen Mather, and William Kent were determined that there should not be a repeat of Hetch Hetchy. In the years to follow there have been numerous attempts by the Bureau of Reclamation, the Army Corps of Engineers, and irrigation interests to invade the national parks, but they have been turned aside, often with the example of Hetch Hetchy. When Idaho and Montana farmers attempted to place two dams in Yellowstone National Park in 1920 for irrigation purposes, *The Outlook*'s editor, Lyman Abbott, broke the story with an editorial headlined "Another Hetch Hetchy."[32] Having established the context, Abbott did not even mention Hetch Hetchy in his story. A mere reference to the battle was enough to warn his readers of another invasion. Lyman Abbott and others, some of them veterans of Hetch Hetchy, succeeded in defeating the threat to Yellowstone.

In the early 1950s a significant threat emerged to the national park system with the Bureau of Reclamation's proposed Echo Park dam in Dinosaur National Monument. With its legacy of Hetch Hetchy the Sierra Club led the fight to save Echo Park. David Brower championed the Sierra Club forces, and he often invoked the names of John Muir and Hetch Hetchy in his confrontations with the engineers of the Bureau of Reclamation. Testifying before a Senate subcommittee Brower asserted that "if we heed the lesson learned from the tragedy of the misplaced dam in Hetch Hetchy, we can prevent a far more disastrous stumble in Dinosaur National Monument." By 1956 the Bureau of Reclamation abandoned its plans, and the memory of Hetch Hetchy had much to do with it.[33] In early 1914 a despondent John Muir had predicted that some good would come from the loss of Hetch Hetchy, and indeed it did.

The Echo Park struggle was as much the beginning as the end of dam controversies on the Colorado River. In his effort to save Echo Park, Brower tacitly consented to the sacrifice of Glen Canyon. As workers raised the great dam, Brower regretted his action. When in the early 1960s the Bureau proposed two more dams on the Colorado, Brower girded for action. Supporting the Bureau was Secretary of the Interior Stewart Udall. Beholden to his state of Arizona, the secretary was considered an environmentalist, and had even written a popular environmental history, titled *The Quiet Crisis*. In his book Udall noted that the Hetch Hetchy Valley "was flooded out, but those who had fought a losing fight for the principles of park preservation served notice on the country that its outdoor temples would be defended with blood and bone."[34] Of course, the lessons of history, even when one writes them, do not always influence action. Udall remained committed to the Marble Canyon and the Bridge Canyon dams. However, neither Udall nor his Director of the Bureau of Reclamation, Floyd Dominy, could overcome those who fought with "blood and bone." Brower organized and publicized his way to victory, motivated by the memory of Hetch Hetchy.

Less tangible, but no less significant, there has been a growing appreciation by Americans for national parks and grand scenery. Americans realized that nature is finite, and once lost, cannot be easily replaced. The Hetch Hetchy fight has lost little of its symbolic importance in almost a century. It constantly reminds many Americans that the sanctity of our national parks and scenic lands must be defended. There will always be those who can find sufficient reason for invasion of a park or monument. Yet, because of the memory of the Hetch Hetchy loss, such inroads will not be easy, and in most cases, will be impossible.

In recent years the Hetch Hetchy fight has entered a new phase. In 1987 President Reagan's Secretary of the Interior, Donald Hodel, posed a dramatic question. Why not consider the removal of the O'Shaughnessy Dam and the restoration of the Hetch Hetchy Valley? It was a shocking idea, and one that no knowledgeable or responsible person had considered. Even David Brower admitted that after the construction of the O'Shaughnessy dam, he "just gave up." Now a responsible government official had suggested studying the idea of removal, thus creating "a second Yosemite Valley." The San Francisco Mayor, Diane Feinstein, reacted strongly, labeling Hodel's suggestion "the worst thing since the sale of arms to the ayatollah [Khomeini]." David Brower led those who lauded the secretary's suggestion as a move that would "correct the biggest environmental mistake ever committed against the National Park System." Many, of course, speculated on the motives of Reagan's interior secretary, who lacked strong credentials within the environmental community.[35] Yet, twenty years later, Hodel is a strong supporter of restoration, and there is every indication that his "epiphany" was based on his love of nature and his belief in the national park system.

After all the talking and posturing was done, two studies resulted. The California state legislature authorized $100,000 for the state Department of Water Resources to estimate the economic and environmental impacts of tearing down the dam. The Department of the Interior carried out its own study, entitled "Hetch Hetchy: A Survey of Water & Power Replacement Concepts." The California study focused on the difficulties and issues involved with the physical restoration of the valley. The Interior Department study examined the possibility of water and power replacement, should the decision be made to remove the dam. Neither study claimed to be comprehensive, and Hodel and other leaders recognized that a feasibility study, authorized by Congress, would be necessary before any decision could be made. The California Department of Water Resources study nicely summarized the issue, concluding that both sides were right, but one side was just a little more right than the other:

> John Muir was right: the Hetch Hetchy Valley was gorgeous and would have provided incredible recreational opportunities. San Francisco was also right: the Hetch Hetchy Valley would make an exceptional municipal reservoir site. In 1913, Congress decided that San Francisco was "more" right and the Hetch Hetchy Dam was allowed. For the people of the 1980s, the issue of restoring Hetch Hetchy involves trade-offs between several very important public needs: recreation, aesthetics, high quality drinking water supplies, hydroelectric energy, and cost. We conclude that the existing Hetch Hetchy system is more valuable to society than a restored Hetch Hetchy.[36]

Secretary Hodel had planted a seed, but maturation was not yet possible. The George H. W. Bush presidency (1989–93), with Manuel Luhan presiding as interior secretary, had no interest in pursuing Hodel's pet project. Furthermore, the Sierra Club gave Hodel little support. The restoration idea died of neglect. However, there were a few people who considered the issue only moribund. By the 1990s more and more environmentalists questioned the feasibility of old dams, and removal and restoration became less a foolish idea and more an attractive alternative. In October 2000, a few members of the Sierra Club, bolstered by Hodel's vision and Brower's enthusiasm, formed "Restore Hetch Hetchy." The group is committed to a "win–win" solution in which the great dam is removed and the valley restored, yet San Francisco will receive replacement water and power.[37] The City of San Francisco has chosen to ignore "Restore Hetch Hetchy" and continues to laud its system and spend many millions of dollars on its maintenance and improvement. During the first decade of the twenty-first century, however, the idea of restoration of natural areas has gained in popularity, and the submerged Hetch Hetchy Valley will continue as a touchstone, reflecting the needs of San Francisco, but also acting as a barometer of the nation's environmental attitudes.

Notes

1   Michael M. O'Shaughnessy, *Hetch Hetchy: Its Origin and History* (San Francisco: privately printed, 1934), 52.

2   "O'Shaughnessy Dam Dedication," *Municipal Record* 16 (19 July 1923), in SF City Engineer, 92/808 C, carton 4, folder "O'Shaughnessy Dam Dedication scrapbook," Bancroft Library, University of California, Berkeley.

3   For material on today's fight, see www.RestoreHetchHetchy.com.

4   See "A Brief in the Matter of Reservoir Rights of Way for a Domestic and Municipal Water Supply . . . " (27 July 1907), 2, 4–5, in *Reports on the Water Supply of San Francisco, 1900–1908*, Board of Supervisors, 1908, in San Francisco Room, San Francisco Public Library.

5   Secretary Hitchcock to President Roosevelt, 20 February 1905, ibid., 7, 21, 31.

6   *Congressional Record*, 63rd Cong., 1st Sess., 3 October 1913, 6041.

7   Gifford Pinchot to Marsden Manson, 28 May 1906, in *Reports on the Water Supply of San Francisco, 1900–1908*, Board of Supervisors, 1908, in San Francisco Room, San Francisco Public Library.

8   Josiah Dwight Whitney, *Yosemite Guide-Book: A Description of the Yosemite Valley and the Adjacent Regions of the Sierra Nevada, and the Big Trees of California* (published by authority of the California State Legislature, 1869), 111–13.

9   John Muir, "Hetch Hetchy Valley," *Overland Monthly*, 11 (July 1873), 46.

10 John Muir, *The Yosemite* (New York: Modern Library, 2003 ed.), 262.

11 Gifford Pinchot, *Breaking New Ground* (Seattle: University of Washington Press, 1972 ed.), 103.

12 Samuel Taylor Coleridge, "Rime of the Ancient Mariner" (1797), Part 2.

13 Quoted in Emily Wortis Leider, *California's Daughter: Gertrude Atherton and Her Times* (Palo Alto, CA: Stanford University Press, 1991), 257.

14 James P. Walsh and Timothy J. O'Keefe, *Legacy of a Native Son: James Duval Phelan and Villa Montalvo* (Saratoga, CA: Forbes Mill Press, 1993), 120.

15 James Phelan to Mabelle Gilman, 8 May 1906, in James Phelan Papers, 1880–1930, MSS C-B 800, box 1, Bancroft Library, University of California, Berkeley.

16 Wanda Muir to John Muir, Alameda, AZ, 10 April 1906, in John Muir Papers, Microfilm, Reel 16, 1906–7.

17 Kevin Starr, *Endangered Dreams: The Great Depression in California* (New York: Oxford University Press, 1996), 279.

18 "Sierra Club Beginnings," n.d., printed article by Ethel Olney Easton, with "Recollections of John Muir," typescript, no. 134, Regional Oral History Office, University of California.

19 Holway R. Jones, *John Muir and the Sierra Club: The Battle for Yosemite* (San Francisco: Sierra Club, 1965), 47–49.

20 An original pamphlet is in the DeGolyer Library, Southern Methodist University. Few of the pamphlets have survived.

21 *San Francisco Call*, 11 February 1909.

22 Muir to William Colby, 21 October 1909, in John Muir Papers, Microfilm, Reel 18, 1909.

23 Jones, *John Muir and the Sierra Club*, 123.

24 *The Hetch Hetchy Water System for San Francisco*, 1912 report by John R. Freeman (San Francisco: Rincon Publishing Company for the Board of Supervisors, 1912). I was so impressed with the size and weight of the report that I asked David Farmer, former director of Southern Methodist University's DeGolyer Library, if he might weigh the volume. He took it to the adjacent post office and on his returned announced: five pounds, eight ounces.

25 See George Norris, *Fighting Liberal: The Autobiography of George W. Norris* (New York: Macmillan, 1945).

26 *U.S. v. City and County of San Francisco, 1940*, 587 U.S., 7, 11 (1940).

27 *Congressional Record*, 63rd Cong., 2nd Sess., Vol. 51 (December 5, 1913), 274.

28 The "wilderness versus development" thesis was advanced by Roderick Nash in his well known book *Wilderness and the American Mind*, first published in 1965 by the Yale University Press. A number of environmental historians have accepted this thesis, but the evidence does not support it.

29 The best statement of what the defenders wanted is William Colby's brief in response to the Freeman Report. Relevant portions can be found in Jones, *John Muir and the Sierra Club*, and Robert W. Righter, *The Battle over Hetch Hetchy: America's Most Controversial Dam and the Birth of Modern Environmentalism* (New York: Oxford University Press, 2005).

30 See Righter, *The Battle over Hetch Hetchy*, 134–66.

31 Ibid., 167–90.

32 "Another Hetch Hetchy," *The Outlook*, 7 July 1920, 448.

33 See David Brower, *For Earth's Sake: The Life and Times of David Brower* (Salt Lake City: Peregrine Smith Books, 1990). For the Echo Park story, see Mark W. T. Harvey, *A Symbol of Wilderness: Echo Park and the American Conservation Movement* (Seattle: University of Washington Press, 2000); for the Glen Canyon story see Jared Farmer, *Glen Canyon Dammed: Inventing Lake Powell and the Canyon Country* (Tucson: University of Arizona Press, 1999); and for the Marble and Bridge Canyons dam fights see Byron E. Pearson, *Still the Wild River Runs: Congress, the Sierra Club, and the Fight to Save Grand Canyon* (Tucson: University of Arizona Press, 2002).

34 Stewart Udall, *The Quiet Crisis* (New York: Holt, Rinehart and Winston, 1963), 343–44.

35 Righter, *The Battle over Hetch Hetchy, 216–241.*

36 California State Legislature, Assembly Office of Research, *Restoring Hetch Hetchy* (1988), 40–41.

37 For current information as well as historical materials and photographs, see www. restorehetchhetchy.org.

CHAPTER 6

Rethinking Reclamation

How an Alliance of Duck Hunters and
Cattle Ranchers Brought Wetland Conservation
to California's Central Valley Project

PHILIP GARONE

Between the 1780s and the 1980s, the United States, exclusive of Alaska and Hawaii, lost more than half of its original inheritance of over 220 million acres of wetlands.[1] Although definitions of wetlands vary, they are distinguished by three main components: the presence of water, soil conditions that often differ from adjacent uplands, and the presence of vegetation adapted to wet conditions.[2] In addition to providing habitat for migratory waterfowl and a wide variety of other wetland-dependent animals and plants, wetlands provide immense ecological benefits, including the recharge of aquifers, the absorption and storage of floodwaters, and the improvement of water quality. Most of the wetlands lost in the United States were "reclaimed," drained and converted to agricultural use. In the seventeen western states, including California, much of this transformation has been orchestrated by the U.S. Bureau of Reclamation, an agency created within the U.S. Department of the Interior by the Reclamation Act of 1902.[3] Operating under the mandate of the Reclamation Act, which was intended to open up the West for agricultural settlement, the Bureau has constructed reclamation projects that include dams, reservoirs, power plants, and irrigation canals, and that have brought millions of acres into cultivation, but often at considerable ecological cost. Because of their environmental consequences, many of these projects were— and remain—controversial.

The Bureau of Reclamation did not prioritize wildlife in its early projects, some of which reclaimed parts of national wildlife refuges. President Theodore Roosevelt created the Lower Klamath Wildlife Refuge, on the California–Oregon border, in 1908 as one of the first national wildlife refuges established primarily for the benefit of migratory waterfowl. Yet in 1917 the Bureau drained Lower Klamath Lake to create agricultural land, drastically reducing the refuge's wetland habitat, increasing mortality rates for waterfowl, and initiating decades of controversy in the Klamath Basin between wildlife advocates and the federal government that continued into the twenty-first century.[4] Other Bureau projects threatened to drown, rather than drain, wilderness areas. During the post-World War II era, the Bureau of Reclamation initiated an unprecedented era of dam-building intended to provide irrigation water and hydroelectric power but that also threatened to flood wilderness areas throughout the West. In the early 1950s, opposition from the Sierra Club, the Wilderness Society, and a concerned public prevented the Bureau from constructing Echo Park Dam on the Green River in Colorado's Dinosaur National Monument, the first major dam project to be halted in the postwar era.[5] Preservation of Dinosaur National Monument was indeed a seminal victory for the advocates of wilderness preservation and marks a major chapter in the history of American environmentalism. But the fight to protect public lands from the consequences of reclamation projects is but one strand of American environmentalism. At approximately the same time that wilderness advocates were challenging the Bureau's plans to flood *public* lands in Colorado's Echo Park Valley, a different kind of coalition was challenging the Bureau's plans to terminate water supplies to *private* lands in California, the most important block of wetlands remaining in the Central Valley.

Once replete with at least 4 million acres of permanent and seasonal wetlands, California's Great Central Valley is of particular importance to the migratory waterfowl of the Pacific Flyway, one of the four north–south bird routes that span North America from the arctic to the tropics. Pacific Flyway waterfowl populations fluctuate annually, but have averaged over 6.6 million since accurate counts began in 1955.[6] This number, though impressive, represents only a fraction of the estimated tens of millions of birds that filled nineteenth-century skies before much of their wetland habitat was lost. The 400-mile-long Central Valley, lying between California's Coast Ranges to the west and the towering mountains of the Sierra Nevada to the east, comprises two smaller valleys, the Sacramento Valley in the north and the San Joaquin

Valley in the south. It is drained by rivers of those same names, whose confluence near the center of the valley forms the Sacramento–San Joaquin Delta,
an inland estuary that extends westward to San Francisco Bay (Figure 6.1). As
they have done for millennia, several million ducks and geese, representing
approximately 60 percent of the entire waterfowl population of the Flyway,
as well as hundreds of thousands of shorebirds and other wetland-dependent
birds spend their winters in the relative warmth of the Central Valley, where
temperatures rarely fall below freezing.[7]

The loss of Central Valley wetlands began shortly after California state-
hood in 1850. Over the next century, reclamation for agriculture, by local,

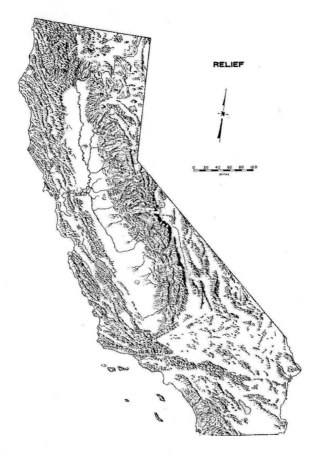

Figure 6.1 Relief map of California. Occupying the center of the state, the Central Valley
is drained by the Sacramento River in the north and the San Joaquin River in the south.
The rivers join near the center of the valley to form the Sacramento–San Joaquin Delta.
Source: Warren A. Beck and Ynez D. Haase, *Historical Atlas of California* (Norman:
University of Oklahoma Press, 1974).

regional, state, and federal projects led to the destruction of over 90 percent of the Central Valley's wetlands, reducing the total to less than 400,000 acres.[8] By the mid-twentieth century, the single most important block of remaining wetlands in the Central Valley encompassed approximately 100,000 acres in the lower San Joaquin Valley, in a region known locally as the "Grasslands."[9] When those wetlands were threatened by California's most massive reclamation and irrigation enterprise, the Central Valley Project, constructed and operated by the Bureau of Reclamation, an unlikely coalition of duck hunters and cattle ranchers launched a fifteen-year struggle, the first episode in a multigenerational saga, to save the Grasslands. By calling nationwide attention to the seminal place of the Grassland wetlands in the life cycle of the migratory waterfowl of the Pacific Flyway, the duck hunters and cattle ranchers of the Grasslands not only successfully protected the wetlands from destruction, but also caused the Central Valley Project to take into account for the first time its effects on fish and wildlife. The efforts of this small but committed group of individuals served as a harbinger of changing societal values about wetlands, helped to halt the unparalleled loss of wetlands in California, and set the stage for future conservation and restoration efforts that ultimately led to international recognition of the importance of the Grassland wetlands for the protection of biodiversity.[10] Their story is therefore as integral a part of American environmental history as the stories of those who fought to preserve wilderness areas.

Historically, the Grasslands have provided a freshwater haven for both migratory and resident waterfowl. Swollen by winter rains and spring snowmelt, the San Joaquin River cyclically renewed the Grassland wetlands as it overtopped its banks and flooded the low-lying Grasslands, located to the west of the river.[11] This natural seasonal pattern was first altered during the nineteenth century by the enterprises of Henry Miller and Charles Lux. These self-made "cattle kings" were the largest and most influential landowners in the San Joaquin Valley during the second half of the nineteenth century. By 1881, under the auspices of the Swamp and Overflowed Lands Act of 1850 and other provisions for the sale of public land, Miller and Lux had accumulated holdings in the vicinity of the Grasslands that extended for sixty-eight contiguous miles along the west side of the San Joaquin River, and were from five to forty miles wide.[12] While continuing to take advantage of natural winter and spring flooding, Miller and Lux introduced the practice of fall flood irrigation by diverting part of the flow of the San Joaquin River onto the Grasslands. This activity nurtured winter grasses for their cattle and, at the same time, attracted millions of migratory waterfowl arriving from the north.[13]

For as long as Miller and Lux held on to their Grassland properties, the region remained a land of flood-irrigated pastures and thousands of cattle that grazed on them, of seasonal lakes and ponds and millions of ducks and geese that wintered on them, and of waterfowl hunters who leased shooting privileges on them. Only after 1926, with both partners dead and the firm sinking toward bankruptcy, did Miller and Lux, Inc., begin to divide its land into small parcels for sale to duck clubs and cattle ranchers. The firm expressly marketed its land as a waterfowl hunter's paradise, and, in its land sale pamphlets, made clear the connection between organized duck hunting and cattle raising that had come to define the Grasslands region.[14] The new owners of these Grassland properties coexisted symbiotically; the cattlemen leased shooting privileges to the duck clubs, and the duck clubs leased grazing privileges to the cattlemen. In years when sufficient water was available, they continued the practice of fall flood irrigation, maintaining the annual cycle that made the Grasslands a haven for waterfowl from early fall through spring.

The annual flooding of the Grasslands, by human enterprise and by natural overflow, might have continued indefinitely, except for one fateful provision. In almost every purchase deed, Miller and Lux, Inc., had retained title to their water rights, reserving the right to use their water on the lands "until such time as it could be diverted to other lands of higher agricultural productivity or disposed of otherwise."[15] That time soon came to pass. After decades of planning, California's Central Valley Project was poised to become a reality by the late 1930s. Originally conceived by the State to divert water from the relatively well-watered Sacramento Valley, across the Sacramento–San Joaquin Delta, to the more arid San Joaquin Valley, the Project was taken over by the federal government in 1935 and reauthorized two years later for construction by the U.S. Bureau of Reclamation.[16]

Of great consequence to the Grasslands, one component of the Central Valley Project called for construction of a dam and reservoir on the San Joaquin River at Friant, close to where the river emerges from the Sierra Nevada onto the eastern edge of the San Joaquin Valley floor. Most of the river flow would be diverted north and south from the reservoir, via the 37-mile-long Madera Canal and the 153-mile-long Friant–Kern Canal, respectively, to develop and support agriculture on the fertile soils on the east side of the valley (Figure 6.2). With its flow diverted, the river below Friant Dam would essentially run dry, cutting off water supplies to downstream lands, including those of the non-agricultural Grasslands, located more than sixty miles downriver. Before the Bureau of Reclamation could begin construction of Friant Dam, however, it needed to acquire the water rights of the downstream landowners.

Figure 6.2 Friant Dam on the San Joaquin River, with Lake Millerton beyond. The Madera Canal is in the upper left, and the Friant–Kern Canal is in the right foreground, dwarfing the trickle of the river that remains below the dam. Source: U.S. Bureau of Reclamation.

On 27 July 1939, the firm of Miller and Lux entered into a Purchase Contract with the U.S. Bureau of Reclamation by which it received $2,450,000 for its water rights to more than a quarter million acres of land in the lower San Joaquin Valley, including 98,234 acres of the Grasslands that it had sold to duck clubs and cattle ranchers. By an Exchange Contract of the same date, the Bureau agreed to provide substitute water to a portion of the lands that had lost their water rights in the sale, to be drawn from the Sacramento–San Joaquin Delta and transported to the lower San Joaquin Valley by a feature of the Central Valley Project, the Delta–Mendota Canal, yet to be constructed (see Figure 6.3). This substitute water would be delivered only to those higher-value lands that were either croplands or "controlled" grasslands, irrigated pastures maintained by developed sloughs and canals.[17] The 98,234 acres of the Grasslands were neither. The poorly drained, saline and alkali soils of the Grasslands were not well suited for agriculture and were "uncontrolled" grasslands, subject to the natural seasonal overflow of the San Joaquin River.[18] Although Miller and Lux, Inc., agreed to continue to provide free water until 1944, the year in which the San Joaquin River would first be impounded behind Friant Dam, the duck clubs and cattle companies of the Grasslands now faced the impending loss of their water supply.

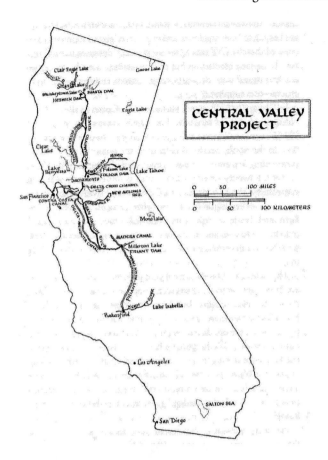

Figure 6.3 The main features of the Central Valley Project. Note especially the locations of the Friant–Kern Canal and Madera Canal, and of the Delta–Mendota Canal, which delivers "substitute" water from the Sacramento–San Joaquin Delta to the lower San Joaquin Valley. Source: Norris Hundley Jr., *The Great Thirst: Californians and Water: A History*, rev. ed. (Berkeley: University of California Press, 2001).

The Battle for Grasslands Water

Miller and Lux's sale of its water rights in 1939 therefore precipitated a new era in the Grasslands, one that threatened the extirpation of this paradise for waterfowl. In early March, a few months prior to the sale, representatives of the Grasslands owners arranged to meet with Harold Ickes, Secretary of the Interior, and John Page, U.S. Commissioner of Reclamation, in Fresno, California, to discuss the impending water situation. Ickes and Page advised the Grasslands owners to form some type of public body for the purpose of applying for water from the Bureau of Reclamation, suggesting that such provision would need to be included in the Central Valley Project plan if they hoped to acquire water subsequent to the completion of Friant Dam. Responding to this advice, representatives of the various duck clubs and cattle ranching interests in the Grasslands met at the California Hotel in Fresno on 15 March, and voted to create the San Joaquin Grass Lands Mutual Water Users Association, the name of which was quickly shortened to the Grass Lands Association.[19]

The officers and board of directors of this new organization were men of influence in the Grasslands and surrounding communities. Most were avid duck hunters. Al Jessen, President of the Security First National Bank in Fresno, became President of the Association (Figure 6.4). Henry Wolfsen, a prominent cattleman from Dos Palos, near the southern edge of the Grasslands, assumed the office of Vice President. George Fink, a banker from the small town of Crow's Landing and President of the Gustine Gun Club, joined the board of directors. Fink had long been a proponent of waterfowl habitat

Figure 6.4 Al Jessen, President of the Grass Lands Association and its successor, the Grass Lands Water Association, on a good hunting day. Source: J. Martin Winton Special Collection on Water Use and Land Development, San Joaquin College of Law, Clovis, California.

protection, and had attended the founding meeting of the waterfowl conservation organization Ducks Unlimited in Chicago in 1937. Claude Rowe, an attorney for the City of Fresno, joined the board and served as counsel for the Association. Rowe was a member of the National Board of Directors for the Izaak Walton League, one of the nation's oldest conservation organizations, and a director of the Fresno County Sportsmen's Association.[20] By late 1944, the organization, now renamed the Grass Lands Water Association, encompassed over 62,000 acres, and represented over 5,000 individuals.[21]

The members of the Grass Lands Water Association were initially hopeful that they would be able to negotiate a water contract with the Bureau of Reclamation that would be acceptable to the Bureau as part of its overall plan for the Central Valley Project. The hope for negotiation and accommodation was a result of a number of statements written by Charles Carey, Regional Director of the Bureau, during the fall of 1944, suggesting that the Bureau would be able to provide water to the Grasslands in the future, either by releases from Friant Dam or by delivery from the Sacramento–San Joaquin Delta.[22] Unfortunately for the Grasslands interests, Charles Carey died during the summer of 1945, and was replaced as the Bureau's Regional Director by Richard Boke, who would take a much less sympathetic stance toward providing water for the Grasslands.

Throughout the remainder of the 1940s, the Grass Lands Water Association, with support from the U.S. Fish and Wildlife Service, attempted to negotiate a permanent settlement with the Bureau of Reclamation. Although both agencies were housed within the Department of the Interior, the Fish and Wildlife Service often found its conservation mission to be at odds with the Bureau's reclamation mission. In 1945 the Service's Director, Ira Gabrielson, wrote a memorandum to the Bureau of Reclamation Commissioner, Harry W. Bashore, in which he recommended that the Grasslands receive 100,000 acre-feet of water annually, and urged that "The grasslands area must be preserved or the migratory waterfowl of the Pacific Flyway, a national resource, will suffer seriously."[23] Yet neither the Association's lobbying efforts nor support from the U.S. Fish and Wildlife Service were adequate to secure a permanent contract from the Bureau. Anticipating the time when the full supply of the Central Valley Project's water would be required on agricultural lands elsewhere, the Bureau was willing to negotiate only annual contracts for releases from Friant Dam, leaving the Grasslands interests in a continual state of uncertainty about their economic future and the fate of the region's wildlife. By 1947, its efforts to negotiate with the Bureau still fruitless, the Grass Lands Water Association prepared to use the courts. On 20 October 1947 their counsel, Claude Rowe, filed the suit, *Hollister Land and Cattle Company and Yellowjacket Cattle Company v. Julius A. Krug et al.*, in U.S. District Court.[24]

The Hollister suit hinged in part on California's dual system of water rights, which incorporates both riparian and appropriative rights. The doctrine of riparian rights, the origins of which can be traced back to English common law, was recognized by the first California legislature in 1850.[25] Riparian rights guarantee owners of land bordering a stream the full natural flow of that watercourse. The competing doctrine of appropriative rights, which allow for the diversion of water from a stream to non-adjacent lands, was first developed in California in the early 1850s on the public lands of the state's mining districts during the Gold Rush, and was quickly embraced by irrigators in the Central Valley.[26] The plaintiffs in the Hollister suit were owners of lands riparian—adjacent—to the San Joaquin River. Rowe stressed the dual nature of the lands of the Grass Lands Water Association as both cattle pasture and habitat for the migratory waterfowl of the Pacific Flyway. Rowe argued that the plaintiffs and their predecessors in title had "reasonably and beneficially" used San Joaquin River water for over sixty years for domestic use, drinking water for cattle, and the irrigation of pasture. The requirement for the reasonable and beneficial use of water had been added to the state's constitution in 1928, but the use of water for the preservation of wildlife had not yet been elevated to beneficial use status, a shortcoming the Grasslands owners hoped to rectify.[27] Rowe contended that the Secretary of the Interior, Julius Krug, and other federal officials had illegally, and in excess of their authority, constructed Friant Dam across the San Joaquin River, impounded and stored the waters of the river behind it, and, with the Madera and Friant–Kern canals nearing completion, would soon transport nearly the full volume of the river away from the lands of the plaintiffs. The physical removal of the waters of the San Joaquin River was particularly grievous because these waters were to be used on lands that neither were riparian to the San Joaquin River nor possessed any appropriative rights to the river's flow. With the filing of the Hollister suit, the Grass Lands Water Association had thrown down the gauntlet to the Bureau of Reclamation.

A Small Green Book Raises the Stakes

In March 1947, as construction of the Central Valley Project proceeded, the U.S. Fish and Wildlife Service and the U.S. Bureau of Reclamation agreed to conduct a joint study to determine the importance of the 98,234 acres of the uncontrolled Grasslands to waterfowl and to recommend measures for perpetuating the waterfowl habitat of the lower San Joaquin Valley. Three and a half years would pass before the release of the final report, "Waterfowl Conservation in the Lower San Joaquin Valley, California: Its Relation to the Grasslands and the Central Valley Project," in October 1950.[28] Known as the

"Green Book," the report enumerated several highly controversial recommendations unfavorable to the Grasslands landowners, and effectively propelled the battle to the U.S. Congress, where hearings on the future of the Grasslands would be held for three consecutive years.[29] The Green Book thus served as the linchpin in the Grasslands controversy, and as a catalyst for its eventual resolution.

The authors of the Green Book fully recognized the importance of the Grasslands to waterfowl and other waterbirds. They noted that the area "provided waterfowl with good breeding conditions and excellent wintering habitat" and that, in addition to waterfowl, other common resident and migratory species in the Grasslands included long-billed curlews, black-necked stilts, American avocets, dowitchers, killdeer, white pelicans, sandhill cranes, great and snowy egrets, black-crowned night herons, and great blue herons.[30] The Green Book left little doubt of the ecological importance of privately owned wetlands such as those in the Grasslands, acknowledging that:

> The vast bulk of waterfowl habitat in California is in private ownership, with much of it under the control of duck clubs. Consequently, duck clubs will always shoulder a share of the responsibility for perpetuating the waterfowl resource with their Federal and State governments.[31]

This joint responsibility was especially true in the lower San Joaquin Valley, where the lone public refuge in 1950, the Los Banos Waterfowl Refuge, was limited in its effectiveness by its small size of only 3,000 acres. The Green Book recommended the provision of water for a proposed expansion of the Los Banos Refuge and for a proposed federal waterfowl management area to the east of the San Joaquin River, which in 1951 became the Merced National Wildlife Refuge. While providing for water supplies for these *public* refuges, and despite affirming the need to sustain the Grasslands, the Green Book did not recommend water deliveries from the Central Valley Project to those *private* lands, as they had not been included within the scope of the Central Valley Project. Instead, in what would prove to be its most inflammatory passage, the report recommended that the Grasslands owners develop, at their own expense, irrigation drainage water and groundwater sources "to perpetuate the Grasslands area as waterfowl habitat."[32]

A "class" element may have influenced, at least in part, the Green Book's recommendations to supply water to public waterfowl refuges but not to private wetlands. Sportsmen in the United States have been active supporters of the conservation of wildlife and wildlife habitat since at least the 1870s.[33] Drawn from the upper classes of society, sport hunters promoted a gentlemanly "code of conduct" that outlined acceptable hunting practices, and they lobbied for the creation of wildlife reserves and the passage of conservation laws that regulated hunting. Yet, despite aiding the recovery of wildlife populations, new legislative restrictions on hunting often criminalized the activities of hunters of much more modest means who relied on wild game for subsistence rather than sport.[34] From its origins, therefore, conservation was tinged with elitism. The Green Book noted that there was little public hunting in the Grasslands. Most of the remaining land that had once been available for public waterfowl hunting in the lower San Joaquin Valley had been reclaimed. Unattached hunters, those not affiliated with private duck clubs, therefore experienced increasingly limited hunting opportunities. As the number of these dispossessed hunters grew, they increased their demands for more public waterfowl hunting in California. The report suggested that more publicly owned waterfowl areas, on which controlled hunting might be permitted, would offer a solution to this problem.[35]

In light of the assurances that the Grasslands interests had received for the provision of Central Valley Project water—from the Bureau of Reclamation's Charles Carey in 1944 and from the Fish and Wildlife Service's Ira Gabrielson in 1945—it is hardly surprising that the Grass Lands Water Association and its members reacted bitterly to the 1950 Green Book's recommendation that they rely on drainage water and groundwater to maintain their seasonal wetlands. Indeed, the decision to withhold Central Valley Project water appeared to the Grasslands interests as a change in policy and an abnegation of promises and statements of support that various federal officials had made to them over the previous years. The Green Book's recommendation indicated a retreat from more recent statements as well, including a letter from Secretary Krug to President Truman, in which Krug stated that the Central Valley Project included plans for the preservation and propagation of fish and wildlife, and that "every effort will be made to preserve fish and wildlife resources."[36]

To Washington!

Having failed to sway the Bureau of Reclamation, and now that the formerly supportive Fish and Wildlife Service, under its new Director, Albert Day, had accepted the conclusions of the Green Book, the duck hunters and cattle ranchers of the Grasslands took their fight to Washington, D.C. They hoped that they would be able to influence Congress to pass legislation that would override the Bureau's resistance to protecting private wetlands in California. On 17 April 1951, Congress held the first of three pivotal hearings on the Grasslands water situation. Called by California Congressmen Jack Anderson and (Allan) Oakley Hunter, the hearing was held before the 82nd Congress's House Subcommittee on Irrigation and Reclamation of the Committee on Interior and Insular Affairs. Clair Engle of California, Chairman of the Subcommittee, presided. Rice growers on the fringes of the Grasslands, cattlemen, and duck clubs, each for their own reasons, supported the Grasslands; opposition originated primarily from agricultural interests outside the Grasslands who feared a reduction in their water deliveries should the Grasslands win a larger share of the scant resource.

Among those testifying for the Grasslands was Earl Harris of Santa Cruz. A prosperous haberdasher by profession, Harris had been a member of the Grass Lands Water Association's board of directors since 1949.[37] Harris expressed his frustration with the "arrogant and dictatorial policy of the Bureau of Reclamation" in its administration of the Central Valley Project, a charge that would be often repeated at the hearings.[38] He argued both for the economic importance of supporting the Grasslands with water and for the federal government's stewardship responsibility for the nation's natural resources. Harris presented numerous letters in support of the continued delivery of water to the Grasslands. R. E. Des Jardins, President of Cal-Oro Rice Growers, Inc., based in the south Grasslands, had written to Harris of the importance of Grasslands water in preventing severe crop depredations by migrating ducks every September and October.[39] John Baumgartner, President of the California Cattlemen's Association, had written to Oscar Chapman, the new Secretary of the Interior, stressing the need for livestock water, without which hundreds of head of cattle would need to be moved out of state to, quite literally, greener pastures.[40] Harris offered a particularly damning written statement by George W. Fink, now Secretary-Manager of the Grass Lands Water Association. Fink enumerated once again the broken promises by federal officials, and argued that the recommendations of the Green Book represented a complete reversal of these earlier positions, and that the federal government had abandoned its responsibilities to the Grasslands, leaving its owners to "take care of the Pacific coast flight of wild ducks and geese which under congressional statutes is the duty of the Secretary of the Interior, the Commissioner of Reclamation, and the United States Fish and Wildlife Service."[41]

Speaking next for the Grasslands was J. Martin Winton (Figure 6.5), who was destined to become one of the most important—and most vocal—spokesmen for the preservation of the Grasslands. Winton grew up hunting ducks and geese with his family in the vanishing wetlands of the Tulare Basin (the southern San Joaquin Valley) and in the wetlands around the small city of Los Banos, in the heart of the Grasslands. Winton was a pharmacist by profession, and a lifelong duck hunter devoted to the protection of waterfowl lands in the Grasslands. By the time he journeyed to Washington to speak before the Subcommittee on Irrigation and Reclamation, he had already

Figure 6.5 J. Martin Winton (left) and Earl Harris in Washington, D.C., to testify on behalf of the Grasslands before the House Subcommittee on Irrigation and Reclamation, April 1951. Source: J. Martin Winton Special Collection on Water Use and Land Development, San Joaquin College of Law, Clovis, California.

established significant conservation credentials. A member of the Hollister Land and Cattle Company duck club, Winton was chairman of the waterfowl committee for the Sportsman's Council of Central California, chairman of the San Joaquin Valley committee for Ducks Unlimited, and a member of the Izaak Walton League. Later, in 1952, he joined the board of directors of the Grass Lands Water Association, and served on the board of the Association's successor, the Grassland Water District, and as president of that new organization for over twenty years from 1957 until his retirement in 1978.[42]

Most of Winton's accomplishments on behalf of the Grasslands still lay ahead when, despite his already impressive credentials as a conservationist, he introduced himself to the Subcommittee as "just a duck hunter." Winton explained the importance of the Pacific Flyway and the ways in which hunters supported the maintenance of flyway populations by contributions to Ducks Unlimited and by fees paid for state hunting licenses and federal duck stamps. He pointed out that since 1944 the Grass Lands Water Association had been purchasing the water necessary to protect the waterfowl lands of the Grasslands and in some years had provided the water needed by the adjacent Los Banos Refuge as well. Winton was critical of the Green Book's recommendation to create a federal refuge in the Grasslands, while at the same time denying water to the private waterfowl lands there. He also called attention to the issue of rice growers reclaiming marginal land on the fringes of the Grasslands, and the unusual support that they were now providing for the maintenance of Grassland water. With more land under cultivation and less land for waterfowl, the rice growers were suffering from increasingly serious crop depredations. Every fall, enormous flocks of ducks, seeking resting and feeding areas, descended on the rice fields and devoured part of the maturing rice crop before it could be harvested. Therefore, even as they reclaimed the waterfowl lands of the Grasslands, the rice growers lobbied to protect those lands that remained. Winton was fiercely opposed to agricultural development in the Grasslands area, and argued that water should be made available only "for the growing of natural grass and waterfowl management," not for agricultural crop use.[43]

Winton had raised a key point about the threat agriculture posed to the Grasslands. Not only was the rice economy consuming ever more critical wetlands, but, more importantly, agricultural enterprises beyond the Grasslands were poised to carry away its historical water supply. These agricultural interests throughout the San Joaquin Valley had their own concerns over the provision of additional water for the Grasslands, which they expressed to the Subcommittee in the form of telegrams and letters. Irrigation districts served by the Madera Canal and the Friant–Kern Canal argued that, especially in the current drought year, water should not be released from Friant Dam for wildlife when it was so desperately needed for croplands. The agricultural interests contended that, as an irrigation and reclamation agency, the Bureau's highest priority should be to deliver water to croplands and not to wetlands, highlighting the fact that the crux of the Grasslands issue was how limited supplies of water would be distributed among competing claimants.

Richard L. Boke, Regional Director of the Bureau, then addressed the Subcommittee and attempted to refute the contentions of the Grasslands representatives. Boke argued that, despite Director Carey's earlier assurances, any permanent water supply to the Grasslands would be contingent upon increasing the delivery capacity of the Central Valley Project by the construction of additional storage reservoirs. Boke maintained that the Bureau had been able to provide interim contracts to the Grasslands since 1944 only because the Central Valley Project had not yet been fully in operation. Now that the Madera and Friant–Kern canals, which would carry away most of the flow of the San Joaquin River, were completed, the interim period was over, and, except for diminishing annual deliveries that the Bureau would continue to provide until 1953, the Grass Lands Water Association would now be forced to rely on groundwater and irrigation drainage water, as per the conclusions of the Green Book.[44]

Facing recalcitrance from the Bureau, and with the Hollister suit moving glacially through the courts, the Grasslands interests and their representatives continued to seek legislation that would secure a water supply and that would compel the Bureau to expand its mission to include the protection of fish and wildlife. In March 1952, Congressmen Clair Engle and Jack Anderson introduced bills in the House of Representatives "to authorize works for development and furnishing of water supplies for waterfowl management" in the lower San Joaquin Valley. Significantly, the bills called for the reauthorization of the Central Valley Project. To the Project's previous purposes of improvement of navigation, river regulation, flood control, and storage and delivery of water, would be added the purpose of "delivering and furnishing water supplies for fish and wildlife conservation and management and for other beneficial uses."[45] Both bills were referred to the House Subcommittee on Irrigation and Reclamation; a hearing was scheduled for 6 June.

During the months before the hearing, the Grass Lands Water Association lobbied for the passage of these bills, although both the Association and its supporters had serious reservations. The bills clearly expanded the beneficial use of water to include the conservation and management of fish and wildlife, but did not explicitly provide for a permanent water supply to the private lands in the Grasslands. They were designed instead to provide a water supply for state waterfowl management areas and national wildlife refuges under development in the lower San Joaquin Valley. The California Department of Fish and Game thus supported the bills, as did the U.S. Fish and Wildlife Service. But the Grass Lands Water Association President, Al Jessen, wrote to Clair Engle to remind him that the bill failed to protect the Grasslands, and that the Association had been spending private funds to purchase water from the Bureau of Reclamation to preserve this important link in the Pacific Flyway.[46] Martin Winton reemphasized this point in his testimony during the hearing. Drawing a parallel to perhaps the most widely known human-caused extinction in American wildlife history, Winton argued that "if it had not been for the Grass Lands Water Association, the ducks and geese of this all important wintering ground would have vanished with the passenger pigeon."[47] Although the legislation advanced to the full Committee on Interior and Insular Affairs, it stalled there, and Clair Engle could do little more than promise to reintroduce the bill at the beginning of the 1953 session.

The Grasslands owners turned this delay to their advantage by changing their Grass Lands Water Association into a public water district. Under the California Water Code, such a district would possess clear legal authority to negotiate long-term water contracts with the Bureau of Reclamation once Congress passed legislation compelling the Bureau to enter into such negotiations. On 27 December 1952, at the annual meeting of its stockholders, the Association initiated the formation of a new Grassland Water District.[48] Nearly one year later, on 22 December 1953, the Merced Board of Supervisors granted its approval and the Grassland Water District, the state's only water district created expressly for the preservation of waterfowl, came into existence.[49]

While the Grassland Water District was being organized, in early 1953 Governor Earl Warren called a conference of representatives of federal and state agencies to draft a revised bill acceptable to all agencies concerned.[50] Clair Engle and Oakley Hunter introduced this new bill, which would become known as the Grasslands bill, in the House of Representatives, and on 25 March the Subcommittee on Irrigation and Reclamation held a hearing on the new legislation, marking the third consecutive year that Congress addressed the Grasslands problem.[51] The bill was intended to provide water supplies not only to state and federal management areas, but also to the privately owned Grasslands. Thus, the bill addressed the Grasslands owners' earlier concerns and was a significant improvement over prior legislation. It contained a seminal new provision that its predecessors lacked, one for which the Grasslands interests had been lobbying for years and in anticipation of which they had created the Grassland Water District. The provision authorized the Secretary of the Interior to contract for delivery of Central Valley Project water to public organizations for waterfowl purposes in the Grasslands area of the San Joaquin Valley.

The House of Representatives passed the Grasslands bill on 1 August. The Senate followed a year later, on 11 August 1954. All that now stood between the Grasslands and the legal right to negotiate for a guaranteed supply of water was the signature of President Eisenhower. On 27 August, Eisenhower signed into law the Grasslands Development Authorization Act, paving the way for the Grasslands to enter into a long-term water contract with the Bureau of Reclamation, and ending fifteen years of uncertainty and struggle that had begun with Miller and Lux's sale of its water rights to the Bureau in 1939.[52] In a fitting tribute to the man who had been the most unrelenting force behind the passage of the Grasslands legislation, Martin Winton was presented with the pen Eisenhower used to sign the document.[53]

The Grasslands Development Authorization Act of 1954 reauthorized the Central Valley Project, explicitly stating that, in addition to the purposes enumerated in prior authorizing acts, the waters of the Project are also "for fish and wildlife purposes." Water for fish and wildlife was thus added as a Project purpose for the first time, albeit with the understanding that "delivery of water from the Central Valley Project for waterfowl purposes is to be subordinate to the priority of deliveries of water for agricultural purposes."[54] Despite this caveat, the language of the 1954 act signified a marked advance from that of the 1937 act that had first authorized the construction of the Central Valley Project by the Bureau of Reclamation, which required only that the Central Valley Project "shall include a due regard for wildlife conservation."[55] The duck hunters and cattle ranchers of the Grasslands and their congressional allies had prevailed in forcing the Bureau of Reclamation to reconsider the purposes and goals of the Central Valley Project and to begin to take into account the effects of the Project on wildlife. Their accomplish-

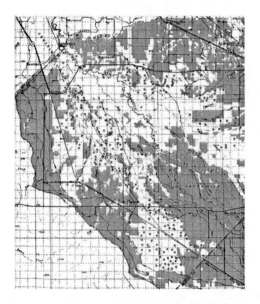

Figure 6.6 Map of the Grasslands of western Merced County, 1957–1958. Shaded areas represent croplands and unshaded areas represent grasslands, which often served dual purposes as cattle ranches and duck clubs. Small circles represent the duck clubs. Note the especially heavy concentrations of clubs to the west of the San Joaquin River. Source: State of California, Department of Water Resources, Division of Resources Planning, in Howard R. Leach, "The Wildlife and Fishery Resources in Relation to Drainage Disposal Problems in the San Joaquin Valley" (California Department of Fish and Game, 1960).

ments call attention to the often overlooked role that protest from relatively small, locally based organizations of conservation-minded citizens has played in influencing national environmental policy.

The most important task now facing the Grassland Water District was the negotiation of a permanent contract with the Bureau for Central Valley Project water. Martin Winton led the negotiations for the Grasslands beginning shortly after the passage of the 1954 Grasslands Act, but final execution of the contract would be subject to the prior resolution of the Hollister suit that had initiated the legal struggle over Grassland water rights. Toward that end, in January 1956, the Grassland Water District passed a resolution for the dismissal of the case, and, on 13 September 1956, the District and the U.S. Bureau of Reclamation entered into a permanent contract for 50,000 acre-feet of fall water to be delivered annually from the Delta–Mendota Canal, the 117-mile-long canal that the Bureau had constructed to deliver substitute water from the Sacramento–San Joaquin Delta to the lower San Joaquin Valley.[56] Although this quantity of water was only about half of what was desirable for optimal management, the Grasslands owners would be able to continue the tradition of fall flood irrigation and the annual transformation of the region into wetland habitat for Pacific Flyway waterfowl. (See Figures 6.6 and 6.7.)

Figure 6.7 Flooded grasslands near South Dos Palos. This photograph, taken in late August 1958, on flooded duck club lands, illustrates the marshy conditions and excellent waterfowl habitat in the Grasslands created by controlled flooding in the late summer and fall, and then sustained by seasonal rains until the spring. Source: Photograph by Howard R. Leach, California Department of Fish and Game. Used with permission.

The Grasslands Today

The 1954 Grasslands Act and the water contract that followed two years later represented a pivotal step toward the permanent protection of the Grassland wetlands. A generation later, during the early 1980s, the Grasslands and the federal wildlife refuges in the lower San Joaquin Valley weathered a second challenge, again precipitated by the operations of the Central Valley Project—the lethal poisoning of thousands of waterfowl and other waterbirds by selenium, a naturally occurring element that is toxic in high concentrations. Leached by irrigation water from the soils of the west side of the San Joaquin Valley, the selenium was delivered through drainage systems to the ponds of the newly created Kesterson National Wildlife Refuge and to the canals of the Grassland Water District.[57] In part as a result of this environmental nightmare, which attracted national media attention and called into question the wisdom of supplying wetlands with degraded agricultural wastewater from reclamation projects, Congress passed the groundbreaking Central Valley Project Improvement Act (CVPIA) of 1992.[58]

The far-reaching Central Valley Project Improvement Act ushered in a new era in California water history. Passed in the sixth year of a prolonged drought, and supported by a nascent coalition of environmental groups and urban lobbyists, the CVPIA was intended to increase the efficiency of the operation of the Central Valley Project and to distribute limited water resources more equitably among agricultural users, city dwellers, and the natural environment. The CVPIA included provisions for the protection and restoration of fish and wildlife habitat in the Central Valley and the protection of the estuary that extended from San Francisco Bay to the Sacramento–San Joaquin Delta. Of paramount importance, the Central Valley Project Improvement Act reauthorized the Central Valley Project once again. The Grasslands Act of 1954, promoted by a small group of duck hunters and cattle ranchers, had included the use of the waters of the Central Valley Project for fish and wildlife as a Project purpose for the first time. The 1992 Central Valley Project Improvement Act, supported by a much broader coalition, built upon the successes of that earlier generation of waterfowl enthusiasts and their allies, and offered a much higher level of protection, adding the "mitigation, protection, and restoration of fish and wildlife" as an *equal* priority among the Central Valley Project's purposes. The act dramatically increased the provision of Project water to the Central Valley's national wildlife refuges, state wildlife management areas, and the Grassland Resource Conservation District.[59]

By 2007, the greater Grasslands region consisted of over 160,000 acres of wetland and wetland-related habitat distributed among national wildlife refuges, state wildlife areas, a state park, and nearly 200 privately owned parcels, most of which are waterfowl hunting clubs in the Grassland Water District.[60]

In recent decades, as cattle prices have fallen and economic incentives such as conservation easements have become more prevalent, ranching has declined in the Grasslands and most properties are now managed year-round for waterfowl purposes. More than half a century of public and private efforts to protect the Grasslands, dating back to the formation of the Grass Lands Association in 1939, have brought international recognition to this region of the lower San Joaquin Valley. As an acknowledgment of the importance of the Grasslands not only to migratory waterfowl but also to migratory shorebirds, on 29 April 1991 the Western Hemisphere Shorebird Reserve Network officially recognized the Grasslands region as an International Reserve.[61] The coup for the Grasslands came on 2 February 2005, when the region, known since the late 1990s as the Grasslands Ecological Area, was designated a Ramsar Wetland of International Importance. This coveted designation, one of only twenty-two in the United States as of 2007, was awarded under the Convention on Wetlands of International Importance, the official title of the Ramsar Convention, named after its place of adoption in Iran in 1971. Ratified by the United States in 1986, this global treaty, with over 150 signatory nations, provides an international framework for wetland protection.[62]

The Ramsar designation recognized the unique ecological contribution of the Grasslands Ecological Area. In addition to its wetlands and the more than two dozen species of waterfowl they harbor, the area contains a variety of ecological communities, including riparian cottonwood and willow forests, riparian oak woodlands, vernal pools, alkali sinks, and native alkali grasslands. This matrix of habitats supports numerous species of wading birds, raptors, and other wildlife and plant species, several dozen of which are classified as federally threatened or endangered, or as otherwise sensitive species.[63] The number and diversity of protected species in the Grasslands Ecological Area reflect the importance of the area not only for waterfowl but for biodiversity in general.

The wetlands of the Grasslands will face continuing challenges in the near future. Urban encroachment brought on by rapid population growth in the San Joaquin Valley threatens the region. Global climate change seems destined to change much of the precipitation in the Sierra Nevada, upon which California largely relies for its water supply, from snow to rain, affecting the timing of runoff and impacting the state's ability to store adequate water supplies in its reservoirs.[64] But despite these challenges, Californians appear committed to protecting their remaining wetland heritage. Were it not for the relentless efforts of a band of duck hunters and cattle ranchers who challenged the inevitability of the destruction of their lands for the "greater good" of irrigated agriculture, there would today be much less of that wetland heritage to protect.

Abbreviations

AGWD   Archives of the Grassland Water District, Los Banos, California

CEP   Clair Engle Papers, Meriam Library, Special Collections, California State University, Chico

JMW   J. Martin Winton Special Collection on Water Use and Land Development, San Joaquin College of Law, Clovis, California

M-GLWA   Minutes of the Grass Lands Water Association

M-GWD   Minutes of the Grassland Water District

SLNWRC   San Luis National Wildlife Refuge Complex archives, Los Banos, California

Notes

1 T. E. Dahl, "Wetland Losses in the United States, 1780s to 1980s" (Washington, DC: U.S. Department of the Interior, Fish and Wildlife Service, 1990), 1. For a history of wetlands in the United States, see Ann Vileisis, *Discovering the Unknown Landscape: A History of America's Wetlands* (Washington, DC: Island Press, 1997).

2 W. J. Mitsch and J. G. Gosselink, *Wetlands*, 3rd ed. (New York: John Wiley & Sons, 2000), 26.

3 32 Stat. 388. Until 1923, the Bureau of Reclamation was called the Reclamation Service. For irrigation and reclamation history in California and the larger West, see Norris Hundley Jr., *The Great Thirst: Californians and Water: A History*, rev. ed. (Berkeley: University of California Press, 2001); Donald J. Pisani, *From the Family Farm to Agribusiness: The Irrigation Crusade in California and the West, 1850–1931* (Berkeley: University of California Press, 1984); Donald Worster, *Rivers of Empire: Water, Aridity, and the Growth of the American West* (New York: Pantheon Books, 1985).

4 Robert M. Wilson, "Directing the Flow: Migratory Waterfowl, Scale, and Mobility in Western North America," *Environmental History* 7(2) (2002), 247–48; Nancy Langston, *Where Land and Water Meet: A Western Landscape Transformed* (Seattle: University of Washington Press, 2003), 83–87.

5 See Mark W. T. Harvey, *A Symbol of Wilderness: Echo Park and the American Conservation Movement* (Seattle: University of Washington Press, 2000).

6 R. E. Trost, J. S. Gleason, and T. A. Sanders, "Pacific Flyway Data Book—Waterfowl Harvest and Status, Hunter Participation and Success in the Pacific Flyway and United States" (Portland, OR: U.S. Fish and Wildlife Service, 2007), 96.

7 U.S. Fish and Wildlife Service, "Concept Plan for Waterfowl Wintering Habitat Preservation: Central Valley, California" (Portland, OR: U.S. Department of the Interior, Fish and Wildlife Service, 1978), 1.

8   W. E. Frayer, D. D. Peters, and H. R. Pywell, "Wetlands of the California Central Valley: Status and Trends—1939 to Mid-1980s" (Portland, OR: U.S. Department of the Interior, Fish and Wildlife Service, 1989), 27.

9   "Grasslands" is spelled with a capital "G" to distinguish the seasonally flooded area from the more than 200,000 acres of grasslands in the lower San Joaquin Valley as a whole.

10 For the long tradition of American hunters as conservationists, see John F. Reiger, *American Sportsmen and the Origins of Conservation*, 3rd ed. (Corvallis: Oregon State University Press, 2001). For a more critical view of hunters, see Thomas R. Dunlap, *Saving America's Wildlife: Ecology and the American Mind, 1850–1990* (Princeton, NJ: Princeton University Press, 1988).

11 The natural permanent and intermittent ponds and marshes of the Grasslands are subject to desiccation during the hot, dry San Joaquin Valley summer. The permanent water areas shrink considerably, while the seasonal water areas usually dry completely and support only alkali scrub vegetation or turn into barren alkali or mud flats.

12 Elliott & Moore, *History of Merced County, California* (San Francisco: 1881), 96. For a detailed study of Miller and Lux, see David Igler, *Industrial Cowboys: Miller & Lux and the Transformation of the Far West, 1850–1920* (Berkeley: University of California Press, 2001), 66.

13 U.S. Department of the Interior, "Waterfowl Conservation in the Lower San Joaquin Valley: Its Relation to the Grasslands and the Central Valley Project" (Washington, DC: U.S. Department of the Interior, 1950), 17–23.

14 Miller and Lux pamphlet: "California Irrigated Lands in the Western San Joaquin Valley," no date, but *c*. 1920s. Box 12, Folder 2, Frank Latta Collection: Skyfarming Collection, Huntington Library, San Marino, California.

15 U.S. Department of the Interior, "Waterfowl Conservation in the Lower San Joaquin Valley," 18.

16 49 Stat. 1028; 50 Stat. 844.

17 U.S. House of Representatives, "Central Valley Project Documents: Part Two: Operating Documents" (House Document No. 246, 85th Congress, 1st Session, 1957), 555–89; M. Catherine Miller, *Flooding the Courtrooms: Law and Water in the Far West* (Lincoln: University of Nebraska Press, 1993), 173.

18 U.S. Department of the Interior, "Waterfowl Conservation in the Lower San Joaquin Valley," 26–27.

19 Al Jessen, "Grass Lands Association History," 1939. Box 9, Folder 3, JMW.

20 Howard R. Leach, "An Historical Account of Waterfowling, San Joaquin Valley, California: 1870–1970" (1997), 60.

21 Jessen, untitled document, 1944. Box 9, Folder 3, JMW.

22 For example, Carey to Anthony C. Mattos, General Manager, Western Cooperative Dairymen's Union, 22 September 1944. Box 16, Folder 8, JMW.

23 Gabrielson to Bashore, 5 June 1945. An acre-foot is 325,851 gallons.

24 S.D. Cal., No. 680-ND, unpublished, 20 October 1947. Reflecting the dual nature of land use in the Grasslands, many of the duck clubs were designated as "land and cattle" or "cattle" companies.

25 1850 Cal. Stats. Ch. 95.

26 1851 Cal. Stats. Ch. 5.

27 Cal. Const. Art. X, Sec. 2, originally Cal. Const. Art. XIV, Sec. 3 (1928, amended 1976).

28 U.S. Department of the Interior, "Waterfowl Conservation in the Lower San Joaquin Valley."

29 The term "Green Book" was adopted from the report's green covers.

30 U.S. Department of the Interior, "Waterfowl Conservation in the Lower San Joaquin Valley," 17, 52.

31 Ibid., 59.

32 The Green Book estimated that the Grasslands owners would need to develop 150 wells at a cost of $6,000 per well, for a total development cost of $900,000. The additional cost of pumping the groundwater would be approximately $2.25 per acre-foot, far higher than the $1.50 per acre-foot that the Grass Lands Water Association had been paying since 1948 for its annual contracts for water with the Bureau. U.S. Department of the Interior, "Waterfowl Conservation in the Lower San Joaquin Valley," 111–12, 118; M-GLWA, 18 November 1947, AGWD.

33 See Reiger, *American Sportsmen and the Origins of Conservation.*

34 This tension within the conservation movement has been revealed by the works of several historians, including Louis S. Warren, *The Hunter's Game: Poachers and Conservationists in Twentieth-Century America* (New Haven, CT: Yale University Press, 1997); Karl Jacoby, *Crimes against Nature: Squatters, Poachers, Thieves, and the Hidden History of American Conservation* (Berkeley: University of California Press, 2001).

35 U.S. Department of the Interior, "Waterfowl Conservation in the Lower San Joaquin Valley," 62–63.

36 Krug to Truman, 29 July 1948, in U.S. Bureau of Reclamation, "Central Valley Basin: A Comprehensive Report on the Development of the Water and Related Resources of the Central Valley Basin" (U.S. Department of the Interior, Bureau of Reclamation, Senate Document 113, 81st Congress, 1st Session, 1949), 6.

37 M-GLWA, 8 November 1949, AGWD.

38 U.S. House of Representatives, Subcommittee on Irrigation and Reclamation of the Committee on Interior and Insular Affairs, *Hearing on Central Valley Project Water Problem Relating to the Grasslands Area in the San Joaquin Valley, Calif.*, 82d Congress, 1st Session, 17 April and 3 May, 1951, 7.

39 Des Jardins to Harris, 11 April 1951, ibid., 7–8.

40 Baumgartner to Chapman, 10 April 1951, ibid., 8.

41 Statement of George Fink, 20 February 1951, ibid., 10–12.

42 M-GLWA, 8 July 1952, AGWD; Lloyd Carter, "J. Martin Winton: A Short Biography," JMW.

43 *Hearing on Central Valley Project Water Problem*, 22–27.

44 Ibid., 48–62.

45 H.R. 7177 and 7178.

46 Jessen to Engle, 21 May 1952. Box 139, Folder 2, CEP.

47 Statement of J. Martin Winton, 6 June 1952. Box 1, Folder 25, JMW.

48 M-GLWA, 27 December 1952, AGWD.

49 The provisions governing California water districts are collected in the California Water Code, Sections 34000–38501.

50 The agencies included the U.S. Bureau of Reclamation, U.S. Fish and Wildlife Service, California Division of Water Resources, California Water Projects Authority, California Department of Fish and Game, California Fish and Game Commission, and Wildlife Conservation Board.

51 H.R. 4213.

52 68 Stat. 879.

53 Lloyd Carter, "J. Martin Winton: A Short Biography," JMW.

54 U.S. Senate, "Authorizing Works for Development and Furnishing of Water Supplies for Waterfowl Management, Central Valley Project, California. Senate Report No. 1786, to Accompany H.R. 4213" (U.S. Senate, 83d Congress, 2d Session, 1954), 1.

55 50 Stat. 844.

56 M-GWD, 10 January 1956, AGWD; "Contract Between the United States of America and the Grassland Water District," in U.S. House of Representatives, "Central Valley Project Documents: Part Two: Operating Documents," 39–42. The original cost of the water was $1.50 per acre-foot; it was made free of charge in perpetuity by the Fish and Wildlife Improvement Act of 1978. 92 Stat. 3110.

57 For a fuller treatment of selenium toxicity at Kesterson and in the Grasslands, see Philip Garone, "The Fall and Rise of the Wetlands of California's Great Central Valley: A Historical and Ecological Study of an Endangered Resource of the Pacific Flyway" (Ph.D. dissertation, University of California at Davis, 2006). The scientific literature is too extensive to cite, but for journalistic accounts see Russell Clemings, *Mirage: The False Promise of Desert Agriculture* (San Francisco: Sierra Club Books, 1996); Tom Harris, *Death in the Marsh* (Washington, DC: Island Press, 1991).

58 The CVPIA is Title 34 of the Reclamation Projects Authorization and Adjustment Act of 1992, a large omnibus water bill authorizing a total of $2.4 billion for projects throughout the Western states. 106 Stat. 4706.

59 The Grassland Resource Conservation District includes approximately 75,000 acres, encompassing most of the Grassland Water District as well as all or part of several neighboring state and federal refuges.

60 The Grasslands Ecological Area consists of the San Luis and Merced national wildlife refuges, the Los Banos, Volta, and North Grasslands wildlife areas, and the Great Valley Grasslands State Park, and over 100,000 acres of private lands in or

adjacent to the Grassland Water District and/or the Grassland Resource Conservation District.

61 Narrative Report, 1991, Grasslands Wildlife Management Area, 43. SLNWRC.

62 Ramsar Convention Bureau, *Directory of Wetlands of International Importance* (Gland, Switzerland: Ramsar Convention Bureau, 1990).

63 "Information Sheet on Ramsar Wetlands," 14 January 2005. Compiled by Kim Forrest, Refuge Manager, SLNWRC.

64 Christopher B. Field, Gretchen C. Daily, Frank W. Davis, Steven Gaines, Pamela A. Matson, John Melack, Norman L. Miller, "Confronting Climate Change in California: Ecological Impacts on the Golden State" (Cambridge, MA, and Washington, DC: The Union of Concerned Scientists and The Ecological Society of America, 1999).

CHAPTER 7

A Twisted Road to Earth Day

*Air Pollution as an Issue of Social Movements after
World War II*

FRANK UEKOETTER

When environmental awareness and activism reached record heights in 1970, air pollution was one of the key issues. Earth Day celebrations frequently referred to pollution problems, and hearings on air pollution drew mass audiences everywhere. In Cleveland, the Air Conservation Committee of the Tuberculosis and Respiratory Disease Association of Cleveland and Cuyahoga County started a newsletter, which noted in its first issue that "Clevelanders have every right to be militant about pollution"; on other occasions, the Air Conservation Committee sounded a "breathers alert."[1] In Missoula, Montana, environmentalists staged what they called "the first anti-pollution 'fly-in' in the nation" on 8 March 1970, when thirteen planes circled a nearby pulp mill. One month later, a University of Montana ecology group called "the Environmentalists" chose four issues for a three-week long observance that overlapped with the national Earth Day celebrations, and pollution figured alongside population, pesticides, and recycling on their agenda.[2] It was by all means fitting that on 18 December 1970 an air pollution hearing in the State Health Building in Atlanta, Georgia, voted as its first item of business to move to the nearby Central Presbyterian Church because the original conference room did not have sufficient space for all participants. After all, the move not only mirrored the unexpected turnout at that hearing but also a crucial shift of the arena. From now on, decisions on air pollution issues would no longer be taken at obscure meetings in administrative buildings but in plain view of the public.

It is difficult to imagine that this outburst of civic activism all over the country could have happened spontaneously. Going through contemporary statements, it is all too easy to note a feeling of impatience and disaffection that obviously had deeper roots. Polls had shown a growing discontent in the years before 1970. According to polls conducted by the Opinion Research Corporation, the proportion of respondents who saw air pollution as "very serious" or "somewhat serious" grew from 28 percent in May 1965 to 48 percent in November 1966 and 55 percent in November 1968. The figures become even more dramatic when one focuses on city dwellers, among whom fully 86 percent saw air pollution as a "serious" problem in 1968.[3] In the light of these figures, it is tempting to favor a rather simplistic interpretation of the rise of environmentalism, namely the notion of a groundswell of criticism that was gathering force through the 1960s and finally exploded in 1970. However, such a reading would ignore that the 1960s saw not only the rise of a new environmental community but also the demise of an existing tradition of civic protest. Since the Progressive era, city dwellers had pressed for aggressive measures against the urban smoke nuisance, and this tradition of civic activism was still active far into the postwar years. Even more, the smoke abatement tradition was a civic crusade as well as a regulatory tradition, and both had roots in an elite tradition of municipal politics that was somewhat at odds with the broader civic base of the nascent environmental movement. The two traditions also favored different political styles: whereas environmentalists usually sought to "get tough" on pollution, the smoke abatement tradition saw air pollution control as a matter of gentlemen's agreements among great, public-spirited citizens.

With that, it seems insufficient to argue that the environmental movement essentially raised a previously "neglected" topic. A more appropriate reading sees an elite-based tradition of cooperative environmental regulation being challenged by a growing mainstream concern about pollution that favored faster measures and, by implication, a more adversarial political approach. In fact, it seems that such a distinction is much easier in hindsight than from a contemporary perspective: much of the new environmental style grew out of existing traditions, with all the inconsistencies and compromises that a gradual change of modes of thinking and action implies. It was not until 1970 that the camp of anti-pollution activists clearly divided into a large group of environmentalists who were attacking industry and a small minority of smoke abatement traditionalists who stuck to defending industry. Before that, most citizens involved in the fight against air pollution were actually somewhere in between, discontented with the dominant political approach but not yet ready for a full-scale attack on cooperative air pollution control. The road to Earth Day was a twisted one, and it was by no means a one-way street.

The Smoke Abatement Tradition

Civic organizations have called for measures against smoke and air pollution since the late nineteenth century. As early as 1880, the Citizens' Association of Chicago supported a drive against the coal smoke nuisance.[4] For the Progressive reform movement of the early 1900s, smoke had been one of a whole host of urban reform issues, and the result was a mixture of success and accommodation: smoke abatement found an institutional home in municipal agencies for "smoke inspection," but it progressed far less rapidly than reformers would have hoped.[5] The relevance of these Progressive era campaigns is twofold: first, the smoke abatement movement reached its apogee with spectacular campaigns in St. Louis and Pittsburgh around 1940, and these campaigns were still in living memory throughout the early postwar years.[6] Second, more than half a century of activism had defined certain patterns of civic protest, and these traditions remained vibrant far into the 1960s, when environmental sentiment was slowly getting into full swing. In fact, some of the organizations that had sustained smoke abatement during the Progressive era were still around in the postwar era.

One example was the Smoke Abatement League of Cincinnati, founded in 1906 and renamed the Air Pollution Control League of Greater Cincinnati after World War II. With that, its roots went back to the times when smoke abatement was still nothing short of a civic crusade. An early circular reported proudly that the League had hired one of the best lawyers in town "to 'fight the case to the bitter end.'"[7] But activists eventually realized that rhetoric of this kind earned it few friends, and gradually adopted a more conciliatory line of action. "There was a time when harsh, severe measures were the best, the only ones to employ; . . . but that time should have passed," the League declared in its annual report for 1911.[8] One year later, the League supported a new local ordinance that stressed education and cooperation of local industries and created a City Smoke Department, headed by a trained engineer.[9] "The Department tries to be helpful and has the friendship and co-operation of many of the owners and operators of furnaces," Cincinnati's chief smoke inspector Charles W. Heath noted in 1916.[10] However, the Department continued to monitor smoke emissions and punished recalcitrant smoke offenders; in fact, the Smoke Abatement League maintained its own force of inspectors until 1930 in order to both support the city smoke inspector and monitor his performance.[11] From 1915, the Smoke Abatement League of Cincinnati received funds from the Community Chest, Cincinnati's central fund for philanthropic endowments.[12]

Cooperation and education remained the key pillars of the League's work after 1945. "Education is the most important factor in any program of air purification," the Smoke Abatement League noted in its report for 1949.[13] In fact, the League influenced air pollution control nationwide when it launched a national Smoke Abatement Week, and the League's secretary, Charles N. Howison, became chairman of the National Smoke Abatement Week Committee in 1949.[14] The event, soon renamed Cleaner Air Week, became a key event of air pollution control in the 1950s and 1960s; for example, Cleaner Air Week in October 1965, still organized under the auspices of Charles Howison, was celebrated in eighty-six U.S. cities and Brampton, Ontario.[15] The event stood out for emphasizing cooperation with industry: "It is teamwork that will help solve the problem," the brochure for Cleaner Air Week 1960 declared, and the list of suggested activities included "industry tours for air pollution control progress of your community plants."[16] The Air Pollution Control League of Greater Cincinnati also continued to fill an important role locally. "This is the only place we have to turn to for assistance when we have air pollution problems," Albert W. Van Sickle, Health Commissioner of the City of Hamilton, Ohio, noted as late as January 1969.[17] But when, a year later, support for environmental issues virtually exploded, the League was anything but pleased: "Finger pointing is the order of the day among many interests in air conservation," the League noted and bemoaned "today's tendency to polarize public thinking on social problems."[18]

Similar traditions of activism existed in Pittsburgh, most prominently with the Civic Club of Allegheny County. The Club had established a committee on the smoke nuisance as early as April 1906 and, although it never entertained a network of inspectors like Cincinnati's Smoke Abatement League, its record against smoke was impeccable.[19] "The Civic Club has for years been actively interested in some plan whereby the smoke evils may be minimized, has had a standing committee on the subject, and has co-operated in every movement . . . to secure the passage and enforcement of an ordinance requiring the use of smoke consumers by our industrial plants and railroads," a clubwoman noted in 1912.[20] When the Pittsburgh Smoke Commission considered drastic action against domestic smoke in 1941, the Club organized a full session with witnesses in support of the project, a meeting that concluded with the reading of a Club resolution declaring that "the Civic Club of Allegheny County registered its disapproval of smoke conditions over forty-five years ago."[21] The United Smoke Council of Allegheny County, which offered public support to the ensuing campaign in Pittsburgh, presented itself as "an outgrowth of a smoke committee of the Civic Club" and became affiliated with the powerful Allegheny Conference on Community Development in November 1945.[22] But in spite of this proud tradition, it monitored the rise of environmentalism with notable distrust. In a circular of June 1971, the Civic Club of Allegheny County complained about the costs of air pollution control with words that one would expect from industrial lobbyists rather than from an old-time smoke crusader:

> Unfortunately, many of the advocates of instant pollution abatement appear to be either politically motivated, directly or indirectly, or to be oblivious of or without appreciation of the effect of the economic disruptions in these specific localities. To crusade for environmental quality is currently in vogue and has created a multitude of economically naive "experts."[23]

At a hearing in 1969 where environmentalists assaulted a proposed set of rules and regulations for Allegheny County, Samuel Rosenbach, Secretary of the Civic Club, criticized "the apparent emotional anti-industry stand" of his fellow speakers and sternly declared, "We must recognize that industry is the backbone of our economic well-being."[24]

To be sure, few associations could claim a similar tradition of activism. In fact, few organizations sustained the fight against smoke for a decade or more; usually, energy was lapsing after two or three years of activism. However, the two clubs were by all means typical for the social composition of the coal smoke abatement movement, which usually drew its strongest support from members of the social elite of a city. Progressive era municipal reform has long been recognized as an upper-class project, and many crusaders against the smoke nuisance were listed in upper-class visiting lists such as the Blue Book.[25] The exclusive character of the movement became at times visible in notes about activism: for example, when the Women's City Club of Cleveland conducted a series of smoke observations in the 1920s, the women drew on a type of help that would have been unavailable to middle-class or working-class activists: "On occasion they set their chauffeurs to watching when the ladies took occasional time out to shop," an internal history of the Women's City Club recorded.[26] The Smoke Abatement League of Cincinnati emphatically proclaimed in its annual report for 1912 that it included "all classes of our people," but in order to see through this rhetoric it is sufficient to look at the list of professions that went along with this statement: citing "bishops, clergymen, judges, lawyers, physicians, teachers, manufacturers, banks and bankers, merchants, hotel-keepers, railroad and coal men, together with many leading women," the exclusive character of the membership roster was utterly clear.[27] In many cities, real estate interests played a pivotal role, no doubt because urban smoke was detrimental to downtown real estate values. In 1941, a woman who had first-hand experience about the St. Louis anti-smoke campaign told a smoke meeting in Pittsburgh, "The biggest boosters for it were the St. Louis Real Estate men. They said people were moving out of town—now they are moving back." Thus, her recommendation for Pittsburgh was: "We should interest our real estate group."[28]

To be sure, recent research has revealed that smoke was also an issue in organizations and newspapers that did not belong to the upper class.[29] But even in the light of this multitude of voices, there is no use denying that smoke abatement as it was represented in municipal politics was an elite project. Characteristically, the Civic Club of Allegheny County found it necessary to inflate the support rate among poor Pittsburgh citizens, claiming a 55 percent approval rate in "the lowest-income family group" at the aforementioned hearing before the Pittsburgh Smoke Commission on 28 March 1941.[30] When a more independent survey was conducted in 1946, the approval rate among individuals of low income stood at 36 percent (though it grew to 62 percent within two years).[31] However, if smoke abatement was an elite project, the preference for cooperation and education was anything but surprising; after all, that meant that anti-smoke activists came from the same social strata as the owners and managers of large polluting companies. At its core, smoke abatement was a project of self-education within the municipal elite: it presupposed a local business community that would listen to and support reasonable, cooperative policies in the interest of the general citizenry. From such a point of view, the business community was not so much a polluter as it was a group of corporate captains who would adhere to a gentlemen's agreement.

It does not need long explanations to show that this smoke abatement strategy could achieve change only in the long run. But at the same time, it is important to note its two important attractions. First, it meant that cooperative smoke abatement could enjoy the support of large parts of the business communities, not a small achievement in light of the fact that they were, after all, the polluters. The cooperative atmosphere in most major cities was worlds away from the bitter conflicts that were fought between metal smelters on the one hand and farmers and forest interests on the other in the American West.[32] Second, the cooperative strategy moved beyond the smoke issue once coal smoke ceased to be the major air pollutant in postwar American cities. Smoke abatement became the model for the fight against other pollutants: if smoke could be fought in a cooperative way, why shouldn't the same approach apply to other pollutants as well? Few things illustrate this prevailing mode of thinking better than the stance of business periodicals from the late 1940s through the 1960s, which generally came out strongly in support of pollution control. As early as 1948, *Chemical Engineering Progress* published an article noting that industry had "an obligation to the community to do everything reasonable to minimize atmospheric pollution."[33] During the same year, *Business Week* published the following warning after the Donora catastrophe, which claimed some twenty lives after the emissions from a zinc smelter became trapped under an inversion layer: "The Donora 'death smog' could happen in your town—given the right combination of smoke, hilly terrain, and foggy weather."[34] Some seventeen years later, *Fortune* published an essay entitled "We Can Afford Clean Air", with the full backing of the editorial board.[35] The National Association of Manufacturers even published a glowing account of the Pittsburgh air pollution control program in 1962.[36] Of course, nice words in business periodicals did not secure effective measures by themselves, but these quotations show that those industrialists who ignored or downplayed the demands of pollution control did so in defiance of a broad business consensus: a good corporate citizen takes care of pollutants that disturb its neighbors.

The Environmental Challenge

Sketches of environmental groups usually start with remarks on their goals and rhetoric. But with the class bias of the smoke abatement tradition so apparent, it might be worthwhile to start an analysis with a view to the social background of the protesters. If the smoke abatement tradition was firmly rooted in an elite tradition of environmental politics, it is crucial to see that the social basis of pollution protests was slowly changing in the postwar years. In fact, that change had been evident in the Pittsburgh campaign against domestic smoke: the 1941 Report of the Mayor's Commission for the Elimination of Smoke included eight pages with a long list of civic organizations who had come out in support of the anti-smoke drive, including organizations such as the Disabled Veterans of the World War and the International Brotherhood of Firemen and Oilers, who clearly could not be suspected of an elite background.[37] Increasingly, concerned middle-class citizens took the role that business leaders had played during the age of smoke. Whereas the strong man behind the Citizens' Association of Chicago was Marshall Fields, the formation of the Cleaner Air Committee of Hyde Park-Kenwood in 1959 went back to the South Side resident Laura Fermi, who, as widow of the physicist Enrico Fermi, was part of an academic middle class.[38] In Cleveland, the Chamber of Commerce had stood behind smoke abatement during the Progressive era, whereas Casimir Bielen, a key community activist during the late 1950s and 1960s, was a school principal.[39]

To be sure, this transformation of the social background of anti-pollution protests did not make the environmental cause a broad issue that knew no boundaries. For instance, concern about air pollution among workers remained meager. It was not until 1969 that the United Steelworkers of America became the first union to organize an air pollution conference.[40] Likewise, African Americans were rarely to be found among the activists. Even Freddie Mae Brown, president of "Black Survival Inc.," an integrated African American environmental initiative founded in St. Louis around 1970, declared in an interview with other environmentalists:

> The existence of qualitative, quantitative and up-to-date information about environmental problems within the black community is appallingly scarce. It is felt by many black people that other problems such as housing, education and employment are so crucial that they require the immediate and ongoing thrust of black leadership.[41]

Characteristically, a 1966 study of air pollution complaints in Chicago showed "a heavy [geographic] weighting of sources reflecting the complaints of north side residents, especially those living along the lake shore," a fact that the authors saw as "suggesting that factors such as those of a socio-economic nature influence the complaint rate."[42] Yet even this result mirrored a new social basis of air pollution control: traditionally, business-oriented smoke abatement had focused first and foremost on the Loop, and not on the residential North Side.

Thus, air pollution concerns were slowly becoming a mainstream issue in postwar America, and the social basis of environmental activism broadened significantly. Once again, it is important to see this development not only from a teleological perspective, as a trend pointing towards what would one day be the environmental movement. From the perspective of the smoke abatement tradition, this change in the anti-pollution movement's social composition implied a tacit but fundamental challenge for the reigning polity: could air pollution control continue to work according to a gentlemen's agreement if it involved not only corporate captains but, well, middle-class Americans? It was one thing to have managers, experts, and politicians agree on a certain approach, but a different thing to have a manager listening to enraged citizens: the former was pretty much business as usual in 1950s America, whereas the latter was, from the viewpoint of a self-confident business elite, an almost humiliating act. With that, the divergent visions of air pollution in postwar America were not only the result of different worldviews—they were also rooted in different positions in America's class society.

Thus, civic protest took on a new tune after the late 1950s: it was more impatient, more adversarial, more disaffected with cooperation than traditional civic activism. To be sure, leagues and associations overwhelmingly continued to advocate a cooperative strategy. For example, a group named Clear Air Clear Water Unlimited, founded in the Greater Minneapolis–St. Paul area in 1956, noted in its list of accomplishments for 1957 that it had "gained cooperation of key industrial leaders who appreciate the vital importance of anti-pollution regulations," and generally "sought understanding of industry."[43] When New York State's Hudson River Conservation Society changed its Certificate of Incorporation in 1961 in order to reflect a growing concern with pollution and recreation, it even included a statement declaring it society policy "to cooperate with industry and where necessary to seek its regulation."[44] In Cleveland, Casimir Bielen, acting as secretary of the Southeast Air Pollution Committee, declared in 1960, "We agree with a policy of peaceful cooperation with industry if it is not at the expense of our home owning community."[45] And yet the qualification was already revealing: cooperation was not a self-evident approach, let alone a celebrated one, but rather a strategy that one might employ as long as it worked. In fact, only one year later, Casimir Bielen, then writing for the newly founded Ohio Pure Air Association, launched a staunch attack on "local self-control" in a letter to the editor: "The cooperative policy advocated for many years by the City Air Pollution Department is nothing more than a policy of giving industry its way at the expense of the general health and welfare of the entire community."[46]

The Ohio Pure Air Association soon became more moderate, however, and even offered a "Best Neighbor Award" to Jones & Laughlin Steel Company in 1965 "for their continuous efforts to voluntarily reduce air pollution by modernizing their facilities with the latest engineering and technical devices to reduce air pollution."[47] Cooperation continued to be the strategy of choice for citizens, administrators and industry alike, but it was a new kind of cooperation: it was no longer a gentlemen's agreement among good corporate citizens but rather the path of least resistance for the time being. With business stressing its moral obligation to curb pollution, and with the entire system of air pollution control being oriented towards cooperation, it was simply the easiest way for enraged citizens to work within the system, if only because lobbying for a different regulatory model was obviously a difficult and time-consuming endeavor. It gives an impression of the ambivalent stance towards cooperation in many of the new civic associations that Cleveland's Buhrer Air Pollution and Civic Association noted in its Spring 1962 newsletter, "We really do believe that the fact that industry knows that 678 persons are aroused, and organized, and sitting at the top of Jennings Rd. hill; has a constructive effect in strengthening industry's 'Social Conscience'."[48] In retrospect, that was a curious hybrid of the cooperative rhetoric emanating from the age of smoke and the "get-tough" approach that the new environmental sentiments inspired. Characteristically, the newsletter proudly cited "increasing industrial efforts to meet their social responsibilities," only to end with a call for a strict air pollution code and complaints about the slow pace of change.[49] It wasn't that citizens were generally distrustful of industrialists and experts, but they did not really trust them either.

The rift between citizens and the business community becomes clear only when one compares the lukewarm support from civic leagues with the emphatic praise that corporate captains and officials were offering for cooperative air pollution control. In a review of its program, the Allegheny County Bureau of Smoke Control was jubilant about "a definite, almost about-face in the attitude of industry," even going so far as to declare, "Were it not for the cooperation of industry, this Bureau might as well turn out its lights and close its doors."[50] Thus, there was a notable divergence of opinion between the views of "insiders" in industry and pollution control departments on the one hand and the "outsiders" in the growing number of civic leagues on the other, and the issue of cooperation was one of several where views and attitudes diverged. Generally, it seems that the gap between citizens and the regulatory establishment was not so much about different opinions as it was about different topics, for the divergence of themes and issues was unmistakable. For industrialists and regulators, the key themes were technical standards and timetables, along with the myriad of technical details that every active pollution control program comprises. With nationwide investments into air pollution control equipment lying in the range of $850 million per year in the mid-1960s, it should be clear that there was a huge number of technical issues waiting to be discussed within the regulatory establishment.[51] In contrast, civic protest focused overwhelmingly on the effects of air pollution, and specifically on the health hazards. Furthermore, the interest in health risks implied a tacit abdication from smoke abatement traditions, in which protest had usually emerged from cleanliness and property concerns. "The medical argument against air pollution always was a hard sell," environmental historian Adam Rome noted on the prevailing attitudes during the age of smoke.[52] But that was changing around 1960, as a statement before the Federal Power Commission by Mrs. Chauncy D. Harris, speaking on behalf of the Cleaner Air Committee of Hyde Park-Kenwood, demonstrated in 1964:

> Five years ago we began our fight against air pollution because we were weary of the dirt. Today we are continuing because we feel that the evidence is becoming overwhelming that our health and that of our children demand it.[53]

With that, there was a clear rift of rhetoric and interests among those concerned about air pollution, and it generally grew throughout the 1960s. The debate over air pollution problems followed a course that many societal debates took during the 1960s. Maurice Isserman and Michael Kazin spoke of a "Civil War of the 1960s" in their synthesis of the decade, thus drawing attention to a general trend toward divisive and antagonistic patterns of political debate.[54] To be sure, environmental issues were not prominent on the political agenda during most of the 1960s, and Isserman and Kazin barely mention them before the events of 1970.[55] And yet environmental debates, and specifically those on air pollution, did not remain untouched by a general escalation of rhetoric. In August 1965, the rock song "Eve of Destruction" rose to the top of the U.S. charts, and drastic, even apocalyptic rhetoric also emerged in debates over air pollution issues.[56] At a general meeting of the Metro Clean Air Committee in Minneapolis, participants discussed a scenario in which "air pollution is cutting off rays from the sun which is lowering the temperature and by the year 2000 we may have an ice age."[57] Other groups went public with their horror scenarios. "Some experts warn that as many as 10,000 people may die prematurely in the near future in one of the largest cities of the world which are blanketed by smog," a newsletter from the Conservation Foundation declared in 1966, adding that New York City and Los Angeles were "among the leading candidates for such a disaster".[58]

In 1971, Joseph Sax gave a name to this rift between the regulatory establishment and the environmental community when he chastised the former for its "insider perspective." Sax argued that industrialists and bureaucrats were overwhelmingly focusing on technical issues and had grown uninterested in the effects of air pollution that bothered the "outsiders," i.e. the general public.[59] Sax's critique was quite on the mark, not the least because his interpretation did not discount the efforts of industry, as so many other environmentalists did around 1970. Sax acknowledged that regulators and businessmen had made significant advances against pollutants but argued that, in evaluating and planning these policies, the regulatory establishment had grown insensitive to the demands of enraged citizens. But once again, there is good reason to doubt that this clash between "insiders" and "outsiders" was an inevitable conclusion of history. With the rift between insiders and environmentalists, it was perhaps inevitable that discussions over air pollution problems would grow more adversarial; but that does not mean that the clash would inevitably escalate to the extent that it did in 1970. It was one thing to argue that air pollution was a health hazard and that progress against the problem was too slow, but another one to argue that "What our industrial leaders deserve is a jail sentence for the crime they are committing against society", as a radio station with the ABC network in Chicago declared in a broadcast of November 1969.[60] In fact, environmentalists were still seeking cooperative approaches on the eve of the environmental revolution. As late as December 1968, the general meeting of the Metro Clean Air Committee decided unanimously to move "closer to the Minnesota Association of

Commerce and Industry," arguing that, "If we work together, we'll get more accomplished."[61] Cooperative air pollution control was clearly in trouble during the 1960s, but it was not doomed until shortly before the environmental revolution of 1970.

Cooperative air pollution control might have survived into the 1970s if it had not been for two developments of the late 1960s. One of them was a general swing of civic activism towards environmental issues, which had a lot to do with developments in other fields that had previously captured the public's attention, most prominently Vietnam and civil rights. The Vietnam war had dominated the 1968 presidential election, but the debate was clearly losing steam as it shifted from winning the war towards ending it after the Tet Offensive. Similarly, the civil rights struggle "passed into another stage characterized by bickering and shouting" after Martin Luther King's assassination on 4 April 1968, and participation of whites became next to impossible.[62] With that, a pattern of civic activism from these issues spilled into environmental discussions, and ecological themes looked all the more attractive to late 1960s activists because they offered to heal the wounds of previous disputes: in the light of the bitter civil rights struggle, it was refreshing to talk about an issue that concerned the very survival of whites and blacks alike, and in fact of every human being. Or that is how it looked to white middle-class citizens, for African Americans showed limited interest in sharing an all-encompassing ecological vision. When an editor asked Cleveland's mayor, Carl Stokes (the first black mayor of a major U.S. city), for a statement on pollution problems for a college handbook in the summer of 1970, he sourly replied, "Attention to ecological problems should not become a cop-out. The war on poverty, on hunger, and on inadequate health care should be America's first priority."[63] The early environmental movement was nowhere nearly as color-neutral as it saw itself.

The second event that doomed cooperative air pollution control had to do with previous legislation, specifically the federal Air Quality Act of 1967. As was common during the reign of cooperative air pollution control, industry, and specifically coal interests, had had an exceeding influence in the formulation of the Act, so much so that some saw it as "coal's law."[64] One of the stipulations that industry had successfully advocated was that state ambient air quality standards would need to become the subject of a public hearing.[65] The idea was obviously to provide an opportunity for industry to influence the process of standard setting, and give well-prepared lobbyists a chance to prevent unduly harsh standards. The initiative was thus testimony to an industrial community that was proud of its long history of splendid cooperation with experts and regulators, and generally convinced that cooperation represented the one rational approach to pollution troubles. However, environmentalists quickly saw these hearings as a golden opportunity, with federal officials playing a key role in efforts to get a good turnout. "I cannot emphasize too strongly the importance of public hearings in the implementation of this Act. They serve as the principal forum for all viewpoints to be heard and considered by both the public, and by the public servant," John Middleton, Commissioner of the National Air Pollution Control Administration, declared on numerous occasions.[66] As it turned out, these efforts were successful, and overwhelmingly so, for the hearings pursuant to the Air Quality Act became dominated by concerned citizens everywhere. The environmental movement's collective memory emphasizes the Earth Day celebrations on 22 April 1970, but the experience of hearings packed with enraged environmentalists was no less impressive. "Let the polluters know that to expect us to sacrifice human lives on their behalf is unrealistic," Congressman Abner J. Mikva declared at one of the first hearings in Chicago on 5 August 1969.[67] A month later, a Pittsburgh hearing attracted some 400 citizens, a quarter of them women, who heard the first speaker denounce the proposed standards as "legalized murder."[68] With that, there was no longer any way back to the cozy atmosphere of cooperation that had prevailed during the age of smoke.

The Underside of Success: Afterthoughts about the Environmental Revolution

The huge turnout in the air pollution hearings of 1969/70 was clearly a success for the nascent environmental movement, and an event that was instrumental in the passage of the federal Clean Air Act Amendments in late 1970. That story has been told numerous times, and there is no need to repeat it here. Of course, the rivalry between President Nixon and Senator Edmund Muskie was instrumental as it resulted in a "policy escalation" toward ever tougher provisions, but with the law of air pollution having been revised only three years earlier, the issue might not have appeared on the radar screen of either player if vigorous citizen protests in all parts of the country had not demonstrated the political vibrancy of the issue.[69] But while environmental sentiments were clearly inspiring politicians in 1970, the same cannot be said of concepts from the environmental community. Staunch as it was in its attacks on weak bureaucrats and standards, the environmental movement was notably poor in ideas about strategies and approaches that would do better. In fact, it was not until after the passage of the Clean Air Act Amendments that environmentalists began to advocate a regulatory strategy, most prominently through the creation of the Coalition to Tax Pollution in the summer of 1971.

This Coalition seems to be a forgotten chapter in the history of the environmental revolution, but it offers some valuable lessons on the downside of what was undoubtedly an important boom time that continues to fascinate environmental activists to the present day.[70] The Coalition's concern is already striking in its own right: after all, the Coalition was advocating a market-based approach to environmental regulation that did not become part of federal air pollution legislation until the Clean Air Act Amendments of 1990.[71] Furthermore, the Coalition to Tax Pollution drew support from a wide array of environmental associations. Corporate members were the National Audubon Society, the Federation of American Scientists, Environmental Action, Friends of the Earth, Zero Population Growth, the Wilderness Society, and the Sierra Club, as well as thirty-five local organizations from twenty-three states.[72] The idea also won support from economists, and the Coalition published a special brochure comprising accolades from scholars as diverse as James Tobin, Wassily Leontief, Paul Samuelson, and Milton Friedman—probably the only time that the latter came out in support of an environmental initiative. "I think it is appropriate for government to impose taxes on polluters to make it worth their own while to reduce the amount of pollution," Friedman told a Coalition interviewer.[73] With this kind of backing, it should come as no surprise that the Coalition to Tax Pollution eventually won a hearing with the Ways and Means Committee of the U.S. House of Representatives in March 1973. "To replace present policies the Coalition advocates using taxes to internalize the full social and environmental costs of producing goods," Laurence I. Moss, vice president of the Sierra Club speaking on behalf of the Coalition, pointed out on this occasion, criticizing the fact that, "at present, these costs, though real, are not included in the costs incurred by the polluter, or in the market price of the goods produced." As a start, the Coalition proposed a tax of 20¢ per pound of sulfur.[74] In a brochure of December 1971, the Coalition already gave thought to possible follow-up campaigns once it had established the sulfur tax: "Other pollutants for which pollution taxes would be particularly appropriate are BOD (biological oxygen demand—a measure of water pollution) and nitrogen oxides (another serious air pollutant)."[75]

The rise of the Coalition to Tax Pollution shows that the year 1970 was not only a time of environmental activism but also a time of rapid institutional learning. In a way, environmentalists were taking a crash course in environmental regulation, and the Coalition was a first result of these efforts. Environmentalists were surprisingly frank in acknowledging that they were still learning the nuts and bolts of environmental policy. Speaking in front of a congressional committee, Michael McCloskey, executive director of the

Sierra Club, readily admitted that environmentalists had seen taxes as merely "licenses to pollute" until very recently:

> Traditionally conservationists have been reluctant to consider economic factors in relation to controlling industrial pollution. They have been fearful that shifting the focus to these factors tends to move the discussion into an arena which is basically more favorable to the pleas of polluters.[76]

It may be surprising to find such innocence on regulatory issues in a movement that had been gathering momentum for more than a decade, but it is important to note that the setting of early environmental activism had not encouraged reflections on these kinds of issues. Faced with a regulatory establishment that favored cooperation and negotiations behind closed doors, activists of the late 1950s and 1960s generally came to accept this setting without much enthusiasm, trying to work within the system mostly because everything else was obviously an uphill job. In other words, the nascent environmental movement never came into a position to take major policy decisions until 1970; before that, policy decisions had already been taken, by representatives of a smoke abatement tradition that was distant from, though not necessarily at odds with, the guiding ideas of the environmental community. With that, there was no need to learn about environmental regulation until 1970, but then the need was suddenly urgent in order to keep pace with a rapid sequence of events.

Of course, there is no way to say whether the sulfur tax would have been a success. In fact, the prospects for a tax-based approach look somewhat meager when one recognizes that the idea itself was not new. As early as 1959, the Rand Corporation had presented a concept for a "smog tax" for Los Angeles, and Californians had not made use of it even though conditions for regulatory innovation were more favorable in Los Angeles than anywhere else in the country.[77] The concept certainly has the charm of having been tried successfully two decades later: in 1990, Congress created an emissions trading program for sulfur oxides, and assessments after ten years drew a highly favorable picture.[78] And yet there is no way to know whether market-based approaches would have worked with similar efficiency in the early 1970s; in fact, the sulfur oxides emissions trading program probably would not have become such a shining success itself if it had not been preceded by two decades of frustrating command-and-control regulation. In any case, the Coalition to Tax Pollution eventually lost its momentum, and the idea of a sulfur tax drowned somewhere along the tumultuous environmental and political events of 1973 and 1974.[79] In fact, the summer of 1971 may have been a bad time for a policy initiative on air pollution: after major legislation in 1967 and 1970, the bar was exceedingly high for yet another change of the law. When environmental activism was at its peak in 1970, with Nixon and Muskie competing on who was the better environmentalist, a sulfur tax probably would have flown through Congress on the momentum of environmental sentiments, but that moment had gone by unused. The environmental community had learned quickly in 1970, but probably not quickly enough.

Notes

1 Western Reserve Historical Society, Cleveland, Ohio Mss 4370 Container 10 Folder 169, Newsletter, Air Conservation Committee, Cleveland, vol. 1 issue 1 (1970), p. 2, and pamphlet of the Air Conservation Committee of 2 January 1970.

2 University of Montana, Missoula, Montana, Special Collections, Maureen and Mike Mansfield Library Mss 43 Box 1 Folder 48, *The GASP Newsletter*, April 1970, p. 2n.

3 Hazel Erskine, "The Polls: Pollution and its Costs," *Public Opinion Quarterly* 36 (1972), 121.

4 Citizens' Association of Chicago, *Annual Report 1880*, 8.

5 For an exhaustive discussion of the smoke abatement movement, see David Stradling, *Smokestacks and Progressives: Environmentalists, Engineers, and Air Quality in America, 1881–1951* (Baltimore: Johns Hopkins University Press, 1999), and Frank Uekoetter, *The Age of Smoke: Environmental Policy in Germany and the United States, 1880–1970* (Pittsburgh: University of Pittsburgh Press, 2009).

6 Cf. Joel A. Tarr and Carl Zimring, "The Struggle for Smoke Control in St. Louis: Achievement and Emulation," in Andrew Hurley (ed.), *Common Fields. An Environmental History of St. Louis* (St. Louis, MO: Missouri Historical Society Press, 1997); Joel A. Tarr, *The Search for the Ultimate Sink: Urban Pollution in Historical Perspective* (Akron, OH: University of Akron Press, 1996), 232–53; Sherie R. Mershon and Joel A. Tarr, "Strategies for Clean Air: The Pittsburgh and Allegheny County Smoke Control Movements, 1940–60," in Joel A. Tarr (ed.), *Devastation and Renewal: An Environmental History of Pittsburgh and Its Region* (Pittsburgh: University of Pittsburgh Press, 2003): 145–73.

7 Public Library of Cincinnati and Hamilton County, Rare Book Room, Pamphlet File, Air Pollution Control League of Greater Cincinnati, circular to members from Matthew Nelson, 28 June 1907.

8 Smoke Abatement League of Cincinnati, *Annual Report for 1911* (s.l., n.d.), 10.

9 Smoke Abatement League of Cincinnati, *Annual Report 1912*, 5n. See also Walter M. Squires, "Smoke Abatement Activities in American Cities: Cincinnati," *Heating and Ventilating Magazine* 14(10) (October 1917), 33.

10 *Williams' Cincinnati Directory, June 1916: Sixty-Sixth Annual Issue* (Cincinnati: Williams & Co., 1916), 13.

11 Cincinnati Historical Society Mss qA 298 Box 1 Folder 4, Charles N. Howison, "The History of a Citizens Organization for Cleaner Air," 27 July 1954, p. 1.

12 Cincinnati Historical Society Mss. qA 298 Box 1 Folder 3, Charles N. Howison, Executive Secretary, Air Pollution Control League of Greater Cincinnati, Press Release of 9 June 1955, p. 3.

13 Cincinnati Historical Society Mss qA 298 Box 1 Folder 1, The Smoke Abatement League, Annual Report for 1949, p. 3.

14 Cf. ibid., p. 5 and Cincinnati Historical Society Mss qA 298 Box 1 Folder 2, Howison to all officials in charge of air pollution control and to members of the Smoke Prevention Association of America, 10 September 1949.

15 Historical Society of Western Pennsylvania Archives, Senator John Heinz Pittsburgh Regional History Center, Pittsburgh, Mss 285 File "Smoke Control—General," help stop air pollution. Cleaner Air Week, 23–29 October 1966, p. 3.

16 Historical Society of Western Pennsylvania Archives Mss 285 File "Smoke Control—General," Cleaner Air Week, 23–29 October 1960, *Air Pollution Control Association Handbook*, pp. 2-1 and 2-8.

17 Cincinnati Historical Society Mss qA 298 Box 1 Folder 2, Notes on Meeting with Representatives of the Community Chest Board and Trustees of the Air Pollution Control League of Greater Cincinnati on 31 January 1969, p. 4.

18 Cincinnati Historical Society Mss qA 298 Box 1 Folder 4, Charles N. Howison, "Cleaner Air: The Community Commitment to the Seventies," 29 October 1970, p. 6.

19 Civic Club of Allegheny County, *Fifteen Years of Civic History. October 1895–December 1910* (s.l., n.d.), 33.

20 Archives of Industrial Society, University of Pittsburgh Libraries 83:7 Ser. I FF 1, Mrs. Franklin P. Iams to Mr. C. W. A. Veditz, 18 March 1912.

21 Pittsburgh City Council Archives, Proceedings, Hearing before the Pittsburgh Smoke Commission, 28 March 1941, p. 42.

22 Historical Society of Western Pennsylvania Archives Mss 285 File "Smoke Control—General," David N. Kuhn, Secretary, United Smoke Council, Smoke Elimination via the United Smoke Council, p. 1.

23 Historical Society of Western Pennsylvania Archives Mss 122 Box 1 Folder 5, *Communicator, Civic Club of Allegheny County* vol. 1 no. 5 (June 1971), p. 2.

24 Ibid., *Monthly Bulletin, Civic Club, Allegheny County* vol. 3 no. 3 (October 1969), p. 3.

25 Samuel P. Hays, "The Politics of Reform in Municipal Government in the Progressive Era," *Pacific Northwest Quarterly* 55 (1964), 159. Compare, for instance, the "List of Subscribers and Donors" in *Annual Report, the Smoke Abatement League of Cincinnati, Hamilton County, Ohio: For the Year Ending December 31, 1910*, pp. 10–15, with entries in *Social Register Cincinnati & Dayton 1910*.

26 Western Reserve Historical Society, Cleveland, Ohio Mss 3535 Box 1 Folder 4, "Women's City Club: History," p. 9.

27 Smoke Abatement League of Cincinnati, *Annual Report for 1912* (s.l., n.d.), p. 3.

28 Archives of Industrial Society 70:2 Add. 1971 Box 11 Folder 182, Smoke Meeting – 2-20-41 – 4:00 P.M., p. 7.

29 Cf. Angela Gugliotta, "Class, Gender, and Coal Smoke: Gender Ideology and Environmental Injustice in Pittsburgh, 1868–1914," *Environmental History* 5 (2000), 165–93; Angela Gugliotta, "How, When, and for Whom Was Smoke a Problem in Pittsburgh?," in Tarr (ed.), *Devastation and Renewal*, 110–25.

30 Pittsburgh City Council Archives, Proceedings, Hearing before the Pittsburgh Smoke Commission, March 28, 1941, p. 24.

31 Archives of Industrial Society 80:7 Box 1 FF 5, Pittsburgh Bureau of Smoke Prevention, "Report on Stationary Stacks: Year 1948," p. 7.

32 Cf. John D. Wirth, *Smelter Smoke in North America: The Politics of Transborder Pollution* (Lawrence: University Press of Kansas, 2000); Donald MacMillan, *Smoke Wars: Anaconda Copper, Montana Air Pollution, and the Courts, 1890–1924* (Helena: Montana Historical Society Press, 2000); Timothy LeCain, "The Limits of 'Eco-Efficiency'. Arsenic Pollution and the Cottrell Electrical Precipitator in the U.S. Copper Smelting Industry," *Environmental History* 5 (2000), 336–51; M.-L. Quinn, "Industry and Environment in the Appalachian Copper Basin, 1890–1930," *Technology and Culture* 34 (1993), 575–612.

33 W. C. L. Hemeon, "Air-Pollution Control," *Chemical Engineering Progress* 44(11) (November 1948), 18.

34 *Business Week* 1003 (20 November 1948), 21. On the Donora catastrophe, see Lynne Page Snyder, "The Death-Dealing Smog over Donora, Pennsylvania: Industrial Air Pollution, Public Health, and Federal Policy, 1915–1963" (Ph.D. dissertation, University of Pennsylvania, 1994), and her essay, "Revisiting Donora, Pennsylvania's 1948 Air Pollution Disaster," in Tarr (ed.), *Devastation and Renewal*, 126–44.

35 Edmund K. Faltermayer, "We Can Afford Clean Air," *Fortune* 72(5) (November 1965), 158–63, 218, 223–24.

36 National Association of Manufacturers, *Cinderella City: How Community Action Transformed Pittsburgh's Smoke-Stained Identity* (New York: s.n, 1962).

37 Archives of Industrial Society 69:14 Box 2 Folder 26A, "Report of the Mayor's Commission for the Elimination of Smoke," pp. 23–30.

38 Donald L. Miller, *City of the Century: The Epic of Chicago and the Making of America* (New York: Simon & Schuster, 1996), 233; Cleaner Air Committee of Hyde Park-Kenwood Records, Department of Special Collections, University of Chicago Library Folder 1, Laura Fermi, The Cleaner Committee, 1960, p. 1; ibid. Folder 4, Statement of the Cleaner Air Committee of Hyde Park-Kenwood before the Special Subcommittee on Air and Water Pollution of the Senate Committee on Public Works, 30 January 1964, p. 1.

39 Cleveland Chamber of Commerce, *Report of the Municipal Committee on the Smoke Nuisance* (s.l.: s.n., 1907); Western Reserve Historical Society Mss 4074 Folder 4, Ohio Pure Air Association, "For Immediate Release," 7 November 1965, p. 2.

40 Metro Clean Air Committee Records, Minnesota Historical Society, St. Paul, Minnesota Box 2 Folder "Unions", "Poison in our Air: National Conference on Air Pollution, United Steelworkers of America," 25 and 26 March 1969, p. 8.

41 Becker Medical Library, Washington University School of Medicine, St. Louis FC 12 Helen T. Graham Papers Series 7, 12/3/1/7, *Alert: by the Coalition for the Environment, St. Louis Region* vol. 1 no. 9 (March, 1971), p. 2.

42 Chicago Historical Society, Northeastern Illinois Planning Commission Records Box 83 Folder 3, Citizen Complaints of Air Pollution— Northeastern Illinois, 1 April 1966, p. 3.

43 Minnesota Historical Society Microfilm 1594, *News Letter Clear Air Clear Water Unlimited*, January 1958, p. 4.

44 Hudson River Conservation Society Papers, Franklin D. Roosevelt Presidential Library, Hyde Park, New York, Container 20 Folder "Financial Matters: Minute Book 1956–68," Minute Book, p. 69.

45 Western Reserve Historical Society Mss 4074 Folder 6, Southeast Air Pollution Committee, Casimir Bielen, Secretary, to Southeast Community Council, 18 February 1960.

46 Ibid. Folder 4, Ohio Pure Air Association, Casimir Bielen, secretary, letter to the editor, 1 February 1961.

47 Ibid. Folder 4, Ohio Pure Air Association, "For Immediate Release," 7 November 1965. The same press release also announced a "Citizen Award" for Casimir Bielen, still executive secretary of the association, "for being the most informed citizen concerning air pollution."

48 Western Reserve Historical Society Mss 4456 Box 7 Folder 114, *Buhrer Buzz: Official newsletter of the Buhrer Air Pollution and Civic Association*, Spring 1962 issue.

49 Ibid.

50 Archives of Industrial Society 80:7 Box 1 FF 1, County of Allegheny, Bureau of Smoke Control, "A Review of Program," 18 June 1951, p. 2.

51 National Archives of the United States, College Park, Maryland RG 90 A 1 Entry 11 Box 34 Folder "LL-2-1—Bills and Acts Part 2," Division of Air Pollution Control, "A Review of the New Jersey Air Pollution Control Program," August 1966, p. 7.

52 Adam W. Rome, "Coming to Terms with Pollution: The Language of Environmental Reform, 1865–1915," *Environmental History* 1(3) (July 1996), 16.

53 Cleaner Air Committee of Hyde Park-Kenwood Records Folder 5, Rebuttal Testimony of Mrs. Chauncy D. Harris, p. 6.

54 Maurice Isserman and Michael Kazin, *America Divided: The Civil War of the 1960s* (New York: Oxford University Press, 2000).

55 More generally, Adam Rome noted the dearth of references to environmentalism in conventional narratives of the 1960s: Adam Rome, " 'Give Earth a Chance': The Environmental Movement and the Sixties," *Journal of American History* 90 (2003), 525n.

56   Todd Gitlin, *The Sixties: Years of Hope, Days of Rage* (New York: Bantam, 1987), 195.

57   Metro Clean Air Committee Records Box 1 Folder "General" no. 1, Metro Clean Air Committee, General Meeting Minutes, 16 September 1969, p. 2.

58   Milwaukee Urban Archives, University of Wisconsin-Milwaukee, Milwaukee, Wisconsin, Milwaukee Series 44 Box 2 Folder 12, The Conservation Foundation, CF Commentary, 15 July 1966, p. 1.

59   Cf. Joseph L. Sax, *Defending the Environment: A Strategy for Citizen Action* (New York: Knopf, 1971).

60   Chicago Historical Society, Leon Mathis Despres Papers Box 88 Folder 5, WLS Viewpoint, "Clean Air is a Right, Not a Privilege."

61   Metro Clean Air Committee Records Box 1 Folder "General" Nr. 1, Minutes of the Metro Clean Air Committee General Meeting, 17 December 1968, p. 3.

62   Terry H. Anderson, *The Movement and the Sixties: Protest in America from Greensboro to Wounded Knee* (New York: Oxford University Press, 1995), p. 193.

63   Western Reserve Historical Society Mss 4370 Box 21 Folder 367, Carl B. Stokes to Mr. Aubrey N. Brown Jr., Editor, *Presbyterian Outlook*, 17 July 1970.

64   Richard H. K. Vietor, *Environmental Politics and the Coal Coalition* (College Station: Texas A&M University Press, 1980), p. 149.

65   Robert G. Dyck, *Evolution of Federal Air Pollution Control Policy 1948–1967* (Ph.D. dissertation, University of Pittsburgh, 1971), pp. 222, 253.

66   Delaware Valley Regional Planning Commission Records, Urban Archives, Temple University, Philadelphia Acc. 650 Box 44, John T. Middleton, "Air Pollution: Where Are We Going?" Presented at a conference on environmental pollution sponsored by the Junior League of Los Angeles and the Rand Corporation, Los Angeles, California, 6 December 1969, p. 7.

67   Chicago Historical Society, Leon Mathis Despres Box 87 Folder 1, Statement of Honorable Abner J. Mikva of Illinois before the Air Pollution Control Board on Proposed Ambient Air Quality Standards, August 1969, p. 3.

68   Historical Society of Western Pennsylvania Archives Mss 285 File "Smoke Control—General," Marshall Bridgewater, Memorandum on the September 9, 1969 Hearing on Proposed Air Pollution Control Standards, 12 September 1969, p. 1.

69   Cf. Charles O. Jones, *Clean Air. The Policies and Politics of Pollution Control* (Pittsburgh: University of Pittsburgh Press, 1975), 180. See also J. Brooks Flippen, *Nixon and the Environment* (Albuquerque: University of New Mexico Press, 2000).

70   Revealingly, the Coalition to Tax Pollution has even escaped the attention of scholars who specifically looked at the history of the emissions trading system: see Hugh S. Gorman and Barry D. Solomon, "The Origins and Practice of Emissions Trading," *Journal of Policy History* 14 (2002), 293–320.

71   Cf. Walter A. Rosenbaum, *Environmental Politics and Policy*, 4th ed. (Washington, DC: CQ Press, 1998), pp. 196n.

72 Oregon Historical Society, Portland, Oregon Mss 2386 Box 19 Folder 11, Coalition to Tax Pollution: Cooperating Organizations, attachment to Kathy Fletcher to "cooperating organizations," 19 January 1972.

73 Department of Special Collections, Charles E. Young Research Library, University of California, Los Angeles, California Collection 1199 Box 85 Folder 4, Coalition to Tax Pollution, "The Sulfur Tax: Economists Favor Taxing Pollution," 25 May 1972, pp. 2, 5n, 8. Quotation p. 2.

74 Oregon Historical Society Mss 2386 Box 19 Folder 11, Coalition To Tax Pollution, Washington, DC, 20 March 1973, "For Immediate Release: Coalition Seeks to Make Tax Policy More Responsive to Environmental Needs," p. 2.

75 The Bancroft Library, University of California, Berkeley, California BANC MSS 71/103 c Container 141 Folder 2, "Coalition to Tax Pollution, Turning the Tables on Polluters," December 1971, p. 2.

76 University of California, Los Angeles, Department of Special Collections, Collection 1199 Box 85 Folder 4, Statement of Michael McCloskey on Economic Incentives to Control Environmental Pollution before the Subcommittee on Priorities and Economy in Government of the Joint Economic Committee, 12 July 1971, p. 1.

77 D. M. Fort, W. A. Niskanen, A. H. Pascal, and W. F. Sharpe, *Proposal for a "Smog Tax"* (Santa Monica: RAND, 1959). On air pollution control in Los Angeles, see James E. Krier and Edmund Ursin, *Pollution and Policy: A Case Essay on California and Federal Experience with Motor Vehicle Air Pollution 1940–1975* (Berkeley: University of California Press, 1977), and Marvin Brienes, "The Fight Against Smog in Los Angeles, 1943–1957" (Ph.D. dissertation, University of California Davis, 1975).

78 Cf. A. Denny Ellerman, Paul L. Joskow, Richard L. Schmalensee, Juan-Pablo Montero, and Elizabeth M. Bailey, *Markets for Clean Air: The U.S. Acid Rain Program* (Cambridge: Cambridge University Press, 2000).

79 Cf. John F. Burby, "White House, Activists Debate Form of Sulfur Tax," *National Journal* 4 (1972), 1643–50, 1663–71.

CHAPTER 8

A Call to Action

Silent Spring, Public Disclosure, and the Rise of Modern Environmentalism

SARAH L. THOMAS

Several months after the publication of *Silent Spring*, Rachel Carson praised the public response to her best-selling book in a speech to the Garden Club of America.[1] She commended not only the increased awareness about the dangers of pesticides and the government's heightened attention to address these hazards, but also the growing tendency among the public to demand access to information and to insist on change. Referring to the public response to *Silent Spring*, she stated:

> The most hopeful sign is an awakening of strong public interest and concern. People are beginning to ask questions and to insist upon proper answers instead of meekly acquiescing in whatever spraying programs are proposed.[2]

The statement illustrates Carson's commitment not just to conveying the potential risks associated with pesticides, but also to encouraging an informed public to participate in decisions regarding the application of scientific innovations. As such, it highlights Carson's engagement with important intellectual and political questions of the 1960s regarding the relationship between science, the public, and democratic decision-making.

Silent Spring represented a significant contribution to debates about science and its role in society in the 1960s. Like other scholarly works of the era, notably Thomas Kuhn's *The Structure of Scientific Revolutions* (1962), *Silent Spring* was part of a cultural–political movement that altered the prevailing views of science of the time, reshaping ideas about the nature of scientific inquiry and about the role of science in society.[3] Carson challenged the pervasive belief in scientists' beneficence, the disinterestedness of their research, and, most importantly, the openness and certainty of their findings. The degree of scientific uncertainty about pesticides and scientists' failure to communicate this uncertainty to the public were important messages of *Silent Spring* and were central to Carson's critique of the scientific community. In addition, Carson's work expressed an explicit concern for the role of science in society, particularly its effects on the public. Carson strongly rejected science removed from democracy, or science as "the prerogative of only a small number of human beings isolated and priest-like in their laboratories" as she described in 1952.[4] She also protested the idea that the public should be treated as "guinea pigs" as a part of the scientific endeavor.[5] As such, she emphasized the critical importance of public access to information about both scientists' findings and the nature and degree of uncertainty in their findings. Only with access to such important information could a mobilized, politically engaged public make knowledgeable decisions about the level of environmental risk it was willing to accept.

The fact that *Silent Spring* engaged so strongly in contemporary questions regarding science and its role in society helped give shape to the approaches and tools that defined environmentalism after World War II. In particular, Carson's work contributed to a growing emphasis on access to information and public participation, both of which emerged as key tenets of the new environmentalism. The "right to know" and public decision-making were central to key pieces of federal environmental legislation during the 1960s and early 1970s.

This examination of *Silent Spring*'s engagement with the broader intellectual discourse of the 1960s seeks to deepen the understanding of the book's significance to its historical moment and to the environmental awakening it helped to shape. In doing so, it builds on two of the many veins of scholarship that now exist regarding *Silent Spring*.[6] First, it draws on analyses of Carson's relationship to modern environmentalism and to America's burgeoning ecological consciousness. Many historians, notably Donald Worster, situate Carson among earlier ecologists and analyze her role in raising the public's awareness about the environment. Worster maintains that, like Aldo Leopold's *The Sand County Almanac* (1949), Paul Ehrlich's *The Population Bomb* (1968), and Barry Commoner's *The Closing Circle* (1971), Carson's work was instrumental in encouraging Americans to reconsider their relationship to nature and to usher in modern environmentalism.[7] Other scholars also have come to refer to *Silent Spring* and modern environmentalism in the same breath, describing Carson's work as an "epoch-making book" that "led to an effective environmental movement."[8]

This article also draws on a second body of scholarship that considers Carson in relationship to shifting notions of science in the postwar era, particularly mounting public concerns about the health effects of scientific innovations. Biographer Linda Lear argues that much of Carson's importance stems from her challenge to prevailing postwar ideas about science. In particular, she identifies Carson's critical role in highlighting the "moral vacuity" of the government and scientists who failed to acknowledge the dangers of pesticides and in exposing the culture of science that "arrogantly claimed dominion over nature."[9] Other scholars note that debates about dangerous chemicals that gained notoriety after the cranberry crisis of Thanksgiving 1958, the thalidomide scare of 1962, and the decade-long controversy over radioactive fallout influenced the public's acceptance of Carson's work.[10] As one scholar argues, the public was "prepared" to "understand the basic concepts underlying Rachel Carson's *Silent Spring*."[11] Recent scholarship also analyzes the vehement response Carson elicited from the chemical industry and the scientific establishment, which portrayed her book as "unscientific" and insisted that her claims were "distorted, selective, overstated, alarmist, hysterical, and reliant on scare tactics."[12] In addition, scientists also invoked Carson's gender to undermine the legitimacy of her writings, questioning why "a spinster with no children is worried about genetics."[13]

Despite the importance of the existing scholarship on *Silent Spring*, there is more to understand about Carson's ideas about science and her contributions to environmentalism. A closer analysis of Carson's place within the robust intellectual discourse on science in the 1960s will elucidate her particular concerns about science and its role in society and will highlight her importance to broader debates of the era. It also will provide a more detailed understanding of the ways in which Carson, and her assessment of science and society, shaped modern environmentalism. In challenging many of the prevailing ideas about science, Carson raised specific questions about information and public participation in decision-making in a scientific age, questions that ultimately led many environmentalists to emphasize the need for greater public access to information and increased public participation in decisions regarding the environment and public health.

Carson dedicated much of her career to providing the public with accessible scientific information about the natural world. This devotion was predicated on a deep belief in the importance of science in daily life, likely a result of the nature study traditions she experienced as a child.[14] Yet the Progressive era institutions that encouraged nature study as a method of promoting conservationist values also championed the importance and authority of technical expertise. This second phenomenon created a culture of "leaving it to the experts," which Carson regarded as intellectually problematic and socially dangerous. "Science is not something that belongs in a compartment of its own, separated from everyday life," she asserted in 1952. "The materials of science are the materials of life itself."[15] This idea guided much of her professional life. After receiving a master's degree in zoology from Johns Hopkins in 1932, Carson devoted her career to working as an editor and biologist for the Fish and Wildlife Service. In 1951, she published *The Sea Around Us*, an eloquent, scientific description of the marine world for which she received the National Book Award. She also published the best-seller *The Edge of the Sea* in 1955, detailing scientific elements of the marine world. In writing *Silent Spring*, Carson again sought to provide the public with important scientific information, this time about the negative effects of pesticides and other chemicals.[16] In doing so, Carson worked hard to ensure the scientific integrity of the book. She thoroughly researched the existing data on pesticides, collaborated with other scientists in compiling and verifying facts, and welcomed scientists' input on draft versions of *Silent Spring*.[17] (See Figure 8.1)

Despite her devotion to science, Carson confronted many of the dominant postwar notions about science and the nature of scientific inquiry in *Silent Spring*. For one, she mounted a strong challenge against the broadly held belief that scientists' work was always in the public's interest. This faith in the beneficence of science pervaded postwar America. As the scholar Don Price asserted in 1965, most Americans believed that "what's good for science is good for the nation."[18] After all, scientific and technological advances, including those by the chemical industry, appeared to be an integral part of the nation's booming postwar prosperity and Americans' improved quality of life. Yet *Silent Spring* provided ample evidence of the ways in which scientific applications could have new and unanticipated consequences, many of which could be quite dangerous for the nation's public. As Carson persuasively demonstrated, the chemical effects of pesticides not only threatened the health of birds and wildlife, they also imperiled Americans' soil, water supplies, and very bodies.

Carson not only chronicled the potential hazards of pesticides, she made sure to show that the scientific community allowed these dangers to persist. Incorporated into her explanations of chemicals' harmful effects were accounts of scientists who failed to protect the public good and even failed to acknowledge that any danger existed. In a strongly worded critique, Carson related a decision by a committee of the Federal Drug Administration to al-

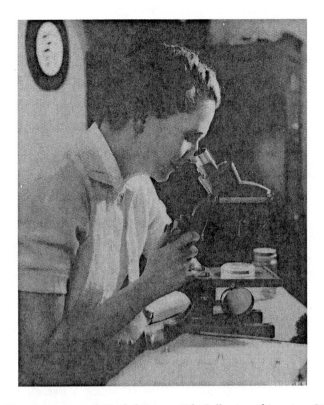

Figure 8.1 The scientist at work: Rachel Carson. Yale Collection of American Literature, Bienecke Rare book and Manuscript Library, Yale University, New Haven, CT. Rachel Carson, 1962. Phoograph by Brooks Studio. Used by permission.

low a certain chemical to be marketed for two years while the agency determined whether the chemical was a carcinogen. "Although the committee did not say so," Carson wrote, "its decision meant that the public was to act as guinea pigs, testing the suspected carcinogen along with the laboratory dogs and rats."[19] Through this condemnation, Carson asserted that the public was not always the beneficiary of scientific advances; in fact, in some instances it had become an object of scientific experiments.

What made scientists' disregard for the public's welfare more egregious was the fact that, on occasion, they knowingly denied evidence about the dangers of pesticides and other chemicals. Carson's account of wildlife losses due to pesticide applications is representative of this belief. She described how wildlife biologists "assert that the losses [to wildlife] have been severe and in some cases even catastrophic."[20] Despite significant evidence, however, scientists within the control agencies, tended "to deny flatly and categorically that such losses have occurred, or that they are of any importance if they have."[21] In Carson's mind, government agencies also were at fault for misrepresenting the risks associated with pesticides, even when the data suggested that they were significant. Carson cited an aggressive spraying campaign in the southern United States to kill the fire ant. After the campaign, scientists accumulated data about its impacts. She wrote that the studies "revealed losses running all the way up to complete destruction of wildlife in the treated areas."[22] Nonetheless, the Department of Agriculture "brushed away all evidence of damage as exaggerated and misleading."[23] In presenting such cases, Carson highlighted the reality that neither the scientific community nor government agencies always had the public good in mind. In doing so, one scholar has commented, Carson effectively demonstrated "the failings of the inner circle of science and government charged with protecting the public against health threats."[24]

Closely tied to Carson's challenge to the notion of scientists' beneficence was her belief that scientists could be influenced by personal biases and, more problematically, by their economic ties to industry. As such, Carson confronted another deeply held tenet of the time, most clearly articulated in Robert K. Merton's description of the scientific ethos, namely the disinterestedness of science.[25] Whereas the public traditionally viewed scientists as disinterested researchers, discovering observable and objective facts, Carson highlighted the fact that their training and their economic ties strongly influenced their findings. For instance, in relating the disparate conclusions of biologists and entomologists concerning the effects of pesticides on wildlife populations, Carson argued that the different training and mentality of the scientists explained the discrepancies in their conclusions. As she noted, an entomologist was not "psychologically disposed to look for undesirable side effects" of specific control programs.[26] In short, scientists *had* interests, and these interests shaped both the questions they asked and the way the interpreted the answers.

More pointedly, Carson maintained that scientists' affiliations and funding directly shaped their interpretation of data. In a striking passage in *Silent Spring*, Carson challenged the perceived objectivity of scientists, writing:

> Inquiry into the background of some of these men reveals their entire research program is supported by the chemical industry. Their professional prestige, sometimes their very jobs, depends on the perpetuation of chemical methods. Can we then expect them to bite the hand that literally feeds them? But knowing their bias, how much credence can we give to their protests that insecticides are harmless?[27]

Far from viewing scientists as "isolated and priest-like," Carson illustrated the considerable forces that influenced scientists' work. These forces were results of scientists' training and disposition, but they were also results of powerful, well organized companies with particular agendas. For Carson, the reality that major chemical companies were "pouring money into the universities to support research on insecticides" helped to explain the "otherwise mystifying fact that certain outstanding entomologists are among the leading advocates of chemical control."[28] The sharp response *Silent Spring* elicited from the chemical industry, and from scientists within their influence, certainly underscored Carson's belief in the lack of disinterestedness among scientists. As scholars effectively demonstrate, the chemical industry launched a concerted and vicious campaign to discredit the findings in *Silent Spring* and Carson personally. Subsequent claims that Carson was "hysterical," that the book was "fantasy," and that the country would "return to the Dark Ages" without pesticides hardly squared with notions of scientists working objectively, without strong personal interests, on scientific discovery.[29]

Carson's skepticism of both scientists' beneficence and their disinterestedness paralleled and, in some cases, contributed to ideas held by other important scholars of her time. As Charles Rosenberg argues, Carson, Thomas Kuhn, and other commentators on science were part of "the same political discourse" in which "science and technology became . . . a kind of social nemesis."[30] Like Carson, scholars of the 1960s began to question science's role as "the ultimate provider of the means through which to attain a better life."[31] Price, for instance, in *Scientific Estates* (1965), challenged the pervasive belief in science's benefit to the broader public. He wrote, "The simple reassurance that science is bound to be good for you is not likely to be adequate, especially in view of the new potentialities for both good and evil."[32] Other intellectual and political leaders of the time expressed similar concerns about science. C. P. Snow's famous depiction of "The Two Cultures," published in 1961, warned of the "great gulf" between science and the humanities and of a "possible monopoly of scientific advice to high political authority."[33] Similarly, in his farewell address, President Eisenhower expressed concern that the nation might "become captive of a scientific–technological elite."[34] Inherent in these concerns was the belief that scientists might not always act out of disinterestedness or with the public good in mind. Not only did Carson share these worries, the information she provided directly influenced scholars' thinking on such matters. Price, in fact, alluded to Carson's work in describing the dangers presented by scientific advances. "Our popular worries about intercontinental missiles and radiation fallout, in which our alarm can be directed against an alien enemy, are bad enough," he wrote. "But to these worries we have added the fear that scientists are about to use chemistry to poison our crops and rivers [and] biology to meddle with our heredity."[35]

Moreover, scholars maintained that although scientists possessed technical expertise this knowledge did not grant them an inherent moral authority or an ability to make wise policy decisions on behalf of the public good. As one scholar observed in 1965, "A scientist may have a PhD in molecular biology and have little interest in or understanding of ethical issues."[36] Likewise Price, directly citing Carson's discussion of the fire ant, asserted:

> You can readily invent chemicals to kill a pest like a fire ant but it is . . . very much harder to decide how to staff the Department of Agriculture so as to get the right mixture of chemical and biological and political judgment involved in the decision to use it or not.[37]

These concerns led scholars to debate directly the role of science in policy decisions. Ralph Lapp, an important scholar of the time, expressed strong concerns about the risks of allowing a scientific elite to control public policy. "We face the real danger of a layered society in which a scientist elite fraction floats up on top and dominates our policy-making," he argued.[38] In order to preserve democracy in an age dominated by science, the country needed to maintain a "democratic dialogue" in which "expert-citizens" alerted the public to possible dangers and in which the public fulfilled its duty to "listen, to translate, and to debate."[39] Price agreed, maintaining that the "scientific estate" should not have exclusive authority over decision-making. "It is abundantly clear," he wrote, "that some type of decisions have to be made, not by professionals using scientific techniques, but by other kinds of individual thought and collective deliberation."[40]

Carson certainly shared this concern about the role of science in society, and *Silent Spring* represented an important contribution to the discourse about science and democratic decision-making. Carson clearly rejected the notion that scientists or government agencies alone should make decisions about scientific applications. After all, the decision to apply chemicals was "not only scientific but moral" and the potential health effects resulting from the decision would be borne by the broader public.[41] This reality made the question of decision-making crucial. Carson wrote, "Who has made the decision that sets in motion these chains of poisoning . . . Who has decided— who has the *right* to decide—for the countless legions of people who were not consulted . . . ?"[42] Carson strongly maintained that this right lay with the public and that citizens should have the right to a "democratic dialogue" in which they participated in decisions that dearly affected them. The very presentation of *Silent Spring*, a book directed at the public as opposed to policy makers and politicians, underscored Carson's deep conviction that citizens should be consulted and should play a critical role in such important decisions.

Given this view, Carson maintained that public access to reliable and accurate information about scientific applications, about both the information scientists possessed (but often withheld from the public) and the level of uncertainty about their data, was critical. For only with reliable information could the public participate effectively in decision-making or even demand political action and policy changes in the first place. "The public must decide whether it wishes to continue on the present road," insisted Carson, "and it can do so only when in full possession of the facts."[43]

Not surprisingly, then, information and the lack thereof dominated Carson's discussion of science and society in *Silent Spring*. For one, Carson severely criticized occasions when the scientific community and government agencies withheld or misrepresented information to the public. She recounted, for instance, a case in which a reservoir popular with fishermen was treated with pesticides in order to kill the gnat population. The public was not consulted about the project, yet still was "forced either to drink water containing poisonous residues or to pay out tax money for the treatment of the water to remove the poisons—treatments that are by no means foolproof."[44] Withholding information about the spraying and its risks, especially given the potential dangers, represented a violation of the public trust. "We have subjected enormous numbers of people to contact with these poisons," Carson chastised, "without their consent and often without their knowledge."[45]

What troubled Carson were not just instances in which scientific information was withheld from the public, but also the degree of scientific uncertainty about the effects of pesticides on natural ecosystems and the human body before they were introduced into the environment. The lack of information resulted, in part, from scientists' myopia or inattention to the interaction of various chemicals. Carson described how scientists only examined the effects of individual chemicals in laboratories and failed to research how they might interact in everyday situations. "The common salad bowl may easily present a combination of organic phosphate insecticides," she explained. Of great concern was the fact that "the full scope of the dangerous interactions of chemicals is as yet little known."[46] Yet the lack of information also was due to the inability of biologists to keep pace with the rapid introduction of new pesticides. For, Carson wrote, "the chemists' ingenuity in devising insecticides has long ago outrun biological knowledge of the way these poisons affect the living organism."[47]

The lack of information was so alarming because it was the public who would bear the potential health risks resulting from the scientific uncertainty. Consequently, even though the knowledge about pesticides' dangers was less than certain, the public had a right to know about the information—and the lack of information—that existed.

Indeed, in Carson's view, it was partly on account of the uncertainty of scientific knowledge that the public deserved greater access to information and a greater role in decisions affecting it. Quoting the French biologist and activist Jean Rostand, Carson wrote, "The obligation to endure gives us the right to know."[48]

Given Carson's belief that public access to information was a critical element of ensuring democratic decision-making, it is not surprising that she praised the public's increasing demands for information and its calls to political action in the speeches she gave subsequent to the publication of *Silent Spring*. As she stated in a lecture to the Kaiser Foundation in 1963:

> I for one would like to see the American public treated like individuals, capable of hearing the truth about the hazards that exist in the modern environment, and capable of making intelligent decisions as to prudent and necessary measures that ought to be taken.[49]

In fact, she consistently commented favorably on instances when the public started to question authority and to "insist upon proper answers instead of meekly acquiescing."[50] Carson praised such demands for better information, regarding them as key components of broader calls for political action. In a speech to the Federation of Homemakers in 1963, Carson claimed that the "most heartening" part of the letters she received was "the number of people who want to do something. And this is a personal and active thing. They don't merely ask 'why doesn't the government correct the problem?' They ask, 'what can I do to help?'"[51] Carson's emphasis on the actions of individual citizens is particularly striking in light of government efforts to solve the problems with pesticides. By 1963, federal agencies were starting to consider action against pesticides and many state legislatures had begun to enact stricter pesticide regulations. Although Carson regarded these government actions as important, she consistently placed greater emphasis on the "reappearance of a sense of personal responsibility."[52] Carson put such significance on personal knowledge and action because she believed they were critical to ensuring democratic processes.

What is striking in analyzing the responses to *Silent Spring*, and what provides further evidence of the importance of Carson's emphasis, is the subsequent focus placed on information. Indeed, the issue of information and the lack thereof was a dominant theme both of a primary journalistic response to Carson's work, a CBS broadcast in April 1963, and of private letters to Carson. The CBS broadcast, entitled "The Silent Spring of Rachel Carson" and reported by Jay McMullen and Eric Sevareid, was instrumental in bringing

Silent Spring and the surrounding controversy to the attention of the public. CBS estimated that 10 to 15 million people viewed the program, "a huge number of whom had not read the book but were concerned and confused by what they had been reading."[53] The CBS report proved to be highly influential. According to Lear, the broadcast "shattered months of comparative quiet in Washington on the pesticide issue" and prompted scores of angry letters to federal agencies "decrying their lack of scientific evidence about the long term effects of what they were doing."[54]

In their broadcast, Sevareid and McMullen clearly echoed Carson's concern for the lack of adequate information on the dangers of pesticides and her critique of occasions when scientists withheld existing information from the public. The reporters related cases in which scientists disagreed about their interpretation of information and in which their assertions appeared false. In describing the influence of Carson's book, for instance, they compared a scientist who argued that *Silent Spring* "should be ignored" with a Nobel Prize-winning scientist who praised Carson's book.[55] Likewise, in the first part of the show, they included statements by several government scientists dismissing the claims of *Silent Spring*. The commissioner of the Federal Drug Administration, for instance, asserted that to his knowledge there had been no "human injuries caused by an amount of pesticide on a food product which did not exceed the tolerance."[56] Similarly, a toxicologist with the Public Health Service insisted that "there is no evidence that the small doses of pesticides that we do get are causing any harm."[57] Yet, by the end of the report, such assertions of scientific knowledge appeared inadequate. As Sevareid pointed out, the number of deaths from pesticides had not been reported since 1957 and "the total number of injuries and illnesses caused by pesticides each year is unknown."[58]

Indeed, the dominant message of the broadcast was the lack of concrete information about pesticides. The reporters asked government officials a multitude of questions about pesticides from the number of non-fatal pesticide poisonings in the country to the effects of pesticides on soil and water. Repeatedly, the government scientists displayed their ignorance on the subject. In a characteristic exchange, McMullen questioned Dr. Page Nicholson from the Public Health Service about the effects of pesticides on water and aquatic life:

McMullen: Do you know how long the pesticides persist in the water once they get into it?

Nicholson: Not entirely.

McMullen: Do you know the extent to which our groundwater may be contaminated right now by pesticides?

Nicholson: We don't know that either, nor do we know if concentration may be occurring in ground water.

McMullen: Do you know the effect of long-term exposure of pesticides in aquatic life?

Nicholson: Not completely.

McMullen: Do you know how pesticides may inter-react within water organisms?

Nicholson: This, too, is an area where we need to know more.[59]

Such responses resonated strongly with Carson's concerns about the lack of certainty regarding the dangers of pesticides. Moreover, the reporters' ultimate conclusion that "scientist after scientist has pointed to an appalling scarcity of facts concerning the effects of pesticides on man and his environment" clearly underscored Carson's central message.[60]

Like Carson, the reporters also emphasized the need for greater disclosure to the public about the known and unknown dangers in order that it might determine the future course of action about pesticides since it assumed the risks associated with them. During an exchange, McMullen subtly criticized officials' disregard for the public's welfare. Questioning the Secretary of the United States Department of Agriculture about the lack of information given to the public, he asked, "During the past years, do you think that the public was sufficiently appraised of the potential hazards of pesticides?"[61] When Secretary Freeman responded that the public would not have been "receptive" to such information, McMullen pointedly retorted, "In what ways would it not be receptive to learning that it may possibly be facing a health hazard?"[62]

Six weeks later, in a second broadcast on the controversy surrounding *Silent Spring*, CBS reported on the conclusions of a paper issued by the Federal Council on Science and Technology. The paper vindicated Carson's claims. According to the council, Sevareid stated, "Little is known about the long-term and cumulative effects of pesticides on people. Experimental data is scanty and data on children non-existent."[63] Sevareid concluded the broadcast by echoing Carson's concern for the lack of scientific information. "There is danger in the air, and in the waters, and in the soil, and the leaves and the grass," he stated. "Both *Silent Spring* and the council's report," he said, "tell us we must know far far more about it. We must police it more firmly. There must be many changes in procedures, technical and governmental. There must be new laws and regulations."[64]

Private letters sent to Carson subsequent to *Silent Spring*'s publication also emphasized the lack of information; in these letters, the focus was less on scientific uncertainty and more on the failure of scientists and the government to alert the public to the dangers of pesticides. Indeed, the letters exhibited a marked preoccupation with the issue of knowledge and a pervasive anger that the public had not been informed about the potential dangers of pesticides. In a characteristic letter, Elizabeth Aleck wrote, "What is so alarming is that we are not told about these things."[65] Expressing a similar outrage at the lack of information, Sally Reahard claimed that the danger of pesticides "is much more serious than the fall out menace . . . at least that receives national publicity."[66] Other respondents suggested that such information was consciously withheld from the public. Audrey Newcomb stated, "I have been familiar with many of the facts that went into this article for some time but for the most part these have been suppressed from popular magazines and from newspapers."[67] Judith Jay agreed, stating, "Too large a segment of the population has been in ignorance of these hazards."[68]

Indeed, most readers regarded Carson's book as a public service for the very fact that it alerted citizens to the potential dangers around them. Walter Rosenberg, for one, thanked Carson for the public service she performed in warning Americans "who were heretofore largely or completely unaware of the dangers" of pesticides. He went on to compare her to the muckrakers of the early twentieth century.[69] Other letters centered on the fact that Carson confirmed citizens' own concerns about the dangers of pesticides. Dorothy Pernell wrote that "many of us have been convinced of the harm of all the items" in *Silent Spring* and that the book was "just what was needed to document our opinion."[70] Thus, many respondents regarded Carson's role as critical in helping to inform the public.

It also is clear from the letters that Carson's emphasis on public disclosure and action resonated with the public. One of the most dominant themes of the letters, in fact far more prominent than expressions of fear about pesticides, was a desire to inform others about the content of *Silent Spring*. A strong contingent of respondents focused their energies on conveying the information to friends, the government, and citizen organizations. Many expressed their belief that "the message must be passed on" and that they "should like to see to it that this information is distributed wherever it is needed."[71] Private citizens informed Carson that they had written to senators, representatives, and officials in government agencies. In addition, respondents expressed a desire to act on the information. "Never before have I read anything that moved me to serious thought and action," wrote David Peat.[72]

The responses to *Silent Spring*, by prominent journalists and by private citizens, demonstrate the extent to which Carson's specific concerns about public access to scientific information, both the known and unknown risks of pesticide, and to public action dominated discussions about the book after its publication. This fact certainly underscores *Silent Spring*'s importance to the history of environmentalism. They also provide insight into the importance of *Silent Spring* for modern environmentalism.

Indeed, *Silent Spring*'s engagement with fundamental questions of the 1960s regarding science and democratic decision-making were critical in shaping American environmentalism. For one, Carson's presentation of the limits of scientists' beneficence, disinterestedness, and claims to secure knowledge influenced the changing ideas about science that evolved in the decades after World War II. Just as Carson exposed the limits of scientists' knowledge about and concern for the effects of pesticides, so too did other environmental problems expose the reality that scientists often had limited information or differing interpretations of the information that existed. In this way, the emerging environmental issues of the 1960s and 1970s exposed what the historian Samuel P. Hays calls "the frontiers of scientific judgment."[73] The suggestion that scientists often lacked the information necessary to assess the impacts of science and technology on the environment and public health became a dominant part of environmentalists' dialogue about science. Likewise, Carson's call for greater information about these unknown impacts was a critical part of the environmental agenda. "There was little data about water or air quality or patterns of land use, and health monitoring was equally skimpy," observed Hays. "Environmentalists urged that public funding help fill the gaps."[74]

More significantly, environmentalists' emphasis on the right to know and the belief in the importance of public disclosure stemmed directly from Carson and the discourse of the 1960s.[75] As Hays notes, "The control of information was the crucial element in environmental politics."[76] The value environmentalists came to place on the public's right to know reflected Carson's influence. "The issue," explains Hays, "was no longer simply the right to speak and be heard, but the right to have access to information that was crucial for successful public action."[77]

The concern for access to information is evident in the legislation that followed *Silent Spring*. The Freedom of Information Act (FOIA), enacted in 1964, partially reflected this tug-of-war over information. Although the basis for and intent of FOIA preceded the environmental movement, it was clearly and explicitly designed to ensure public access to information. It had important consequences for environmentalism as it provided a means through which the public could gain the information that was "necessary for political action."[78] The emphasis on public access to information also played a prominent role under the National Environmental Policy Act, enacted in 1969. The act emphasizes the full disclosure of information to the public—actions affecting the quality of the environment have to be revealed, in order for federal agencies to analyze the impacts adequately, but they do not have to be prevented. NEPA's focus on disclosure as opposed to mitigation has received criticism, but the law reveals the fundamental importance of public access to information to environmental politics. As the scholar David Vogel notes, the emphasis on public information, an echo of the Progressive era, was based on "a great deal of faith in the efficacy of disclosure as a mechanism for disciplining both business and government."[79]

The emphasis on public disclosure also was predicated on the belief that the public should be involved in environmental decisions that affected it. Only with adequate information could public participation in the political process be effective. Indeed, through its provisions for public disclosure, NEPA opened the way for citizens and environmental groups to protest a range of environmental projects to their public representatives and to government agencies. It also provided a powerful tool for a new litigious group of environmental organizations to contest environmental projects and decisions through the courts. Even more traditional elements of conservation were affected by this emphasis on public participation. A critical component of many resource management plans since the 1960s has been public participation. Management plans under federal agencies require extensive public review and comment periods, requirements that are clearly part of the effort to ensure public participation in decision-making processes. Thus, the emphases on both public disclosure and public participation are key elements of modern environmentalism.

At the time of *Silent Spring's* publication, Supreme Court Justice William O. Douglas called it "the most revolutionary book since *Uncle Tom's Cabin*" and claimed that it would be "the most important chronicle of this century for the human race."[80] Douglas's prediction proved true in more ways than one. Certainly, *Silent Spring* was important in raising awareness about the specific issue of pesticides and in helping to launch modern environmentalism. Yet, as with so many elements of environmental history, the book possessed a broader and deeper significance to American intellectual and political history than generally acknowledged by historians. *Silent Spring* reflected and explicitly engaged central intellectual questions of the era and Carson made important contributions to ideas about the relationship between science and democracy. Her focus on public disclosure and public participation also helped to shape the political tactics that would drive much of the environmental activism leading up to and beyond the first Earth Day in April 1970. In doing so, she empowered generations of citizens to ask questions, seek proper answers, and demand change.

Notes

1   *Silent Spring* first appeared in serial form in *The New Yorker* on 16, 23, and 30 June 1962. Houghton Mifflin published the book in September 1962. For more on the

publication of *Silent Spring*, see Priscilla Coit Murphy, *What a Book Can Do: The Publication and Reception of Silent Spring* (Amherst: University of Massachusetts Press, 2005).

2 Rachel Carson speech to Garden Club of America, 8 January 1963, box 101, Rachel Carson Papers. Yale Collection of American Literature, Beinecke Rare Book and Manuscript Library, Yale University, New Haven, CT. Copyright © 1998 by Roger Allen Christie. Used by permission.

3 As Charles Rosenberg notes, Carson and Kuhn were both part of a cultural–political movement that brought science into the "realm of the temporal, the contingent, and the negotiated." Charles Rosenberg, *No Other Gods: On Science and American Social Thought*, rev. ed. (Baltimore: John Hopkins University Press, 1997), xi.

4 Rachel Carson National Book Award Speech, 29 January 1952, box 101, Rachel Carson Papers. Copyright © 1998 by Roger Allen Christie. Used by permission.

5 Rachel Carson, *Silent Spring*, 40th Anniversary Edition (Boston: Houghton Mifflin Company, 2002), 224. Copyright © 1962 by Rachel L. Carson. Used by permission.

6 An excellent and extensive scholarship exists on *Silent Spring* and Rachel Carson, ranging from analyses of the media response to the book to investigations of Carson's private life. Linda Lear provides an excellent biography of Carson and a thorough account of the publication of and response to *Silent Spring* in Linda Lear, *Rachel Carson: Witness for Nature* (New York: Henry Holt and Company, 1997). Maril Hazlett and Julia Corbett also offer strong analyses of the response to *Silent Spring*, particularly the gendered attacks from the chemical industry. See Maril Hazlett, "Woman vs. Bugs: Gender and Popular Ecology in Early Reactions to *Silent Spring*," *Environmental History Review* 9 (2004), 701–29, and Julia B. Corbett, "Women, Scientists, Agitators: Magazine Portrayal of Rachel Carson and Theo Colborn," *Journal of Communications* 41 (2001), 720–49. For the purpose of this article, however, I will focus primarily on the literature examining Carson's notions of science and her relationship with modern environmentalism.

7 See Donald Worster, *Nature's Economy: A History of Ecological Ideas,* 2nd ed. (Cambridge: Cambridge University Press, 1994), 347. Stephen Fox argues that the new conservation movement could "be dated" to the controversy surrounding *Silent Spring*. Stephen Fox, *John Muir and His Legacy: The American Conservation Movement* (Boston: Little, Brown, and Company, 1981), 292.

8 Margaret Rossiter, "Science and Public Policy since World War II," *Osiris* 1 (1985), 291.

9 Linda Lear, "Introduction," in Rachel Carson, *Silent Spring*, 40th Anniversary Edition, xv and xvi.

10 See Rossiter's "Science and Public Policy since World War II" for an analysis of the cranberry crisis of 1958 and the thalidomide scare. Ralph Lutts describes Carson in relation to the decade-long debate over radioactive fallout. See Ralph Lutts, "Chemical Fallout: Rachel Carson's *Silent Spring*, Radioactive Fallout, and the Environmental Movement," *Environmental Review* 9 (1985), 212.

11 See Lutts, "Chemical Fallout," 212. See also Michael Egan, *Barry Commoner and the Science of Survival: The Remaking of American Environmentalism* (Cambridge, MA: MIT Press, 2007), 47–48.

12 See Murphy, *What a Book Can Do*, 106. For more detailed studies of the gendered response to Carson see Hazlett's "Woman vs. Bugs" and Corbett's "Women, Scientists, Agitators."

13 Murphy, *What a Book Can Do*, 106.

14 For a discussion of nature study and its influence on Carson, see Lear, *Rachel Carson*, 14.

15 Rachel Carson National Book Award Speech, 29 January 1952, box 101. Rachel Carson Papers.

16 Carson's interest in DDT and other pesticides started during World War II, but it was a 1957 lawsuit over aerial spraying on Long Island that sparked her effort to publish on the topic. After E. B. White declined her suggestion that he address the matter, Carson decided to write on the issue herself. Lear, *Rachel Carson*, 328.

17 See Lear, *Rachel Carson*, 400.

18 Don K. Price, *Scientific Estates* (London: Oxford University Press, 1965), 3.

19 Carson, *Silent Spring*, 224.

20 Ibid., 86.

21 Ibid.

22 Ibid., 165 and 166. For a detailed analysis on the fire ant episode, see Johua Blu Buhs, *The Fire Ant Wars: Nature, Science, and Public Policy in Twentieth-Century America* (Chicago: University of Chicago Press, 2004).

23 Carson, *Silent Spring*, 166.

24 Corbett, "Women, Scientists, Agitators," 724.

25 Robert K. Merton, *Social Theory and Social Structure*, revised and enlarged edition (Glencoe, IL: Free Press, 1957), 552. Merton's notion of a scientific ethos describes a set of norms held by the scientific community. These include universalism, communism, disinterestedness, and organized skepticism. For an excellent account of Merton's formulation of the scientific ethos see David A. Hollinger, *Science, Jews, and Secular Culture: Studies in Mid-Twentieth Century American Intellectual History* (Princeton, NJ: Princeton University Press, 1996), 80–96.

26 Carson, *Silent Spring*, 86.

27 Ibid., 259.

28 Ibid., 258 and 259.

29 For an account of responses to Carson's work see Murphy, *What a Book Can Do*, 104. Also consult Lear, *Rachel Carson*, 430. Claims about the "Dark Ages" were made by Dr. White-Stevens in CBS Report, "The Silent Spring of Rachel Carson," April 3, 1963, p. 21, folder 1329, box 75, Rachel Carson Papers. Used with the permission of CBS News Archives.

30 Rosenberg, *No Other Gods*, xii.

31 Ibid.

32 Price, *Scientific Estates*, 4.

33 In ibid., 11.

34 Quoted in ibid., 11.

35 Price, *Scientific Estates*, 4.

36 Ralph E. Lapp, *The New Priesthood: The Scientific Elite and the Uses of Power* (New York: Harper and Row, 1965), 152.

37 Price, *Scientific Estates*, 128.

38 Lapp, *The New Priesthood*, 3.

39 Ibid., 153.

40 Price, *Scientific Estates*, 132.

41 Carson, *Silent Spring*, 99.

42 Ibid., 127.

43 Ibid., 13.

44 Ibid., 50.

45 Ibid., 12.

46 Ibid., 32.

47 Ibid., 25.

48 Ibid., 13.

49 Speech to Kaiser Foundation, 18 October 1963, box 99, Rachel Carson Papers. Copyright © 1998 by Roger Allen Christie. Used by permission.

50 Speech to Garden Club of America, 8 January 1963, box 101, Rachel Carson Papers.

51 Speech to Federation of Homemakers, 1963, box 99, Rachel Carson Papers. Copyright © 2007 by Roger Allen Christie. Used by permission.

52 Ibid.

53 Lear, *Rachel Carson*, 450.

54 Ibid., 450 and 451.

55 Transcript of CBS Report, "The Silent Spring of Rachel Carson," 3 April 1963, pp. 11 and 12, folder 1329, box 75, Rachel Carson Papers. Used with the permission of CBS News Archives.

56 Ibid., p. 7.

57 Ibid., p. 8.

58 Ibid., p. 14.

59 Ibid., pp. 20–21.

60 Ibid., p. 29.

61 Ibid., p. 12.

62 Ibid.

63 Transcript of CBS Report, "Verdict on Silent Spring," 15 May 1963, p. 26, folder 1340, box 75, Rachel Carson Papers. Used with the permission of CBS News Archives.

64 Ibid., p. 31.

65 Letter from Elizabeth Aleck, 28 June 1962, folder 1609, box 91, Rachel Carson Papers.

66 Letter from Sally Reahard, 9 July 1962, folder 1609, box 91, Rachel Carson Papers.

67 Letter from Audrey Newcomb, 18 June 1962, folder 1609, box 91, Rachel Carson Papers.

68 Letter from Judith Jay, 5 July 1962, folder 1609, box 91, Rachel Carson Papers.

69 Letter from Walter Rosenberg, 6 July 1962, folder 1609, box 91, Rachel Carson Papers.

70 Letter from Dorothy Pernell, 13 July 1962, folder 1609, box 91, Rachel Carson Papers.

71 Letter from Mrs. Harold Restwick, 9 July 1962, folder 1609, box 91, Rachel Carson Papers.

72 Letter from David Peat, 3 July 1962, folder 1609, box 91, Rachel Carson Papers.

73 Samuel P. Hays, *Beauty, Health, and Permanence: Environmental Politics in the United States, 1955–1985* (Cambridge: Cambridge University Press, 1987), 254.

74 Ibid., 249.

75 Scholars of various disciplines have produced many important studies on the complex dynamic between scientific expertise and public participation. Yet these analyses tend to focus on the period after 1970. See Frank Fisher, *Citizens, Experts, and the Environment: The Politics of Local Knowledge* (Durham, NC: Duke University Press, 2000) and Sylvia Noble Tesh, *Uncertain Hazards: Environmental Activists and Scientific Proof* (Ithaca, NY: Cornell University Press, 2000). Brian Balogh's *Chain Reaction: Expert Debate and Public Participation in American Commercial Nuclear Power, 1945–1975* (Cambridge: Cambridge University Press, 1991) does explore the confrontation between expert debate and public participation during earlier years but his concern is with commercial nuclear power.

76 Hays, *Beauty, Health, and Permanence*, 320.

77 Ibid., 538.

78 Ibid., 537.

79 David Vogel makes an explicit link between public interest movements of the late twentieth century and reformers of the Progressive era. His description of the public interest movement could easily include Carson. See David Vogel, "The Public-Interest and the American Reform Tradition," *Political Science Quarterly* 95 (1980), 607–27.

80 Advertising material for *Silent Spring* in folder 1329, box 75, Rachel Carson Papers.

CHAPTER 9

Ball of Confusion

Public Health, African Americans, and Earth Day 1970

SYLVIA HOOD WASHINGTON

Despite altruistic efforts to unite the various progressive movements that survived the 1960s, the civil rights movement and the environmental movement eyed each other with some trepidation as they entered the 1970s. On 22 April 1970, the first Earth Day became a watershed celebration for the newly emergent environmental movement and a "rousing success" that included over 20 million participants nationwide. It was a movement that would dramatically change the way most Americans lived and did business into the new millennium. But Earth Day was also a call to action to protect a planet whose industrial and exploitative practices were spiraling desperately out of control. This notion was captured elsewhere as well. Two weeks after Earth Day, on 7 May 1970—a week after President Richard Nixon had announced that the United States would send troops into Cambodia, and a few short days after four students had been killed at Kent State University—Motown, the foremost African American recording studio, released the Temptations' song, "Ball of Confusion, That's What the World is Today." With lyrics such as "Segregation, determination, demonstration, integration/Aggravation, humiliation, obligation to our nation," it became an immediate hit, reaching #2 on the R&B charts and #3 on the pop charts, in large part because it aptly captured the tension and confusion in American society that had grown from the numerous and ever-evolving cultural, political, and social revolutions. That the world was a ball of confusion struck a chord with many Americans, but the song and its lyrics were more effective at drawing immediate connections between the various social movements that sought to remedy the situation.

In spite of the overwhelming public response to Earth Day, the most famous and most widely circulated African American periodical, *Ebony* magazine, paid little attention to the newly emerging environmental movement or the first national celebration of Earth Day on 22 April 1970. Indeed, *Ebony*'s April 1970 issue maintained its focus on the continuing struggles of the civil rights movement. Instead of any acknowledgment of environmental discourse the cover showed an image of the slain preeminent civil rights leader, Reverend Dr. Martin Luther King. *Ebony*'s focus reflected the concerns of mainstream African American leaders who felt that the civil rights movement should remain paramount to their constituency over and above parallel movements such as the women's movement and the environmental movement. Younger and more radical civil rights activist groups such as the Black Panther Party, however, openly embraced certain concerns and tenets of the emergent environmental movement as long as they were in line with their own revolutionary ethos. Like today, the response to the environmental movement and environmental concerns by African Americans was in no way singular and monolithic. The historical evidence shows that the response among African Americans during this period was in fact was as diverse as their ethnic, racial, class, political, and religious backgrounds.[1] This diversity in response among African Americans to the environmental movement yesterday and today has not been elucidated and revealed in current environmental or African American historiography. Neither has this information been adequately documented in the literature that has been produced by environmental justice scholars. For example, the Brookings Institute scholar Christopher H. Foreman Jr., in his recent monograph, *The Perils and Promise of Environmental Justice*, using very little historical evidence has erroneously conflated a few statements made by a handful of African American *male* politicians and leaders during this period as being representative of the environmental stance taken by the entire African American community irrespective of class, gender, color, or age during this period.[2]

The story is far more complicated; there was no singular or monolithic African American response to environmentalism or to the first Earth Day. Unlike the 1970 issue of *Ebony*, the biographies and autobiographies of mainstream African American leaders such as the Reverend Dr. Martin Luther King Jr., Reverend Ralph Abernathy, Reverend Andrew Young, Reverend Jesse Jackson Jr., Whitney M. Young, Mayor Carl B. Stokes of Cleveland, Ohio,

New York Congresswoman Shirley Chisholm, and Mayor Richard Hatcher of Indiana, as well as the histories of civil rights and activist groups, do yield information, albeit limited, on their views of the environmental movement and its primary tenets. This essay will demonstrate that although a large percentage of African Americans and their older and more conservative leadership in the 1970s was presented by the news media during this period as ignoring or rejecting Earth Day and the publicly articulated objectives and goals of the environmental movement, they did not, in fact, reject the idea of environmental activism. They concurred, but from a different perspective, with the objectives of one of the chief organizers of Earth Day, Denis Hayes. Hayes, according to the environmental historian Hal Rothman in his cogent monograph, *The Greening of a Nation? Environmentalism in the United States since 1945,* wanted an "environmental movement [in which] all people [would] have a stake no matter their politics."[3] African Americans did believe that they had a stake in an environmental movement, and ironically today's current environmental goal of sustainable communities mirrors their original vision of a more inclusive and realistic environmental agenda. On Earth Day 1970, African Americans wanted an environmental movement whose primary objective included protecting or optimizing the "human habitat" as well as protecting nonhuman and nonsentient life. The early schism in the perspectives and goals of the mainstream environmental movement (i.e. biocentrism and protection of nonhuman habitats) from those of the civil rights leaders and the leaders of the environmental movement (i.e. anthropogenic goals and creation of sustainable human environments) occurred much earlier than existing accounts note, and would later result in the birth of the environmental justice movement by the end of the 1970s.

By 1970, many African American political and civil rights leaders were concerned that the environmental movement shifted both national attention and discourse away from the civil rights movement. They eyed suspiciously the "environmental movement" that was being touted by the media because it seemed to suddenly emerge in the wake of the racial demonstrations and riots, civil disturbances that grew from the frustrated demands of the declining civil rights movement. This suspicion was fueled by the way in which Earth Day was developed and promoted. Earth Day organizers consciously created a celebration that would be embraced by the "Silent Majority," as a means of broadening the environmental movement's appeal. They achieved this end by intentionally mixing and capitalizing upon "1960s ideology and the rhetoric of moral suasion with the tactics of the declining and struggling civil rights movement."[4] When newly elected African American politicians were interviewed in 1970 by the national media on the topic of the environmental movement, they did not hesitate to express their disdain and disappointment over the country's sudden embrace and focus on environmental issues so soon after the assassinations of leading civil rights leaders and deaths of political activists.

For example in a 1970 *Businessweek* essay, Mayor Stokes did not dismiss the importance of pollution control but poignantly argued that a higher priority for the American government should be providing "adequate food and housing" for the poor and marginalized.[5] Likewise in 1971, within one year of the first Earth Day, Whitney M. Young Jr., head of the National Urban League, stated that:

> The war on pollution is one that should be waged after the war on poverty is won. Common sense calls for reasonable national priorities and not for inventing new causes whose main appeal seems to be in their potential for copping out and ignoring the most dangerous and pressing of our problems.[6]

Mayor Hatcher of Gary, Indiana, offered a similar sentiment in an August 1970 *Time* magazine article on "The Rise of Anti-Ecology." Hatcher bitingly complained that "the nation's concern with the environment has done what George Wallace was unable to do: distract the nation from the human problems of Black and Brown America."[7] This disenchantment with the ecocentric perspective of the environmental movement was most clearly articulated by Huey Newton, the founder and icon of the controversial Black Panther Party (BPP). In his 1974 essay, "Dialectics of Nature," Newton found the new environmental movement suspect and difficult to embrace because:

> Human beings are the component left out of the survival equation by the environmentalists except in generalized "underdeveloped" nation statistics, and as objects of blame for the whole mess, in the industrialized countries, and, of course as suicidal breeders in the colonies.[8]

Yet in contrast to the mainstream and older African American politicians, Newton asserted that the environmental concerns of the mainstream environmental movement were still valid and relevant for the Black Panther Party and the African American community despite its ecocentricity. The essay was rooted in his observations and analyses of the 1970s oil and energy crisis and the concomitant pollution that was occurring on land and in the ocean as a direct result of oil production, especially the strip-mining process that was being used extensively by the American shale oil industries. Citing the recent and devastating environmental impacts to the marine ecosystems of Great Britain's Land's End on 18 March 1967 from the 36 million gallon oil spill of the *Torrey Canyon*, Newton warned that "The ocean promises to be the ultimate challenge to nations to co-exist on a watery planet whirling through space."[9] The environmental challenge according to Newton was "international as well as national in scope" since recent advancements in marine technology were associated with increased activities and desires for the economic exploitation of ocean resources, or its utilization for transportation and military purposes. As a result of this increase in demand for ocean resources to drive the global economy, nations would eventually, in Newton's view, have to "learn how to preserve marine sources as well as their respective [national] tempers."[11]

Newton firmly believed that environmental concerns were endemic to the revolutionary and intercommunalist ideologies of the Black Panther Party because party members felt that "ecological spoliation" was derived from rampant and reactive capitalism and saw "pollution for what it is—war against nature, war against people, against the race itself, against the unborn."[12] According to Newton, exploitation of natural resources for economic growth and dominance was the root cause of the world's environmental problems. His 1974 essay also asserted that intercommunalism, the primary philosophy of the Black Panther Party, was "founded on the basic concept of the unity of nature underlying and transcending all arbitrary national and geographic divisions."[13] For Newton, the human community regardless of color or nationality would continue to suffer from the unregulated economic exploitation of nature unless everyone regardless of color or class became engaged in both global and national environmental struggle to protect the world's commons.

Population Control and Family Planning

African Americans were not in consensus by any means over one of the key tenets of the modern environmental movement, family planning and population control, by Earth Day 1970. Their debate over the issue was in no small way influenced by the history of forced sterilization of African Americans in the United States that had begun in the early twentieth century and the disproportionately higher mortality rate among women of color from illegal abortions. The division among African Americans in the 1970s was also along gender lines. Some, especially African American males, such as the popular comedian and social critic Dick Gregory, charged that population control was part of a sinister revival of racist-inspired eugenic public policy, whereas others (more women than men), such as Congresswoman Shirley Chisholm, viewed it as a means of reducing the burdens of poverty and promoting better health for black women.

In her autobiography Chisholm reiterated her legendary question concerning population control that she had put to black male leadership during this period:

> Which is more like genocide . . . my black brothers . . . the way things are, or the conditions I am fighting for in which the full range of family planning services is freely available to women of all classes and colors, starting with effective contraception and extending to safe, legal termination of undesired pregnancies, at a price they can afford?"[14]

Her position in favor of birth control and legalized abortion was based in part on contemporary studies, such as that by Edwin M. Gold for the period 1960–62, which showed that "abortion was the cause of death in 25 percent of white cases, 49 percent of the black ones, and 65 percent of the Puerto Rican ones."[15]

Dick Gregory's response to Chisholm, "My Answer to Genocide," which appeared in *Ebony* magazine in the early 1970s, "advocated large black families as insurance against black extermination." Leery of whites' motives for family planning, Gregory warned the readers that, "Now that we've got a little taste of power, white folks want us to call a moratorium on having children."[16] Gregory was not alone in his open suspicions about family planning. The civil rights activists Jesse Jackson Jr. and Fannie Lou Hamer made similar statements. In 1972 Jackson, head of Operation PUSH (People United to Save Humanity), also alluded to the irony of the government's sudden interest in family planning for African Americans. His suspicions were rooted in his observation that the government's interest had occurred "simultaneously with the emergence of African Americans and other nonwhites as a meaningful force in the nation and the world."[17] Both Gregory's and Jackson's stances on population control efforts, although less dramatic, were similar to the BPP's warning of black genocide. BPP member Evette Pearson's January 1969 essay "In White America Today" blatantly asserted that the country "Shrewdly, cunningly . . . starts to do you in. Genocide. Planned Parenthood, Birth Control, Vietnam War, Prostitution . . . Genocide. Dig, it black men. It is time to deal with the situation, Educate your woman to stop taking those pills."[18]

In her landmark monograph, *Killing the Black Body: Race, Reproduction and the Meaning of Liberty*, Dorothy Roberts observes that the resurgence in the promotion of population control occurred in the 1960s, when the controversial "eugenics theory was revived ... by genetic explanations of racial differences by scientists such as Arthur Jensen and William Shockley."[19] Roberts points out that these renewed racist eugenic theories of the 1960s were soon followed by books in the early 1970s such as Edgar R. Chasteen's *The Case for Compulsory Birth Control* and the well known biologist Garrett Hardin's *Exploring New Ethics for Survival*, which argued that "supporting children gave the government the right to strip their parents of the capacity to produce more."[20] African Americans' fear of population control, which was a critical component of the modern environmental movement in the 1970s, seems to have been well grounded. According to Roberts's study the greatest level and growth in sterilization in the African American community occurred between 1970 and 1980. Sterilization cases rose from 200,000 in 1970 to over 700,000 in 1980.[21] Numerous reports began to surface in the 1970s about routine and undisclosed acts of sterilization on poor black women across the country. "In April 1972, the *Boston Globe* ran a front page story reporting the complaint by a group of medical students that Boston City Hospital was performing excessive and medically unnecessary hysterectomies on black patients."[22] In July 1973 the abusive sterilization of African Americans was exposed by a lawsuit filed by the Southern Poverty Law Center on behalf of two black teenage girls, fourteen-year-old Minnie Lee Relf and her twelve-year-old sister Mary Alice Relf. Both girls unwittingly had been intentionally sterilized by the federally funded Community Action Agency of Montgomery, Alabama, through long-term injections of the experimental contraceptive Depo Provera.[23] The Relf lawsuit brought to light the "shocking magnitude of sterilization abuse across the South. Judge Gerhard Gesell found that an estimated 100,000 to 150,000 poor women like the Relf teenagers had been sterilized annually under federally funded programs."[24] "On September 21, 1975 The New York Times Magazine reported that doctors in major cities across the country were routinely performing hysterectomies on mostly black welfare recipients as a form of sterilization, a practice that came to be known euphemistically among medical insiders as the 'Mississippi appendectomy.'"[25]

Despite these findings African Americans around the country still remained divided (primarily along gender lines) on population control. A 1970 study of the use and approval of birth control in Chicago revealed that "80 percent of the black women in Chicago interviewed approved of birth control and 75 percent were practicing it,"[26] even in the Black Panther Party, which had made a national call for "sisters to abandon birth control . . . picket family planning centers and abortion referral groups and to raise revolutionaries."[27] Black Panther female activists such as Toni Cade, however, would argue in 1970 that despite the party line, the right to choose birth control should be determined only by black women. Cade's position was echoed and supported by many of her contemporary female activists such as Dr.

Dorothy Brown, the first black female general surgeon in the United States and a Tennessee state representative, and by Angela Davis. Davis's position on the matter was cogently described in her chapter, "Racism, Birth Control and Reproductive Rights," in her classic *Women, Race and Class*, which also called for abortion rights along with an end to sterilization.[28] Davis stated in this essay that "Birth control—individual choice, safe contraceptive methods, as well as abortions when necessary—is a fundamental prerequisite for the emancipation of women."[29]

Black Environmentalism, 1970: Economy, Housing and the Built Environment

As African American political and intellectual leaders saw it, the Vietnam War, the quest for women's rights, and now the ecological fad all diverted crucial attention and resources away from the root problem of structurally embedded racism in the United States. There was also a belief at this time that the nation's inordinate attention to the environmental movement and the first Earth Day was, in fact, a manifestation of its desire to escape from the discourse of civil rights—a discourse that had increasingly focused on full participation in the political economy for African Americans. Even after the 1964 Civil Rights Act and the 1968 Fair Housing Act, the majority of African Americans still lived in racially segregated communities with poor or inadequate environmental infrastructures even if they had the financial means to escape the ghettos. By Earth Day 1970, they were still blocked from the more environmentally sound white suburbs because of race-based redlining policies employed by the real estate industry, the federal government, and the banking industry.[30] Therefore their focus was improving environmental conditions by creating what we now refer to as "sustainable communities." Environmental concern was perceived by many as an interest that ignored the ways in which the political economy created environmentally marginalized spaces for people of color and the poor. Numerous African American leaders, radical or conservative, argued that it was full participation in the political economy and the enforcement of legal and extralegal fair housing policies that were the ultimate means of solving the environmental problems for the vast majority of African Americans. The fact that these critical civil rights issues were not part of the environmental movement's discourse in the 1970s made it less relevant for them. African Americans believed that the national shift away from the civil rights movement and to the environmental movement only further exacerbated the "ball of confusion."

The Reverend Dr. Martin Luther King's 1966 Chicago campaign for "open housing" and for better housing conditions in the city's slums foreshadowed the common and persistent and complaint among many African Americans on Earth Day 1970 that a large percentage of their population was compelled to live in unhealthy and unsafe environmental habitats because of their inequitable participation in the political economy. King demanded a resolution of these problems through economic enfranchisement. In *The Autobiography of Martin Luther King Jr.*, edited by Clayborne Carson, King recounted the dismal conditions stemming from environmental and economic disenfranchisement. King observed as a slum tenant that:[31]

> Too soon you began to see the effects of this emotional and environmental deprivation. The children's clothes were too skimpy to protect them from the Chicago wind, and a closer look revealed the mucous in the corners of their bright eyes, and you were reminded that vitamin pills and flu shots were luxuries which they could ill afford. The "runny noses" of ghetto children became a graphic symbol of medical neglect in a society which had mastered most of the diseases from which they will too soon die. There was something wrong in a society which allowed this to happen.

After taking up residence in a notorious Chicago slum community with his family, King understood more clearly that African Americans living in the slums were trapped by an existing economic system that had them paying "more rent in the substandard slums of Lawndale than the whites paid for modern apartments in the suburbs."[32] As King explained, African Americans living in the slums were "confined to an isolated community" that "no longer participated in a free economy, but was subject to price fixing and wholesale robbery" by the merchants who serviced the community.[33] Even if they were able to move out of the "vicious circle" of poverty and economic exploitation, according to King, and "get just one foot out of the jungle of poverty and exploitation, [they were] subject to the whims of the political and economic giants of the city," which immediately and impersonally crushed all hopes for their future economic and hence environmental success.[34]

Congresswoman Shirley Chisholm, the first African American woman elected to Congress, held a slightly different opinion about the relationship between economic and environmental enfranchisement. Unlike her male counterparts, Chisholm cautioned that:

> It will do black Americans absolutely no good to be politically and economically enfranchised into a system that systematically denies human values and destroys the environment that sustains life. By affirming and fighting for the values that are life sustaining, black politicians can

become the vanguard of the forces that save this country, if it is to be saved.[35]

For Chisholm economic enfranchisement was not a magic bullet for the social and environmental ills of the black community. The more critical problem was the dehumanizing and ecologically destructive worldview of the body politic, one that had to be changed for the salvation of all citizens and their environments. Chisholm also pointed out during this period that African American women's primary concern with sustainable communities was the root cause of their lack of interest in the emerging women's movement. According to Chisholm,

> In the view of many black women, [Betty] Friedan and other white women's right activists were zeroing in on issues that would benefit white women only, particularly issues dealing with personal fulfillment. . . . the issues that [black women] care about—[are] improved housing and transportation, better health care and nutrition, welfare, and the like—[and these] were not priorities of white women, who'd never had to worry about the basics of life.[36]

By 1970 the BPP's national program and local program had produced and published manifestos calling for environmentally sustainable black communities. The fourth point in the party's October 1966 BPP Platform and Program stated that they wanted "decent housing, fit for shelter of human beings" and that "if white landlords will not give decent housing to our black community, then the housing and the land should be made into cooperatives so that our community, with government aid, can build and make decent housing for its people."[37] Two of the ten points of the January 1970 "Ten Point Health Program of the Young Lords" in New York were clearly environmental demands for the community. Points seven and eight of this program called for "'door to door' preventive health services emphasizing environment and sanitation control, nutrition, drug addiction, maternal and child health care" and "education programs for all the people to expose health problems— sanitation, rats, poor housing, malnutrition, police brutality, pollution and other forms of oppression."[38] The Panthers wanted economic control of their environment to ensure sustainable development for optimal living environments.

Black Media and the Environmental Movement

The *Chicago Defender*, the most prominent black local and national newspaper in the United States during this period, ran during April 1970 several essays that either emphasized black people's concern and involvement with environmental problems or revealed how black people were being perceived as environmental problems by the larger community. On April Fools' Day, 1 April 1970, the newspaper featured a front page editorial decrying the eviction of "Negroes from their homes because of 'scandalously high' real estate prices which were a result of residential segregation." This same editorial was accompanied by a satirical cartoon titled "Ghetto Litterbugs," which showed Sheriff Woods dumping miniaturized black people and their furnishings from their homes like a person emptying trash onto a street.[39] One day before Earth Day 1970, the *Defender* ran a photographic essay about the visit of Special Presidential Assistant Robert J. Brown and his Task Force on Aid to Disadvantaged Communities to the black and severely economically depressed suburb of Robbins, Illinois. The *Defender* essay pointed out that Robbins was suffering from environmental health problems; its land "cannot be drained off into public waterways because the standing water is full of sewage. This extreme health hazard was blamed for causing a resident to contract hepatitis."[40] The following day—Earth Day—the paper's front headline story depicted black residents trying to protect and secure their existing living space from being condemned by the City of Chicago. The story pointed out that when the city's "board-up services attempted to cover windows and doors [of a contested building] the neighbors took over the building and burned the boards, while children attached signs of 'Black Power' to the trees."[41] A day after Earth Day the newspaper featured an article about the renowned black scientist Dr. Percy L. Julian's appointment to an ecology panel in Chicago. The essay pointed out that "Dr. Julian was named to a distinguished 12 man panel formed by the Common Wealth Edison Company. The new panel will assist the company in formulating policies and carrying out programs of action to benefit the environment."[42]

Black Municipal Leaders' Response to Earth Day and the Environmental Movement

By April 1970, the only African American leaders who had the power to influence or make public policy and governmental decisions that would be environmentally beneficial to the African American communities on a day-to-day basis were elected officials, especially mayors such as Carl B. Stokes in Cleveland, Ohio, and Richard Hatcher in Gary, Indiana. Although they were relatively new to their elected political offices—they had both been elected in the fall of 1967—their biographies and autobiographies reveal that their chief concerns focused on providing sustainable housing and sustainable communities. In a chapter titled "The 'Real' Estate," in his autobiography *Promises of Power* (1973), Stokes is explicit: "Another arena which I hoped to crack down was slum-landlordism." According to Stokes his administration

> did move forcefully on demolition of old abandoned buildings, doubling the number of torn down buildings . . . Vigorous enforcement of the housing authority building code added millions of dollars to the tax duplicate and cleaned up some of the worst eyesores and safety hazards in the poorer neighborhoods.[43]

What is absent in both Stokes's most recent biography, *Carl B. Stokes and the Rise of Black Political Power* by Leonard Moore, and his autobiography, *Promises of Power*, is the critical role that he played in environmental protection in Cleveland's metropolitan area, and particularly the launching of the 1972 Clean Water Act.[44] Moore's narrative is unfortunately typical of most African American historical narratives about the black experience in the post-Reconstruction period and throughout the twentieth century. African American history has resolutely stayed with the historical paradigm of poverty, political and economic disenfranchisement of the "black" community and has rarely mentioned other issues such as the environment and environmental disparities. The burning of the Cuyahoga River in Cleveland, Ohio, was considered the galvanizing event that led directly to the creation of the Clean Water Act. When the Cuyahoga River burst into flames in the city's industrial district known as the Flats on 22 June 1969, Carl B. Stokes was the recently elected mayor of Cleveland.[45] Jonathan Adler points out in his seminal environmental history of the Cuyahoga River, "Fables of the Cuyahoga: Reconstructing a History of Environmental Protection," that although the river had already become recognized as one of the most polluted rivers in the nation before Stokes took office in 1967 he "pledged a greater commitment to pollution concerns than his predecessor."[46]

Within one year of his taking office, "In November 1968, voters approved a $100 million bond issue to finance river cleanup and protection [which] passed by a two-to-one margin."[47] Among the projects financed by the bond issue were sewer system improvements, storm water overflow controls, harbor improvement facilities, and an improved debris removal program. City officials welcomed the vote, calling it a "mandate" for the city to clean up the river, as well as an opportunity "to ask for strict enforcement of state and federal anti-pollution laws." The bond issue failed under the Stokes administration because of "unfavorable interests" and a lack of matching funds from both the state and federal governments.[48] Stokes's administration also sought to convince state officials to locate a state water pollution control office in Cleveland at city expense. Cleveland made significant strides toward environmental improvement in 1968 and 1969. In addition to the bond issue and the creation of the Clean Water Task Force—both before the June 1969 fire—the city enacted "one of the strongest air pollution codes in the country." By 1970 Stokes found his administration embroiled in a lawsuit filed by the citizens of the city over the city's liability for controlling water pollution. As a result of this lawsuit he found himself "testifying before Congress in 1970 . . . [and] calling upon Congress to enact federal legislation so that the city would have more control over local water quality."[49]

Mayor Stokes's highest priorities continued to be those that focused on the environmental conditions in poor and minority neighborhoods. When criticized about administration efforts to act more aggressively in fighting environmental pollution in 1970, Stokes stated that, as Mayor, he was more concerned with resolving the "many more serious crises which affect the lives of my constituents to a greater degree than air and water pollution. . . . [such as] housing, jobs, food, clothing and the ability to live in a society free of racial hatred." Mayor Stokes also expressed "hope that the amount of concern over the environmental crisis [would] not overshadow these more basic and in many ways more difficult social problems."[50] Despite these articulated concerns for improving the environmental conditions of poor and minority communities, by Earth Day 1970 Stokes would find himself embroiled in an intense environmental debate with the African American middle-class community Lee-Seville. This little-known debate has often been referred to as an intraracial class struggle but a closer examination of the documentation reveals an intense debate that was centered on the lack of equitable environmental infrastructures in middle-class African American communities on the far southeast side of the city.[51]

Richard G. Hatcher's mayoral administration in Gary, Indiana, was also known for its efforts to create sustainable communities through housing development and for its direct involvement in improving the overall environmental conditions of the city. In his biography of Hatcher, *Black Power, Gary Style*, Alex Poinsett points out that after two years in office in February 1970 Hatcher had managed to bring $35 million in federal funds to the city "for education, manpower programs, urban renewal, code enforcement, neighborhood facilities, poverty programs, law enforcement, health and beautification."[52] Hatcher had also by this time increased the inspection of substandard housing units from "less than six thousand per year to more than fifty thousand per year."[53] Like Stokes, Hatcher was committed to improving the environmental conditions of Gary's impoverished communities;

his commitment has been well documented by Andrew Hurley's seminal monograph, *Environmental Inequalities, Class, Race and Industrial Pollution in Gary, Indiana, 1945–1980*. Under his administration Gary's air quality had improved by 34 percent in 1969.[54] By the time Hatcher had taken office the environmental pollution problems of the city were well recognized locally and nationally. To address the city's environmental issues Hatcher established a Beautification Commission that was specifically tasked to deal with "wide scale blight in the city."[55]

Conclusion

If "Ball of Confusion" touched a nerve with music listeners by identifying the time's racial and ecological sensibilities, it was not alone. The dual concern and tension among African Americans over the state of both the political economy and the environment during this time frame was also captured by one of Motown's most popular artists, Marvin Gaye. In 1971 Gaye released what is considered to be "his most successful solo album," *What's Going On*. The album contained two of his greatest hits, "Mercy, Mercy Me (the Ecology)" and " Inner City Blues (Make Me Wanna Holler)."[56] Today "Mercy, Mercy Me" is recognized as one of the most touching "ecological" songs of this era along with John Denver's "Calypso." The ecocentricity of this song was evident in its lyrics; it asks "Where did all the blue skies go?" and comments on "poison in the wind" that blows in from all directions. The centrality of the need for greater participation in the political economy among African Americans during this period explains why Gaye's "Inner City Blues" was also a hit that same year. The lyrics of this song clearly elucidated the total disenfranchisement felt by many African Americans at this time as well as their concern over the country's shift in priorities away from the civil rights movement. Millions of copies of both songs were sold because they struck a strong responsive chord among African Americans. They articulated the two most critical and perennial issues in their community. African Americans really were environmentally conscious and cognizant of their own environmental plight and they believed that it could be redressed only by their full and equal participation in the nation's political economy.

Caretaker[57]

(Black Panther poem, n.d.)

We are not owners of Mother Earth;
We are merely caretakers for future generations.

We must let our forests grow.
We must let our animals roam.
We must let our rivers flow.
We should take only what we need.
We must pick only flowers for today;
We must leave some for tomorrow.
We must save the future for our children's children.
We must let the salmon swim and the buffaloes roam.

—Tolbert Small

Notes

1 According to Shirley Chisholm's autobiography, *Unbought and Unbossed* (Boston: Houghton Mifflin Company, 1970), 149–50: "In 1970 there were about 1500 black elected officials in the United States, about 600 of them in the South . . . the ten black members of Congress [who] must be considered significant mainly for their symbolic value. They are so few that, even were they more unified into a bloc than they are, their effect would be negligible—except for that which they exert as individuals . . . There are now more than 450 school board members, more than 450 city councilmen and other local officials, and some 200 state officials, chiefly legislators. There are 55 mayors, 100 county officials, and 175 judges, marshals and sheriffs."

2 Christopher H. Foreman, *The Promise and Peril of Environmental Justice* (Washington, DC: Brookings Institution Press, 1998).

3 Hal K. Rothman, *The Greening of a Nation: Environmentalism in the U.S. since 1945* (New York: Wadsworth, 1997), 123.

4 Ibid.

5 *Businessweek*, 14 November 1970.

6 Ibid.

7 Quoted in Foreman, *Promise and Peril*, 15.

8 David Hilliard and Donald Weise (eds.), *The Huey P. Newton Reader* (New York: Seven Stories Press, 2002), 308–9.

9 Ibid., 307. For the *Torrey Canyon* disaster see http://greennature.com/article228.html: "On the morning of March 18, 1967, the T/V Torrey Canyon ran aground on Pollard Rock on Seven Stones Reef off Lands End in England due to the master's negligence. The entire cargo, approximately 860,000 barrels (references range between 857,600 and 872,300 barrels), was released into the sea or burned during the next twelve days."

11 Hillard and Weise, *The Huey P. Newton Reader*, 307.

12 Ibid., 304.

13 Ibid., 311.

14 Chisholm, *Unbought and Unbossed*, 122.

15 Ibid., 116.

16 Dorothy Roberts, *Killing the Black Body: Race, Reproduction and the Meaning of Liberty* (New York: Pantheon Books, 1997), 98.

17 Ibid., 99.

18 Philip S. Foner (ed.), *The Black Panthers Speak* (1970; Cambridge, MA: Da Capo Press, 1995), 25–26.

19 Roberts, *Killing the Black Body*, 89.

20 Ibid., 89.

21 Ibid., 90.

22 Ibid., 91.

23 Ibid., 93.

24 Ibid.

25 *Eugenics in America: A Brief History*, www.sntp.net/eugenics/eugenics_america. htm.

26 Roberts, *Killing the Black Body*, 101.

27 Ibid.

28 Ibid.

29 Angela Davis, "Racism, Birth Control, and Reproductive Rights," in Marlene Gerber Fried (ed.), *From Abortion to Reproductive Freedom: Transforming a Movement* (Boston: South End Press, 1990), 15; also available at www.questia.com/ PM.qst?a = o&d = 94199582.

30 Nancy A. Denton and Douglass S. Massey, *American Apartheid, Segregation and the Making of the Underclass* (Cambridge, MA: Harvard University Press, 1996).

31 Clayborne Carson (ed.), *The Autobiography of Martin Luther King, Jr.* (New York: Intellectual Properties Management, Inc in association with Warner Books, 1998), 300–1.

32 Ibid., 301.

33 Ibid.

34 Ibid.

35 Chisholm, *Unbought and Unbossed*, 149.

36 Lynne Olson, *Freedom's Daughters: The Unsung Heroines of the Civil Rights Movement from 1830 to 1970* (New York: Touchstone Books/Simon and Schuster, 2001), 367.

37 Foner, *The Black Panthers Speak*, 2.

38 Ibid., 238.

39 *Chicago Defender*, 1 April 1970.

40 *Chicago Defender*, 21 April 1970.

41 *Chicago Defender*, 22 April 1970.

42 *Chicago Defender*, 23 April 1970.

43 See Ch. 8 in Carl B. Stokes, *Promises of Power, Then and Now* (Cleveland: Friends of Carl Stokes, 1989), 120–21.

44 Leonard N. Moore, *Carl B. Stokes and the Rise of Black Political Power* (Urbana: University of Illinois Press, 2002).

45 Sierra Club, *The Clean Water Act at 30* (www.sierraclub.org/scoop/
    clean_water_act.asp). "The event, subsequently reported in the national media, is
    generally considered to be a galvanizing moment in America's environmental his-
    tory, one that led directly to the passage of the Clean Water Act in 1972."

46 Jonathan Adler, "Fables of the Cuyahoga: Reconstructing A History of Environ-
    mental Protection", *Fordham Environmental Law Journal* 14, 20.

47 Ibid., 20–21.

48 Ibid., 22.

49 Ibid., 40.

50 Ibid., 25, quoting a letter from Carl B. Stokes, Mayor, City of Cleveland, to Bernard
    N. Sroka, 12 August 1970, on file with Western Reserve Historical Society in
    Cleveland, Ohio.

51 For a cogent description of the environmental debate between Stokes and Lee-
    Seville please read my dissertation, *Packing Them In: A 20th Century Working
    Class Environmental History* (PhD dissertation, Case Western Reserve Univer-
    sity, 2000), and my essay "Wadin' in the Water: African American Struggles for
    Environmental Equality in Cleveland, OH, 1915–70," in Sylvia Hood Washington,
    Heather Goodall, and Paul Rosier, *Echoes from the Poisoned Well: Global Memories
    of Environmental Injustices* (Lanham, MD: Lexington Books, 2006).

52 Alex Poinsett, *Black Power Gary Style: The Making of Mayor Richard Gordon
    Hatcher* (Chicago: Johnson Publishing Company, 1970),150–51.

53 Ibid., 151.

54 Ibid., 152.

55 Ibid., 170.

56 "Paying Tribute to Marvin Gaye," http://tracy_prinze.tripod.com/
    atributetomotown/id11.html.

57 Black Panther Party poem, undated and found on their contemporary website
    page at www.itsabouttimebpp.com/BPP_Poetry/poetry_tolbert_small_2.html.

CHAPTER 10

"Save French Pete"

Evolution of Wilderness Protests in Oregon

KEVIN R. MARSH[1]

On 15 November 1969, "Mobilization Day," Vietnam moratorium demonstrations brought out the largest anti-war crowds of the era. Over 700,000 marched in Washington, D.C., that day and many more across the nation. Three days later, another set of moratorium marches occurred in Eugene and Portland, Oregon's two largest cities.[2] This second call for a moratorium was not aimed at the war; it was aimed at logging in the valley of French Pete Creek in the western Cascade Mountains. Forest Service historian Gerald Williams surmised that this was the first public demonstration against national forest policy ever held. In Eugene, an estimated crowd of 1,500, comprising students from the University of Oregon and community members, marched to the headquarters of the Willamette National Forest. A new student organization, Nature's Conspiracy, coordinated the rally with support from the community-based Save French Pete Committee. One agency official observed at the time, "Never again will it be 'business as usual' for the Forest Service."[3] Another observer described the crowd as "bearded, long-hair students, . . . girls with long stringy hair, and clean-cut persons as well." Messages printed on the signs they carried included "Make Love, Not Lumber" and "Keep Oregon Green—Save French Pete." The same day, a smaller group marched from Portland State University to the regional office of the Forest Service, where they met with the regional forester Charles Connaughton.[4]

The two moratorium demonstrations—anti-war and anti-logging—were not isolated incidents. Environmental protestors clearly borrowed from the rhetoric and organizing strategies of the anti-war marches. Idaho senator Frank Church in 1970 "urged citizens to form a 'moratorium movement' to save the environment." Denis Hayes, the lead organizer of Earth Day, found direct inspiration in the Vietnam moratorium demonstrations the previous November.[5] In addition, both demonstrations represented established political movements that attracted large numbers of new participants from the counterculture of the late 1960s. Although organizers were delighted at the growing numbers and corresponding publicity, they struggled to maintain a cohesive political strategy. Whereas this was not a beginning for either the fight over French Pete Valley or broader environmental activism, the growing connections between the environmental movement and counterculture activists represented a shift throughout the country and began to change the nature of well-established wilderness campaigns. This confluence, according to historian Robert Gottlieb, "served as a transition to a new environmental politics in which the question of Nature could no longer be separated from the question of society itself."[6]

Figure 10.1 Overlooking the valley of French Pete Creek. Beginning in 1968, wilderness activists focused on the unique character of this as one of the few remaining valleys in the western Cascades with no roads or logging sites. Photo by Samuel Frear, courtesy of the National Archives and Records Administration—Pacific Alaska Region. Found in Region 6 History Collection, Box 76, Folder: 2430 timber Sales French Pete, Proposed FY 68+69 [3 of 5].

By 1969, the cultural protestors of the era infused the older conservation community with a new and vital force of supporters. The campaign to pass the Wilderness Act, approved into law in 1964, focused on increasing public participation in and political accountability for land use decisions, removing from the Forest Service its sole authority to define wilderness areas. The established movement against bureaucratic autonomy opened doors to challenge administrative decision-making that the anti-authoritarian members of the counterculture eagerly walked through. This shift provided a tremendous boost in visibility and political effectiveness for the environmental movement, but it also changed the nature of environmental debate, adding a far broader range of concerns and a more radical set of strategies. These two branches of environmentalism helped fuel the most successful era of environmental reform from the late 1960s to the early 1980s, but the lingering divisions between them also defined some of the biggest challenges for the environmental movement into the twenty-first century. The French Pete debate, which had been the focus of an active citizens' campaign since at least 1954, reflected how environmental protest changed around 1970 and illustrated much of the external power and the internal divisions of this new era of environmentalism.[7]

French Pete Creek valley was once a forgotten drainage, lost in the myriad of similar, heavily wooded valleys in the western slope of the Cascade Range. At its confluence with the South Fork of the McKenzie River the elevation is 1,900 feet. The highest reaches of the drainage top out at nearly 5,000 feet. The forests that stood at the center of this political debate were not unusual either in their size or in their commercial value. The trees, mostly Douglas fir, were relatively young at about 100 years old. Sheepherders, including the creek's namesake, used the upper slopes extensively well into the twentieth century to graze their flocks, and they often set fire to these areas to improve grazing conditions. Few claimed that this was an absolutely pristine environment, but for many it was a place of tremendous solitude, aesthetic beauty, and convenient recreation.

In the 1930s, Bob Marshall identified French Pete and surrounding valleys as significant landscapes, worthy of protection by the U.S. Forest Service. Marshall was an early advocate within the agency for protection of wilderness areas, particularly for setting them aside from road building in the 1930s. He urged foresters to protect pristine areas "before some damn fool chamber of commerce or some nonsensical organizer of unemployed demands a useless highway to provide work and a market for hotdogs and gasoline."[8] As head of the national Division of Recreation and Lands for the Forest Service, Marshall was instrumental in convincing the Forest Service in 1938 to add French Pete and over 55,600 acres in surrounding forested valleys to the existing Three Sisters Primitive Area, first established in 1937.[9]

Marshall also used his position in the Forest Service to promote a more rigorous and well-defined policy for protecting wildlands, the U-Regulations, which were approved in 1939. Under these new rules, areas over 100,000 acres could be labeled wilderness areas and could only be created or revised by authority of the Secretary of Agriculture, rather than just the chief of the Forest Service. The regulations for wilderness areas were stricter than those governing the primitive areas; road building and logging would not be allowed as they often were in primitive areas.[10]

As it profoundly shaped so many other aspects of American history, World War II marked a watershed of change for wilderness and the timber industry. Prior to the war, most timber came from private lands owned by corporations such as Weyerhaeuser, Pope and Talbot, and the Northern Pacific Railway Company. Production on these lands peaked in the 1920s, after which companies faced lethargic markets during the Great Depression and scarce supplies, having already cut much of their timber. After the war, the federal government's role greatly increased as a supplier of timber. In the Willamette National Forest in Oregon both the sale of timber and the volume of timber cut more than quadrupled between 1945 and 1955, and these figures continued to rise significantly in following decades.[11]

The Forest Service, led by Bob Marshall, planned to redesignate primitive areas under the new U-Regulations before the war; however, the 38-year-old Marshall's untimely death in 1939 and World War II delayed such action. After the war, reclassification of these lands occurred in the context of dramatically increased demands for commercial timber production. The Forest Service sought to maximize production by making all potential forests open to timber sales. Thus, when the agency proposed reclassification of the Three Sisters Primitive Area to the stronger protection of Wilderness Area in 1954, it removed from within the old boundary 53,000 acres of commercial timberlands. This was most of the land that the Chief of the Forest Service had added in 1938 under Marshall's inspiration.[12]

The response to the Forest Service's attempts to reduce the size of the protected area sowed the seeds of environmental protest movements over logging in the postwar era. Local hiking clubs and university scientists had been aware of the developing Forest Service plan for three years, and they reacted quickly in 1954 to organize in opposition. Karl Onthank, a leader with the local Obsidians hiking club, and his wife Ruth, active with the Eugene Natural History Society, hosted a meeting that year in their Eugene living room. Together with geologists, botanists, labor organizers, and others, they formed the Friends of the Three Sisters Wilderness. Karl Onthank, who was also dean of students at the University of Oregon, described the group's leadership as "mostly scientists who know something of our Cascade Mountains and are interested in seeing a little [of] them preserved for future enjoyment in their natural state and for scientific study."[13] The Friends of the Three Sisters established a model for site-specific, grassroots activism that historian Samuel P. Hays later called "the key to the success of wilderness action."[14]

As required by the U-Regulations, the Forest Service organized a public hearing in Eugene on its proposal in February 1955. This was the first major public hearing on national forest management in the Northwest in the postwar era, and activists came from around the region and across the country to voice their protest. So many came that an unexpected second day was needed to hear the testimony. Among those testifying on the second day was Howard Zahniser, executive secretary of the Wilderness Society, who came from Washington, D.C., "to represent the national interest."[15] The size of the crowd was testimony to the growing concern over increasing threats to public lands throughout the country. Forest Service officials later expressed surprise at the number of people supporting preservation. Although troubled by an earlier lack of unity among wilderness advocates, Karl Onthank came away from the hearing pleased. "Finally," he wrote, "perhaps chiefly as a result of the hearing rather than in advance of it, which would have been much better, we really did get together and presented a solid front and we have been much more successful."[16]

The emergence of the Friends of the Three Sisters and the widespread opposition to Forest Service plans for the area represent a remarkable shift in alliances within the conservation movement. Through the first half of the twentieth century, the Forest Service had allied with conservationists throughout the country. Stewardship was the priority of the agency and its leaders represented the leadership of the conservation movement, often portrayed in opposition to the cut-and-run practices of corporate timber harvesters. By the 1930s, the Forest Service had created the modern system of wilderness preservation and the leading voices for preservation—Aldo Leopold, Arthur Carhart, and Bob Marshall—were all agency employees. However the shift within the Forest Service during and after World War II to become the main champion of increased timber harvests placed it at odds with its former allies, who were frightened by the changes that began to transform previously undeveloped forest lands. Beginning in the 1950s, the alliance and trust were eroding away and the rest of the century would see increasing animosity between a growing environmental movement and the increasingly timber-oriented Forest Service. The Three Sisters debate was one of the earliest rifts in this relationship.[17]

Regional leaders of the Forest Service, accustomed to cooperative relations with conservationists and hiking clubs, expressed among themselves surprise at the animosity generated against their proposal. In a meeting two months following the public hearing, they admitted that they had not been aware of the views of either wilderness advocates or the timber industry and were genuinely shocked at the opposition. One forestry journal referred to the change in public attitudes as a "dramatic surprise."[18]

Although wilderness advocates became increasingly well organized during these years, the Forest Service defined the terms of debate and activists remained on the defensive. This pattern characterized what Michael Mc-Closkey, the first Northwest Conservation Representative and later Executive Director for the Sierra Club, identified as the first stage of the postwar wilderness movement. During this time, wilderness advocates were "fighting off attacks on areas already reserved," particularly national forest primitive areas. McCloskey, who was from Eugene, was referring to the Three Sisters controversy. This dominant pattern of the 1950s, he later wrote, "embodied a limited view of the possibilities for conservation." It "was a confession of weakness" by environmental activists.[19] In 1957 the Forest Service moved forward without changing its plan to reduce the size of the protected area. Consequently, the Secretary of Agriculture created the Three Sisters Wilderness Area in February and released 53,000 acres around French Pete to timber sales and road building.[20]

The Three Sisters case became a rallying cry for the national wilderness movement. After their failure, wilderness advocates promoted a stronger national ordinance for wilderness as a way to limit the arbitrary nature of Forest Service administrative designations. Karl Onthank wrote to his colleagues after the Three Sisters verdict, "The decision certainly points up the importance of passing a 'Wilderness Preservation Bill' which will give substantial and durable protection. If it is not passed we can take it for granted we will have this kind of battle on every one of the primitive and the limited areas found in Region 6."[21] The Three Sisters controversy was as much, or more, a catalyst for the Wilderness Act of 1964 as the more famous battle over Echo Park, the successful campaign in 1954 to stop construction of a federal dam in Dinosaur National Monument, Utah. The debate at Echo Park was over policies of development within the national park system, whereas the Wilderness Act focused on the national forests. When Congress moved in 1964 to check the unilateral power of the Forest Service to decide the fate of wilderness areas, the Three Sisters decision served as a model of administrative abuse of power. Howard Zahniser, in direct reference to the Three Sisters wrote, "The intention was that in such an instance in the future the Congress would have a procedural way of preventing such administrative action to eliminate wilderness."[22]

Frustrated by a series of agency decisions like that in the Three Sisters, Congress passed the Wilderness Act in 1964. In that year, however, the Willamette National Forest extended roads and sold timber in the valleys north of French Pete Creek that had been part of the Three Sisters Primitive Area prior to 1957. The Friends of the Three Sisters consistently challenged these developments by sponsoring study trips, organizing public photo displays, supporting scientific research, and filing administrative appeals. Karl Onthank set the tone for this persistence. After the initial loss of 1957, he wrote:

> It seems very important to maintain the attitude that this is just the first round of a battle which is bound to continue for a long time. And if we keep at it we will certainly win much of it in the long run, even though we may take some loses [sic].

He died in 1967 before he could see any sign of long-term victory and before the issue returned to national prominence.[23]

By 1968, French Pete Valley was the only drainage in the lands removed from protection in 1957 that had not seen logging. The uniqueness of its relative ecological health was the basis of a renewed environmental campaign after the Willamette National Forest announced plans early in 1968 to begin building roads and selling timber there.[24] Brock Evans, who became Northwest Conservation Representative for the Sierra Club in 1967, immediately turned to a coalition of veterans who had fought the Forest Service to protect these lands since the mid-1950s. As regional representative, his job was to organize, assist, and coordinate the efforts of local activists. He gathered Richard and Winninette Noyes, Holway Jones, and others in Eugene to form a new organization devoted to preventing logging in French Pete Creek valley. These veterans were exhausted from their years of seemingly fruitless efforts, Evans remembers, but he persuaded them to launch another campaign to challenge once again the decision of 1957.[25]

They formed the Save French Pete Committee to focus attention on this single issue. Their first action was to offer an alternative management plan to create an "intermediate recreation area" in the valley, which would allow neither logging nor road construction. Although it did not offer the firm protection of wilderness designation, this concept seemed to the Committee to be a politically more realistic option given what seemed to be a very limited time frame before cutting might begin. They recruited the support of local congressman John Dellenback, who asked the Forest Service to delay its decision until further public input could be heard. The forest supervisor postponed the timber sales until 1969 and embarked on developing new plans for logging and road building.[26]

As the stalemate over French Pete deepened, Congress became more directly involved. An assistant regional forester in Portland noted, "The French Pete Creek controversy in Oregon has become a national issue." After forest supervisor David Gibney announced plans to reopen timber sales in 1969, Oregon Senators Mark Hatfield and Bob Packwood and Congressman Dellenback requested the Secretary of Agriculture, Clifford Hardin, to intervene, so that more time could be provided for public discussion. Hardin relented, placing a sixty-day delay on the timber sales.[27]

Hatfield and Dellenback requested the delay based on concerns of due process; otherwise, they openly supported Forest Service plans for logging in the area. But Bob Packwood, who won election to the Senate the previous year, began to speak out against logging plans. Packwood understood the political capital of growing environmental awareness, and he sought to take political advantage, declaring, "There has been a dramatic change in public opinion about environmental concern." Holway Jones of the Save French Pete Committee referred to Packwood as "our strongest champion for preservation of wilderness lands."[28] In December 1969, Packwood introduced a bill based on the Save French Pete Committee's proposal for an "intermediate recreation area." Although Forest Service officials made plans to resubmit the timber sale in February 1970, they admitted to representatives of the timber industry that "nothing would be done with the French Pete timber sales until Congress acted upon Packwood's bill."[29]

Advocates of preserving French Pete Creek from logging tried to convince people of the unique and rare qualities of the area that would be lost. This was the "hook" that Brock Evans chose to cultivate public support for the cause of preserving the valley. French Pete was, they claimed, one of three remaining low-elevation valleys at least ten miles long in the Oregon Cascades that had not yet been developed. Representatives in the timber industry argued that the number was actually four, and the Forest Service counted five, but this did not diminish the point of scarcity, when the original count was at least sixty-five.[30] Rhetorically, advocates sought to gain sympathy and support by focusing on saving one of the last remnants of undisturbed low-elevation forests.

In contrast, the costs of not logging the valley would be minor, wilderness activists argued. The 700 million board feet contained in the 19,000-acre drainage represented merely 1 percent of the timber volume available in the Willamette National Forest. The original timber sale proposed in 1968 would have resulted in less than 2 percent of the timber volume harvested annually on that forest. Further, as a relatively young forest of just over 100 years old, it was not among the most valuable of timber stands in the region. "The commercial timber value within French Pete is miniscule when one considers the entire Willamette National Forest," Senator Bob Packwood commented in 1971. "French Pete is little for the Forest Service to give up."[31] As a symbol of the debate over competing values and bureaucratic authority, the valley of French Pete Creek itself became far more important than the sum of its timber. It became a battle over who should determine the appropriate use of national forests.

Despite Packwood's leadership and the increasingly national scope of opposition to its plans, the Willamette National Forest persisted in its determination to develop timber sales in the valley, resting its justification upon both the Secretary of Agriculture's 1957 decision and the broader USFS mandate to maximize timber production. Forest supervisor David Gibney led this campaign with a militant righteousness. Gibney represented the arm of the Forest Service that pushed the timber program into the highest priority in the decades after World War II. He once said, "We must keep every acre of land outside of wilderness fully productive. A decrepit old-growth stand depresses me."[32] Gibney was an "old saw-and-axe" forester to his colleagues and "an extreme timber beast" to wilderness activists. Brock Evans recalled his first meeting with Gibney in July 1967:

> He eyed me coldly, put his feet up on his desk, lit up a black cigar, blew smoke in my face, and said, "I don't like your ethics," and then proceeded to lecture me on the fact that all the forests would turn into a jackstraw of downed logs and rot away unless loggers came to clean them up and cut them down.

Evans soon afterward suggested that public comments be directed to the Chief of the Forest Service and the regional forester, rather than to Gibney: "The forest supervisor is hopeless," he told others.[33]

The polarization of this debate, a microcosm of the broader political and cultural schisms of the late 1960s, was quite unfamiliar to those who had led a determined but civil campaign to protect the Three Sisters. Karl Onthank always trusted in the ability to find compromise.[34] Gibney's approach certainly eliminated any room for compromise in this debate, but even when Zane Smith replaced him as forest supervisor in 1970 and brought a more conciliatory approach with greater opportunity for public input, there was no middle ground on the question of how to manage the French Pete Valley. Until 1977, every agency land use plan for the area included proposals for logging, and the environmental coalition would not accept a plan that did. Although some in the timber industry realized that French Pete was a lost cause for them and suggested that support for its protection could be exchanged for greater logging opportunities elsewhere, most in the industry dug in their heels.[35]

The growing counterculture movement at the time lent support and activists to the French Pete campaign. Young people in this movement rebelled

against an artificial, middle-class, consumer society, and in environmentalism they saw an opportunity to discover authenticity in nature. The historian
Roderick Nash noted in 1973:

> The environmental renaissance of the late 1960s and early 1970s par-
> alleled a deep-rooted questioning of established American values and
> institutions on the part of what some labeled the "counterculture."
> Wilderness and the idea of wilderness played a key role in both social–
> intellectual movements.

The historian Adam Rome argued more recently, "Though the environmental movement drew young people from all parts of the ideological spectrum,
the new cause appealed especially to critics of the nation's cultural and political institutions."[36]

Protests in Eugene to preserve French Pete from logging gave that community a national reputation for environmental activism (Figure 10.2). Activist Bob Wazeka compared Eugene's role in the wilderness movement of
the 1970s to the role of Paris as the center of the western literary world of the
1920s. Nature's Conspiracy organized much of the student environmental
activism during these years. The group was founded in October 1969 to coordinate actions on a broad range of environmental issues from field burning to
nuclear power. On the second anniversary of the original French Pete protest
march, students organized "a community happening" to mark the occasion
and to protest the latest round of Forest Service plans.[37]

For many, the campaign to preserve French Pete was their first introduction to wilderness issues. Andy Kerr, a high school student in the logging
town of Creswell, Oregon, at the time of the first logging moratorium rally in
1969, had little interest in the anti-war protests that week, but the French Pete
debate made him take notice. "What a novel concept," he thought, "part of
the national forest that you don't log." Participation in the second Earth Day
events in 1971 further helped Kerr to develop an awareness of environmental
issues. He went on to Oregon State University in Corvallis in 1973, where he
founded a student environmental center. In 1976 he joined the staff of the
Oregon Wilderness Coalition (OWC) for $50 per month, lobbying to pass a
wilderness bill in Congress that included French Pete. By the 1990s he had
been on the cover of *Time* magazine and burned in effigy in Oregon logging
towns on account of his leadership of the campaign to preserve old growth
forests.[38]

Aesthetic appreciation and recreational opportunities were not what drove
Andy Kerr and his colleagues at OWC. In this way they separated themselves
from the "old guard" of the Sierra Club and the Friends of the Three Sisters
and cultivated some of the divisions that increasingly characterized the na-

Figure 10.2 The debates over proposed logging in the French Pete Creek valley beginning in the late 1960s reflected the growing numbers of citizens and the increasing role of counterculture activists involved in public lands issues. On 18 November 1969 a crowd of up to 1,500 protesters marched from the University of Oregon to the supervisor's office of the Willamette National Forest in downtown Eugene, calling for a moratorium to logging. Photo by S. Frear, courtesy of the National Archives and Records Administration—Pacific Alaska Region. Found in Region 6 History Collection, Box 76, Folder: 2430 Timber Sales French Pete, Proposed FY 70 [3 of 5].

tional environmental movement in later years. OWC produced a button that read, "Wilderness, More than Recreation."[39] The OWC began in 1972 to provide a local coordinating body for grassroots organizing. Several of the early staff members and organizers were biologists by training, and they brought in a strong ecological perspective. The strong presence of scientists in the Friends of the Three Sisters in the 1950s demonstrates that this was not a new awareness, but it was a new emphasis that OWC brought to the public campaign. The economist and forester Randall O'Toole opposed the dominance of clearcutting on public lands, but he also disliked opposition to clearcutting based solely on aesthetic and emotional values. O'Toole recalled, "The wilderness movement in Oregon was changing from one based on emotion to one based on reason."[40] OWC now focused on watershed health, wildlife habitat, and salmon habitat as the intrinsic values of wilderness.

The breadth of environmental concerns beyond simply wilderness preservation and the radical rhetoric of counterculture participants in the campaign were reflected in the pages of Eugene's underground newspaper, *The Augur*.

Coverage ranged from organic gardening to cleaning up urban waterways to freeway expansion, and writers presented the French Pete question as part of the broader issues of ecology. One contributor remembered:

> Our paper helped to unify people and give them a shared vision of what was happening. . . . Struggles of Native Americans to keep the culture of Raven and Eagle alive flowed into saving French Pete Creek with its streamside hiking trail flowed into nutritional information on organic foods.[41]

The growing ties between the counterculture and the environmental movement also generated angry resentment as part of the cultural backlash of the era. Supporters of logging in French Pete turned to this rhetoric to help their case. The North West Timber Association encouraged industry workers to speak out "as the 'Silent Majority.'" One Oregon forester wrote in 1970, "I have no sympathy for those who use conservation and environment issues merely as a medium in which to further the basic goal of creating social chaos in this Nation." Another man in a public hearing mocked French Pete activists as "welfare recipients who have time to look all over the forest and prepare land use plans. Who pays them?"[42]

Counterculture activists also generated conflict with the established wilderness advocates who focused the campaign on human-centered values and practical politics. Division of strategy emerged by 1971 when the Save French Pete Committee's proposal for an intermediate recreation area was opposed by members of Nature's Conspiracy, who sought instead "to put it back in the wilderness." Many in the campaign disliked the angry rhetoric now widely used by younger activists. Thomas Kimball of the National Wildlife Federation warned, "In a democracy the people need to know the facts to make sound decisions about their environment. But whom do they hear the loudest? The militants—the emotionalists—the eco-freaks when they should be hearing the professionals."[43]

Karl Onthank was once disturbed by too many voices calling for different interests in wilderness protection. "Our weakness is our disunity," he wrote to David Brower in 1956.[44] By the mid-1970s, however, a relative cacophony of individuals and interest groups coalesced behind efforts to stop Forest Service plans to build roads and sell timber in the French Pete region. Kirkpatrick Sale wrote of the environmental movement in the 1970s, "The range of interests and causes (not to mention styles and strategies) was absolutely protean, diverse, and varied as no other movement to date." He continued, "The kind of movement that evolved in these years and the kind of public support that sustained it were both largely without precedent, at least in this century." Sierra Club executive director Michael McCloskey referred to this era as "'the glory days' of the environmental movement."[45]

Despite Onthank's earlier concern for unity, the growing diversity of the drive to preserve French Pete gave that movement greater strength. Boundary decisions for new wilderness areas were still concluded by well-dressed lobbyists and congressional staff members in Capitol Hill offices, but the broader social activism that arose out of Eugene provided wilderness advocates in Congress and national organizations with greater leverage to negotiate. Doug Scott came to the movement after reading a pamphlet on French Pete while studying in Michigan in 1968. He later succeeded Evans as Northwest Representative for the Sierra Club and by 1977 had become one of the club's leading lobbyists nationwide. He strongly followed an incremental approach: you take what you can get and then come back for more. Scott at times decried "bomb throwers" on both sides who threatened to cripple negotiations for compromise, but many of those more radical activists provided an essential base of support from which he and others could negotiate. In addition, their principled stands and stated refusal to compromise made moderates such as Scott seem quite reasonable in their demands, thus increasing their political leverage. The sociologist Rik Scarce noted that founders of radical groups "adopted the role of the extremists as a tactic to allow the mainstream groups to look less radical and achieve more protection for the environment."[46]

By 1975, all elements of the campaign to protect French Pete supported an effort to lobby Congress to employ the Wilderness Act to protect the area as wilderness. Partially, the switch was a product of a national battle with the Forest Service over wilderness areas in the eastern United States. Wilderness advocates sought to make sure that undeveloped areas in the east, which had seen heavy use in earlier centuries, be given the same protective status as other wilderness areas. The Forest Service argued that only fully pristine areas should qualify for wilderness status. Critics labeled this the "purity doctrine." To support an intermediate recreation area seemed to fit right into the agency's argument. However, this also could be seen as one example of how the more radical anti-establishment voices in the environmental movement helped to push the agenda further to the political left, as Adam Rome has argued.[47]

In the course of the stalemate over French Pete, the election of James Weaver to Congress in 1974 gave environmentalists an important local vote of support in their efforts. Weaver disagreed with those in the timber industry and Forest Service who based their opposition to wilderness designation for French Pete on principle. He felt it was a small sacrifice for the industry. When Dave Burwell of the Roseboro Lumber Company in Springfield wrote to him objecting to his support for protecting French Pete, Weaver shot back a handwritten response: "Dammit, Dave—I'm back here *fighting* for forest mgmt. funds to *increase* the productivity of our forests and all I hear from you people is bitching about wilderness. Let's get to work and tackle the *real* job."[48] Weaver saw in French Pete an opportunity to preserve wilderness, while expanding timber production elsewhere on the national forests.

The more the Forest Service and timber industry dug in their heels, the longer logging operations were delayed, the more national attention that growing protests brought to the issue, the larger "French Pete" became. Partially because of Forest Service studies as part of the nationally mandated Roadless Area Review and Evaluation, environmental activists agued that significant portions of neighboring valleys should also be protected. These studies identified nearly 11,000 acres of undeveloped land in the Walker Creek valley to the north and a similar amount in the Rebel Creek valley to the south of French Pete. By 1973, "French Pete" had more than doubled to 42,000 acres. Final approval of French Pete as an addition to the Three Sisters Wilderness Area came as part of a national initiative, the Endangered American Wilderness Act signed by President Jimmy Carter in 1978 (Figure 10.3). It was a major victory for wilderness advocates. Gerald Williams argued, "Basically, the back of the Oregon timber industry was broken—it would never have the same power and influence that it once felt and could no longer act with impunity in matters dealing with logging on the national forests."[49]

Divisions that emerged within the wilderness campaign during the French Pete debate began to redefine environmental politics nationwide in the 1980s. The split between moderates and radicals grew wider and more public during efforts to pass a state-wide Oregon Wilderness Bill in 1984. The creation of Earth First! in 1980 was a direct outlet for the frustrations that arose from this growing division nationwide.[50] Partially, this was a gap between generations, old and young. More, it represents a diversity of goals and methods that arose by 1970. The focus of the established wilderness movement was and continues to be on protecting specific sites from development. Ideas brought to the campaign by the counterculture instead challenged the broader social interaction with the natural world and called for a wholesale change in natural resource policy.

Beginning in 1978 with extensive public hearings as part of a second Roadless Area Review and Evaluation (RARE II), the Oregon Wilderness Coalition—which changed its name in 1982 to the Oregon Natural Resources Council (ONRC)—was able to muster a lineup of local citizens who knew each specific area with deep personal knowledge and passion. They created a constituency that did not reflect the dominantly urban, middle-class membership of the Sierra Club in Oregon, and they expressed pride that they represented more than just "the wine and brie set," as Andy Kerr referred to

Figure 10.3 President Jimmy Carter signed the Endangered American Wilderness Act, including the French Pete addition to the Three Sisters Wilderness, into law on 24 February 1978. At the signing ceremony, from left to right behind the president, are Representative Jim Weaver (OR); Nancy Showalter, a member of Weaver's staff; Senator Frank Church (ID); Fred Hutchison, a member of Church's staff; Representative Morris K. Udall (AZ); Doug Scott, Sierra Club Northwest Representative; and Representative Teno Roncalio (WY), chairman of the House Subcommittee on Public Lands. Courtesy: Jimmy Carter Library.

the "old guard in 1985."[51] By cultivating local citizens, including sportsmen and Native Americans, ONRC sought to find the authentic roots idealized by the counterculture.

ONRC also pushed the focus of its arguments for wilderness toward purely ecological issues of habitat and biodiversity and away from the recreational and aesthetic concerns of traditional wilderness campaigns. Although protection of old growth forests had been at the focus of the conservationist agenda since the 1950s, ONRC made it the sole purpose in the 1980s. Andy Kerr expressed some of the passion with which he and his colleagues in Oregon approached this issue:

> By the time the fight came in the 1984 bill, it was God damn it, we want the Middle Santiam *because* it's old growth. Because it *has* the most volume per acre. And we wanted Waldo [Lake] because it *had* the most volume of timber of any roadless area in the debate, in Oregon or anywhere else.

With those areas we got some of the first wildernesses for old growth forests, which was an emerging political concept at that time.

Kerr also cited the Cummins Creek Wilderness, created in 1984 in the Oregon Coast Range, which he claimed was the first wilderness area in the country that did not have a recreational trail in it.[52]

In the 1980s, ONRC dismissed the relatively slow, incremental approach favored by Sierra Club leaders such as Doug Scott. ONRC strongly felt that it could not compromise in the short run, because there might be few forests left to come back for. Openly defying the strategy of the Sierra Club and the Wilderness Society, who feared a political backlash, ONRC in 1983 filed suit in federal court against the Forest Service's RARE II decision in Oregon. Modeled after the state of California's successful lawsuit, this seemed certain to shut down logging operations in all the lands studied under RARE II. To many, this was like throwing gasoline on a fire that seemed on the verge of coming under control, and it exacerbated growing divisions between environmental activists. For ONRC, the intent was clearly to create more pressure on the timber industry and the legislative process, and they were substantially successful. ONRC executive director James Montieth explained, "The lawsuit is the best catalyst we can provide." Others went further by joining the civil disobedience efforts of Earth First!, which debuted in Oregon in the spring of 1983 by blocking road construction into a roadless area in the Klamath Mountains of Southern Oregon.[53] Although the debates and arguments of the 1980s got away from the location of French Pete Creek, their roots lay in that earlier campaign.

Although it is important to acknowledge that the debate over French Pete Creek did not begin in 1969, the influx of new participants changed the nature of the protests. Work by activists like Karl Onthank to challenge the Forest Service and pass the Wilderness Act opened the door for citizen participation in wilderness debates and the cultural shifts of the late 1960s provided a crowd to walk through. New participants brought strength in numbers, but they also brought a conflicting set of values and strategies. Part of the legislative success of the French Pete campaign can be explained by the cooperation of these diverse groups, but that cohesion broke down in the 1980s. Environmentalism is one of the tremendous success stories of political activism of the late twentieth century, carried out in countless places like French Pete. However, the factor that gave it such great strength—its broad inclusion of so many parts of American society—also placed upon it great challenges to maintain unity.

Notes

1 Portions of this essay were adapted from my book, *Drawing Lines in the Forest: Creating Wilderness Areas in the Pacific Northwest* (Seattle: University of Washington Press, 2007).

2 James T. Patterson, *Grand Expectations: The United States, 1945–1974* (New York: Oxford University Press, 1996), 753; "Trouble Flares at Conclusion of Capital Moratorium March," *Portland Oregonian*, 16 November 1969, 1. Marches in Eugene and Portland occurred on Friday 14 November 1969, to allow for protesters to board overnight buses for the rally in San Francisco; see "November Moratorium Local Committee Discusses Plans," *Oregon Daily Emerald*, 30 October 1969, 3.

3 Gerald W. Williams, "The French Pete Wilderness Controversy 1937–78: A Leadership Case Study" (n.d.), copy in author's possession, obtained from Gerald Williams, former chief historian for the U.S. Forest Service, 6, 12–13; Samuel T. Frear to Regional Forester, "French Pete Rally," 17 December 1969, National Archives—Pacific Alaska Region, Seattle (hereafter NA-PAR), RG 95, Records of the U.S. Forest Service, Region 6 Historical Collection, Box 76, Folder: 2430 French Pete, Proposed FY70 [3 of 5].

4 "Crowds Rally for Environmental Change," *Oregon Daily Emerald*, 19 November 1969, 3; Anthony Netboy, "French Pete for the People," *American Forests* 76(5) (May 1970), 18, 56; Dennis M. Roth, *The Wilderness Movement and the National Forests: 1964–1980* (Washington, DC: U.S. Department of Agriculture, Forest Service, 1984), 50; Sierra Club Columbia Group, "French Pete Creek," 12 November 1969, Forest History Society, Durham, NC, Society of American Foresters Records (hereafter SAF), Box 256, Folder: Sierra Club. Estimates of the Eugene crowd range from 500 to 2,000.

5 LeRoy Ashby and Rod Gramer, *Fighting the Odds: The Life of Senator Frank Church* (Pullman: Washington State University Press, 1994), 346; Adam Rome, "'Give Earth a Chance': The Environmental Movement and the Sixties," *Journal of American History* 90(2) (September 2003), 541–49; Denis Hayes, "Earth Day: A Beginning," in editors of the *Progressive* (eds.), *The Crisis of Survival*, 209–14 (New York: William Morrow & Company, 1970); Robert Gottlieb, *Forcing the Spring: The Transformation of the American Environmental Movement* (Washington, DC: Island Press, 1993), 105–11.

6 Gottlieb, *Forcing the Spring*, 6–11, 105.

7 Marsh, *Drawing Lines*, 12–13, 33–36; Williams, "French Pete," 6. A valuable, parallel discussion of how the influx of counterculture activists added both energy and schism to the political campaigns of the New Left can be found in Todd Gitlin, *The Sixties: Years of Hope, Days of Rage* (New York: Bantam Books, 1987), 212–14, 353–61.

8 James M. Glover, *A Wilderness Original: The Life of Bob Marshall* (Seattle: The Mountaineers, 1986), 145. For Marshall's legacy, see also Paul S. Sutter, *Driven*

Wild: How the Fight against Automobiles Launched the Modern Wilderness Movement (Seattle: University of Washington Press, 2002), 194–238.

9   U.S. Department of Agriculture, Forest Service, "Fact Sheet for the Proposed Three Sisters Wilderness Area" (n.d.), NA-PAR, Box 25219, Folder: Three Sisters Wilderness Area 1954–66.

10 Harold K. Steen, *The U.S. Forest Service: A History*, Centennial Edition (Durham, NC: Forest History Society, 2004), 210–13; Roderick Frazier Nash, *Wilderness and the American Mind*, 4th ed. (New Haven, CT: Yale University Press, 2001), 203–6, 220; Glover, *Wilderness Original*, 230–33; Sutter, *Driven Wild*, 252–55. For an extended discussion of Forest Service preservation policies prior to World War II, see James P. Gilligan, "The Development of Policy and Administration of Forest Service Primitive and Wilderness Areas in the Western United States" (Ph.D. dissertation, University of Michigan, 1953).

11 Lawrence C. Merriam, *Saving Wilderness in the Oregon Cascades: The Story of the Friends of the Three Sisters* (Eugene: Friends of the Three Sisters Wilderness, 1999), 3; Lawrence Rakestraw and Mary Rakestraw, *A History of the Willamette National Forest* (Eugene: Willamette National Forest, 1991), 202–3; William G. Robbins, *Landscapes of Conflict: The Oregon Story, 1940–2000* (Seattle: University of Washington Press, 2004), 175–77.

12 Paul W. Hirt, *A Conspiracy of Optimism: Management of the National Forests Since World War Two* (Lincoln: University of Nebraska Press, 1994); Merriam, *Saving Wilderness*, 2; True D. Morse, "Decision of the Secretary of Agriculture Establishing the Three Sisters Wilderness Area," 6 February 1957, NA-PAR, Box 25219, FRC #73A898, Folder: Three Sisters Wilderness Area 1954–66; and E. L. Peterson to Doug McKay, 10 September 1956, University of Oregon Archives and Special Collections, Eugene, OR, Karl Onthank Conservation Papers (hereafter KOP), Box 1, Folder: Three Sisters. Incoming Correspondence. U.S. Secretary of Agriculture.

13 Merriam, *Saving Wilderness*, 4–5; Karl Onthank to Hubert G. Schenck, 7 October 1955, KOP, Box 1, Folder: Three Sisters. Outgoing Correspondence.

14 Samuel P. Hays, *Beauty, Health, and Permanence: Environmental Politics in the United States, 1955–1985* (Cambridge: Cambridge University Press, 1987), 120. Also see Hays, "The Structure of Environmental Politics Since World War Two," *Journal of Social History* 14 (Summer 1981), 719–20.

15 Leslie Tooze, "Opponents to Reductions of Primitive Area Heard," *Portland Oregonian*, 17 February 1955, 5; "Panel Scores Logging Plan for Three Sisters," *Portland Oregonian*, 12 February 1955, 7; Howard Zahniser, "Statement on the Three Sisters Wilderness Area," 17 February 1955, 5, obtained from the files of Doug Scott, in author's possession (hereafter DSP).

16 Karl W. Onthank to Dave Brower, 31 May 1956, 1, KOP, Box 10, Folder: Sierra Club Correspondence. Brower, David R.

17 On Leopold, see Curt Meine, *Aldo Leopold: His Life and Work* (Madison: University of Wisconsin Press, 1988); on Carhart, see Donald N. Baldwin, *The Quiet*

Revolution: Grass Roots of Today's Wilderness Preservation Movement (Boulder, CO: Pruett Publishing Company, 1972).

18 "Notes—Three Sisters Analysis," 26 April 1955, and Information and Education, L. G. Jolley to Supervisor Mt. Baker *et al.*, 10 May 1955, NA-PAR, Box 25219, FRC #73A898, Folder: Three Sisters Wilderness Area 1954–66; "People's Forests . . . For Wilderness—How Much," *Crow's Lumber Digest*, 14 February 1957, 28.

19 Michael McCloskey, "Wilderness Movement at the Crossroads, 1945–70," *Pacific Historical Review* 41(3) (August 1972), 347–48.

20 True D. Morse, "Decision of the Secretary of Agriculture Establishing the Three Sisters Wilderness Area," 6 February 1957, 1, NA-PAR, Box 25219, FRC #73A898, Folder: Three Sisters Wilderness Area 1954–66.

21 Karl W. Onthank to Dr. Olaus Murie *et al.*, 9 February 1957, 2, DSP. USFS Region 6, headquartered in Portland, encompasses all the national forests in Oregon and Washington.

22 Howard Zahniser to Frank Church, 11 April 1961, 4, KOP, Box 1, Folder: Three Sisters. Associated Documents; Kevin R. Marsh, "'This is Just the First Round': Designating Wilderness in the Central Oregon Cascades, 1950–64," *Oregon Historical Quarterly* 103(2) (Summer 2002), 210–33.

23 Karl W. Onthank to Olaus Murie *et al.*, 9 February 1957, 2. On consistent challenges, see Robert M. Storm, "Proposal for Grant from the National Science Foundation," 1, KOP, Box 1, Folder: Three Sisters. Associated Documents; Ruth [Onthank] to Gerry [Sharpe], 9 August 1961, KOP, Box 10, Folder: Sierra Club. Outgoing Correspondence; Karl Onthank, "Problems of Oregon's Central Cascades," *Sierra Club Bulletin* 44(1) (January 1959), 4.

24 USDA Forest Service, Willamette National Forest, "Background: Management of the French Pete Drainage," March 1971, copy included in Willamette National Forest, "French Pete Creek" (1973), bound collection of documents obtained from the files of Gerald W. Williams, national historian, U.S. Forest Service, in author's possession.

25 Brock Evans, interview by author, 28 July 2001; see KOP, Box 10, Folder: Sierra Club. Outgoing Correspondence. Adam Sowards emphasizes the importance of local activism in "William O. Douglas's Wilderness Politics: Public Protest and Committees of Correspondence in the Pacific Northwest," *Western Historical Quarterly* 37(1) (Spring 2006), 41–42.

26 Williams, "French Pete," 4–5; Winninette A. Noyes, "French Pete: Lowland Valley in the Cascades," *The Living Wilderness* 32(104) (Winter 1968–69), 28.

27 J. H. Wood to Assistant Regional Foresters, 26 January 1970, NA-PAR, Region 6 Historical Collection, Box 76, Folder: 2430 French Pete, Proposed FY70 [2 of 5]; Netboy, "French Pete," 18; "French Pete Delay Hailed," *Portland Oregonian*, 19 November 1969, 28; U.S. Department of Agriculture, "Timber Sales Delayed for More Public Discussion," 17 November 1969, NA-PAR, Region 6 Historical Collection, Box 75, Folder: 2430 Timber Sales French Pete [1 of 5].

28 A. Robert Smith, "Conservation Splits Oregon's Senators," *Portland Oregonian*, 23 November 1969, 49; Andy Kerr, "The Browning of Bob Packwood," *Cascadia Times* 1(6) (1995), 2, page number from manuscript obtained from Andy Kerr, in author's possession; Holway R. Jones to Senator Robert Packwood, 4 February 1973, 2, DSP.

29 "French Pete Again," *Western Forester* 15(5) (February 1970), 1.

30 Evans quoted in Kathie Durbin, *Tree Huggers: Victory, Defeat, and Renewal in the Northwest Ancient Forest Campaign* (Seattle: The Mountaineers, 1996), 28; Andy Kerr, interview by author 28 April 2001; Williams, "French Pete," 5; Oregon Wilderness Coalition, "Three Sisters Wilderness Additions," (1973), DSP.

31 Noyes, "French Pete," 26; Kerr, interview by author; Bob Packwood to Clifford Hardin, Secretary of Agriculture, 26 July 1971, NA-PAR, Box 36824, FRC #74B63, Folder: French Pete Creek 2150.

32 Anthony Netboy, "French Pete for the People," *American Forests* 76(5) (May 1970), 59; Irving Brant and Brock Evans, both quoted in Williams, "French Pete," 11. For discussion of the pressures on the Forest Service to increase timber production during these years, see Hirt, *Conspiracy of Optimism*, 249–51.

33 Brock Evans to Gerald Williams, 2 September 1992, 2, quoted in Williams, "French Pete," 11; Brock Evans, "Environmental Campaigner: From the Northwest Forests to the Halls of Congress," interview conducted by Ann Lage, 1982, in Ann Lage (ed.), *Building the Sierra Club's National Lobbying Program, 1967–1981*, (Berkeley: Regional Oral History Office, The Bancroft Library, University of California, 1985), 105; Brock Evans to Mr. Scott (n.d.), handwritten remark in margins of Douglas W. Scott to Supervisor, Willamette National Forest (draft), 10 April 1968, DSP.

34 Onthank, according to his colleagues, was never bitter toward the Forest Service; see Merriam, *Saving Wilderness*, 37. On "the polarized sixties," see Patterson, *Grand Expectations*, 442–57.

35 Williams, "French Pete," 8; Kerr, interview by author. The final Environmental Impact Statement for the Willamette National Forest Plan in 1977 listed the area as "undeveloped roadless recreation area," but by that point environmentalists had lost all faith in the agency and would not accept anything less than wilderness designation.

36 Roderick Nash, "Abstract of 'Wilderness and the Counterculture,'" presented at the Organization of American Historians Convention, Chicago, 13 April 1973, Forest History Society, Durham, NC, US Forest Service Headquarters History Collection, Folder: Wilderness: General—Speeches. Also see Nash, *Wilderness and the American Mind*, 251–54, where he argues more simply that the counterculture embraced the wilderness movement but not that it reshaped the movement. Rome, "Give Earth a Chance," 542.

37 Robert T. Wazeka, "Organizing for Wilderness: The Oregon Example," *Sierra Club Bulletin* 61(9) (October 1976), 52; Doug Newman, "Nature's Conspiracy," *Oregon*

Daily Emerald, 22 October 1969, 4; Kyle Johnson, "French Pete Anniversary: 'A Community Happening,'" *Oregon Daily Emerald*, 18 November 1971, 8–9.

38 Kerr, interview by author. A very similar quotation from Kerr is found in Durbin, *Tree Huggers*, 36; David Seideman, "Terrorist in a White Collar," *Time*, 25 June 1990.

39 Kerr, interview by author.

40 Durbin, *Tree Huggers*, 39–40.

41 Peter Jensen, "At This End of the Oregon Trail," *Serials Review* 16(3) (Fall 1990), 94. For an example of this holistic vision, see "McCall Fails to See War Relating to Ecology," *Eugene Augur* 1(13) (28 April to 12 May 1970), 7.

42 On the broader backlash, see Patterson, *Grand Expectations*, 668–77. North West Timber Association, "Multiple-Use Management: How Does it Affect You?," (n.d.), NA-PAR, Box 76, Folder: 2430 French Pete, Proposed FY70 [3 of 5]; W. B. Ellington to Scott Pirie, 24 February 1970, NA-PAR, Box 76, Folder: 4230 French Pete, Proposed FY70 [2 of 5]; Cynthia Anderson, "Both Sides Hit Forest Plan," *Springfield News*, 22 October 1975.

43 "Free French Pete," *Eugene Augur* 2(18) (5–30 August, 1971): 7; Kimball quoted in H. R. Glascock, "A Forester Views His Profession," Address to the 15th Annual Washington State Forestry Conference, Seattle, 5 November 1971, SAF, Box 244, Folder: Washington State Forestry Conference 1971.

44 Karl W. Onthank to Dave Brower, 31 May 1956, 1, KOP, Box 10, Folder: Sierra Club Correspondence. Brower, David R.

45 Kirkpatrick Sale, *The Green Revolution: The American Environmental Movement, 1962–1992* (New York: Hill and Wang, 1993), 31–32; Michael McCloskey, *In the Thick of It: My Life in the Sierra Club* (Washington, DC: Island Press, 2005), 364.

46 Scott quoted in David Knibb, *Backyard Wilderness: The Alpine Lakes Story* (Seattle: The Mountaineers, 1982), 202; Douglas W. Scott to M. Brock Evans, 15 April 1968, DSP; Douglas Scott, interview by author, 29 April 2001; Rik Scarce, *Eco-Warriors: Understanding the Radical Environmental Movement* (Chicago: Noble Press, 1990), 7.

47 Roth, *The Wilderness Movement: 1964–1980*, 38–46; Scott, *A Wilderness-Forever Future*, 24–25; Scott, interview by author; James Morton Turner, "Wilderness East: Reclaiming History" *Wild Earth* 11(1) (Spring 2001), 19–26; Rome, "Give Earth a Chance," 551.

48 Jim Weaver to Dave Burwell, 10 March 1977; Dave Burwell to Jim Weaver, 16 March 1977; and Jim Weaver to Dave Burwell, 21 March 1977, SAF, Box 276, Folder: Regional Policy Issues: Oregon & Maine-1977. Emphasis and abbreviation retained from original.

49 Williams, "French Pete," 14.

50 Scarce, *Eco-Warriors*, 58.

51 Kerr quoted in Dennis M. Roth, *The Wilderness Movement and the National Forests: 1980–1984* (Washington: U.S. Department of Agriculture, Forest Service, 1988), 26; Kerr, interview by author.

52 Kerr, interview by author, emphasis retained from the original transcript; Roth, *The Wilderness Movement: 1980–1984*, 26, 32–33.

53 Roth, *The Wilderness Movement: 1980–1984*, 24–36; Durbin, *Tree Huggers*, 56–59.

CHAPTER 11

Parting the Waters

The Ecumenical Task Force at Love Canal and Beyond

ELIZABETH D. BLUM

Nobody wants to produce a play about a couple that moved back to Love Canal. . . . Nobody wants to pay twenty dollars to watch people living next to chemical waste! They can see that in New Jersey!
George Fields to Michael Dorsey, *Tootsie* (1982)

Introduction

When the movie *Tootsie* premiered in 1982, audiences would have been very familiar with the story behind the reference to Love Canal. The neighborhood's dilemma flooded the media beginning in the summer of 1978, maintaining a steady stream of news for several years. Although George Fields, Sidney Pollack's character in *Tootsie*, certainly felt no theatergoer would want to see a play about the famous environmental disaster, one religious group, known as the Ecumenical Task Force (ETF), continued their interest and activism in the Niagara Falls, New York, neighborhood even after most of the residents left. Pollack's character, in addition, deftly highlighted an issue with which the ETF quickly became all too familiar: hazardous waste was a national, widespread issue, hardly limited to western New York state. In contrast to other groups involved at Love Canal, the ETF grasped Pollack's point, and plugged away against the variety of toxic waste problems endemic in the area surrounding Love Canal.

The ETF provides an interesting case study within twentieth-century environmental activism. The middle-class, white group evolved from a local, grassroots organization focused on a Christian ethic of helping the unfortunate, to a professional, determined group dealing with complex scientific and legal issues of hazardous waste. Although Pollack's character (and many real-life characters) hoped to brush Love Canal from popular culture, the ETF pressed forward to increase understanding of the environmental problems as well as the connections between environmental and social problems. They presented a sophisticated understanding of environmental issues that flowed from their class status, prior activism, and the balanced gender ratio of the group.[1]

Background: The Story of Love Canal[2]

The sheer magnitude of Niagara Falls mesmerized even the earliest European explorers. Father Louis Hennepin, the first European to describe the falls to his region, exclaimed that the falls cascaded "down after a surprising and astonishing manner, insomuch that the Universe does not afford its Parallel."[3] The falls, he added, made "an outrageous Noise, more terrible than that of Thunder; for when the Wind blows from off the South, their dismal roaring may be heard about fifteen Leagues off."[4]

By the 1800s, 200 years after Hennepin wrote his early description, the falls had caught on as a popular destination for a variety of interests. Newlyweds flocked to the site to gasp in awe as the Niagara River catapulted 2.3 billion gallons of water per hour over an impressive 180-foot precipice. The flowing water also attracted industry. In the late 1800s, Niagara Falls teemed with a great variety of companies interested in harnessing the power of the river to generate electricity. Other entrepreneurs, including businessman William Love, saw other uses for the water. In the 1890s, Love intended to build a canal upstream from the falls that would provide a navigable route from the river to Lake Ontario. Love's plan failed when he ran out of money, but his venture left a large partially dug hole east of Niagara Falls.[5]

The industries around Love's canal produced various consumer goods as well as large amounts of waste products. One prominent local company, Hooker Electrochemical Company (later Hooker Chemical Company), purchased the unfinished canal property during World War II as a place to dispose of some of its chemical waste. The company used the property until 1952, dumping at least 21,000 tons of chemicals, including "caustics, alkalis, fatty acids, and chlorinated hydrocarbons from the manufacture of dyes, perfumes, solvents for rubber and synthetic resins."[6] When they filled the canal, Hooker covered it with dirt and sold the lot to the local school board for a dollar.[7]

In the 1950s and 1960s, Niagara Falls needed new neighborhoods to house workers and new schools for their children. The city constructed a school directly on the canal with the land obtained from Hooker, and a neighborhood, known as LaSalle after the prominent French explorer, sprang up around it. Families flocked to the neat, small starter homes, impressed with the green space, the closeness of the school, and the sense of family pervading the area. Underneath this façade of idyllic family life, Hooker's waste lurked unseen by residents. The invisibility of the waste was temporary, however. The 1970s proved an especially wet decade for the Falls area, and the extra snow and precipitation accelerated the deterioration of the metal barrels the waste had been buried in, causing them to leak, burst, or even push to the surface in some cases.[8]

A young housewife named Lois Gibbs watched the news and combed through the newspapers avidly over the summer of 1978. Gibbs and her husband Harry had moved to the LaSalle neighborhood a few years earlier. Lois enjoyed walking her son Michael to school and playing with her younger daughter Missy during the day while Harry worked at the local Goodyear plant. Over the summer of 1978, however, she began hearing stories, notably from the *Niagara Gazette*'s reporter Michael Brown, detailing problems local families had encountered. The stories related tales of miscarriages, birth defects, sick pets, oily puddles of muck in backyards, and strange odors in basements.[9]

Brown's articles also detailed the history of the canal, which alarmed Gibbs. She tried unsuccessfully to have her son, who attended the school built directly on the waste site, moved to another school, and then organized a campaign in the neighborhood (now better known as "Love Canal") to have everyone relocated. Toward the end of the summer, on 2 August 1978, public officials acknowledged the scope of the problem by declaring an emergency, stating that the "Love Canal Chemical Waste Landfill constitutes a public nuisance and an extremely serious threat and danger to the health, safety, and welfare of those using it, living near it, or exposed to the conditions emanating from it."[10]

After the announcement, Gibbs's campaign, assisted by several other women from the working-class neighborhood, kicked into high gear. They staged rallies, protests, pickets, marches, and letter-writing campaigns. They burned politicians in effigy, appeared on the *Phil Donahue* show, and even took two EPA officials hostage for an afternoon. After several long years, the women won their struggle, as the federal and state governments agreed to purchase their homes and allow them to leave the contaminated area. To help deal with future Love Canals, Congress passed CERCLA, better known as Superfund, a piece of legislation designed to force companies to pay for the cleanup of their waste.[11]

While Lois Gibbs began to attract media attention with her struggles at Love Canal, other groups and individuals joined in the fight as well, swimming upstream against a host of entrenched interests. For example, a group of African American renters fought against the entrenched racism and classism inherent in Niagara Falls during the 1970s as they tried to escape Love Canal as well. The ETF drew the local Judeo-Christian community into the struggle. Each of the group members prominent in the ETF brought with them several common characteristics—a high level of education, middle-class status, a commitment to the Christian church, and a wide experience in other social justice issues. The ETF differed substantially from Gibbs's organization in class status, membership, justification for involvement, and most significantly, their recognition of, and willingness to become involved in, a wider scope of problems laid bare at Love Canal. Their work parted the waters for other anti-toxics organizers interested in using religious faith as a way to promote environmentalism.

Parting the Waters: The ETF's Origins at Love Canal

Water ebbed, flowed, and sloshed through the problems at Love Canal. The furious rush of the river piqued late nineteenth-century industry's interest in harnessing it for electricity. An enterprising businessman hoped to divert some of the water to provide a canal for the area. The failed canal served as a dumping ground for industry, and high levels of precipitation forced the buried waste to the surface and to residents' attention. Drinking water, flooded basements, and yard irrigation proved a potent source of contamination for the residents. Interestingly, experiences with water's destructive power also brought another woman, Sister Margeen Hoffmann, one of the leaders of the ETF, into the struggle at Love Canal.

While Gibbs dealt with the consequences of the water-drenched situation at Love Canal, water issues of a different nature held Hoffmann's attention. After a very destructive flood in the summer of 1978 in Rochester, Minnesota, Hoffmann accepted an assignment from the Catholic Church to direct the Rochester Area Churches Emergency Response (RACER), an ecumenical relief effort for the victims of the Minnesota disaster. Originally slated to last only six weeks, Hoffmann stayed in the assignment for a year, until July of 1979. Hoffmann noted wryly that "Either I am very good at my work . . . that they keep me, or I am very slow to get it done." Her work involved substantially more than the typical response of "just go[ing] out and help[ing] people with their flooded basements and send[ing] people out there and [to] give out quilts." Hoffmann organized an extensive array of volunteers, eventually numbering over 600, who assisted with counseling services for the victims, many of whom had lost everything. They conducted research into the personal effects of disasters on victims, and eventually developed a model used by Church World Service (CWS) as it extended its disaster relief services.[12] In fact, a CWS employee, McKinley Koffman, connected Hoffmann with the ETF, feeling her experience in Minnesota could help the new ETF in New York.[13]

By the time Hoffmann arrived in Niagara Falls in the summer of 1979, most of the nation had become familiar with the story of Love Canal, mainly thanks to Lois Gibbs's effective control of the media. Yet the publicity also generated interest from other quarters. The Reverend Dr. Paul Moore, pastor at the First Presbyterian Church in Lewiston, a community near Love Canal, had been following the news stories with some interest.[14] In the summer of 1978, a year before Hoffmann arrived, Moore toured the Love Canal neighborhood and came away from the visit deeply troubled about the implications of how humans and the natural world interacted. "In Niagara County," he stated firmly in a letter to his congregation after the visit:

> God's law has been broken, his eternal covenant violated, and we are reaping the bitter consequences: ecological disaster and human tragedy. . . . This is God's good earth; not ours. We do not own the earth; we are but stewards of the earth. God has established an eternal covenant with the dwellers on the earth; "Take care of my earth, and you will live; exploit it, and you shall surely die."[15]

Other church members soon shared Moore's interest in the Love Canal problem. Over the winter of 1978 to 1979, Donna Ogg, the church's Director of Outreach Ministries, approached Moore to see what the church could do.[16]

On 22 February 1979, the pair sent a letter to the Buffalo–Niagara Falls area churches requesting a meeting to organize a collective response to the health, financial, and psychological strains at Love Canal.[17] The letter spawned an enthusiastic response among many in the Buffalo–Niagara Falls area of churches. Over 200 people, including area academics, scientists, and Love Canal residents as well as church leaders and lay persons met at the Wesley Church across from the canal on 13 March 1979. At a pivotal moment during the meeting, Moore "asked the question, 'Do you think the churches should become involved here?'" The question was certainly not a simple one. Moore realized that opposition for assistance might emerge from several factions: those who believed that the church should stay out of social activism, and those who felt it unwise to antagonize Hooker Chemical, a major employer in the area with substantial economic power. A majority at the meeting, however, responded positively to Moore's query, agreeing that the church should play a role in the environmental crisis.[18]

A week later, members from over twenty-one religious centers, representing Catholics, Protestants, and Jews, met to form the ETF, formally known as the "Ecumenical Task Force to Address the Love Canal Disaster." The new organization, which quickly elected Paul Moore chairman and Donna Ogg secretary, decided to restrict membership to "representatives of the religious community." The new ETF established five main goals. These included "providing direct aid to residents," "assuming the advocate role in applying political pressure," "gathering and interpreting appropriate data," "seeking reconciliation through justice," and "advocating the complete neutralization of toxic wastes."[19]

Although many of those at the early meetings agreed with Ogg and Moore, the ETF encountered significant resistance to church involvement at Love Canal from some in the religious community. Some congregation members simply felt that churches should stay away from participating in social issues, and stick to "organizing Bible studies."[20] A far more common reaction, especially among those churches in the Niagara Falls area, was that it would become far too political or divisive. Local churches' memberships, of course, included Love Canal residents but also substantial numbers of workers and management of the area chemical companies, including Hooker Chemical. Many felt that assisting the Love Canal residents equated to an overt act of protest against Hooker. Fearful that the company might leave the area entirely, or fire "unsupportive" workers, many Niagara Falls residents maintained a respectful distance from the activism. The Reverend Dr. James Brewster, who led the ETF after Moore departed and was present at the first meetings, stated that:

> there was a direct, and implicit effect [that] if the churches were involved with this [Love Canal], then people might turn away from local congregations, or congregations might lose membership . . . I knew of one instance in which one of the local pastors was called off of our interfaith work because of pressure from the members of his congregation.[21]

The tasks and duties of the organization very quickly overwhelmed Ogg, its only staff member. Therefore leaders decided to hire a full-time executive director and as many staff members as funding permitted to implement the goals and directives of the organization. By May 1979, Ogg reported that

Hoffmann had accepted the executive director position.[22] Sister Margeen not only became the executive director, but also a driving, dominant force behind the organization for the next ten years. As time went on, Hoffmann found the analogy of "the flood, Noah, and the rainbow" important as a way to justify the ETF's work and provide hope for the future.[23] Hoffmann saw the ETF as beginning to lead Love Canalers, and the wider community, out of the "flood" of the hazardous waste problem.

ETF's Justification for Involvement and Activism at Love Canal

The ETF's rationale for involvement at Love Canal centered around its interpretations of the role of the church and Christian theology, but also incorporated elements of ecology, Native American philosophy, and paganism. This diverse philosophy developed by the ETF directly related to the group's gender balance, as well as members' prior activism, class level, and education level. The philosophy also contrasts sharply with the dominant rhetoric emerging from Love Canal's main resident group, which stressed a concern for the health and well-being of children above all else.

To deflect some of the initial resistance from churches, the earliest justifications for the ETF's involvement centered on themes of assisting the oppressed and less fortunate in society, which would have been seen by many as appropriate avenues for church involvement. Early literature and rhetoric of the group described Love Canal residents as "victims," or "unfortunate dwellers," "rejected ones," and even "unwanted citizens."[24] Sister Margeen justified the ETF's presence with the statement:

> churches have a mandate: they *must* be concerned with the welfare of individuals. They must address the concerns of the poor, the needy, and the victimized. They, as *institutional* representatives of God, must be active and responding to the needs of the people.[25]

The ETF proceeded along traditional natural disaster lines during their early work at Love Canal, while pressing politically for permanent voluntary relocation for the area. In a natural disaster, for example, immediate efforts focus on obtaining housing, food, and medical aid for the residents, as well as giving support counseling. The ETF, beginning in the summer of 1979, counseled residents with the emotional costs of the crisis, assisted those moving from their homes, communicated information through a newsletter, set up a phone bank, and provided worship services for hotel residents. The ETF also provided direct financial relief: The monetary grants to families included paying for moving costs, housing, utilities, clothing, phone calls, printing costs, and food, although the largest expense came from the payment of medical bills for four families. In all, during that early period, the group dispensed over $11,000 in direct aid.[26]

In addition to providing direct aid to residents, the ETF also provided a strong advocate's voice during the crisis years of 1979–81. The ETF became a forceful advocate for the African American renters at Love Canal, the most marginalized group in the crisis. The black renters suffered from many of the same problems as the white homeowners, but politicians, doctors, bureaucrats, and the media attended to them far less frequently. Solutions for the renters came much later and with more struggles than for the local whites. The ETF assisted as they could, by contacting numerous politicians at the local, state, and federal levels and maintaining ties with the state and federal bureaucracy. They also kept local congregations informed and updated about Love Canal status and events.[27]

The organization of "Love Canal Sunday" demonstrates this advocacy role. The event was organized for Sunday 3 August 1980 by the United Methodist Conference, and the ETF urged other faiths to participate as well. They suggested that the congregations "pray for all those involved in the Love Canal tragedy . . .[and] take up a special offering for Wesley United Methodist Church . . . An offering may also be taken for the Ecumenical Task Force." The ETF further offered their services as speakers or in providing a videotape explaining the Love Canal problem.[28] Acts such as Love Canal Sunday helped spread awareness of hazardous waste problems outside the immediate community. However strong the ETF advocacy role became, direct aid continued to dominate the ETF until the majority of the residents left the area and the homeowners had their homes purchased.

The ETF struggled with defining the tragedy of Love Canal. In some ways, they attempted to squeeze Love Canal into the definition of a "natural disaster." In order to obtain funding from religious organizations that typically funded disasters, for example, Sister Margeen noted forcefully that:

> Our position [at Love Canal] is the same response given to natural disasters. . . . A disaster is an occurrence such as a tornado, storm, flood, blizzard, civil strife . . . or other situation that causes human suffering or creates human needs that the victims cannot alleviate without assistance.[29]

The organization, however, quickly noticed striking differences between man-made and natural disasters. First and foremost, the ETF noticed the invisible nature of man-made disasters, especially with respect to hazardous waste. "A flood or fire is a well defined disaster," noted Roberta Grimm, ETF member and President of the New York State Church Women United. "[B]ut chemicals leaching through the ground, working into basements, walls and gardens, working their way also into the body of a child, a pregnant woman, a man . . . these are more elusive, hard to see, hard to measure, hard to prove."[30] The church's role was also different. "In addition to care for the people," Brewster stated,

> more emphasis must be given to the political and legal resolution of this human-caused disaster . . . we prod at agencies unprepared and unwilling to share in resolving the crisis. . . . Any uneasiness of the church to deal with business, government, law, and science will thwart efforts to alleviate the sufferings of victims.[31]

The ETF also found a far greater reluctance on the part of people to respond with charity during a man-made disaster, noting "People respond positively and heartily to requests for food and blankets, but when people are fearful, distraught . . . it is not so easy to respond . . . more is required of the human spirit."[32] Along with the differences in gaining response, the ETF also faced ostracism and criticism for its role in the disaster. "Many times the ETF was suspect by members of their congregations," they noted, "by people who refused to believe there was a problem, and even by some religious leaders for asking the questions, and seeking the answers from those who had the information or held public office."[33]

Defining the residents as "victims" certainly played into the vision of Love Canal as a disaster, but the ETF also emphasized empowerment of the residents as a solution to their problems. "If a community is not in control there is no opportunity to get 'back on its feet,'" Hoffmann had learned. "It only makes good psychological sense for a community to . . . make decisions concerning rebuilding, and to plead on behalf of those members who have been ignored, forgotten, or damaged emotionally and physically."[34] John Lynch, a member of the ETF board, noted that the group

> has wisely encouraged the resident's participation in seeking out resources to meet their problems. Probably for the first time, some are involved in community organizations and are doing things for themselves . . . The Ecumenical Task Force has perhaps provided a foundation on which the residents can rebuild their futures.[35]

Hoffman also noted positive effects from local participation. In the late 1980s, she reported that "Niagara is experiencing the exhilaration of the empowerment of people that can shake entrenched institutions."[36]

Moving hand-in-hand with the language of empowerment, the ETF also emphasized environmental health as a fundamental right of citizenship. Paul Moore co-opted elements of Jefferson's Declaration of Independence when he stated:

> Citizens deserve the right to breathe safe, clean air, the right to drink safe, pure water, the right to safe, environmentally clean housing, [and] the right to a safe, clean environment in which to work. When citizens are denied these basic rights of man and nature [he continued], the government had a responsibility to guarantee them.[37]

As the organization struggled with the definition of a disaster, they groped with ways to incorporate Judeo-Christian theology into an environmental context. The ETF needed a strong biblical basis as a means to justify its actions to other congregations and gain support from church funding organizations. Most of the ETF's biblical rationale centered around the concept of stewardship. Moore, the first to articulate and develop this concept for the ETF, said

> I speak as a Christian charged by God in the Scriptures with a cultural mandate to be a careful, meek and responsible steward of this good earth which in the beginning came from the hand of the Creator pure and fresh and clean—a lovely, living thing of exquisite beauty, a magnificent habitat fitted by ingenious design for God's highest creation—the human family—to live, move, have their being, and—in cooperation with their Creator—fashion a social order grounded in justice.[38]

He drew his biblical rationale for this stewardship from a passage in Isaiah:

> The earth lies polluted under its inhabitants, for they have transgressed the laws, violated the statutes. Therefore a curse devours the earth and its inhabitants suffer for their guilt. . . . The earth staggers like a drunken man, its transgression lies heavy upon it, and it falls, and will not rise again.[39]

Others found additional sources reiterating the gloomy prophecy of Isaiah when man's relationship with God's creation was disrupted. They noted that the "prophet Hosea said: 'There is no faithfulness or kindness, and no knowledge of God in the land . . . Therefore the land mourns, and all who dwell in it languish.'"[40]

Donna Ogg reinforced Moore's discussion of stewardship with a clarification of the idea of dominion in Genesis. She said that in giving humans "dominion" over the earth, God "appointed mankind as caretakers over the whole of that creation." Caretakers, Ogg asserted, "accept custody of that creation, accept responsibility for all that is part of creation, . . . [and] allow no one or no thing to mar the pureness, freshness and exquisite beauty of that creation." If a caretaker witnesses God's creation being defiled, "we are required by God to challenge the injustice of such cruel, irresponsible and arrogant behavior," Ogg continued.[41]

Others combined religion and secular sources to explain environmental activism. Brewster explicitly compared Love Canal with Eden, describing the neighborhood as "the garden poisoned." The inspiration for his effort, he stated, came during his discovery of the works of the transcendentalist philosopher Henry David Thoreau. "Thoreau," Brewster noted,

> was . . . suggesting that America could be the kind of Eden which was not apparent in Europe . . . Also, of course, one of the emphases that when you moved to a place like Love Canal, you move there because it is your Eden. . . . an ideal suburban place where you could raise children without the city problems, etcetera.[42]

Donna Ogg picked up on the vision of a paradise lost when she linked the events at Love Canal with Rachel Carson's writings. Carson's groundbreaking *Silent Spring* had a profound effect on many members of the ETF. After reading its opening passage about the ideal community struck silent by a "strange blight," accompanied by illness and the death of wildlife, fish, and vegetation, Ogg drew a direct comparison between Carson's fictional community and Love Canal. Ogg stated that "The community in Carson's fable *does* exist. This community *has* experienced all the misfortunes she describes. The imagined tragedy *has* become a stark reality."[43]

The ETF added even more eclectic justifications for involvement, ranging from a gendered paganism to Native American philosophy to other literature. One of Moore's most quoted passages incorporated a very pre-industrial, pagan philosophy. He stated, in pressing for ecological change:

> I speak for the Earth—our loving mother who gave us birth and faithfully sustains us. I speak for her, because she cannot speak for herself. When, as a vulnerable woman, she is ravaged and raped by brutal exploiters and hear[t]less profit-takers, and then discarded as a worthless, spent

thing—wounded and sore—it is my duty to stoop to her weakness, bind her wounds, and heal her hurt.[44]

Moore's words stress a gendered interpretation of nature, seeing the Earth as a weak, helpless female who has been sexually victimized by men, and yet also needs the help of brave, strong men to keep her alive.[45]

Native American philosophy played a part in ETF rhetoric as well. The ETF quoted a statement recorded by Chief Seattle in 1854 as his tribe contemplated giving some of their land to the advancing whites. As Europeans encroached on Native American land, Chief Seattle noted that

earth is not his [the white man's] brother, but his enemy, and when he has conquered it, he moves on . . . Our God is the same God [as the white man.] . . . This earth is precious to Him, and to harm the earth is to heap contempt on its Creator . . . Contaminate your bed, and you will one night suffocate in your own waste.[46]

Seattle's warning eerily echoed the sentiments expressed in Isaiah. The ETF also quoted a "Mohawk Indian Prayer," which asked:

Oh Great spirit, Creator of all things; . . .
Be kind to us.
Give these people the favor
To see green trees,
Green grass, flowers, and berries
This next spring;
So we all meet again.[47]

The ETF linked Native American beliefs with a closeness to and reverence for nature they found lacking in twentieth-century America.

While the justifications for activism were highly eclectic, discussions of possible solutions tended to be more limited among ETF members. Initially, the ETF focused almost exclusively on technical, scientific solutions as the main answer to hazardous waste, choosing to blame government and corporations for the problems. In October 1980, the board boldly stated that they advocated the "complete neutralization of chemical and radioactive wastes," a goal that limited how the ETF focused on the problem to a certain extent.[48] With a focus on "neutralization," they examined ways to change the waste itself through technology, rather than limit the production of toxics in the first place.

In 1982, for example, the ETF exclaimed "[a]bove ground storage and 'secure' landfills MUST BE ENDED!" Ways to do this included "recycling and waste exchange . . . incineration . . . raw material and energy recovery . . . disassemblage."[49] Each stressed the development of technical, end-of-the-line solutions to the hazardous waste problem. The next year, Roger Cook outlined again the approved ways for dealing with hazardous waste, which

> would include: Chemical treatment (neutralization, precipitation of solids, ion exchange, etc.); Biological treatment to break down organic compounds; Physical treatment to reduce, solidify, or separate (evaporation, carbon absorption, filtration, membrane osmosis, etc.); [and] Thermal treatment (incineration, wet oxidation, pyrolysis, plasma arc, etc.).[50]

Again, early on, the ETF's focus on technology allowed them only to see solutions at the end of the waste stream.

The ETF, with their faith in technology, held that industries had the primary responsibility and duty to deal with, and find solutions for, the problems of hazardous waste. In a resolution proposed by the ETF for their Executive Board, leaders stated that "We ask that the moral conscience of the leaders of our country and . . . concerned citizens demand correction and compensation from our government and corporations and not let profit and politics stand in the way."[51] They also noted that industry should be guided by the principle "that it is morally irresponsible to produce materials or by-products which cannot be either neutralized or absolutely sealed off from the environment forever."[52]

In the first few years of its existence, the ETF generally chose to blame others—corporations and government—for hazardous waste problems. However, as it immersed itself in the complexity of the problems surrounding hazardous waste, it also began to articulate more forcefully a language stressing change within individual consumption practices. Roberta Grimm, an ETF member, stated that "We need to be alert to the life styles we perpetuate, to question waste and extravagance."[53] This language really remained underdeveloped until the mid- to late 1980s. Barbara Hanna, the ETF's executive assistant, articulated the idea of individual responsibility for prevention of hazardous waste most clearly. "Our common household garbage poses a threat," she warned a Methodist audience. "Sanitary landfill capacity is decreasing at a rapid rate. We are faced with a choice of our garbage being incinerated in-toto in a waste-to-energy plant . . . or sorting and separating our household garbage at home." Although Hanna simplified the options somewhat, she certainly demanded that consumers accept responsibility for the waste produced. In addition, she also offered a critique of the incineration process, which the ETF had earlier proposed as a cure-all. Waste-to-energy incinerators, she had learned, "may pose danger not only in the air emissions while burning, but also in the residue ash which must be buried."[54] A year later, she lectured another group on the need to use cloth diapers, limit the use of plastic bags, use paper cups instead of Styrofoam, walk instead of drive, and properly dispose of cleaning agents.[55] Hanna's arguments urged people to think about their actions, consumption habits, and responsibility for the waste they generated, something foreign to the ETF in its early years.

In addition, the ETF also articulated concern for children and future generations as a way to justify activism, a rhetoric often called "maternalism." In the middle of a speech to the Niagara County Legislature, Sister Margeen asked for help from the legislature in passing a law to regulate hazardous waste in a comprehensive way. She lobbied for these laws "for this generation of children and the children yet to be born."[56] Looking back on her involvement with the ETF, Terri Mudd, mother of six, stated that her Love Canal activism, "was a very natural outgrowth of my sense of parenthood."[57] Concern for children also produced a more radical critique. Roberta Grimm and Hoffmann noted that "it is for this generation of children and the children yet to be born that we . . . call to task science and the forces which allow researchers to tinker with the very stuff of life."[58] In addition, the ETF's activities sometimes focused directly on children: they conducted tours of the area for eighth- and ninth-grade classes and planned other educational events.

Maternalism, the dominant and almost sole language of the residents, played a far more muted role in the ETF. Concern for Lois Gibbs and the residents, of course, played an integral role in the ETF's involvement, and yet language stressing children never formed a dominant part of its rationale. Instead, the ETF emphasized justifications and solutions centered on an eclectic mix of assisting victims, Judeo-Christian theology, Native American philosophy, an environmentalist ethic, faith in technology, and the need for individual responses.

Flowing Waters: The ETF Expands Its Activism

As the ETF stepped more deeply into the Love Canal problem, they encountered a crisis in purpose. As it had been originally formed with a single-minded mission to assist at Love Canal, many felt the organization had performed its duty and could disband once the Love Canal "crisis" seemed to dissipate. Others, however, prompted by a growing awareness of the widespread nature of the problem of hazardous waste, saw a permanent role for the church in applying knowledge gained at Love Canal to other communities. After much soul-searching and debate, the ETF decided to continue and broaden its work, formalizing the change with the adoption of a new name. In November 1979, the "The Ecumenical Task Force to Address the Love Canal Disaster" became the "The Ecumenical Task Force of the Niagara Frontier." The By-Laws of the newly formed organization stated "[i]t is the primary purpose of the Task Force to provide relief from the physical, psycho/social, and economic distress of persons living in areas affected by the ecological tragedy of chemical and radioactive contamination."[59] Although work at Love Canal continued over the lifetime of the organization, emphasis in the ETF shifted around 1982 from direct aid there to a more overtly political, legal, and advocacy role regarding hazardous waste in general.

The ETF's Involvement outside Love Canal: Case Studies

Board members and staff encountered numerous horror stories from residents, newspaper stories, and other contacts concerning other Niagara Falls neighborhoods dealing with hazardous waste problems. In addition, as the Love Canal residents fled their homes, they soon realized, and reported to the ETF, that dangerous hazardous waste sites peppered the entire city. Many of these other hazardous waste issues became so complicated and time-consuming that individual board members were assigned specific sites to keep up with and inform the general body about their status. This interaction in outside issues, which clearly distinguished the group from the local residents, included involvement in legal cases, consulting work with other communities, and general education and advocacy efforts.

The situation at Hyde Park, also known as Bloody Run, provided an opportunity for the ETF to publicly demonstrate its increased role and focus on non-Love Canal events through the court system. The case piqued the ETF's interest because the Hyde Park site sat a short distance from the Niagara River, and threatened both American and Canadian water supplies. ETF had also communicated with several Hyde Park residents, including Fred Armagast, whose home abutted the highly contaminated Bloody Run Creek.[60] Jim Brewster drew the straw for the Hyde Park issue when it appeared before the ETF. Brewster remembered that the landfill in northern Niagara Falls

> had an extraordinarily high concentration of dioxin. Probably the most dioxin anywhere in this part of the world, I guess. And it was leaching out of a fairly large dump site directly through bedrock directly to the gorge face of the Niagara River, and you could see discoloration of the shale in the rock face, and eventually this would filter down into the Niagara River affecting water quality, even, for example, especially Canadian cities that would be downstream.[61]

In fact, dioxin levels at Hyde Park had been measured to be higher than all the dioxin used in the Vietnam War. Hooker dumped over 80,400 tons of waste at the site over the years, making Love Canal seem minor by comparison.[62]

The ETF hired an attorney, Barbara Morrison, who appealed to Judge John Curtain to grant them amicus curiae, or "friend of the court," status in May 1981 in a legal case for the residents of Hyde Park. The ETF also began coordinating the various citizens' groups there, keeping them informed and up to date. In getting involved in the legal case, the ETF hoped to benefit the public at large, as well as to "present to the public and the court, the flaws contained in the EPA–Hooker plans on clean-up and containment of the chemicals."[62] Ultimately, they hoped that, "if we can get the court to specify duration of time company must monitor the site, . . . then we will already have more than what the EPA now requires." The ETF saw its amicus status as "the beginning of bringing issues of liability, responsibility and justice to bear for the first time through the courts, on the issue of hazardous waste."[64]

Fourteen months after the court filed the original settlement plan, and after lengthy hearings on the case, Judge John Curtain finally approved the settlement in April 1982. The ultimate settlement agreement reached contained many elements the ETF had pressed for, included plans for remedial construction of the site, and required Occidental Chemical Corporation (Hooker Chemical's legal successor) to "identify the extent of contamination" and do anything necessary "to protect the public health and environment."[65]

The ETF tempered its enthusiasm with the frustration of the realities of legal cases involving a Superfund site, complex scientific issues, and a very wealthy corporation. Cleanup remedies only began in 1985, and included a complex system of wells to suck up waste, drains to collect runoff, and underground walls to contain the site. As had happened at Love Canal, the entire site was fenced off, and the residents moved. Bloody Run Creek was excavated in 1993. The remedial construction continued through 2000. Treatment at the site will run even longer. The EPA estimated that over 1.5 billion gallons of groundwater "will need to be treated over the next 30 years."[66] The ETF had a legal victory under their belts, and yet the organization would not survive to see Hyde Park put to bed.

The ETF's involvement with another Niagara Falls hazardous waste site, known as the "S-area," also concerned water issues and proved a turning point in its involvement in legal wrangling. The S-area, located directly on the Hooker plant site, abutted not only the Niagara River, but also the drinking water treatment facility for the city. Over a period from 1947 to 1961, Hooker dumped 63,000 tons of hazardous waste onto the eight-acre site. It covered the area with "other wastes and debris" for another decade, and then constructed two lagoons on top of it to handle non-hazardous waste. Samples taken around the site revealed that the waste had leaked poisons, namely benzene and dioxin (both highly toxic), into the soil and water. Activists, including the ETF, worried about the dangers to drinking water since the treatment plant lay literally next door. The EPA noted that, although the main threat "to people is the risk from eating fish" from the river, the treatment plant was a "potential public health threat."[67]

As it had at Hyde Park, the ETF pressed for a role in the legal wrangling over the site. By November 1981, they had decided, along with their attorney Morrison, to try for intervenor status in the case. The principle of "intervenor status" allows a non-party in litigation to join as a party to the case if it can show it has property or interests at stake. The ETF hoped that intervenor status would give it a voice in the final agreement in the case against Hooker.[68]

Again, much like in the Hyde Park case, legal action proceeded slowly. After two years, Morrison finally argued for the ETF's intervenor status before Judge John Curtain. Although the judge denied the ETF's request, the group optimistically felt that the process had spread their ideas farther afield. Hoffmann later noted that the application "did much to change the scientific work prescribed by the governments."[69]

As the months stretched into years with the S-area issue, frustration grew within the group. Not only was legal action slow, the ETF found it exceptionally expensive. In January 1984, only a month after the intervenor status had been denied, Hoffmann reported some severe budget problems. The ETF had fallen behind in paying Hoffmann's salary to her order and, because of a lack of funds, had to cancel its annual evaluation conference. Hoffmann even suggested to the board that she continue working out of her apartment with no staff to save money.[70]

Without intervenor status, the S-area case proceeded with the ETF only able to watch on the sidelines. In April 1985, the agreement forced Occidental to clean up the area, which included the construction of buried walls around the areas, drains to collect and manage the runoff, and a cap over the entire area, all of which was completed by 1996. A second agreement in 1991 forced the company to pay for the destruction of the old water treatment plant and the construction of a new $70 million plant.[71] The S-area litigation ended the ETF's direct legal involvement in hazardous waste questions. For the small, underfunded group, litigation proved far too costly and time-consuming for its fragile budget. As a result, the ETF shifted its focus entirely towards education and advocacy efforts after 1984.

Although western New York provided more than enough hazardous waste problems to occupy the organization's resources, groups from around the country called on the ETF from time to time. Consulting work constituted a part of the ETF's work as well. In early 1983, the ETF became aware of another Love Canal-like situation developing in Times Beach, Missouri. Again, water played a strong role in the development of the problem. In 1972, the small community's roads had been sprayed with oil laced with dioxin and other hazardous chemicals. The situation had been exacerbated when the Meramec River flooded in late 1982, destroying homes, but also spreading the highly toxic chemicals. In February 1983, the EPA announced that the federal government, using Superfund monies, would buy the homes from the neighborhood's residents.[72] Yet the government proved less than prompt in providing relief, and hired an appraiser who provided values lower than expected by the residents. As cancer rates and knowledge of illnesses grew, residents continually pressed for replacement value of their homes and health monitoring for themselves and their children.[73] Alderman (later mayor) Marilyn Leistner reported that "we were so frustrated and wanted to fight, but we had no opponent."[74]

Terri Mudd, an ETF board member, felt the situation important enough for the ETF to get involved, and sent the group's annual report to a local religious group that was attempting to organize the community.[75] Although unity remained elusive in the community, the Lutherans at Times Beach succeeded in coming together and forming the Ecumenical Dioxin Response Task Force (EDTRF). The EDRTF promptly invited Sister Margeen and ETF secretary Barbara Hanna to provide assistance in September of 1983.

Hoffmann and Hanna found the residents very reluctant at first to discuss health problems, but extremely worried and upset about the "discrepancies in appraisal values [for their homes] and the unwillingness" of the local appraiser to alter his views. Many of the 802 families came from small, lower-income mobile home communities sprinkled across Times Beach. As had residents at Love Canal, Times Beach residents also became extremely upset about having to leave their homes and deal with health problems, discrimination, and segregation of their children on local school buses as well as "child and wife abuse."[76] The health problems heard by Hoffmann and Hanna included "the stories of birth defects—a child born with half a heart, a mother who died in childbirth, followed by the death of her child 10 months later, the child with his kidneys on the outside [of his body]."[77] The two women from Love Canal, accustomed to hearing stories of harm to children from chemicals, found these stories eerily familiar.

Although the board of the Times Beach organization initially showed "hesitancy on their part as far as time commitment and their competency to get into the technical areas of the problem," Hoffmann and Hanna tried to bolster their resolve, telling them "to be proud of their accomplishments to date and to realize that their technical knowledge will develop as they proceed." The Love Canal representatives had a definite effect on the organization, especially after several residents testified to the board. The EDRTF saw a "180 degree turn" in attitude during the visit, to a "deep commitment" to the residents' cause. Sister Margeen and Hanna, however, were less than satisfied with the situation. In their notes on the visit, they noted that the "similarities between Love Canal and the problems in Missouri are very evident. We were very upset to think that nothing had been learned or improved upon during the past five years."[78]

This anger and frustration failed to reduce their efforts in Niagara Falls, however. During a speech to the Hyde Park residents, Sister Margeen noted:

> I am angry and disappointed and indignant from what I saw in Times Beach and what I am seeing and hearing about Hyde Park—disappointed and angry that the government and our health officials and politicians have not *learned* from Love Canal—that symbol of toxic dumps and pilot of remedial action. The one thing they evidently have not learned is: PEOPLE COME FIRST—BEFORE POLITICS AND CORPORATE PROFITS!

To keep their hopes up, Margeen told them to "[c]ome together to tell your stories, help others tell theirs so this tragedy ends, so your children and their children's children will have a world intended by the Creator. Do not lose hope or heart."[79] At the very least, the ETF provided the activists at Times Beach with some comfort and the knowledge that they were not alone in their struggle, which they did for other communities as well. The Times Beach group rewarded this assistance in late 1987, when they donated all their remaining funds as they disbanded to the ETF.[80]

The ETF's role outside Love Canal also included a distinct educational and advocacy role regarding the dangers of hazardous waste. ETF board and staff members frequently accepted speaking engagements, wrote articles for publications, and occasionally appeared on local or national news programs.[81] As with their other activities, the theme of water often linked many of these issues. In 1988, as her involvement with the ETF wound to a close, Hoffmann delivered a series of Sunday morning radio addresses on a local AM station. She chose water as the focus of her talks. The radio addresses neatly encapsulated much of the ETF's rationale over the previous decade. In addition, they also explicitly laid out some of the enormous contradictions regarding faith, nature, and science with which the ETF wrestled. Hoffmann noted first the pervasive danger to humans from water, both from natural and man-made causes. "We are daily reminded of the power water has to destroy life," she began, noting the occurrence of floods, ice storms, blizzards, as well as chemical spilling into rivers. On the other hand, Hoffmann reminded her readers, "it's through the gift of water that we sustain our bodies, power our plants, raise our crops, and find beauty and economic benefits in the Niagara Cataracts."[82]

She later went further to declare that water "is not merely a decoration of life, it is life itself."[83]

Sister Margeen's radio addresses also touched on the inherent contradictions found in the ETF's activism. First, dealing with government bureaucracies could be extremely frustrating. The "EPA's progress in setting standards [for water quality] has been slow," she lamented, yet she noted that attitudes and actions toward the environment had changed.[84] "We are reaching a point," she concluded, "where we are embarrassed by any talk of domination, whether it be of nature or other peoples." Environmentalists, in addition, were "newly risen to a measure of power."[85] She also discussed the problems of technology in twentieth-century society. The ETF had always stressed technology as a solution to hazardous waste. Of course, technology and science had, in many ways, caused some spectacular toxic problems. "Agribusiness . . . meant more and more chemicals, which have poisoned field workers and the soil," to name one problem.[86] However, "water-borne diseases such as typhoid and cholera have been almost eliminated [by science and] . . . improved methods of testing water . . . have revealed . . . man-made chemicals."[87] On the one hand, science led to chemical problems, yet it could also benefit humanity in many ways.

Adequate funding had always been a struggle for the ETF. Staff members and volunteers dwindled through the 1980s. Having served the group for a decade, Sister Margeen left to return to Minnesota, where she worked for an organ transplant organization. Pat Brown, one of the last remaining staff members, continued the legacy and educational outreach of the ETF even after the organization's demise in 1991 by donating the group's copious papers to SUNY–Buffalo in 1997. Brown's donation allowed the ETF's educational role to continue, even after the group disbanded. Through its activism at Love Canal and beyond, the ETF served as a valuable resource over its lifetime, parting the waters for other environmental groups and communities beleaguered by environmental problems.

Conclusion

The ETF's rationale and involvement at Love Canal and beyond provides an interesting counterpoint to several historians who have looked to Christianity as the root cause of destructive attitudes toward nature in general. Lynn White Jr., in particular, goes beyond other interpretations of the damage done to the natural world by mechanistic Western scientific attitudes.[88] White demonstrates that those attitudes depended on, and proceeded from, historical scientific reliance on religious justification. "Christianity," White believes, "in absolute contrast to ancient paganism and Asia's religions (except, perhaps, Zoroastrianism), not only established a dualism of man and nature but also insisted that it is God's will that man exploit nature for his proper ends." Christianity effectively removed the concept of spirits residing within natural objects, such as trees or rocks, to place them in heaven. White states that "[b]y destroying pagan animism, Christianity made it possible to exploit nature in a mood of indifference to the feelings of natural objects."[89]

More recently, other scholars have added a more nuanced view of the role of religion in environmentalism. Mark Stoll concluded that Protestantism in America has played both a positive and a negative role in American environmental history.[90] Although Stoll acknowledges the early Puritan concern with dominating the land, he also notes that Puritan theology included a view of wilderness as a place of refuge. He finds this Protestant view in many prominent environmentalists of the twentieth century, including Rachel Carson. Christopher Hamlin and John T. McGreevy focus on an attempt by a Catholic organization to promote sustainable agricultural technologies and an economic alternative to capitalism and socialism in the 1930s and 1940s. Although largely unsuccessful in their efforts, the organization's story reveals "the centrality of images of nature in calls for religious renewal" as well as the need to stretch the discussion of religion and environment to a "framework of religious pluralism."[91] Again, though, the case study presented by Hamlin and McGreevy presents a different image of religion's role within the environment from that posited by White.

As with the Catholic organization discussed by Hamlin and McGreevy, history has largely ignored the contributions of the ETF at Love Canal and beyond. At the very least, the ETF serves as a valuable precursor to later influential religious activism in environmental issues, notably the 1987 release of *Toxic Waste and Race*, a pivotal report by the United Church of Christ's Commission on Racial Justice presenting evidence of environmental injustice. In addition, powerful elements of class and gender associated with the ETF's environmental activism distinguished the group from others, particularly the female-dominated, working-class resident group led by Gibbs.

The most striking difference between the two groups involved the ETF's pursuit of environmental matters outside Love Canal. The resident group, obsessed single-mindedly with their relocation, failed to help other groups on a wide scale or express interest in other environmental issues. This wider focus stemmed at least partially from many of the ETF members' personal knowledge and involvement in other environmental areas prior to Love Canal. Donna Ogg had been sensitized to environmental issues from an early age. She describes her parents as "conservationists, when it wasn't the popular thing to be . . . conservationist from the standpoint of caring for the environment themselves, as individuals. . . . [They believed] that they themselves were responsible for taking care of the Earth."[92] As an adult, she followed the trials and tribulations of two waste sites near her home, the Lake Ontario

Ordinance Works (LOOW), as well as the Chemical Waste Management (CWM) site, the only active hazardous waste disposal facility operating in New York state, throughout her participation on Love Canal. Her knowledge of these sites was one reason she was attracted to helping the Love Canal residents. Cook and Moore had both been involved in anti-nuclear activism prior to Love Canal, and had gained an understanding of the toxic hazards of radiation. Very few of the resident group members, on the other hand, had any experience with either environmentalism or social justice issues prior to Love Canal. In addition, once most of them left the area, they tended to drop their environmental activism completely. For the residents, activism was a means to an end, not a way to participate in society. Generally, therefore, the ETF began with a wider understanding of the problems of hazardous waste than did the residents, and saw Love Canal as only a part of a much broader problem rather than the reason for the group's existence, as the residents did.

In addition, because of their greater level of activism prior to Love Canal, and interest in social justice issues, ETF members also connected the environmental problems at Love Canal and beyond with other social justice ills. Hoffmann's prior experience included assisting anti-war protesters in Washington, D.C., and organizing for civil rights work in South Carolina and Chicago, where she became acquainted with Jesse Jackson and Operation Breadbasket.[93] Paul Moore had a "keen sense of injustice," according to his friends, and a longstanding reputation for concern about social justice issues, including anti-nuclear issues and the ordaining of homosexual priests. He maintained a belief that the church should use its energy to help people.[94] As campus minister at the University of Buffalo, James Brewster had worked within the anti-war movement, and assisted in bringing peace back to the campus after widespread rioting and violence caused a brief occupation by the Buffalo Police in March 1970.[95] As a graduate student in sociology in Michigan, Roger Cook had been involved in anti-war demonstrations and activities. In the mid-1970s, he moved to Albany and participated in prison reform efforts.[96]

All of this experience with other systemic social problems had a notable effect on the ETF's involvement. The ETF members had seen the effects of other social ills, and made apt connections between those issues and environmental problems. The ETF also incorporated a theological rationale to explicitly justify the idea of eco-justice through a focus on 'shalom' and stewardship. The ETF described shalom as a "biblical vision . . . when everyone shall sit under his/her vine and fig tree, and '*none shall make them afraid.*'" Elsewhere, they described it as "peace and wholeness."[97] This interpretation of theology allowed the ETF to justify fighting for environmental equality for those groups victimized by hazardous wastes.

Sister Margeen, after having worked in low-income schools in Boston, noted the links between environmental problems and class issues. One of the lessons learned through her work at Love Canal, she noted, was that "the people of poverty and the people of pollution are one people." Other ETF members made more specific links. "Historically," Sister Joan Malone stated, "toxic dump sites have been located in economically depressed areas, among people uniquely unable to bear the resultant financial burdens and who lack political clout."[98] Through pollution issues, Hoffmann saw the line between wealthy and poor nations diminishing. Love Canal was not just a New York problem, she asserted: "[e]qually damning is a growing movement of countries and corporations from the 'developed' world relocating their plants and shipping their toxic wastes to 'underdeveloped' countries where labor can be bought cheaply and strict regulations can be more easily avoided."[99] The resident group, again, since they had little to no experience with social justice issues, never made the connections between environmental hazards and the systemic problems of classism and racism.

In addition, the story of the ETF (especially when compared with that of Gibbs and the resident group) illustrates much about the importance of gender in environmental activism. First, while the residents consistently applied a rhetoric stressing concern over children, the ETF developed a very complicated rationale. Part of this difference stemmed from differences in the demographics of the organizations. Gibbs's group's leadership was almost exclusively working-class white women; although the ETF's staff was predominantly female, the organization's leadership was far more balanced between men and women. This allowed for a greater variety of views in constructing a justification for existence. Paul Moore and Jim Brewster's ideas affected the direction and philosophy of the organization as much as did Hoffmann or Ogg. The residents had no men on a comparable level to Lois Gibbs. More important as a difference, however, were the variations in class status and educational opportunities between the groups. Gibbs's group was solidly working class, with high school diplomas; the ETF's middle-class group had all obtained bachelor's degrees, and many had graduate degrees. Middle-class status had yielded opportunities for college and often graduate education for many in the ETF. This education broadened not only minds, but experiences: the ETF members had participated in party politics, university reform, anti-war and anti-nuclear protests, and civil rights activism all before Love Canal. Their expanded worldview and experience provided a very different context for their activism from the working-class women at Love Canal. Of course, despite these advantages, history remembers Lois Gibbs and her group of residents as the successful party at Love Canal. The language of "protecting children" and NIMBY activism effectively trumped the complicated language centering on transcendentalism, Rachel Carson, Judeo-Christian theology, Native American philosophy, paganism, a faith in science, and a wider understanding of the problem.

Sister Margeen Hoffmann passed away in the summer of 2007. Along with her colleagues, she incorporated her varied past experience into assisting many communities with their tribulations over hazardous waste in America. She led the Ecumenical Task Force for over ten years, pushing the frontiers of an organized, faith-based response to environmental damage. In the years surrounding the emergence of the environmental justice movement, the ETF's construction of a complicated rationale allowed them to make deeper connections with environmentalism, racism, and classism.

Notes

1 I have developed several of the themes presented here in chapter 4 of Elizabeth D. Blum, *Love Canal Revisited: Race, Class, and Gender in Environmental Activism* (Lawrence: University Press of Kansas, 2008). In addition, I am indebted to the invaluable comments provided at the American Society for Environmental History conference in March, 2003, where I presented an early version of this paper, entitled "Messengers of Isaiah: The Christian and Environmental Rhetoric of the Ecumenical Task Force at Love Canal."

2 Several sources provide detailed accounts of Love Canal. Lois Gibbs has published her own first-hand account of the struggle. See Lois Gibbs, *Love Canal: The Story Continues . . .*, 20th anniversary rev. ed. (Stony Creek, CT: New Society Publishers, 1998). Michael Brown, a reporter for the *Niagara Gazette* early in the crisis, published his account in Michael Brown, *Laying Waste: The Poisoning of America by Toxic Chemicals* (New York: Washington Square Press Publications, 1979). I highlight the implications of race, class, and gender in *Love Canal Revisited*. Adeline Levine tells the story from the perspective of a sociologist on site at the time in *Love Canal: Science, Politics, and People* (Lexington, MA: D. C. Heath and Company, 1982). Allan Mazur examines the validity of several sides of the story in *A Hazardous Inquiry: The Rashomon Effect at Love Canal* (Cambridge, MA: Harvard University Press, 1998). Rich Newman focuses on the women of Love Canal in "Making Environmental Politics: Women and Love Canal Activism," *Women's Studies Quarterly* 29 (Summer 2001), 65–84. For a description of hazardous waste science and disposal prior to Love Canal, see Craig E. Colten and Peter N. Skinner, *The Road to Love Canal: Managing Industrial Waste before EPA* (Austin: University of Texas Press, 1996).

3 Louis Hennepin, *A New Discovery of a Vast Country in America*, vol. 1, ed. Reuben Gold Thwaites (Chicago: AC McClung & Co., 1903), 54, available from www.americanjourneys.org/aj-124a (accessed 26 July 2006).

4 Ibid., 55.

5 Mazur, *A Hazardous Inquiry*, 8–9. For information about the history of Niagara Falls, see Michael Vogel, *Echoes in the Mist: An Illustrated History of the Niagara Falls Area* (n.p.: Windsor Publications, 1991); Pierre Berton, *Niagara: A History of the Falls* (Toronto: McClelland & Stewart, 1992); Ralph Greenhill and Thomas Mahoney, *Niagara* (Toronto: University of Toronto Press, 1969); and Margaret Dunn, *Niagara Falls: A Pictorial Journey*, photography by Michael D. Romanowich (Niagara Falls, NY: M. Dunn, 1998).

6 Brown, *Laying Waste*, 5; Levine, *Love Canal*, 10.

7 Blum, *Love Canal Revisited*, 22.

8 Ibid., 22–24.

9 Ibid., 25–26.

10 Levine, *Love Canal*, 28; Blum, *Love Canal Revisited*, 26–28.

11 For more information on the working-class women at Love Canal, see Blum, *Love Canal Revisited*, 31–62.

12 Sister Margeen Hoffman, transcript of telephone interview by author, 3 April 2002, Rochester, Minnesota, 6–7; Hoffman résumé, ETF Collection. Quote is from Hoffman interview, 6.

13 Hoffmann interview, 11–13.

14 James Brewster, transcript of telephone interview with author, 24 July 2001, Tonawanda, New York, 9; Donna Ogg, transcript of telephone interview with author, 24 October 2001, Lewiston, New York, 3–6.

15 Rev. Paul L. Moore, "The Land Is Cursed," Letter from the Pastor, mid-August 1978, CCHW Collection, Tufts University Archives, Medford, Massachusetts.

16 Ogg interview, 2; Hoffmann interview, 21.

17 Paul L. Moore and Donna Ogg, "A Letter of Concern to the Religious Community," 22 February 1979, ETF Collection.

18 Ogg interview, 11–13.

19 Donna Ogg, Minutes—Ecumenical Task Force to Address the Love Canal Disaster, 20 March 1979, ETF Collection. Funding ebbed and flowed from various denominations and church organizations, including the Baptists, Presbyterians, Episcopalians, Lutherans, Roman Catholics, United Methodists, Unitarian Universalists, and Church World Service. Some private foundations also contributed through grants, including the Ruth Mott Foundation and the William H. Donner Foundation. Donna Ogg, Minutes – Ecumenical Task Force to Address the Love Canal Disaster, 2 April 1979, ETF Collection; "Contributions through March, 1980," in Margeen Hoffmann (ed.), *Progress Report of the Ecumenical Task Force of the Niagara Frontier, Inc.* (Niagara Falls, NY: n.p., 1980), 59. ETF Collection.

20 Ogg interview, 12.

21 Brewster interview, 7. To counter this localized opposition, Moore and Ogg wanted to involve regional organizations, such as the Council of Churches, as well as leaders from the Buffalo area, where Hooker's influence might be less felt.

22 Donna Ogg, "Love Canal Update: For Purposes of Informing Your Congregation about the Task Force," May 1979, ETF Collection.

23 Margeen Hoffmann, "Report of the Executive Director," in *Progress Report*, 9; Hoffmann interview, 38.

24 Moore and Ogg, "A Letter of Concern to the Religious Community," ETF Collection.

25 Margeen Hoffmann, Address to the Niagara County Legislature, 1 April 1980, ETF Collection.

26 *Progress Report*, 4–6, 52–54, ETF Collection.

27 Blum, *Love Canal Revisited*, 79–80.

28 "Love Canal Sunday: How to Participate," *United Methodist Reporter: Western New York Conference*, 11 July 1980, ETF Collection.

29 Margeen Hoffman, "Ecumenical Task Force Statement Regarding Love Canal Relocation," 19 October 1979, 2, ETF Collection.

30 Roberta Grimm, "An Advocate Report," in *Progress Report*, 14, ETF Collection (ellipses in original).

31 Brewster, "Preface," in *Progress Report*, 1, ETF Collection.

32 "Model of Response," in *Progress Report*, 7, ETF Collection.

33 Donna Ogg, John Lynch, and Margeen Hoffmann, "Introduction," in Margeen Hoffmann, *Earthcare: Lessons from Love Canal* (Niagara Falls, NY: ETF, 1987), 24, 25, ETF Collection.

34 Margeen Hoffmann, "Time to Risk," in *Progress Report*, 16, ETF Collection.

35 John A. Lynch, "Living with Chronic Disaster: A Psychosocial Perspective," in *Progress Report*, 13, ETF Collection.

36 Margeen Hoffmann and Therese M. Mudd, "Niagara Celebrates Hope with Winds of Change," late 1980s, 9, ETF Collection.

37 Moore, "The Land is Cursed," in *Progress Report*, ii, ETF Collection.

38 Ibid.

39 Ibid. (Passage is from Isaiah, Chapter 24.)

40 "Model of Response," in *Earthcare*, 8, ETF Collection.

41 Donna Ogg, "God's Good Earth," in *Progress Report*, xvi, ETF Collection.

42 James Brewster, "Theological Reflections—Eden and the Love Canal," talk at the ETF Evaluation Day, 12 January 1981, ETF Collection.

43 Donna Ogg, "God's Good Earth," in *Progress Report*, xv, ETF Collection.

44 Moore, "The Land is Cursed," in *Progress Report*, ii, ETF Collection.

45 Carolyn Merchant, *Ecological Revolutions: Nature, Gender, and Science in New England* (Chapel Hill: University of North Carolina Press, 1989).

46 Chief Seattle, "The Earth is Our Mother," 1854, reprinted in *Earthcare*, 97–98. The inclusion of Native American philosophy indicated the complications and even contradictions inherent in ETF language. Chief Seattle placed all parts of the earth as equal spiritually. He stated that "[e]very part of this earth is sacred to my people. Every shining pine needle, every sand shore, every mist in the dark woods, every clearing and humming insect is holy in the memory and experience of my people . . . The shining water that moves in the streams and rivers is not just water,

but the blood of our ancestors . . . " Traditional Christian philosophy espoused a notion of humans as at the top of a spiritual hierarchy.

47 "Mohawk Indian Prayer," in *Earthcare*, 116, ETF Collection.

48 "An ETF Executive Board Statement: On Persons and the Environment," *Common Ground*, October 1980, 3, ETF Collection.

49 Rich Donoughue, Memorandum to Education Committee, 8 June 1982, ETF Collection.

50 Ecumenical Task Force, "Toward a Christian Ethical Response to the Problem of Hazardous Waste," a preliminary paper for the Peace and Justice Commission of the Diocese of Buffalo and for Bishop Edward D. Head, December 1983, 7, ETF Collection.

51 ETF, Proposed Resolution, 15 April 1980, ETF Collection.

52 "Toward a Christian Ethical Response to the Problem of Hazardous Waste," 12, ETF Collection.

53 Grimm, in *Progress Report*, 15.

54 Barbara Hanna, "WNY United Methodist Conference Council," 13 February 1988, 4, ETF Collection.

55 Barbara Hanna, "Necessary Changes in Lifestyles," 13 April 1989, 3–5, ETF Collection.

56 Hoffmann, Address to the Niagara County Legislature, ETF Collection. The rest of the speech dealt with the rationale of the churches' involvement, the ETF's works, and the scope of the problem. Interestingly, in a newspaper article covering the speech, journalists emphasized the maternalistic language rather than anything else. "Task Force Petitions County to Aid Canal," 2 April 1980, newspaper clipping, reprinted in *Progress Report*, n.p., ETF Collection.

57 Terri Mudd, transcript of telephone interview with author, 30 July 2001, Lewiston, New York, 7.

Mudd, like the others at Love Canal, also had a background of activism. A mother of six children, Mudd and her husband, who worked for Hooker Chemical, quickly became frustrated by the lack of a true two-party system in the very Republican-dominated Lewiston area. In response, the Mudds

> really pulled together a two party system [in Lewiston]. . . . They used to say Democrats [here] had their caucuses in a phone booth. And when we first came here, that was so. We managed to kind of make a change in that. It's definitely a two-party environment, now. We still have lesser representation, but every election is a challenge. (Mudd interview, 4)

The two-party system was a vitally important concept for Mudd, simply because she felt that "power corrupts and absolute power corrupts absolutely. And the competition keeps all of that to a minimum. The corruption stays minimal because somebody's nipping at your heels all the time. And we really saw that take effect in our town. First time the Democrats had somebody on the board, it meant everything had to be done differently." She continued to manage political campaigns for more than twenty years after Love Canal. (Mudd interview, 4–5)

58 Roberta Grimm and Margeen Hoffmann, "A Time to Risk," in *Earthcare*, 45, ETF Collection.

59 By-Laws of the Ecumenical Task Force of the Niagara Frontier, 8 November 1979, 1, ETF Collection. In some of the group's literature and papers (and on stationery they could not afford to discard), they continue to refer to themselves with the earlier name, even after the formal adoption of the new name.

60 Brewster interview, 24; Margeen Hoffmann, "Article for OSHA/Environmental Network News," Memorandum to Roger Cook, 19 January 1982, ETF Collection.

61 Brewster interview, 24.

62 Joan F. Malone, OSF, "An American Tragedy: The Corporate Legacy of Love Canal," *The Corporate Examiner*, ICCR Brief, October 1981, ETF Collection; Jim Brewster, "After Love Canal: Redefining the Meaning of 'Disaster,'" *Toxic Substances* [CWS publication] 10 November 1981, 1, ETF Collection.

63 Margeen Hoffmann, "Article for OSHA/Environmental Network News," ETF Collection. Amicus status was granted to the ETF concurrently with two Canadian environmental groups, Pollution Probe and Operation Clean.

64 Margeen Hoffmann, Memo—Internal to ETF Public Policy Committee, "Telephone Conversation with Edward Lawrence, VEATCH program," 12 January 1982, ETF Collection; Hoffmann, "Article for OSHA/Environmental Network News."

65 Barbara Hanna, ETF Board of Directors meeting minutes, 16 October 1984, 3, ETF Collection.

66 U.S. Environmental Protection Agency, "Hooker Hyde Park," EPA ID# NYD000831644, U.S. EPA website, available at www.epa.gov/region02/Superfund/npl/0201306.htm, accessed 1 March 2008.

67 ETF Executive Board Meeting Minutes, 27 October 1981, 2–7, ETF Collection; U.S. Environmental Protection Agency, "Hooker Chemical S-Area," EPA ID# NYD980651087, U.S. EPA website, available at www.epa.gov/region02/Superfund/npl/02021500.htm, accessed 1 March 2008.

68 ETF Executive Board, "Priorities for ETF Activities," 10 November 1981, 1, ETF Collection; Margeen Hoffmann, telephone conversation with Edward Lawrence, 12 January 1982, 2–3, ETF Collection.

69 ETF Board of Directors' Meeting Minutes, 6 December 1983, 3, ETF Collection; Margeen Hoffmann, "Dear Friend of the ETF," September 1984, 1, ETF Collection.

70 "Minimum Budget Possibilities," 10 January 1984, ETF Collection; Margeen Hoffmann, "ETF in Transition," 25 January 1984, ETF Collection.

71 U.S. Environmental Protection Agency, "Hooker Chemical S-Area," EPA ID# NYD980651087, U.S. EPA website, available at www.epa.gov/region02/Superfund/npl/02021500.htm, accessed 1 March 2008.

72 Mark Neilson, "Churches Give Aid to Dioxin Victims," *National Catholic Reporter*, 13 April 1984, 11, ETF Collection.

73 Margeen Hoffmann, "Presentation at Hyde Park Landfill Meeting," 3 October 1983, Niagara Falls, NY, ETF Collection.

74 Marilyn Leistner, "The Times Beach Story," *Synthesis/Regeneration* 7–8 (Summer 1995), available at www.greens.org/s-r/0708/07-09html, accessed 12 August 2007.

75 The religious community was not unified at Times Beach, just as there had been difficulties at Love Canal. ETF members heard about "difficulty between 'fundamentalists and main-line' protestants," in addition to other concerns. (Barbara Hanna, ETF Board of Directors Meeting Minutes, 15 March 1983, ETF Collection.)

76 Margeen Hoffmann and Barbara Hanna, Memorandum regarding "Response Team Consultation Visit to Times Beach Mo. September 27th – October 1, 1983," n.d., ETF Collection; EDRTF meeting minutes, 28 October 1983, ETF Collection; Ruth Moussette and Karl Reko, EDRTF Newsletter, "Reflections on our ministry," October 1984, ETF Collection.

77 Hoffmann, "Presentation at Hyde Park Landfill Meeting," ETF Collection.

78 Hoffmann and Hanna, "Response Team Consultation Visit," ETF Collection.

79 Hoffmann, "Presentation at Hyde Park Landfill Meeting," ETF Collection.

80 Margeen Hoffmann, "Only One Earth," speech given to Episcopal Charities of Western New York, 3 November 1987, 6, ETF Collection. The ETF also made site visits to Olean, Ohio, LeRoy, New York, and Centralia, Pennsylvania. They provided advice to numerous other communities through their hazardous waste hotline.

    In 1983, the EPA provided funds for the permanent relocation of all residents and businesses from the Times Beach site, a process that was completed in 1986. The EPA, which describes the remediation as "one of the most extensive cleanups in Superfund history," reported the finalization of the cleanup in 1997. The site has subsequently become a state park and bird sanctuary. (Environmental Protection Agency, "Times Beach One-Page Summary," available from www.epa.gov/superfund/programs/recycle/success/1-pagers/timesbch.htm, accessed 12 August 2007.)

81 As another example of some of these educational efforts, in October of 1985, the ETF hosted a conference entitled "Blueprint for Action," which brought representatives from activist groups, government, and business together to discuss solutions to hazardous waste problems.

82 Margeen Hoffmann, "Earthcare," radio address on WJJL 1440 AM Radio, 31 January 1988, 2, ETF Collection.

83 Margeen Hoffmann, "If There Is Magic on This Planet . . . ," radio address on WJJL 1440 AM Radio, 6 February 1988, 1, ETF Collection.

84 Margeen Hoffmann, "Water, Water Everywhere, and Not a Drop to Drink," radio address on WJJL 1440 AM Radio, 21 February 1988, 2, ETF Collection.

85 Margeen Hoffmann, "Pushing the Earth Around," radio address on WJJL 1440 AM Radio, 14 February 1988, 2, ETF Collection.

86 Ibid.

87 Hoffmann, "Water, Water Everywhere, and Not a Drop to Drink," 21 February 1988, 2, ETF Collection.

88 Lynn White Jr., "The Historical Roots of Our Ecological Crisis," *Science*, 155 (10 March 1967), 1203–7.

89 Ibid., 1205.

90 See, for example, Mark Stoll, *Protestantism, Capitalism, and Nature in America* (Albuquerque: University of New Mexico Press, 1997). See also Mark Stoll, "Religion 'Irradiates' the Wilderness," in Michael Lewis (ed.), *American Wilderness: A New History* (Oxford: Oxford University Press, 2007). Thomas Dunlap's *Faith in Nature: Environmentalism as Religious Quest* (Seattle: University of Washington Press, 2004) is also very useful on this topic.

91 Christopher Hamlin and John T. McGreevy, "The Greening of America, Catholic Style, 1930–50," *Environmental History* 11 (July 2006), 464–99. Quote is from p. 488.

92 Ogg interview, 8–9.

93 Hoffmann interview, 5–10. Operation Breadbasket, founded in 1962 as a part of Martin Luther King Jr.'s Southern Christian Leadership Conference, sought to improve economic conditions for blacks and to end racist hiring practices. "Operation Breadbasket," *King Encyclopedia*, The Martin Luther King, Jr. Research and Education Institute, available at http://ublib.buffalo.edu/archives/collections/guides/unrest.htm (accessed 28 February 2008).

94 James Brewster, transcript of telephone interview with author, 24 July 2001, Tonawanda, New York, 9; Donna Ogg, transcript of telephone interview with author, 24 October 2001, Lewiston, New York, 3–6. In September 1988, Paul Moore's car was found, by Donna Ogg and others, abandoned near the Falls. His identification, wallet, and other personal belongings remained in the car. Police never located Moore's body, and several people close to him believed that, rather than committing suicide, he simply chose to abandon his life in Niagara Falls and flee to Canada to begin a new existence. He left behind a wife and two children. (Ogg interview, 3–6.)

95 Brewster interview, 2–4; Campus Unrest Collections at the University of Buffalo, available at http://ublib.buffalo.edu/archives/collections/topic.html#unrest (accessed 21 July 2008).

96 Roger Cook, transcript of telephone interview with author, 9 November 2001, Grand Island, New York, 3–5.

97 ETF Board of Directors and Staff, "Preface," in *Earthcare*, 15, 151, ETF Collection. The ETF listed the source for this idea as "a recent 'Prepare' on toxic waste distributed by IMPACT" (ibid.).

98 Joan F. Malone, "A Ten Commandments for Environmental Stewardship: The Lessons Learned from Love Canal," in *Earthcare*, 40, ETF Collection.

99 Grimm and Hoffmann, "A Time to Risk," 44, ETF Collection.

CHAPTER 12

Cancer Valley, California

Pesticides, Politics, and Childhood Disease in the
Central Valley

ADAM TOMPKINS

The signs of future trouble were evident when Connie Rosales gave birth to her little girl in 1981. After arriving home with her child, she received notices from California's Kern County Health Department advising that mothers abstain from giving infants under six months of age any of McFarland's tap water, because the water might be unsafe for such small children. The notices revealed little specific information on the potential health hazards that the water posed; but they worried her nonetheless, especially since she never received any notices during her pregnancy when her child was in utero.[1] Although the town's water supply was not definitively linked to the health crisis that arose in McFarland in the years following, the notices fostered an air of uncertainty in the community. In the following year, 1982, Rosales's neighbor's daughter, Tresa Buentello, developed neuroblastoma—a cancer that affects the sympathetic nervous system of children under ten years of age.[2] Two weeks later, Rosales's fourteen-year-old son Randy was diagnosed with lymphatic cancer.[3] When the number of pediatric cases reached five in the small community of 6,400, the afflicted families recognized that something was amiss, formed a parent group, and convinced the county to investigate the situation. In the following three years, doctors diagnosed a total of eleven cases of childhood cancer in McFarland, as well as a number of cases in other nearby Central Valley communities.[4] Nationally, communities the size of McFarland averaged three cases of cancer in children under twenty during a ten-year time period.[5] McFarland nearly quadrupled the national average for similarly sized communities in a third of the time, which made parents concerned, frightened, and in search of answers. Definite answers proved elusive, but the best evidence pointed towards a handful of pesticides. Had the logic of the Precautionary Principle—which advocates that policy makers act on uncertain evidence to protect the public health—been implemented, then the rate of pediatric cancer in McFarland might well have dropped as the suspected chemicals were regulated off the market.[6]

When the Kern County Health Department undertook an investigation of the cancer cluster, laypeople and healthcare professionals, including the county health department, speculated that pesticides were most likely to blame. The community's close proximity to heavily sprayed fields certainly made pesticides a prime suspect, but the speculations were supported by science as well. A number of previous scientific investigations found several pesticides either to be carcinogenic or to be strongly suspected of having those properties, some of which were subsequently taken off the market and banned in the United States.[7] Recently banned pesticides were DDT (1972), aldrin (1976), dieldrin (1976), chlordane (1978), and heptachlor (1978). The removal of these sprays from the market did little to hush talk about the continued availability and use of carcinogenic pesticides.

Some of the continued talk about carcinogenic pesticides was generated by politico-scientists, who generally believed that scientific knowledge needed to be clearly communicated to the public, if the public was to make informed decisions in their civic participation.[8] Rachel Carson's *Silent Spring* (1962) and Barry Commoner's *Science and Survival* (1963) disrupted the public's faith in science by educating them about the hazards of modern technologies, including agricultural chemicals. These writings helped inform Cesar Chavez and the United Farm Workers about the dangers of pesticides, and they in turn educated migrant field workers during the Delano Grape Strike in the late 1960s.[9] Later politico-scientists carried on the tradition of their predecessors, reaching out to the public in attempt to spark public discussion about the chemical sprays. In 1978, Samuel Epstein published *The Politics of Cancer*, in which he maintained that environmental carcinogens were responsible for 70 to 90 percent of all cancers.[10] Shortly thereafter, Melvin D. Reuber—a leading authority on rodent liver tumors and head of the Experimental Pathology Laboratory at the Frederick, Maryland, Cancer Research Center—began warning rural communities that pesticides were carcinogenic. One of the pesticides that he railed against was malathion, an aerial spray used heavily in California to kill fruit flies.[11] Given the wealth of information and testimonials about pesticides' carcinogenicity, it is no wonder that people speculated that pesticides were the cause of McFarland's health woes.

To the dismay of the McFarland mothers, the investigations into the cause of the cancers proceeded slowly and yielded little in the way of concrete answers. A myriad of possible sources combined with the long periods of latency between the initial exposure to carcinogenic agents and the development of cancer in humans greatly reduces the likelihood that the causal agents will be unequivocally identified in the investigation of cancer clusters.[12] In turn, scientists employ the uncertain language of probability to explain their investigative findings, which can then be easily manipulated to support arguments in the absolutist language of politicians, activists, and industry.[13] The probable but equivocal link between pesticides and cancer and the significant socio-economic implications of that link provided the right combination of uncertainty and gravity for the issue to become vigorously politicized at local, state, and national levels. In McFarland, scientific investigations provided the contestable terrain on which value-laden political battles over the cause of and culpability for the health crisis would take place. The contentiousness of the situation grew over the course of the decade as one politicized faction of families, the United Farm Workers, and sympathetic politicians employed science to support arguments for pesticide reform, while the other contingent, consisting of the governor, growers, and their representative associations, used it to justify maintaining the status quo.

In this type of situation, in which the politicization of a chemical or its effects fosters unbridgeable divisions, scientific studies—in and of themselves—will often prove unable to resolve the issue conclusively. Liora Salter, Professor of Politics and Policy, contends that the "articulation of scientific issues in the context of a situation where interests are being pursued vigorously means that scientific information will be used as a strategic resource by all parties."[14] The cancer historian Robert Proctor more succinctly echoes these thoughts with his characterization of science as an "instrument of public relations."[15] The entanglement of science and politics is evident in the rhetoric and events related to the McFarland cancer cluster. Different interests read wildly different results from scientific data that was itself influenced by politics. To quote Robert Proctor: "As is often the case in science, what one sees has a lot to do with where one is standing."[16] Therefore, a resolution to a problem, such as that in McFarland, is just as dependent on political players' ability to promote a certain interpretation of scientific data as it is on the scientific information itself.

Scholars who have investigated occupational health problems have often found that public involvement in a given issue was a necessary predicate to change. In his investigation of black lung, Alan Derickson, Professor of

History and Labor Studies, argues that the state and public health officials knew about the deleterious effects of coal dust for over fifty years, yet proved reluctant to address the issue of black lung until the "confrontational collective action" of a worker-based social movement necessitated change. He contends that mining played a vital role in supporting the economies of coal-producing states and that the economic rivalry between these states encouraged them to obfuscate findings on the industrial disease.[17] Gerald Markowitz, Professor of History, and David Rosner, Professor of History and Public Health, charge that the lead and vinyl industries also knew about their products' hazardousness and deliberately hid information, controlled scientific research, and bought the loyalty of elected officials with donations of soft money and contributions to political action committees. Moreover, they threatened to relocate their industries if attempts were made to interfere with their business.[18] Robert Proctor and Samuel Epstein identify the same sort of corruptive practices in the field of cancer research, in which industries funded researchers, had their own industry scientists confuse the issue with ambiguous scientific noise, or exerted political pressure to have reports altered.[19] Considering the pervasiveness of these sorts of actions, Epstein maintains that nearly every legislative regulation or reform to protect workers and consumers against cancer had its roots in a public interest group or labor movement.[20] Markowitz and Rosner similarly conclude that the public must use common sense to interpret inconclusive scientific results and demand change through group action.[21]

When Connie Rosales contacted the Kern County Health Department in November 1984, she confronted an agency that was reluctant to act on her suspicions. County officials initially thought that the cancers represented a simple statistical abnormality, rather than a cancer cluster caused by an environmental toxin, and failed to address the situation until May of the following year, when two additional cases were reported.[22] The afflicted children in McFarland experienced a variety of different cancers, a fact that fueled some of the county's initial skepticism. Health officials assumed that the multitude of different cancers signified the lack of a common causal factor.[23] When the department began its investigation of the cluster, there were nine confirmed cases of cancer in persons under twenty-five years old that had been diagnosed within a forty-two-month period. Three of the diagnosed children lived on the same street. Between 1981 and 1983, doctors also reported a dramatic rise in the number of miscarriages, birth defects, fetal deaths, infant deaths, and low birth-weight babies in McFarland.[24] The county allocated $43,000 to conduct tests on the soil, water, and "other types of environmental media in the area."[25] County epidemiologists also began conducting household interviews throughout the community in hopes of identifying common exposure patterns.[26]

In the same year that the county health department began investigating the abnormal pediatric cancer rate, the California State Water Resources Control Board (CSWRCB) released a risk assessment stating that they had discovered evidence of increasing water contamination from the direct discharge of pesticides, runoff from irrigation, over-spraying, and drift. The improper use of pesticides increased the amount of toxins that percolated through the soil and contaminated the groundwater supply.[27] Tests conducted between 1979 and 1984 by the CSWRCB revealed that over fifty pesticides, including many known carcinogens, were found in the groundwater of twenty-eight of the fifty-eight counties in the state.[28] One hundred and fifty-three contaminated wells were discovered in Kern County alone. After making the discovery, the CSWRCB acted on the Precautionary Principle and decided to permanently close more than 100 wells in the Central Valley and leave several others open but with the understanding that they would be used only on an emergency basis when concentrations of dibromochloropropane (DBCP), a pesticide used to control worm damage in crops, dropped below one part per billion.[29] The CSWRCB stated that the "inability to routinely detect many of these chemicals at levels suspected of having long-term chronic effects is a significant weakness in our ability to adequately assess their risks."[30] They concluded that the "difficulty in demonstrating a cause-and-effect relationship between drinking water and cancer is not sufficient cause to conclude that one does not exist" and that prudence should be exercised on the side of caution.[31]

Although the discoveries of the CSWRCB may have increased expectations that the county investigation would reveal a similar chemical culprit, a number of factors made it difficult for scientists to reach concrete conclusions. Initial investigations by the Kern County Health Department suffered primarily from a lack of staff, funding, and interest.[32] Additionally, it proved impossible to isolate variables in the natural environment, so scientists could not state with certainty the root cause of the cancer cluster. In a laboratory, scientists test the relationship between the subject (dependent variable) and the potential sources of disease (independent variables) in a controlled environment. In this situation, scientists isolate and control the independent variable's interaction with the dependent variable in order to prove cause and effect. In the natural environment, experimentation proves much more complex. If, for example, drinking water is suspected as the causal factor of a disease outbreak, it is difficult if not impossible for a scientist to isolate each possible contaminative component in the water and soil and test it in relation to the affected human subject. The problems inherent in this type of investigation intensify further when scientists attempt to ascertain the causes of chronic environmental disease. In contrast to acute illnesses, which generally affect a person shortly after exposure to the contaminative agent, chronic illnesses take time to develop so that there are long periods of latency between initial exposure and the first signs of disease. This creates problems for investigators who attempt to trace a disease back to its causal factor, because time has blurred the linkage between cause and effect.[33] These aspects of the investigation slowed the county's work, which raised the ire of some community members and politicians.

The delays prompted California State Senator Art Torres, head of the Senate Committee on Toxics and Public Safety Management and a former lobbyist for the United Farm Workers, to call a public hearing in July 1985.[34] During the hearing, Torres often strayed in his questioning to bring attention to a rift between himself and California Governor George Deukmejian, a politician who was often portrayed by the media and United Farm Workers (UFW) as being hostile to farmworker concerns.[35] George Deukmejian, Republican, replaced Edmund G. Brown, Democrat, in the governor's office in 1982, at which point the state's relationship with the farmworkers' union deteriorated. The UFW openly accused the governor of being cowed by agribusiness, since growers contributed somewhere between $750,000 and $1,000,000 to his election campaign, which represented approximately 10 percent of his campaign funds.[36] Deukmejian's actions lent credence to the claims of the UFW. He severely limited the effectiveness of the California Agricultural Labor Relations Board, the state equivalent of the National Labor Relations Board, by reducing its budget by 27 percent and by appointing David Sterling, a former legislator who supported numerous grower-backed bills, as the agency's general counsel and Jyrl Anne James-Montgomery, a former growers' attorney, as chairperson.[37]

Some of the governor's other actions promised to have a more direct and negative effect on the community of McFarland, which is probably why Torres decided to dwell on Deukmejian during the hearing. The governor vetoed a bill requiring growers to post signs along the edges of recently sprayed fields until the fields were safe to enter again.[38] Assuring growers that they had "a friend, not an adversary" in office, Deukmejian tried to slip a bill through the legislature that would substantially restrict the public's ability to challenge pesticide spraying in the state.[39] He also vetoed a bill that would have established a cancer registry in Kern County, which, in combination with a pesticide registry database, would have improved the investigative capabilities of health departments. Deukmejian, however, maintained that the registry was not necessary to protect public health.[40] Torres repeatedly referred to the governor's veto during the Senate Committee hearing and urged the health department personnel to communicate the importance of the cancer registry to the governor.[41] It was clear that Deukmejian's decision was bound to have a significant effect on McFarland citizens' ability to definitively track cancer and its causes in their community.[42] Considering the governor's favorable actions towards growers, it is no wonder that the former UFW lobbyist, Senator Torres, became irritated when he sensed that the governor was failing to protect farmworker families once again.

Throughout the proceedings, Torres expressed his extreme dissatisfaction with the Kern County Health Department's seeming lack of urgency and awareness of the situation in McFarland and other potential cancer clusters in the state.[43] The department generally seemed reluctant or unable to consider the multitude of chemicals and chemical combinations in the water supply. Kern County's health officer, Dr. Leon Hebertson, testified that the department did not allocate much in the way of resources to the investigation, partly because they thought that it was a statistical aberration and partly because other issues already overtaxed the department's resources.[44] Torres, obviously flustered from the apparent apathy in the investigation, charged the county health department with lacking the "chutzpah" to get additional funding and support from the state and expressed dismay over the lack of progress in addressing the "toxic time bomb" in the state of California.[45]

One year later, the Kern County Health Department announced that it had concluded its investigation and found nothing that would have substantially heightened the cancer occurrence rate in McFarland. "I think that we have done as thorough a job as we know how to do," Hebertson reported, adding that "there is not anything in the present environment which can explain the cancer cluster."[46] However, county and state health departments postulated that the peak of environmental contamination would have occurred between 1980 and 1983. Despite this estimation, the county health department admitted that it had not examined old records that might have yielded clues about the potential source of contamination.[47] Two years after the community's initial call for an investigation, the department had yet to check the records of the town's water company from the suspected period of contamination to gauge nitrate levels in the water, look over pesticide records in an attempt to ascertain crop-dusting practices near the town, or examine past conditions in the vicinity of a chemical warehouse near several of the victims' homes.[48]

Criticism of the Kern County Health Department grew when Dr. Thomas Lazar, the coordinator of the investigation from December 1985 to August 1986, broke ranks and testified that the department had succumbed to political pressure to complete the investigation quickly, which necessitated overlooking key data. He claimed that the department orchestrated the investigation poorly and ended the study prematurely when faced with outside political pressure.[49] The most disturbing accusation centered on the possible misrepresentation of scientific findings. Lazar maintained that the results of the investigation never indicated that McFarland was a safe environment, as Hebertson's testimony asserted. Lazar claimed that he had discovered approximately 300 additional cases of cancer within Kern County but was rebuffed by Hebertson when he proposed expanding the scope of the study. Hebertson allegedly stated: "I don't want another McFarland. I already have one McFarland too many."[50] Lazar complained that his immediate supervisor even went so far as to give him a baby's bottle, telling him that he was a "crybaby."[51] Such sentiments and actions reveal an unwillingness to take the threat of pesticides seriously and reflect the pro-grower and anti-public health platform of the governor. This is further evidenced by the fact that the department decided not to investigate allegations that crop-dusting planes often sprayed neighborhoods by mistake, despite the fact that they possessed the records from the agricultural commissioner on pesticide application. Increasingly frustrated by the Health Department's response to the McFarland mothers, Lazar quit in February 1987.[52]

Lazar's resignation occurred in the midst of a growing contentious debate about California Proposition 65 and issues relating to public health, pesticides, and other toxins. Public discourse heightened when Senator Torres and two Democratic assemblymen, Gray Davis and Lloyd Connolly, added Proposition 65, the Safe Drinking Water and Toxic Enforcement Act of 1986, to the November election ballot. If passed, the initiative would prohibit the release of cancer-causing chemicals into drinking water, require that employees and the public be warned if carcinogens were to be used in their vicinity, and subject violators to a possible three years in prison and $100,000 in fines.[53] Support for the proposition broke down along predictable lines. Environmentalists, labor unions, and Democrats supported the bill. The petro-chemical industry, the California Farm Bureau, and the Republicans opposed it.[54] Predictably enough, Deukmejian also vocally opposed the proposition and maintained its passage would put an "unbearable burden on farmers and small businesses" and would effectively drive jobs away from the state of California.[55] After the votes were tallied though, Deukmejian found himself in the minority as two-thirds of Californians placed a premium on health and environment and cast their ballots in favor of Proposition 65.[56] Nevertheless, the promise of the Safe Drinking Water and Toxic Enforcement Act failed to materialize for years thereafter because the administration fought to minimize the applicability of the new law. Deukmejian's response to the new law reassured growers that they had "a friend, not an adversary" in office—just as his campaign had promised.

It was in 1986, also, that the UFW chose to incorporate the McFarland cancer cluster into an existing campaign against pesticides in an attempt to pressure politicians and growers to halt the use of a host of carcinogenic pesticides. The UFW collaborated with a core of physicians and scientists to publicize the hazards of pesticides and the carcinogenic nature of some of them. Lazar, the dissenting doctor from the Kern County Health Department, worked directly for the union and tested food for pesticide residues, so that the union would be able to incorporate the data into their campaign.[57] Dr. Marion Moses, a former employee of the UFW and founder of the Pesticide Education Center, also contributed significantly to the pesticide reform efforts by identifying more pediatric cancers in the surrounding area, alerting government investigators to the existence of additional cases, and serving as a source of scientific expertise in the union's media relations.[58]

The United Farm Workers publicized the McFarland cancer cluster in a video entitled *The Wrath of Grapes*, which they made and released in an effort to galvanize public support for pesticide reform. The video opens with ominous music, the whirring of helicopter blades, and the silhouette of a helicopter dropping pesticides on the fields.[59] The carefully crafted montage resembled a reporter's footage from the battlefield. The iconic leader of the UFW, Cesar Chavez, then made the intended linkage clear when he stated: "We're declaring war, war on the pesticides that are poisoning and killing our people." The video emphasized the casualties of the "war"—the cancer-afflicted families of California's Central Valley who told of their personal tragedies and speculated that their children's illnesses were a result of the parents' work in the fields. Connie Rosales, the mother who first brought government attention to the cluster, despaired: "These homes were our dream homes, our piece of the American Dream, and it's almost become a nightmare and we don't know what's happened here. It's out of control." In its whole, *The Wrath of Grapes* offered a strong moralistic argument for greater pesticide regulation.

The California Grape Commission responded by widely distributing another video entitled *Big Fears, Little Risks: A Report on Chemicals in the Environment*. Walter Cronkite, the newscaster often referred to as "the most trusted man in America," was paid $25,000 to narrate the production in which a handful of scientists assured the public that their fears about chemical carcinogens were overblown.[60] According to their logic, the presence and volume of chemicals in the environment remained nearly constant, while science and definitions of "safe" were in a state of constant flux. The video then asserted that these miniscule amounts of chemicals posed no greater threat to the human body than the natural carcinogens found in foods such as peanut butter or mushrooms. Last, it maintained that the body had an amazing defense system that was "designed to live in a world of carcinogens."[61] In contrast to *The Wrath of Grapes*, this video relied on a trusted public figure and a handful of scientific authorities to counter moralistic arguments for reform.

Divergent opinions about the existence and causes of the McFarland cancer cluster hardened in the midst of these events: the inconclusive results from the Kern County Health Department's questionable investigation, the passage of a promising yet increasingly impotent piece of legislation, and the greater involvement of special interest groups such as the UFW and the California Grape Commission. Individuals who expected results confirming that pesticides were the root cause of the cancer cluster became more convinced and vociferous in their assertions that the investigation had been mishandled. A coalition of local residents, sympathetic politicians, and concerned physicians criticized the qualifications and capabilities of the Kern County Health Department, which subsequently caused the government personnel involved with the investigation to become increasingly defensive.[62] Other McFarland residents without direct ties to the cancer-afflicted children simply wearied of negative publicity and desired a return to normalcy.[63] There would be no respite for these residents in the coming months as a contingent of Hollywood celebrities—including Martin Sheen, Edward James Olmos, and Lou Diamond Phillips—voiced their support for the cancer-afflicted families and brought more attention to the health crisis.[64]

Under increasing pressure, Deukmejian agreed to allocate $200,000 to the state Department of Health Services so it could hire a contingent of university scientists to review the previously collected data.[65] Senator Torres characterized the new investigation as a misdirected and fruitless exercise, since many critics maintained the county's study was faulty and incomplete. Even Dr. Raymond Neutra, chief of the State Health Department, admitted that the county workers who had conducted the previous investigations lacked the capability to accurately test the soil and groundwater in the community. Torres also charged that, if the study was to be conducted properly, it would need more than the paltry sum that Deukmejian had allocated for the investigation.[66] In fact, the dollar amount does seem negligible when compared to the budgets of other toxic site investigations. At Love Canal, for example, the EPA spent $5.3 million to collect and analyze air, water, and soil samples over a six-month period in 1980.[67] Considering this, Deukmejian's initial allocation of $200,000 seems insufficient and misplaced, especially since the money was used to review the results of the initial study, which cost only $43,000.

Deukmejian's concurrent actions in response to the passage of the Safe Drinking Water and Toxic Enforcement Act cast doubt on his commitment to identifying the causal agents of the McFarland cancer cluster. Deukmejian tried his utmost to limit the scope and effectiveness of the law, which theoretically would protect thousands of Californians from the ill effects of environmental carcinogens. After the passage of Proposition 65, it was the governor's charge to appoint a twelve-person scientific panel to determine which toxins should be banned. Deukmejian selected two of the scientists recommended by environmental organizations. However, his selection of Bruce Ames for the panel, a vocal and controversial scientist in the biochemistry department at University of California, Berkeley, helped offset the two appointments.[68] Carl Pope, the Sierra Club's political director and co-author of the proposition, went so far as to call the appointment an act of "sabotage" by the governor.[69]

Ames publicly opposed the proposed legislation prior to the election, maintaining that fears about environmental toxins were overblown and that people needed to worry about the cancer-causing potential of serious threats such as sunlight, diet, and tobacco.[70] In a subtle way, his proposed shift in focus would switch critical attention from industrial polluters to individuals who made poor personal choices in their lives. Ames essentially believed that the victim was usually to blame for the disease contracted, so he continued to characterize Proposition 65 as a "thoroughly silly law" even after being selected as an advisor.[71] If Ames held sway over the panel, Californians could be assured that the field of included chemicals would be greatly narrowed.

When the advisory panel completed its study, Governor Deukmejian announced that only twenty-nine chemicals would be banned as a result of the new law. DDT, dioxins, ethylene dibromide (EDB), and other carcinogens failed to make the list.[72]

The governor and his scientific panel selected the included toxins using the strictest interpretation of scientific carcinogen classifications. In order to understand the administration's logic, it is first necessary to understand how chemicals are classified as carcinogenic. The Environmental Protection Agency groups chemicals in one of five different categories: Group A chemicals (*known* human carcinogens) represent those substances that have been the subject of epidemiological tests done on humans yielding conclusive evidence proving them carcinogenic; Group B (*probable* human carcinogens) have strong evidence from animal-based studies to conclude that a chemical is a carcinogen and more limited results from human-based studies; Group C (*possible* human carcinogens) includes chemicals for which there is some positive evidence from animal-based studies though evidence from human-based tests is either lacking or has yet to be completed; Group D lacks sufficient data or tests to determine if a substance is carcinogenic; and Group E (non-carcinogens) shows no evidence of causing cancer in any species.[73] Deukmejian's office reasoned that only those chemicals in Group A should be included.[74] The governor and his advisory panel entirely discounted animal-based studies, premising their decision to not consider the chemicals in Group B or C on the fact that they had not been sufficiently tested on human subjects.

The public, courts, and even members of Deukmejian's administration were not satisfied or convinced by the determinative logic of the governor and his scientific advisory panel. A coalition of labor and environmental groups filed suit charging that Deukmejian's interpretation of the law was negligent and that more than 200 additional substances should be included in the ban. California's Attorney General John Van de Kamp also showed his disapproval of the governor's action on the new law by refusing to represent him in the case.[75] The Superior Court rejected Deukmejian's logic as "strained and tortured" and forced the eventual addition of over 200 more chemicals.[76] By the end of 1989, the list included 307 chemicals—a number substantially larger than Deukmejian's initial twenty-nine.[77] Resolute in his efforts, the governor continued to try to protect agricultural interests by exempting certain chemicals and removing others from the list by process of appeal.[78] Though repeatedly unsuccessful in his efforts, Deukmejian did succeed in stymieing the effectiveness of the Safe Drinking Water and Toxic Enforcement Act for a couple of years. The governor's actions in response to the passage of Proposition 65 and the scant allocation of resources for the McFarland cancer cluster study reveal a pattern of resistance to committing state resources to the protection of the public's health from environmental pollutants.

The governor's resistance did little to help the people of McFarland. By the time the state Department of Health Services concluded its study in early 1988, over a dozen children had been diagnosed with cancer in the small community—six had died. The state inquiry determined that four particular chemicals—dimethoate, fenbutatin oxide, dinitrophenol, and dinoseb—warranted further investigation, because of a dramatic increase in their usage during the estimated window of exposure.[79] In fact, in the months prior to the release of the report, the Environmental Protection Agency suspended the use of dinoseb, because of the potential hazard that it posed to farmworkers' health.[80] However, Kassy Eddington, a spokeswoman for the state Health Services Department, clarified that there was "no smoking gun."[81] Like a number of other cancer cluster investigators, Eddington expressed her doubt that a definite direct link to the causal factor would ever be found, tempering public optimism about a resolution in the near future.[82]

Like the county study before it, critics targeted the state's methodology as both misdirected and insufficient. The UCLA epidemiologist Robert Haile maintained that abnormal cancer rates plagued other parts of the Central Valley and should be considered in the McFarland inquiry.[83] John M. Peters, the director of the Division of Environmental Health at University of Southern California, maintained that there was a fundamental problem with the logic employed in both the county and state investigations, because investigators focused solely on the differences in the surroundings and experiences of affected and non-affected children in McFarland. Because carcinogens do not have the same effect on all people, it was probable that non-affected children were exposed to the carcinogen too, even if they did not develop cancer.[84]

Despite the study's shortcomings, Eddington recognized that the excessively high number of childhood cancers, coupled with the increased incidence of low birth-weight babies and fetal and infant deaths, suggested that "something" may have poisoned McFarland's environment.[85] Investigators discovered a potential lead after surveying ten cancer-afflicted families in McFarland and twenty other local families who showed no signs of cancer.[86] They found that 80 percent of the afflicted children had fathers who worked in the fields between the third trimester of the mother's pregnancy and the date of the cancer diagnosis, whereas only 45 percent of the fathers of non-afflicted children spent any time in the fields during this period.[87] This discovery supported the contention that agricultural chemicals were responsible for the increase in childhood cancer rates. Children are susceptible to parental exposure to carcinogens before conception, in the mother's womb, and after birth. The paternal link is significant because pesticides from the fields can be carried into the home on the father's clothes and shoes, which would subsequently expose the rest of the family to the hazards of the workplace. These carcinogenic substances can even enter the mother's breast milk through her contact with the father's clothing, thereby exposing the child to carcinogens in the daily dietary intake of food from the mother.[88] Given the way in which cancer develops and manifests itself in a population, this disparity in the percentage of affected families did not definitively prove a link between a work-related parental exposure to a carcinogen and the development of the disease in children; but it is suggestive that there probably was one.[89] The epidemiologists Alice Whittemore of Stanford and Hal Margenstern of UCLA believed the finding was sufficient to warrant further inquiry.[90]

Following the release of the inquiry's results in January 1988, the politicization of the pesticides and the cluster intensified noticeably when Senator Art Torres squared off with the Republican governor again. Deukmejian agreed to pledge another $200,000 toward expanding the research and offered an additional $136,000 to fund free medical screening of elementary school children in McFarland.[91] Torres characterized the amount as utterly insufficient and maintained that $2 million was needed for a proper investigation. Torres then introduced a bill to create a new state agency, the Center for Environmental Disease Control (CEDC), comparable to the national Centers for Disease Control in Atlanta. The agency would act as an umbrella organization to facilitate the coordination of environmental studies and improve communication between different state agencies.[92] It would also provide $466,000 for clinic services, medical assistance, and cancer screening. However, Deukmejian vetoed the bill, claiming that existent programs were capable of providing the necessary support. In response, Torres charged that the governor's office was gripped by "political paralysis," proving itself unable to address the "growing epidemic of cancer."[93]

During this time the United Farm Workers stepped up their visibility in the community, which did not always sit well with residents, some of whom felt that the union was not deeply committed to the affected families and used their tragedies for political gain. Connie Rosales claimed that images of their suffering children were used to drum up funds for the UFW boycott, while the families received little in the way of direct union support. Many residents chafed at the union's intensified efforts, claiming that their actions overstepped the bounds of acceptability, particularly in cases when their political statements entered into the realm of private personal affairs. In a particularly irksome case, twenty-five UFW members showed up at the funeral of Mario Bravo, a fourteen-year-old victim of hepatoblastoma, and marched in procession from the mortuary to the cemetery. Many attendees, including Bruno's mother, felt such actions disrespected the family's privacy.[94] Since the union did not address the everyday needs of the community by providing services such as transportation and daycare, other union actions came off as opportunistic.[95] The UFW and its affiliate the National Farm Worker Ministry defended their actions, maintaining that they were engaged in a larger struggle for pesticide reform and never claimed to be a direct service organization.[96] The disagreements between McFarland residents and the UFW reveal that, to some extent, the cancer-afflicted families in McFarland had become marginalized subjects in a larger political battle.

The funeral incident may have been insensitive, but the union generally succeeded in generating sympathetic attention for the cancer-afflicted victims of McFarland. In July 1988, Cesar Chavez began what became a thirty-six day fast to bring attention to "the scourge of poisons that threaten our people and our land and our food."[97] Chavez, too weak to speak or walk on his own, broke his fast at a liturgy attended by approximately 8,000 farmworkers. Chavez urged his supporters to follow his striking act of self-sacrifice by committing to fast for three days before passing the fast along to someone else, so that the fast would go on in hundreds of different places carried on by millions of different people. Chavez hoped that the chain would continue as a sign of protest against a harmful food production system until pesticide usage was curtailed.

The Reverend Jesse Jackson Jr., in the midst of a bid for the Democratic presidential nomination, stood by Chavez's side when he broke fast on 21 August and was the first to take up the chain. At campaign stops in the Bakersfield area," Jackson used the opportunity to rail against President Ronald Reagan and the environmental policies of his administration. He urged local officials and the community to work together for "environmental justice" and pledged that he would do everything that he could to increase government involvement in the battle against cancer in McFarland.[98] Jackson's reference to "environmental justice" referred to an emergent movement in the late 1980s that sought to ameliorate the disproportionate exposure that poor and minority groups had to environmental toxins.[99] The linkage was appropriate considering that McFarland's population was 94 percent Hispanic with an annual per capita income of $6,056, a figure well below the 1989 state average of $19,929.[100]

Although Jackson's rhetoric of "contamination and corruption" alienated some town officials, continued public pressure and the discovery of additional pediatric cancers in the surrounding area necessitated continued state action.[101] Marion Moses identified six more incidences of cancer in children around the small town of Earlimart—fifteen miles north of McFarland. The union contacted the affected families and discovered that in each case at least one parent, if not both, worked in the grape fields.[102] The union's findings prompted the state to examine the situation and confirm the existence of another cluster. Differing estimates between the state and the UFW placed that rate of cancer occurrence between three and twelve times over the expected norm.[103] The Earlimart cancers represented the latest of a series of alleged clusters in the Central Valley.[104] Still the chief of environmental epidemiology at the state Department of Health Services refused to make the connection between pesticides and cancer, claiming that evidence was still lacking.[105] As the number of cases of childhood cancer continued to grow in the valley, the investigations seemed to be stuck in an inconclusive standstill.

The elusiveness of concrete answers served as a catalyst for more heated and hostile exchanges between the groups with a staked interest in the outcome. Chavez asserted that the close association between agribusiness and the state hampered the investigation, because state officials spent "all of their time apologizing for the agricultural industry."[106] Gonzalo Ramirez, the father of an eleven-month-old cancer victim, charged: "The ranchers don't want just produce, they want it bigger and better no matter what the cost—even our daughter."[107] The growers blistered at their continued demonization by the UFW and cancer-afflicted families. Vineyard owner George Zaninovich vented, "I think people think we walk around with a vat of boiling chemicals and we dip grapes in them."[108] Meanwhile, many of the non-afflicted families in the cluster towns grew weary of the negative attention to their communities and resented discussions about environmental toxins, especially as they began to feel the economic pinch from slackened commerce.[109] In one case,

Dan Shepherd, a resident of Fowler, a town in the suspected cluster, was effectively driven out of town when he began to clamor for an investigation into local pediatric cancers. Community residents boycotted his business and left anonymous death threats until the Shepherd family moved to another town nearby. Community divides over the issue of pesticides were so pervasive that town meetings could not be held without degenerating into shouting matches between conflicting interests.[110]

Since the possibility of establishing a sure link between the Central Valley cancer cluster and its root cause(s) was slim, regulatory legislation targeting suspected pollutants stood as the best possible "remedy" to the situation. The Safe Drinking Water and Toxic Enforcement Act of 1986 represented one such attempt to address issues of toxins and public health, but the legislation became mired in a legalistic struggle over the extent of its reach and implementation. John Van de Kamp and Carl Pope then co-sponsored California Proposition 128—the Environmental Protection Act of 1990—in part to reduce the effects of carcinogenic pesticides on human health, in much the same way that the Federal Coal Mine Health and Safety Act of 1969 was passed to reduce the number of cases of black lung. Nicknamed the "Big Green" initiative, Proposition 128 would have, among other things, gradually phased out agricultural pesticides known to cause cancer or reproductive harm. Senator Art Torres asserted that the legislation would help solve McFarland's health problem, which he maintained was caused by pesticides, by eliminating four of the chemicals viewed with "high levels of suspicion" in the cancer cluster investigation.[111] Proposition 128 would also have transferred the authority to establish and regulate pesticide-related health standards from the Department of Food and Agriculture to the Department of Health Services in an effort to alleviate any administrative conflicts of interest. The proposition further benefited farmworkers through the planned establishment of a farmworker health and safety program and the removal of the agricultural exception from the state right-to-know laws, which had been implemented to ensure that workers knew about hazardous chemicals in the workplace.[112]

Most notably, though, Proposition 128 would have shifted pesticide policy from one premised on acceptable risks to one based strictly on health standards. The cost–benefit analysis weighed the perceived benefits of a chemical against its potential harm as a health and environmental hazard, which involved a fair degree of subjectivity. Critics argued that the determinative latitude that pesticide regulators employed in their analysis still allowed some potentially dangerous chemicals to find their way to the market. Furthermore, scientists judged the hazardousness of a chemical by the health risks that it posed to adults, rather than children, whose high rates of cell proliferation made them more vulnerable to mutagenic substances.[113] These factors led proponents of the proposition to conclude that, "although certain carcinogenic pesticides have been restricted or had their uses canceled, numerous pesticides known to cause cancer continue to be applied on food crops."[114] The proposition would address this problem by only taking into account the risk factors of chemicals, considering the more susceptible nature of children's bodies in the process. In essence, Proposition 128 represented a fundamental shift in policy thinking and embodied one of the basic tenets of the Precautionary Principle. Rather than having to prove the hazards of a chemical to get it off the market, manufacturers would now have to prove that it posed no threat in order to get it on the market.[115]

Support for the proposed paradigm shift in public health policy divided along predictable lines within the voting public. Proposition 128 represented a substantial threat to pesticide manufacturers and growers, so they opposed it, whereas Art Torres, environmental organizations, and the United Farm Workers supported the initiative.[116] If the propostion had passed, roughly 350 of the 2,300 chemicals used in California agriculture would have be banned. Faced with such prospects, well-funded oppositional organizations—such as the Agricultural Council of California, California Women for Agriculture, and the California Chamber of Commerce—actively opposed the legislation and succeeded in garnering enough support to defeat both the proposition and some of the politicians who had actively supported it, including Van de Kamp.[117] As a result, chemically intensive agriculture continued relatively uninterrupted as the residents of McFarland still waited for help from the state.

Investigations into the McFarland cancer cluster continued for nearly a decade, but science proved incapable of identifying the specific cause of the problem. The uncertainty in scientific results encouraged debate about the cluster to grow in the political realm, where there were two possible courses of action. The state could adopt the Precautionary Principle and ban chemicals with probable health risks or it could maintain the status quo until such time as a definitive link was made between certain chemicals and cancer. Affected families and activists lobbied for the former, arguing that enough evidence existed to rationally conclude that pesticides were responsible for the abnormal cancer rate among McFarland children. They subsequently demanded that the most probable suspects be outlawed. Conversely, those with an interest in maintaining uninterrupted levels of high agricultural productivity and those with an interest in the economic health of the petrochemical industry argued that a direct link between the causal agent and the affected children needed to be established before any product was taken off the market. Since science proved unable to provide such linkage, they pushed for a delayed response and argued that the state should exercise constraint in its legislative action in regards to business. Both sides employed scientific data to strengthen their arguments—arguments that stood in stark contrast to one another. The inconclusive nature of most health research virtually guaranteed this result.

The historian Linda Nash faults science for the lack of closure in McFarland, arguing that the pervasiveness of germ theory, with its emphasis on a singular link between a specific pathogen and disease, and the general inability of scientists to operate outside of that theoretical framework obfuscated the cause of the cluster.[118] Her claims are convincing, but they shift focus away from the political factors that played such a critical role in addressing the cancer cluster. Politicians authorized investigations, controlled the studies' funding, played an indirect role in the scope and nature of the studies, and proposed responsive legislation. Likewise, citizens and interest groups played a near-equal role in the generation of a scientific inquiry and the duration of investigative studies. Given this, a solution to McFarland's health woes depended on the outcomes of contentious political debates that were fueled by uncertain scientific results. California voters defeated what was perhaps the best possible solution to the problem, Proposition 128 with its embedded ideas of the Precautionary Principle. After this election, proponents of pesticide regulation failed to muster the political support that they had in the 1980s. Despite the setback from the election loss, President Clinton's signing of the Food Quality Protection Act of 1996 set more stringent pesticide residue limits on food in an effort to better protect children and infants and provided those seeking pesticide reform with a new tool to use in their efforts to protect the health of children and communities.

Notes

1   California Legislature, Senate Committee on Toxics and Public Safety Management, *Childhood Cancer Incidences McFarland* (Sacramento: Joint Publications, 1985), 37.

2   Ibid., 38; Russell Clemings, "Town Where Cancer Lives," *Fresno Bee*, 14 February 1988, A1.

3   *Childhood Cancer Incidences McFarland*, 38; Elliot Diringer, "Central Valley Town's 'Cluster' of Cancer," *San Francisco Chronicle*, 31 October 1986, 1.

4   "2 Small Towns' Mysterious 'Clusters' of Cancer," *San Francisco Chronicle*, 31 October 1985, 16; "10-Year-Old Cancer Victim Involved in Study Dies," *Fresno Bee*, 19 March 1986, B2.

5   Russell Clemings, "Cancer Cluster Still Not Solved; McFarland Health Study Inconclusive," *Fresno Bee*, 30 October 1986, B2.

6   For a discussion of the Precautionary Principle, see Carolyn Raffensperger and Joel A. Tickner, "Introduction," in Carolyn Raffensperger and Joel Tickner (eds.),

Protecting Public Health and the Environment: Implementing the Precautionary Principle (Washington, DC: Island Press, 1999).

7   Policy Research Project on Pesticide Regulation in Texas, *Pesticides and Worker Health in Texas* (Austin: University of Texas at Austin, 1984), 17–19. See also Ephraim Kahn, "Pesticide Related Illness in California Farm Workers," *Journal of Occupational Medicine* 18(10) (October 1976), 693; Irma West and Thomas H. Milby, "Public Health Problems Arising from the Use of Pesticides," *Residue Reviews* 11 (1965), 142, 155; G. M. Wang, "Evaluation of Pesticides Which Pose Carcinogenicity Potential in Animal Testing, II: Consideration of Human Exposure Conditions for Regulatory Decision Making," *Regulatory Toxicology and Pharmacology* 4 (1984), 362; Harrison A. Stubbs, John Harris, and Robert C. Spears, "A Proportionate Mortality Analysis of California Agricultural Workers, 1978–79," *American Journal of Industrial Medicine* 6 (1984), 305, 306; Brad Heavner, *Toxics on Tap: Pesticides in California Drinking Water Sources* (San Francisco: Californians for Pesticide Reform, 1999), 53.

8   Michael Egan, *Barry Commoner and the Science of Survival: The Remaking of American Environmentalism* (Cambridge, MA: MIT Press, 2007), 5, 10, 11.

9   In the late 1960s and early 1970s, articles on pesticides appeared regularly in the union's newspaper, *El Malcriado*. One article in *El Malcriado* extensively quoted a Commoner speech. See "Judge Hides the Dangers of Pesticides," *El Malcriado: The Voice of the Farmworker* (Delano, CA), 1 January 1969, 5. For other examples, see: "Poison! Nitrates Still Pollute Water; City Studying Problem With All Its Might," *El Malcriado*, 26 April 1967, 10; "DDT Poisoning Becomes a National Concern," *El Malcriado*.

10   Samuel S. Epstein, *The Politics of Cancer* (San Francisco: Sierra Club Books, 1978), 23.

11   Keith Schneider, "Whistleblower's Revenge," *The Progressive* (October 1985), 19.

12   Sylvia Noble Tesh, *Uncertain Hazards: Environmental Activists and Scientific Proof* (Ithaca, NY: Cornell University Press, 2000), 5.

13   Liora Salter, "The Public Role in Pesticide Registration," in James A. Dosman and Donald W. Cockcroft (eds.), *Principles of Health and Safety in Agriculture* (Boca Raton, FL: CRC Press, 1989), 218, 220.

14   Ibid., 218.

15   Robert N. Proctor, *Cancer Wars: How Politics Shapes What We Know and Don't Know About Cancer* (New York: Basic Books, 1995), 102.

16   Ibid., 34.

17   Alan Derickson, *Black Lung: Anatomy of a Public Health Disaster* (Ithaca, NY: Cornell University Press, 1998), xii, 21, 60.

18   Gerald Markowitz and David Rosner, *Deceit and Denial: The Deadly Politics of Industrial Pollution* (Berkeley: University of California Press, 2002), 300.

19   Proctor, *Cancer Wars*, 59, 80, 102; Epstein, *The Politics of Cancer*, 262, 300.

20   Epstein, *The Politics of Cancer*, 430.

21   Markowitz and Rosner, *Deceit and Denial*, 304–6.

22   *Childhood Cancer Incidences McFarland*, 5, 23.

23   "2 Small Towns' Mysterious 'Clusters' of Cancer," 16; Atul Gawande, "The Cancer-Cluster Myth," *New Yorker*, 8 February 1999, 36. Scientific thinking at this time generally held that cancer was "probably not one disease but a spectrum of diseases with common features but different—though proximate—causes" (Epstein, *The Politics of Cancer*, 22). Such thinking would not necessarily prevent scientists from concluding that pesticides caused the abnormal increase in childhood cancers, though, because they recognized the potential of different chemicals to interact with one another in different ways and also thought that carcinogens affected different people in different ways (ibid., 22–25). Recent scientific thinking about cancers more fully recognizes that variant cancers may potentially have a common causal agent as catalyst. In *How Scientists Explain Disease*, Paul Thagard, Professor of Philosophy and Psychology, states that there is an increasing recognition that at the most fundamental level "no matter what form a cancer takes, it remains a malady of genes, and most, if not all, causes of cancer act by damaging genes directly or indirectly." Thagard adds that the new Cancer Explanation Schema assumes that cancer is caused by the interaction of multiple variables with different genes that are affected by different hereditary and environmental factors. (Paul Thagard, *How Scientists Explain Disease* [Princeton, NJ: Princeton University Press, 1999], 33, 34). Viewed within this theoretical framework, it seems plausible that the multiple forms of cancer in McFarland developed in response to a single carcinogen or a combination of chemical carcinogens. According to data recorded on pesticide use from 1991 to 1994, nine probable carcinogens and thirty-seven possible carcinogens were sprayed in California. This same study revealed that "hundreds of thousands of children living in areas with high agricultural pesticide use have greater potential for exposure than their more urban counterparts" (Robert B. Gunier, Martha E. Harnly, Peggy Reynolds, Andrew Hertz, and Julie Von Behren, "Agricultural Pesticide Use in California: Pesticide Prioritization, Use Densities, and Population Distributions for a Childhood Cancer Study," *Environmental Health Perspectives*, 109(10) (October 2001), 1072, 1075).

24   *Childhood Cancer Incidences McFarland*, 32; "2 Small Towns' Mysterious 'Clusters' of Cancer," 16.

25   *Childhood Cancer Incidences McFarland*, 10.

26   "2 Small Town's Mysterious 'Clusters' of Cancer," 16.

27   David B. Cohen and Gerald W. Bowes, *Water Quality and Pesticides: A California Risk Assessment Program*, vol. 1 (Sacramento: State Water Resources Control Board, 1984), 28.

28   David B. Cohen, "Ground Water Contamination by Toxic Substances: A California Assessment," *ACS Symposium Series* (Washington, DC: American Chemical Society, 1986), 499, 513; "2 Small Towns' Mysterious 'Clusters' of Cancer," 16.

29   Cohen, "Ground Water Contamination," 502, 503; "2 Small Towns' Mysterious 'Clusters' of Cancer," 16.

30   Cohen, "Ground Water Contamination," 519.

31 Ibid., 520.

32 *Childhood Cancer Incidences McFarland*, 11, 25. Russell Clemings, "McFarland Cancer Study Criticized by Coordinator," *Fresno Bee*, 3 April 1987, B1.

33 For further discussion, see Francis Chinard, "History, Occupational Health, and Medical Education," in Helen E. Sheehan and Richard P. Weeden (ed.), *Toxic Circles* (New Brunswick, NJ: Rutgers University Press, 1993), 266.

34 California Latino Caucus, "Latino Legislative History and Purpose: Historical Overview of the Latino Caucus," http://democrats.assembly.ca.gov/latinocaucus/history_purpose.htm.

35 Ibid., 2, 12, 28; "Back to Basics: Boycott Table Grapes," *National Farm Worker Ministry Newsletter*, 13(3) (September 1984), 1.

36 "California Farmworkers: Back to the Barricades?" *Businessweek* (26 September 1983), 86; Evan T. Barr, "Sour Grapes: Cesar Chavez 20 Years Later," *New Republic*, 193(20) (25 November 1985), 22; *The Wrath of Grapes*, narrated by Mike Farrell, produced by Lorena Parlee and Lenny Bourin, United Farm Workers of America, AFL-CIO, production of Volunteer Staff of UFWofA, videocassette, 1986.

37 "Back to Basics," 1; "California Farmworkers," 86; Barr, "Sour Grapes," 22; George Deukmejian, speech to the Nisei Farmers League, 8 February 1985, Special Collections, Institute of Governmental Studies Library, University of California, Berkeley, 2.

38 Susan Ferris and Ricardo Sandoval, *The Fight in the Fields: Cesar Chavez and the Farmworkers Movement*, ed. Diana Hembree (New York: Harcourt Brace and Company, 1997), 237.

39 Leo C. Wolinsky, "Senate OKs Shield on State's Pesticide Use," *Los Angeles Times*, 12 September 1985, Part 1, p. 3; Deukmejian, speech to the Nisei Farmers League, 2; Leo C. Wolinsky, "Bill to Curb Challenges to State Pest Spraying Pushed," *Los Angeles Times*, 10 September 1985, Part 1, 20; George Deukmejian, speech to the Visalia Agricultural Symposium in Visalia, California, 17 April 1985, Special Collections, Institute of Governmental Studies Library, University of California, Berkeley, 1.

40 John Balzar, "Governor's Veto Holds in Feud on Toxic Waste," *Los Angeles Times*, 33.

41 *Childhood Cancer Incidences McFarland*, 12.

42 For a discussion of the utility and limitations of cancer registries in environmental disease investigations, see Sylvia Noble Tesh, *Uncertain Hazards: Environmental Activists and Scientific Proof* (Ithaca, NY: Cornell University Press, 2000), 31, 32.

43 *Childhood Cancer Incidences McFarland*, 7, 11, 15, 16.

44 Ibid., 23, 25.

45 Ibid., 27.

46 "Cancer Cluster Still Not Solved; McFarland Health Study Inconclusive," B2.

47 Ibid., B2; "Central Valley Town's 'Cluster' of Cancers," 1.

48 "Cancer Cluster Still Not Solved; McFarland Health Study Inconclusive," B2.

49 Amy Pyle, "State Will Expand Probe; Duke Requests Further Study of Cancer Cluster," *Fresno Bee*, 17 December 1987, B1.

50 Lazar's estimate seems exceptionally high, though other cancer clusters were discovered in the surrounding area in the years following. Russell Clemings, "State Broadens Its Cancer Probe," *Fresno Bee*, 1 October 1987, B8; "McFarland Cancer Study Criticized by Coordinator," B1.

51 "McFarland Cancer Study Criticized by Coordinator," B1.

52 Ibid., B1.

53 Dirk Werkman, "Big 5 Might Steal Election Show," *Daily News of Los Angeles*, 27 July 1986, 1.

54 John Marelius, "Toxics Issue Draws Much Heat—Proposition 65 is Central Topic in California Campaigns," *San Diego Union*, 2 November 1986, A6.

55 William Endicott, "Duke Opposes AIDS Initiative Pay Limit, Clean Water Proposals Also Criticized," *Sacramento Bee*, 3 September 1986, A1.

56 Marc Lifsher, "Panel Disagrees on List of What to Ban in Water—Scientific Testimony Conflicts on Which Chemicals Are Most Harmful," *Orange County Register*, 1 April 1987, A3.

57 "State Broadens Its Cancer Probe," B8.

58 "Chavez's New Plea to Ban Pesticides," *San Francisco Chronicle*, 15 September 1989, A4; "4th Valley Town Added to Childhood Cancer List," *Sacramento Bee*, 24 September 1989, A1.

59 For details see n. 36.

60 Proctor, *Cancer Wars*, 150.

61 American Council on Science and Health, *Big Fears, Little Risks: A Report on Chemicals in the Environment*, narrated by Walter Cronkite, produced by Film Counselors Associates, Inc., videocassette, 1989.

62 Russell Clemings, "McFarland Parents Demand New Childhood-Cancer Study," *Fresno Bee*, 17 October 1987, B1.

63 Jim Boren, "Jackson Urges Unity in the McFarland Crisis," *Fresno Bee*, 25 May 1988, A1.

64 Pat Hoffman, "Cesar Chavez's 'Fast for Life,'" *Christian Century*, 12 October 1988, 896, 897.

65 Ibid.; "State Will Expand McFarland Probe; Duke Requests Further Study of Cancer Cluster," B1.

66 "State Will Expand McFarland Probe; Duke Requests Further Study of Cancer Cluster," B1.

67 New York State Department of Health, "Love Canal: A Special Report to the Governor & Legislature: April 1981," revised October 2005, www.health.state.ny.us/environmental/investigations/love_canal/lcreport.htm.

68 "Duke's Toxic List Called Too Short," *Sacramento Bee*, 28 February 1987, A1.

69 Proctor, *Cancer Wars*, 150.

70 Leslie Roberts, "A Corrosive Fight Over California's Toxic Law," *Science* 243 (20 January 1989), 307.

71 Ibid., 306.
72 "Duke's Toxic List Called Too Short," A1.
73 Sandra Steingraber, *Living Downstream: An Ecologist Looks at Cancer and the Environment* (Reading, MA: Addison-Wesley, 1997), 125.
74 Mitchell Benson, "Governor Releases Toxics List But Coalition Says Roster is Incomplete," *San Jose Mercury News*, 28 February 1987, 1A.
75 Ibid., 1A.
76 "Alice in Waterland," *Fresno Bee*, 2 August 1989, B6; "Deukmejian Loses Appeal on Toxics," *San Francisco Chronicle*, 22 July 1989, A13.
77 Jennifer Kerr, "Toxic Substance Warnings Are Now Ubiquitous Part of Consumer-Scene," *Daily News of Los Angeles*, 12 November 1989, N10.
78 "Alice in Waterland," B6; "Court Rejects Bid to Drop Chemicals From Toxics List," *Daily News of Los Angeles*, 23 July 1989, N13.
79 Russell Clemings, "McFarland Cancer Report Yields 2 Clues," *Fresno Bee*, 30 January 1988, A1.
80 "Pesticides Studied in Town's Cancers; Large Quantities of Four Chemicals Used in Kern Community's Fields," *Sacramento Bee*, 30 January 1988, A1.
81 Russell Clemings, "Families Await New McFarland Cancer Report," *Fresno Bee*, 23 January 1988, A1.
82 "Pesticides Studied in Town's Cancers; Large Quantities of Four Chemicals Used in Kern Community's Fields," A1; Daniel Smith and Raymond Neutra, "Approaches to Disease Cluster Investigations in a State Health Department," *Statistics in Medicine* 12(1193), 1760; Gawande, "The Cancer-Cluster Myth," 36.
83 Russell Clemings, "McFarland Cancer Panel Will Look at Other Towns," *Fresno Bee*, 9 April 1988, A1.
84 Ibid., A1. Samuel Epstein would likely support this contention. In discussing the causes of cancer, he maintains that carcinogens affect different parts of the population in different ways and with different force. Epstein, *The Politics of Cancer*, 22, 23.
85 "Pesticides Studied in Town's Cancers; Large Quantities of Four Chemicals Used in Kern Community's Fields," A1.
86 "McFarland Cancer Report Yields 2 Clues," A1.
87 "Pesticide Study Links Cancer, Work in Fields," *San Francisco Chronicle*, 30 January 1988, A4; "Pesticides Studied in Town's Cancers; Large Quantities of Four Chemicals Used in Kern Community's Fields," A1.
88 Steingraber, *Living Downstream*, 39, 65. Recent scientific studies, including some on pesticides, have established some links between parental occupational prenatal exposure and the development of cancer in children: John A. Newby and Vyvyan Howard, "Environmental Influences in Cancer Aetiology," *Journal of Nutritional and Environmental Medicine* 15(2&3)(2006), 92, available at http://201.216.215.170/isde.org/images/pdf/newby%26howardenvinflcanceraetiologyjenm2006.pdf (accessed 16 August 2007).

89 Regarding the development of cancer, Atul Gawande, Professor of Surgery and Health Policy and Management, states: "Cells have a variety of genes that keep them functioning normally, and it takes an almost chance combination of successive mutations in these genes—multiple 'hits,' as cancer biologists put it—to make a cell cancerous rather than simply killing it . . . Even when people have been subjected to a heavy dose of a carcinogen and many cells have been damaged, they will not all get cancer." Gawande, "The Cancer-Cluster Myth," 36.

90 "McFarland Cancer Report Yields 2 Clues," A1.

91 "Deukmejian Explains Cancer-Aid Veto," *Daily News of Los Angeles*, 2 October 1988, N14.

92 Amy Pyle, "McFarland Cancer Study Spurs New Efforts," *Fresno Bee*, A1.

93 "Deukmejian Explains Cancer-Aid Veto," N14.

94 "Town Where Cancer Lives," A1.

95 Bill Donnelly, "'They're Using Our Children'—Couple Say UFW Exploits Victims," *Fresno Bee*, 3 July 1989, B1.

96 "Town Where Cancer Lives," A1.

97 "Cesar Chavez Fasts for Life," *National Farm Worker Ministry Newsletter*, 17(1) (Summer 1988), 1.

98 "Jackson Urges Unity in McFarland Crisis," A1.

99 Robert Gottlieb, *Environmentalism Unbound: Exploring New Pathways for Change* (Cambridge, MA: MIT Press, 2001), 62.

100 Mark Arax, "Baffling Cancers Divide Small Farming Town," *Contra Costa Times* (Walnut Creek, CA), 17 August 1997, A16; U.S. Bureau of the Census, *Statistical Abstract of the United States: 1991* (Washington, DC: Government Printing Office, 1991), 442.

101 "Jackson Urges Unity in McFarland Crisis," A1.

102 Elliot Diringer, "5 Children of Farm Workers New Cancer Cluster in Farm Town," *San Francisco Chronicle*, 14 September 1989, A1.

103 Marilyn Lewis, "Third Cancer Cluster Hits Central Valley Kids," *San Jose Mercury News*, 14 September 1989, 1A.

104 Diringer, "5 Children of Farm Workers New Cancer Cluster in Farm Town," A1.

105 Lewis, "Third Cancer Cluster Hits Central Valley Kids," 1A.

106 Ray Sotero, "Bias Charged at Pesticide Rally," *Fresno Bee*, 19 December 1989, B1. Adolf Nava, a community activist and physician in Earlimart, spoke of a more sinister state presence. He claimed that he spent much time interviewing the families of victims in attempt to find a common link, but that Tulare County health officials warned him that they would ruin his career in Visalia if he didn't "shut up." Philip J. Garcia, "The Legacy of an Unseen Killer—Ag Workers Feel Victimized by Cancer, System," *Sacramento Bee*, 17 February 1991, I1.

107 "4th Valley Town Added to Childhood Cancer List," A1.

108 Ibid.

109 "Town's Cancer Cluster Cause Still a Mystery," *Press-Telegram* (Long Beach, CA), 13 July 1992, B4.

110 "4th Valley Town Added to Childhood Cancer List," A1.

111 Art Torres, *Proposition 128: Analysis of Pesticide Use and Regulation* (Sacramento: Senate Committee on Toxics and Public Safety Management, 1990), 2, 7, 8.

112 Senate Toxics and Public Safety Management Committee, *Proposition 128: Environmental Protection Act of 1990* (Sacramento: Senate Office of Research, 1990), 1, 6, 7.

113 Newby and Howard, "Environmental Influences in Cancer Aetiology," 37.

114 *Proposition 128*, 8, 10, 23.

115 Ibid., 8; Ken Geiser, "Preface: Establishing a General Duty of Precaution in Environmental Protection Policies in the United States: A Proposal," in Carolyn Raffensperger and Joel Tickner (eds.), *Protecting Public Health and the Environment: Implementing the Precautionary Principle* (Washington, DC: Island Press, 1999), xxiii.

116 *Proposition 128*, 6; John Howard, "Where are They Now? Former State Attorney General John Van de Kamp," *Capitol Weekly News*, 8 December 2005, 2; Joe Rosato, "State is Sued Over Pesticides; Warnings Were Allegedly Ignored," *Fresno Bee*, 6 September 1990, B2.

117 Howard, 2; Matthew E. Kahn and John G. Matsusaka, "Demand for Environmental Goods: Evidence From Voting Patterns on California Initiatives," *Journal of Law and Economics*, 40 (April 1997), 170.

118 Linda Nash, *Inescapable Ecologies: A History of Environment, Disease, and Knowledge* (Berkeley: University of California Press, 2006), 7, 12, 207.

CHAPTER 13

"It Seems Like We Should Be on the Same Side!"

Native Americans, Environmentalists, and the Grand Canyon

WILL MCARTHUR[1]

"Indian lover," an exasperated Jeff Ingram shouted at Don McIver while storming out of the room at a meeting of the Grand Canyon Chapter of the Sierra Club. Clearly, the 5 January 1974 chapter meeting was not going well. Club members were particularly anxious to discuss some controversial legislation pending in Congress. Their deliberation centered on two bills that were both designed to enlarge Grand Canyon National Park and consolidate several parcels of public land within the park. The controversy resulted from the fact that attached to each bill was a proposal to return some land from the National Park and a nearby National Forest to the Havasupai Tribe, whose land had been incorporated into various public lands ninety-two years before.[2]

Ingram was a tenacious environmentalist with a deep commitment to protecting the Grand Canyon.[3] A decade prior to Ingram's ugly outburst, David Brower, who became the first executive director of the club in 1952, chose him to be the club's first field representative in the Southwest. Both Ingram and Brower were among a group of leaders that set the tone for the club during the 1950s and 1960s as "hard-driving and uncompromising" with their approach to environmental politics.[4] Together with other leaders such as Mike

301

McCloskey, Martin Litton, and Brock Evans, they pulled the club through a series of galvanizing events beginning with the battle over a dam at Echo Park in Dinosaur National Monument (in the first half of the 1950s) and on through a fight over the placement of dams in the Grand Canyon, lobbying for the passage of the Wilderness Act, fighting for the creation of Redwood National Park in northern California, and blocking the creation of a nuclear power plant at Diablo Canyon on the California coast (all in the 1960s).

These battles all required mobilized grassroots memberships, coalition building, and the use of the media. These techniques, though they required great effort, proved so effective that by 1967 the New York Times noted a transformation of the organization from a "fairly genteel outfit to the 'gang-busters' of the conservation movement."[5] Ultimately, the injection of the issue of race into the environmental debate during the battle over the Havasupai land transfer sorely tested these techniques and their effectiveness.

The test came after immense changes in the Sierra Club at work in the 1960s and the first years of the 1970s. The most noticeable change was that the club enjoyed phenomenal growth during these years prior to the Havasupai legislation. They began the 1960s with 35,000 members and by 1972 claimed 137,000 members. By the last half of the 1960s, the club was growing at around 30 percent a year.[6]

The environmental historian Adam Rome connects this explosive growth of environmentalism in the 1960s to "the revitalization of liberalism, the growing discontent of middle-class women, and the explosion of student radicalism and countercultural protest." Although environmentalism was never the primary concern of any of these groups, environmental concern played a role in each of these movements.[7] Many of these movements also shared common commitments to racial equality and social justice. Thus, concerns about the environment, racial equality, and social justice were all an integral part of the decade's reform movements.[8]

Many of the new members who joined the club in the 1960s and 1970s had already participated in one of the many significant social movements that ran the gamut from civil rights to feminism. Richard Cellarius came to the Sierra Club with the belief that concern over the environment, war in Southeast Asia, and civil rights were all "threads of the same" systemic problem.[9] In 1970, he gave a speech calling for a new environmental ethic that recognized that social and environmental problems have the same roots.[10] Another member, Doris Cellarius, was an active feminist who supported the anti-war movement while a member of the Sierra Club.[11] A survey of Sierra Club members in 1978 found that 18 percent said they were active in civil rights efforts and sympathized strongly with blacks.[12] A more broadly worded survey of environmental group members in 1980 showed this cohort remained strongly liberal, with 80 percent of those surveyed supporting civil rights activism, the anti-war movement, and feminism.[13]

In addition, many of the new members joining the Sierra Club in the 1960s were young students. By 1972, the largest single occupational group in the Sierra Club was students (nearly one of every five members was a student). A number of studies confirm that the university-educated segment of the population has tended to be more liberal on racial and ethnic issues.[14]

The presence of these Movement environmentalists significantly changed the dynamics of environmentalism.[15] Their interest in fighting for both environmental and social justice and their unique values regarding race revealed some of both the problems and possibilities of seeking to simultaneously address social and environmental problems. Finally, their story illuminates some of the real diversity within environmentalism and offers a clearer picture of the development of environmentalism in the 1960s and 1970s.

A Very Definite Uncertainty

White miners, ranchers, and government agents steadily encroached on the territory of the Havasupai, who wintered in Cataract and Havasu Canyons and summered on the Coconino Plateau above the canyons on the Southwest of the Grand Canyon.[16] A government decree eventually left them with a mere 518.6 acre reservation, and the loss of most of their resources left them impoverished.[17] Over the years, the Grand Canyon region was parceled off into private, state, and federal lands that included two national monuments, a national recreation area, two national forests, and a national park. In 1973, after decades of petitions for the return of their homeland, the Havasupai met with Senator Barry Goldwater (R-AZ), who had spent years working to consolidate all of the federal Grand Canyon lands into a single national park. Goldwater agreed to help. Realizing the potential opposition from environmentalists, he asked Morris Udall (D-AZ) for his help in the House.[18] On 20 March 1973, Udall in the House and Goldwater in the Senate introduced bills to enlarge Grand Canyon National Park and to return some of the land from the rearrangement to the Havasupai.

After more than twenty-one months spent battling over the controversial bills, President Gerald Ford signed the legislation that changed Grand Canyon National Park, Public Law 93–620, on 3 January 1975. The legislation doubled the size of the park by adding to it lands from Grand Canyon National Monument, Marble Canyon National Monument, Lake Mead National Recreation Area, and a small area of Kaibab National Forest. The act also transferred 185,000 acres from Park and Forest Service lands to the

Havasupai Indian Reservation and allowed them restricted use of 93,500 acres within the Park.

When Goldwater and Udall introduced the bills, environmental organizations expressed near universal support for the park expansion legislation, except for one provision: the plan to transfer land to the Havasupai.[19] This created a dilemma for the new Movement environmentalists who came to the issue with concerns for both the environment and for social justice. Some of them were troubled by being asked to choose between the plight of the Havasupai and protecting the Grand Canyon. Some environmentalists grasped about for help in making some kind of informed decision.[20] For example, Gordon Rands, one of those young university students who joined the Sierra Club and brought with him liberal commitments to both social issues and the environment, wrote to Udall pleading for guidance while away from Arizona attending the University of Michigan. Up to this point, his values on social and environmental issues had not appeared to him to conflict. Now the young scholar felt he was being forced to choose between the two. He carefully articulated the dilemma:

> I am very concerned about the precedent of giving established parkland to any group. . . . The issue of social justice however is also important, and few groups have received so little as native Americans. Increasingly, aims of the environmental movement and those of Indians [sic] are coming into conflict—a troublesome situation for one who supports both movements.

Rands, it would later prove, was not the only one looking to reconcile commitments to both social justice *and* the environment.[21]

The Sierra Club, however, was also home to thousands of veterans of a movement at the height of its political power, who saw the environment as the most important concern and all others merely appendages to it. Having fought tooth and nail for every victory, much of the leadership and some of the members worried about becoming sidetracked by other issues or having their message diluted. Sticking to this vision of preservation in the face of intense opposition, these environmentalists voiced a variety of reasons for opposing the Goldwater and Udall bills' intention to return land to the Havasupai.

One of the major arguments that environmentalists used to oppose the transfer was that the Havasupai had "no legal right" to this land. Earlier, the Indian Claims Commission had found that the Havasupai were illegally deprived of over 2,250,000 acres and offered them 55 cents an acre in compensation. In 1969, advised by their lawyer that if they refused the money they would get nothing, the tribe voted to accept the payment, though the members continued to affirm that they wanted the land above all. Only a small portion, just over $650, was promised to each member, with the rest amounting to little more than a block grant to the Bureau of Indian Affairs on behalf of the Havasupai. They still desperately wanted their land back, and at the time the land transfer bills were introduced, the Havasupai had yet to receive even a dime of the settlement. Nevertheless, they had given up their claims, environmentalists argued, and now it was public land, and as such belonged to everyone; to turn some of it over to Havasupais would be to defraud "Americans of all races."[22]

Rather than focus on this legal issue, the Havasupai relied on a strategy that spoke deeply to the new Movement environmentalists joining the ranks of the Sierra Club. To be sure, debates over their legal right to the land were nothing new. Over the decades, the Havasupai and their supporters had made dozens of petitions filled with carefully honed legal and historical arguments for the return of their homeland. However, now they turned to a new and far more compelling argument for their legal rights to the land, an argument well designed for a post-civil rights movement world: they framed their loss of land and resulting poverty as the result of injustice and made moral appeals to justice for returning their homeland.[23] This effort brought them new and surprising allies, among them many environmentalists.[24]

This strategy had deep roots. The legal and civil rights scholar Robert A. Sedler argues that a concern for social injustice was one reason that some whites supported African American civil rights. Leaders such as Martin Luther King Jr. successfully used moral appeals to solicit aid from people outside the movement.[25] The Havasupai acutely understood that many Americans in the 1960s shifted their thinking about race and poverty, and began to recognize the need for greater justice and equality for minorities. Oscar Paya, Tribal Council Chair and former World War II paratrooper, lamented to the chairman of the Senate Indian Affairs Subcommittee, "Sadly, when we present economic, legal and historical arguments, no one listens to them." Now that it was clear that their position was "*morally*, historically and economically sound," Paya took this new approach and urged Udall to do what was "right *morally* and possible politically." Nevertheless, he made no apologies that those appeals to morality and justice sounded emotional. "Indeed we are emotional about a place we have called our home for 13 centuries," the tribal chairman freely admitted.[26]

A few environmentalists lamented this change in the racial atmosphere and began to complain about the growing attention to matters of race and justice by environmentalists.[26] After reading a defense of Havasupai land claims written by Senator Ted Kennedy (D-MA), Martin Litton, who had just completed eight years of service on the Sierra Club's Board of Directors (BOD), sent a scathing letter to the editor of the *LA Times* that railed against what he termed Kennedy's "bleeding heart language." That view of Havasupai history was "irresponsible drivel," Litton fumed, leading to an "unreasoning, senseless outcry over Indian 'rights.'"[28] However, though he and others were loath to admit it, race and social justice were becoming an integral part of the conversation over environmental issues. The environmental movement was filling up with "Indian lovers" of all sorts who believed that environmentalism and social justice were inextricably linked.

These changes meant that many environmentalists who continued to oppose the transfer of land to the Havasupai felt compelled to explain, again and again, that they were neither racists nor inconsiderate of the tribe's plight. Brock Evans, the head of the Sierra Club's lobbying efforts in Washington, D.C., since 1973, tried to assure the public that the Sierra Club did care about the Indians. "We agree," he avowed, "that it is important for all Americans to make sure that Indian peoples have a decent standard of living, and are treated fairly within our society."[29] John McComb, the head of the Sierra Club in Arizona, likewise urged "compassionate, thoughtful attention" to the problems of Native Americans, yet he warned that "guilt feelings" had "given rise to an emotion-laden atmosphere in which the facts are ignored and obscured."[30]

These Sierra Club leaders at the time seriously underestimated the convincing power that the moral arguments about justice carried, as well as the larger implications of facing an opponent with these powerful weapons in its arsenal. In their fight for land, the Havasupai and their supporters portrayed the Sierra Club, which came to represent all the opposition by environmentalists, as privileged urban dilettantes more concerned with recreation than with the basic human right to survival. A tribal council member pointedly noted:

> We heard this [John] McComb bragging about how he has spent all of 180 days in the Grand Canyon, but he is just a city man like all the rest thinking about taking these lands away from our people so he can come up once or twice a year and have some recreation on them. . . . Recreation! We are talking about survival while they talk about recreation.[31]

Many of the environmentalists working to oppose the land transfer remained convinced that the Havasupai wanted much more than simple justice. They argued that listening to such claims would be foolish and even dangerous. The transfer of public lands to the Havasupai would set a "very dangerous precedent," opening a "Pandora's Box" of claims to millions of acres from other Native American and Hispanic groups whose lands were formerly incorporated into public lands.[32] The great fear was then that returning these lands would undo a great deal of what environmentalists had fought for in protecting public lands from exploitation. For example, Michael McCloskey, Sierra Club Executive Director, expressed concern that with the return of land, the impoverished Havasupai would "be sorely tempted to mortgage these invaluable scenic and recreation values in order to alleviate their immediate economic problems"—an open invitation "for ill-conceived and destructive tourist developments" that would "produce visual blight on the scenic vistas of the Grand Canyon . . . [and] do irreparable harm to its fragile beauty."[33] Some opponents went so far as to suggest that the Havasupai were merely dupes of corporations waiting to pounce on the land and its resources. It was all "a ploy" to exploit the unpopularity of appearing to be "unkind to Indians," Friends of the Earth's David Brower warned. The plan to return land was, he said, "a cigar-store Indian of the proportions of a Trojan Horse, being wheeled in kindness within the walls."[34] Out of this cigar-store Indian/Trojan Horse would pour forth corporate interests ready to go to work. The national Sierra Club issued a press release with a picture of the canyon, labeled with their most ominous fears: "Motels? Factories? Dams? Tramways?"[35] The main concern of McCloskey and Brower, like many of the environmentalists, was to preserve the landscape against real and perceived threats, and they all feared that the land transfer was just such another threat.

Nevertheless, local members of the Sierra Club were willing to sit down with the Havasupai people and talk over the issues. On 2 December 1973, members of the Grand Canyon Chapter from Arizona agreed to meet with the Havasupai in Flagstaff, where they talked with tribal representatives about the tribe's plans for the use of the land. In spite of the tribe's consideration for careful use of the land, John McComb, leader of the club in Arizona, remained obdurate. The veteran of many Capitol Hill battles, McComb knew how to stand his ground. However, many of the Club members in the Arizona delegation responded in favor of the Havasupai's compelling and convincing description of their plans to utilize the lands only for survival and not to fulfill some grandiose commercial dreams. Some of these Sierra Club members, converted to Havasupai supporters, began to confront McComb, right there in the meeting; they questioned his, and by extension the Sierra Club's, inflexibility when it came to dealing with the Havasupai and their intransigence in the face of their appeals for justice.

This changing attitude regarding the Havasupai claim spread quickly throughout the grassroots of the Grand Canyon Chapter and even made some inroads in the leadership of the club at the national level. A week following this first meeting with Havasupai, on 9 December, the Chapter's Flagstaff Group (a group is a local division of a chapter) met to reconsider its official position. They ended by passing a resolution urging the return of "appropriate federal lands" to the Havasupai.[36] Next, Don McIver of Phoenix, among those at the 2 December meeting, agreed to lead a group of interested representatives from the Prescott, Phoenix, and Tucson groups to the reservation to discuss their concerns. On 30 December, this assemblage of Sierra Club members toured the reservation, observed conditions generally, and learned about "tribal life and land use." On the 31st, they met with the Tribal Council and other Havasupai and listened to the plan for managing the plateau lands. Following this meeting, the Prescott and Phoenix Groups passed resolutions of support.[37]

By the spring of 1974, following an extensive national media campaign that largely favored the Havasupai cause, other divisions further up from the grassroots within the Sierra Club came out in public support of the Havasupai. On 30 March, the club's National Native American Issues Committee issued an official statement of their desire to "help a people survive" who had agreed to "reasonable environmental constraint."[38] A few days later, members of the Southwest Regional Conservation Committee, meeting together with representatives from across the Four Corners, officially asked the national BOD to reconsider the Club's official position, but the BOD refused the request in spite of the large base of support for the Havasupai within the Sierra Club.[39]

The club's leadership, with their bulwark of opposition quickly evaporating, struggled to present a united front. The national staff, at the behest of the BOD, issued press releases and lobbied Congress, repeating their firm opposition to the land transfer. They worked overtime in an attempt to convince the nation that in spite of the clearly visible division of opinion, the "Sierra Club position has not changed at all."[40]

A national media campaign made their job all the more difficult. The campaign, begun in the first half of 1974, brought in crucial support for the Havasupai. The Association for American Indian Affairs (AAIA), helped organize the campaign. Like the Havasupai, the AAIA kept a focus on the theme of justice and argued that environmental concerns and regard for the survival and well-being of the tribe could all be satisfied. The media campaign took in their small paper, *Indian Affairs*, read mostly by liberals concerned with Native American affairs, and included national newspapers such as the *Los Angeles Times* along with a network television program on CBS that reached much of the nation.[41] One of the attention-grabbing pieces in the media came from Massachusetts Senator Ted Kennedy, whose editorial for the *LA Times* argued that Americans had "an opportunity to right an ancient wrong" perpetrated on "helpless" people "condemned to live in stark isolation and poverty" in an "intolerable" situation, which included being driven from the plateau and having their homes burned. He concluded that "simple justice" demanded that Congress return some of their original land.[42] Perhaps the most sympathy for the Havasupai cause came from a *60 Minutes* program, "Canyon Shadows," which aired on 24 February 1974.[43] The show employed stark and powerful language that simplified the complex issues and made supporting the Havasupai an issue of equality, of right and wrong.[44]

Jeff Ingram later lamented that the *60 Minutes* episode was the moment that "the Havasupai issue pole-vaulted past us."[45] Michael McCloskey recalled that all the media attention brought on the club a "torrent of angry comments in publications sympathetic to the tribe" and "an influx of critical letters"— many of them from Sierra Club members.[46] Letter after letter repeated the same theme: justice for the Havasupai.[47]

All this favorable media attention and lobbying by the Havasupai helped them pull together a powerful liberal coalition. Letters from labor and teachers' unions, civil liberties organizations, churches and synagogues, university professors, and, of course, from Indian tribes across the country poured into the offices of Udall, Goldwater, and the Sierra Club, calling for support of the tribe, "on the basis of human justice," and condemning the Sierra Club and their allies for their "callous and exploitative attitude."[48]

The fact that so many of these negative comments came from former allies such as Kennedy made this situation particularly troubling for the Sierra Club. Michael McCloskey, ever the political pragmatist, recognized the dire consequences for environmentalism when such potential and former allies were driven away. "There is a big problem brewing for us on such questions," he acknowledged, "because we will lose the urban liberal support in Congress that we need whenever one of these questions comes up." This had the potential for the development of what he called "an unholy alliance": an alliance "between industry-oriented conservatives and enough urban liberals to squeeze the center out of its majority position."[49]

Nevertheless, just when it seemed that the tide had turned in favor of the Havasupai, at the end of August 1974, the Arizona Governor's Office did something that nearly devastated the Havasupai position. The tribal council had recently submitted an application for grant monies. As a condition of the grant, they endured yet another study of their reservation, the permit land, and its economic potential for the tribe.[50] The grant writers from the governor's office suggested helpful ways for the tribe to increase their income by expanding tourism and other enterprises. Whether out of ignorance or disingenuous design, the report, in suggesting ways to expand the tribe's commercial interests, seemed to echo the language of environmentalists who had predicted that if given the chance, Havasupais would open the land to commercial exploitation.[51] It was not long before news of the study made it to opponents of the transfer, who made political hay with it. "The Havasupai are on record" one writer avowed "as favoring tramways and dams."[52] The report seemed to confirm the worst fears of environmentalists opposing the transfer, who misinterpreted it as a master plan for runaway commercial development.

The Havasupai quickly moved into damage control. Chairman Paya was adamant about the Havasupai position:

> We have been informed of the *maliscious* [sic] and *false representations* being made concerning the Havasupai Tribe and the Draft Economic Study. . . . This is to assure you that the draft study does not have our approval and does not reflect our view. We pledge to use the land according to the statute, rules and regulations setforth [sic] by Congress and the Secretary of the Interior.[53]

A careful review of the study reveals that the governor's office was fully aware that this was the Havasupai position, in spite of their recommendations. It shows that the governor's planners believed that the tribe should adopt a similar business model to the one used at the South Rim by the National Park Service; however, the objects of the study, the Havasupai themselves, were opposed to turning Havasu Canyon and the Plateau above it into Grand Canyon Southwest™. Pages after noting the potential revenues to be developed with increased access to Havasupai lands, the study does reluctantly admit that their suggestions that the tribe build a road or an aerial tramway connecting Supai village to the plateau were deeply resented. Daniel Kaska, tribal sheriff for the Havasupai, son of the first tribal chairman and the chairman himself in the 1960s, made it clear to the study team, "This canyon is our living room. How would you like a tramway in your living room[?]"[54] In spite of this, environmentalists opposed to the Havasupai land transfer read the study selectively, continuing to be convinced that the tribe sought the land only for commercial exploitation in a manner that would ultimately destroy its environmental values.

Conclusion

As early as September 1973, a few environmentalists began suggesting that the opposing sides might be reconciled by placing environmental restrictions on the transferred lands to prevent the development that environmentalists feared would sully the Canyon lands.[55] The tribe itself shrewdly recognized that this would bolster their position and assure hesitant environmentalists of their commitments to caring for the land, so they asked Congress to set environmental restrictions.[56] With the tribe's reluctant support, Congress decreed that the Havasupai could use the land "for agricultural and grazing purposes," but they had to "develop and implement a plan for the use of this land." The decree explicitly forbade mining and logging while requiring all other uses be approved by the Secretary of the Interior. "[E]xcept for the uses permitted," the law stated, "the lands . . . shall remain forever wild and no uses shall be permitted under the plan which detract from the existing scenic and natural values of such lands."[57] Initially, the national Sierra Club attacked the restrictions as "insufficient to prevent degradation of the park values," but relented after facing wave upon wave of opprobrium for their opposition to the Havasupai. These legal restrictions provided a reassuring compromise to members wishing to reconcile their desire to preserve the land and to be just to the Havasupai.[58]

When the dust settled and the transfer was complete, it became clear that throughout this episode the Sierra Club had proved more complex than suggested by the common stereotype of environmentalists as elitist, middle-class whites, concerned only with preserving wilderness and wildlife while remaining blissfully ignorant or unwilling to address the problems of the poor and people of color. Although few environmentalists would fully embrace "environmental justice"—attempts to rectify inequitable exposure to pollution and waste and unequal access to environmental resources—many members were beginning to recognize the connections between social and environmental problems and worked to solve them.[59]

When it was all over, it became clear to some Sierra Club leaders that refusing to come to terms with the connections between social and environmental issues threatened to cripple their ability to work as effectively as they had in the past. Though past decisions by the club had always yielded dissatisfied members who threatened to withdraw their membership if the leadership did not address one issue or drop another, this affair threatened the very grassroots foundation of the club. In addition to the conflicts between members and leaders, this case was so divisive that club members had even explored splitting the Grand Canyon Chapter in two.[60] The position of the Sierra Club leadership also cost them crucial support from many traditional allies including university professors and church groups committed to the environment. In addition, club leadership lost the ability to utilize the media to gather support for their position.

As a result, some Sierra Club leaders came to regret their involvement in opposing the Havasupai. Years later, McCloskey publicly admitted, "We dropped the ball on that one."[61] Brock Evans, though he remained unapologetic regarding his role in fighting against the land transfer, would later try to distance himself from the "unpleasant battle." He placed the blame for the fiasco on others. "I didn't like that issue at all," Evans claimed, shifting responsibility to Jeff Ingram who was "very strong on the subject." Clearly uncomfortable with what happened, Evans took the I-was-just-doing-my-job defense. Opposing the transfer was club policy; he would explain over a decade later that "I was the chief lobbyist so I did my duty."[62]

In spite of the decisions by the Sierra Club leadership at the time to oppose its grassroots members, the Havasupai benefited from a rapidly growing environmental movement that attracted increasing numbers of people with socially liberal sympathies. Meeting face to face with members of the Sierra Club and using the national media, the Havasupai were able to gain widespread support with a message of justice. Their message took advantage of a new climate of acceptance for both environmental and civil rights issues.

Typical of Movement environmentalists, Sue Bradley and her husband, both self-professed "ardent environmentalists" and "supporters of the Sierra Club," stood by the Havasupai "in the name of justice." Sue Bradley was not alone when she lamented, "I hate to see environmentalists and Indians battling each other. It seems like we should be on the same side! As an environmentalist, I would like to balance my feelings about nature, etc. with social concerns."[63] Perhaps she might agree with the observation of the environmental historian Dan Flores: "In the best philosophical sense, choosing between humans and nature is a non sequitur."[64]

Notes

1   The author wishes to thank Peter Iverson, Paul Hirt, Brian Gratton, Aaron McArthur, Kevin Marsh, and Sara Dant, who offered helpful suggestions on earlier versions of this essay. The research and writing of this essay was partially supported by grants from the Charles Redd Center and from the Arizona State University Graduate College.

2   "Sierra Club Votes to Support the Havasupai," *Canyon Shadows* (3 February 1974). The story of Havasupai dispossession and the controversy over transfer has been handled briefly a number of times. Most useful in this analysis were Stephen Hirst, *Life in a Narrow Place* (New York: David McKay, 1976); Barbara J. Morehouse, *A Place Called Grand Canyon: Contested Geographies* (Tucson: University of Arizona Press, 1996); Robert H. Keller Jr. and Michael F. Turek, *American Indians and National Parks* (Tucson: University of Arizona Press, 1998); John Martin, "From Judgment to Land Restoration: The Havasupai Land Claims Case," in Imre Sutton (ed.), *Irredeemable America* (Albuquerque: University of New Mexico Press, 1986), 271–300; and John Carter Freemuth, "The History of S. 1296: The Enlargement of Grand Canyon National Park" (M.A. thesis, Claremont Graduate School, 1975).

3   For Ingram's recollections on his involvement with Havasupai/Grand Canyon legislation, see Jeff Ingram, *Hijacking a River: A Political History of the Colorado River in the Grand Canyon* (Flagstaff, AZ: Vishnu Temple Press, 2003), 73–94.

4   Mark Harvey, *A Symbol of Wilderness* (Seattle: University of Washington Press, 2000), 291.

5   "Sierra Club's 75th," *New York Times*, 11 December 1967.

6   Membership figures are based on Stephen Fox, *John Muir and his Legacy: The American Conservation Movement* (Boston: Little, Brown and Co., 1981), 315; Robert Cameron Mitchell, Angela G. Mertig, and Riley E. Dunlap, "Twenty Years of Environmental Mobilization: Trends Among National Environmental Organizations," in Riley E. Dunlap and Angela G. Mertig (eds.), *American Environmentalism: The U.S. Environmental Movement, 1970–1990* (Philadelphia: Taylor & Francis, 1992), 12.

7   Adam Rome, " 'Give Earth a Chance': The Environmental Movement and the Sixties," *Journal of American History* 90 (September 2003), 527. On the 1960s roots of environmentalism, see Stephen Fox, *The American Conservation Movement: John Muir and His Legacy* (Madison: University of Wisconsin Press, 1985), 322–25; Robert Gottlieb, *Forcing the Spring: The Transformation of the American Environmental Movement* (Washington, DC: Island Press, 1993), 81–114; Hal K. Rothman, *The Greening of a Nation? Environmentalism in the United States since 1945* (Fort Worth, TX: Harcourt Brace College Publishers, 1998), 83–107; Susan R. Schrepfer, *The Fight to Save the Redwoods: A History of Environmental Reform, 1917–1978* (Madison: University of Wisconsin Press, 1983), 163–69; and Thomas Raymond Wellock, *Critical Masses: Opposition to Nuclear Power in California, 1958–1978* (Madison: University of Wisconsin Press, 1998), 92–102.

8   Cf. Rome, "Give Earth a Chance," 527.

9   Richard Cellarius, *National Leader in the Sierra Club and The Sierra Club Foundation, 1970–2002, Sierra Club President, 1988–1990* (Berkeley: Regional Oral History Office, the Bancroft Library, University of California, 2005), 35, 229.

10   For a copy of the speech, see ibid., 227–31.

11   Doris Cellarius, *Sierra Club Volunteer Leader: Grassroots Activist and Organizer on Hazardous Waste Issues* (Berkeley: Regional Oral History Office, the Bancroft Library, University of California, 2005), xix, 62–63.

12   Schrepfer, *The Fight to Save the Redwoods*, 165. For the official summary of this research, see Mitchell/Resources for the Future Survey, Folder 10, Carton 119, Subject Files, Michael McCloskey Papers, BANC MSS 71/295 c, The Bancroft Library, University of California, Berkeley (this collection is identified hereafter as SCMP).

13   Walter A. Rosenbaum, *Environmental Politics and Policy* (Washington, DC: CQ Press, 1985).

14   Eric P. Kaufmann, *The Rise and Fall of Anglo-America* (Cambridge, MA: Harvard University Press, 2004), 196–97.

15 In using this terminology, I am following Terry H. Anderson, *The Movement and the Sixties* (New York: Oxford University Press, 1995) who treats the various social movements of the 1960s as part of a larger effort he calls "The Movement."

16 A useful overview of early Havasupai lifeways can be found in Douglas W. Schwartz, "Havasupai," in Alfonso Ortiz, ed., *Southwest*, vol. 10 of *Handbook of North American Indians*, ed. William C. Sturtevant (Washington, DC: Smithsonian Institution, 1983), 13–24.

17 Martin, "From Judgment," 273–78.

18 Morehouse, *A Place Called Grand Canyon*, 105.

19 Freemuth, "The History of S. 1296," 19; Jeffrey Ingram to Morris K. Udall, July 10, 1974, Folder 5, Box 125, MS Collection 325, Morris K. Udall Papers, University of Arizona Libraries Special Collections, Tucson, Arizona (this collection is identified hereafter as MKU); Ann Roosevelt, "The Grand Canyon Giveaway," *Not Man Apart*, 4(16) (November 1974), 6.

20 See, for example, Robert Z. Norman to Morris K. Udall, 2 September 1974, Folder 3, Box 125, MKU. After reading about the debate in the *Sierra Club Bulletin*, Steven Galef declared that it left him with "a very definite uncertainty." Steven A. Galef (Member of the County Board of Legislators, Westchester County, New York) to Barry Goldwater, 3 October 1973, MSS 1, Barry M. Goldwater Papers, Arizona Historical Foundation, Hayden Library, Arizona State University, Tempe, Arizona (this collection is identified hereafter as BG). This collection was unprocessed at the time I consulted it.

21 Gordon P. Rands to Morris K. Udall, 10 October 1974, Folder 2, Box 125, MKU. Rands would keep these commitments. He is currently an Associate Professor of management at Western Illinois University, where he specializes in studies of ecological sustainability. By 2003, the student was now mentor, from participating in a national teach-in on global warming to leading a discussion on "The Relationship of Social Justice to Environmental Protection." "WIU Joins National Teach-In on Global Warming," Western Illinois University Press Release, 14 January 2008, www.wiu.edu/newsrelease.sphp?release_id = 5956, accessed 25 April 2008; "Western Dialogue Discussions Highlight Social Justice Theme," Western Illinois University Press Release, 18 September 2003, www.wiu.edu/newsrelease.sphp?release_id = 2046, accessed 25 April 2008.

22 Reed Secord (Western Wilderness Association, President) to Morris K. Udall, 14 May 1974, Folder 6, Box 125, MKU; Elizabeth B. Barnett (Sierra Club, Rio Grande Chapter, Chair) to Manuel Lujan (Representative from New Mexico), 8 May 1974, Folder 1, Box 187, MKU.

23 Gary C. Bryner, "Assessing Claims of Environmental Justice: Conceptual Frameworks, in Justice and Natural Resources," in Kathryn M. Mutz, Gary C. Bryner, and Douglas S. Kenny (eds.), *Justice and Natural Resources: Concepts, Strategies, and Applications* (Washington, DC: Island Press, 2002), 31–55, describes five frameworks that represent the most common approaches that advocates and

scholars use to approach injustice: civil rights, distributive justice and ethics, public participation, social justice, and ecological sustainability frameworks.

24   Keller and Turek recognize that ethical claims created "a campaign that outflanked even the veteran David Brower." Unfortunately they neither explain what this means nor explore its implications for environmentalists. Keller and Turek, *American Indians and National Parks*, 169.

25   Robert A. Sedler, "Claims for Reparations for Racism Undermine the Struggle for Equality," *Journal of Law in Society* 3(1). (2002), 119–32. Sedler here draws on the work of Edmond Cahn, *A Sense of Injustice* (Bloomington: Indiana University Press, 1964). Cahn was a tax lawyer turned philosopher who recognized that the law could be used to serve injustice. To counteract that force, the law should feed off empathy for victims of injustice and thus serve justice; see Bruce S. Ledewitz, "Edmond Cahn's Sense of Injustice: A Contemporary Reintroduction," *Journal of Law and Religion* 3(2) (1985), 279, 282–83. For Cahn, this was not just an emotional response, but an amalgam of scientific rationalism and morality—a mixture he called "a blend of reason and empathy" (Cahn, *A Sense of Injustice*, 26), in which justice is an "*active process* of remedying or preventing what would arouse the sense of injustice" (ibid., 13–14, emphasis in original). This phenomenon (a sense of justice) has been recognized by scholars of feminism: a trait exploited internally by "consciousness-raising" that offers "a collectively defined sense of injustice" that plays off "moral shock." Jo Reger, "Organizational 'Emotion Work' through Consciousness-Raising: An Analysis of a Feminist Organization," *Qualitative Sociology* 27(2) (Summer 2004), 206, 213.

26   Oscar Paya to James Abourezk (Senate Indian Affairs Subcommittee, Chairman), 13 December 1973, BG; Oscar Paya to Morris K. Udall, 17 March 1974, Folder 7, Box 125, MKU. Italics added.

27   Ernest L. Youens (Sierra Club, Grand Canyon Chapter, Executive Committee) to Morris K. Udall, 21 May 1974, Folder 1, Box 187, MKU.

28   Martin Litton (Grand Canyon Dories) to Editor *Los Angeles Times*, 12 June 1974, Folder 14, Box 187, MKU.

29   Statement of Brock Evans, Director of Washington Office Sierra Club Regarding Legislative Proposals to Transfer Portions of Grand Canyon National Park and Kaibab National Forest to the Havasupai Indian Tribe, Washington, DC, 12 September 1974, Folder 14, Box 187, MKU.

30   John A. McComb (Sierra Club, Southwest Representative) to Editor *Arizona Daily Star*, 26 September 1974, Folder 16, Box 187, MKU.

31   Statement by Havasupai Tribe Before the United States House of Representatives Committee on Interior and Insular Affairs Subcommittee on National Parks and Recreation, 12 November 1973, Folder 16, Box 187, MKU.

32   "Grand Canyon Bill Heads for House Interior Committee," National News Report, Sierra Club Press Release, 28 June 1974, BG; Ernest L. Youens to Morris K. Udall, 4 November 1974, BG; D. D. Cutler, "Indian Raids on Public Lands," *American*

Forests Magazine (December 1974); Linda Finn to Barry Goldwater, 19 December 1974, BG.

33 Michael McCloskey (Sierra Club, Executive Director) to "Congressman," 7 October 1974, Folder 4, Box 187, MKU. Cf. John A. McComb to Editor *Arizona Daily Star*, 26 Sept 1974, Folder 16, Box 187, MKU.

34 David Brower, "They're After the Grand Canyon Again? The Grand Canyon!" *Not Man Apart* 4(8) (July 1974), 7–8.

35 Sierra Club National News Report, 23 August 1974, Folder 46, Carton 212, Subject Files, Paul Swatek Papers, Sierra Club Members papers, SCMP.

36 "Tribe Makes Major Gains in Land Fight," *Canyon Shadows* (30 December 1973).

37 "Sierra Club Votes to Support the Havasupai."

38 "Havasupai Fight Attracts National Support," *Canyon Shadows* (29 May 1974).

39 "Sierra Club Committee Backs Havasupai Claim," *Durango Herald* (8 April 1974). John McComb was at this meeting and fought hard against the proposal to ask the national organization to reconsider. The Ft. Lewis anthropologist Dr. Robert Euler addressed the group before a vote on McComb's proposal. Euler pointed out to the assembled clubbers the irony of a "group of white people sitting here . . . discussing the fate of the Havasupai." On the BOD decision see, Board Actions, National News Report, Sierra Club Press Release, 10 May 1974, BG. The chair of the club's Native Rights Committee requested that the BOD withdraw the question from the agenda at their next meeting in May 1974, apparently in an attempt to let the chapter and its committee's position stand as the official position of the club. See Michael McCloskey Telegram to Morris K. Udall, 4 April 1974, Folder 6, Box 125, MKU.

40 Michael McCloskey Telegram to Morris K. Udall, 25 April 1974, Folder 6, Box 125, MKU.

41 "The Havasupai: Prisoners of the Grand Canyon," *Indian Affairs* 88 (March–April 1974), 1–2, 7. Over ninety newspapers across the country wrote favorable pieces in the spring and summer of 1974. See "Organizations Supporting Havasupai Tribe," n.d., Folder 11, Box 187, MKU.

42 Edward Kennedy, "A Chance to Right an Ancient Wrong," *Los Angeles Times*, 9 June 1974, F2.

43 Keller and Turek, *American Indians and National Parks*, 169. The Barry Goldwater Papers contain a transcript of the episode. "Who Owns the Grand Canyon," *60 Minutes*, 6(7), as broadcast over the CBS Television Network, 24 February 1974, BG.

44 After discussing the *60 Minutes* piece at the following BOD meeting, the Board decided to draft a letter to respond to the numerous inquiries that resulted from the exposure to the harsh glare of the media. See Joan Cutter, Office of the Executive Director, to Richard A. Marston, 10 May 1974, Folder 20, Carton 94, Correspondence, Michael McCloskey Papers, SCMP.

45 Ingram, *Hijacking a River*, 86.

46 J. Michael McCloskey, *In the Thick of It: My Life in the Sierra Club* (Washington, DC: Island Press, 2005), 199.

47　Many of the letters from Sierra Club members urging the club to change its position on the Havasupai land transfer date to the weeks following the *60 Minutes* broadcast and explicitly reference the show. See, for example, William A. Coffin to McCloskey, 25 February 1974, Folder 14, Carton 107, Conservation Correspondence, Conservation Department Records, Sierra Club records, BANC MSS 71/103 c, The Bancroft Library, University of California, Berkeley (this collection is identified hereafter as SCR); James E. Kearns to SC, 25 February 1974, Folder 14, Carton 107, Conservation Correspondence, Conservation Department Records, SCR. For an example of the response to these member letters, see Michael McCloskey to Charles J. Weber, 25 March 1974, Folder 14, Carton 107, Conservation Department Records: Conservation reference files, SCR.

48　Quotations are from Vernon O. Woolf (Lima–Troy Area United Auto Workers Community Action Program (UAW-CAP) Council, President) to Barry Goldwater, 13 June 1974, BG, and Jerrold E. Levy (University of Arizona, Department of Anthropology) to Editor *Arizona Daily Star*, 8 October 1974, Folder 2, Box 125, MKU. Udall's office compiled a list of organizations that supported the Havasupai sometime after 19 August 1974. See "Organizations Supporting Havasupai Tribe"; Winifred J. Hearn (The Committee on Indian Affairs of the New York Meeting of the Religious Society of Friends, Legislative Chairwoman) to Morris K. Udall, 30 September 1974, Folder 2, Box 125, MKU. See also William L. Brown (Des Moines Valley Friends Meeting, Clerk) to Morris K. Udall, 19 July 1974, Folder 4, Box 125, MKU; Bernard Kligfeld (Temple Emanu-El of Long Beach, Rabbi) to Morris K. Udall, 5 December 1974, Folder 1, Box 125, MKU; Patricia P. Reifsnyder (Germantown Friends School, Teacher) to Morris K. Udall, 7 October 1974, Folder 2, Box 125, MKU; Roger Baldwin (American Civil Liberties Union, Founder) to Morris K. Udall, 25 October 1974, Folder 2, Box 125, MKU; Lucy Wilson Benson, Martha S. Greenawalt, and Ruth L. Sims to James A. Haley, 3 May 1974, Folder 7, Carton 65, National Parks and Reserves, Subject Files, Sierra Club National Legislative Office Records, BANC MSS 71/289 c, The Bancroft Library, University of California, Berkeley; Sterling Mahone (Hualapai Tribal Council, Chairman) to Morris K. Udall, 26 April 1974, Folder 7, Box 125, MKU; Eugene A. Begay (United Southeastern Tribes) to Morris K. Udall, 5 April 1974, Folder 6, Box 125, MKU; Bishop Indian Board of Trustees (Owens Valley Paiute-Shoshone Band) to Barry Goldwater, 26 March 1973, BG.

　　Arizona was home to many of the country's top anthropologists, several of whom had studied and lived among Havasupai. The list of letters written to support the Havsupai is a who's who of southwestern anthropology. See, for example, Bernard L. Fontana (Arizona State Museum, Ethnologist) to Morris K. Udall, 22 April 1974, Folder 1, Box 187, MKU; James L. Axtell (Sarah Lawrence College, Department of History) to Morris K. Udall, 16 July 1974, Folder 4, Box 125, MKU; Keith H. Basso (University of Arizona, Department of Anthropology) to Morris K. Udall, 17 April 1974, Folder 7, Box 125, MKU.

49　Michael McCloskey to James Moorman, 12 September 1974, Folder 20, Carton 94, Correspondence, Michael McCloskey Papers, SCMP.

50 Freemuth, "The History of S. 1296," 20.

51 See notes 33–35 above.

52 Goldie Otters to Morris K. Udall, 21 September 1974, Folder 2, Box 125, MKU.

53 Oscar Paya Telegram to Morris K. Udall, 10 October 1974, Folder 4, Box 187, MKU. Italics added.

54 Governor's Office of Economic Planning and Development, "Havasupai Comprehensive Plan," 30 August 1974, Folder 4, Box 187, MKU. A copy can also be found in Folder 19, Carton 188, Conservation Reference Files, Conservation Department Records, SCR.

Martin Litton was unconvinced by the disavowal, believing it to be part of a devious plan. Sure, their attorney said "that they would never countenance 'any dams, tramlines, or railroad which would flood, harm, or otherwise damage the environment of our land or disturb the life-way of our people,'" he argued, but "the 'resolution' can be dismissed as meaningless" because "the Havasupais can, in response to the exigencies of the moment, reverse themselves as abruptly as any politician." Martin Litton, "What does the Havasupai Tribe Really Want?," *Arizona Republic*, n.d., BG.

55 Frank A. Webster (Izaak Walton League of America, Director) to Morris K. Udall, 7 September 1973, Folder 12, Box 187, MKU. Goldwater's original bill did place some restrictions on the transfer. See Freemuth, "The History of S. 1296," 8.

56 "Havasupais Ask for Our Help," *Akwesasne Notes*, n.d., BG.

57 *Congressional Record—House*, 93rd Cong., 2nd sess., 10 October 1974, 35202.

58 "The Grand Canyon—In Danger Again!," National News Report, Sierra Club Press Release, 22 June 1973, BG; Morris K. Udall to Janet L. Moench (Sierra Club), 15 October 1974, Folder 2, Box 125, MKU.

59 The best introduction to the history of environmental justice is Michael Egan, "Subaltern Environmentalism in the United States: A Historiographic Review," *Environment and History* 8 (February 2002), 21–41.

60 Susan E. Miller to Dan S. Leath, 29 July 1974, Sierra Club Chapters Files, SCR.

61 Michael McCloskey, Question and Answer, "Contested Public Landscapes: The Importance of Names and Ownership Boundaries in Federal Land Management," American Society for Environmental History annual meeting, St. Paul, MN, 31 March 2006.

62 Brock Evans and W. Lloyd Tupling, *Building the Sierra Club's National Lobbying Program, 1967–1981* (Berkeley: Regional Oral History Office, the Bancroft Library, University of California, 1985), 254–56.

63 Sue Bradley to Morris K. Udall, 5 September 1974, Folder 3, Box 125, MKU.

64 Dan L. Flores, "Environmentalism and Multiculturalism," in Hal K. Rothman (ed.), *Reopening the American West* (Tucson: University of Arizona Press, 1998), 36. Cf. Patricia Nelson Limerick, "Hoping against History: Environmental Justice in the Twenty-first Century, in Justice and Natural Resources," in Mutz *et al.* (eds.), *Justice and Natural Resources*, 353; James P. Sterba, "Reconciling Anthropocentric and Nonanthropocentric Environmental Ethics," *Environmental Values* 3(3) (1994), 229–44.

Index